FOUR LAMAS OF DOLPO
Volume I

To my friend, Carl Stacey

FOUR LAMAS OF DOLPO Volume I

Autobiographies of Four Tibetan Lamas

edited & translated
by
David L. Snellgrove

Orchid Press

David L. Snellgrove
Four Lamas of Dolpo: Autobiographies of Four Tibetan Lamas (16th-18th Centuries)
Volume I: Introduction and Translations

First published, Bruno Cassirer & Harvard University Press, Oxford/Cambridge 1967
Second edition, Himalayan Book Seller, Kathmandu 1992

Third edition © Orchid Press 2011

ORCHID PRESS
P.O. Box 1046,
Silom Post Office,
Bangkok 10504, Thailand
www.orchidbooks.com

Protected by copyright under the terms of the International Copyright Union: all rights reserved. No part of this publication may be reproduced in any form or by any means, electronic or mechanical, including photocopying, recording, or by any information storage or retrieval system without prior permission in writing from the publisher.

Front cover image: Chorten, monastery at *Shes*, Dolpo, Nepal.
Back cover image: Chortens at *Sa-ldang*, Dolpo, Nepal.
Both images © Franck Zecchin, 2003, all rights reserved. Reproduced by kind permission of Franck Zecchin.

ISBN 978-974-524-142-8

CONTENTS

List of Illustrations and Maps   *page* vii
Preface to Second Edition   ix
Preface to First Edition   xi-xiii

INTRODUCTION
   I. The Land and its People   1
   II. Philosophy and Religion   17
   III. Life in Dolpo 1960 61   34
   IV. The Four Biographies   68

THE TRANSLATIONS
   I. The Biography of Lama Merit Intellect   79
   II. The Biography of Lama Religious Protector
      Glorious and Good   125
   III. The Biography of Lama Glorious Intellect   183
   IV. The Biography of Lama Lord of Merit   231

TIBETAN INDICES
   Divinities   274
   Texts & Rituals   278
   Personal Names   282
   Place Names   286
GENERAL INDEX   292
ILLUSTRATIONS
MAPS
ABOUT THE AUTHOR

ILLUSTRATIONS

Symbols of long life, p. 110
Powerbolt-Terror, p. 182
Double powerbolt in the form of a cross, p. 273

FOLLOWING INDEX :
1. Ascending the valley leading from the upper Bar-rong (Barbung) valley to the pass towards Tarap.
2. View eastwards towards the upper Bar-rong valley and the great massif separating Dolpo from the Kāli Gandakī.
3. Bridge across the Bar-rong (Barbung) River at Trhim-nyer.
4. The village of Tsharka.
5. Breaking camp in the upper Bar-rong (Barbung) valley.
6. Final ascent of the pass towards Tarap.
7. Descending the other side of the main pass from Bar-rong (Barbung) to Tarap.
8. Sonam Panden and the author on the pass between Tarap and Nang-khong.
9. The Nang-khong Valley. View southwards from above Saldang.
10. The 'Residence of Great Happiness' at Namdo in Nang-khong.
11. Water supply for men and animals from the frozen river at the 'Residence of Great Happiness'.
12. Our host, the Lama of the 'Residence of Great Happiness' with Pasang Khambache.
13. Our second Sherpa assistant Pasang at Nyisal.
14. Yang-tsher Monastry.
15. Nyisal Village on its 'alp' overhanging the gorge (below Ban-tshang).
16. Reciting the liturgy at Yang-tsher.
17. Images and torma (sacrificial cakes) on the altar at Yang-tsher.
18a. The ransom-offering in the form of an effigy of a yak, moulded of tsamba and butter.
18b. Placing the ransom-offering on the temple roof at Yangt-tsher.
19a. Women (wearing hone-spun blankets) and men dancing in the courtyard of Yang-tsher Monastery.
19b. Masked dancers.
20. Two religious brethren of Tarap.
21. A Dolpo woman weaving woollen home-spun.

22. Norbu and the second Pasang by the 'tomb' of our horse Tshering in the lower Nang-khong Valley.
23. Nomad refugees from the north (Byang-thang) encamped outside the 'Residence of Great Happiness'.
24. View of Harp Monastery high up the gorge opposite Tsa.
25. The mummified corpse of the Precious Lama of Shang in Tr'a-gyam Monastry at Namgung.
26. Image of Chos-skyabs dpal-bzang ('Religious Protector Glorious and Good'), made soon after his death.
27. Women of Nyisal, replaiting hair after a monthly wash.
28. The young niece of the Lama of the 'Residence of Great Happiness'.
29. The scribe, Tshe-ring Ta-shi.
30. Washing a length of newly woven home-spun.
31. Nomad women with children and a nun.
32. Nyi-ma Tshe-ring, chief man of Dolpo until his death in 1963.
33. Images of Shākyamuni, 'Powerbolt-in-Hand' and 'Lotus-in-Hand' at Yang-tsher Monastery.
34. Temple banner of the Buddha 'Boundless Light'.
35. 'Lotus-born'.
36. 'Red Fury' with 'Lotus-born' above him and the 'Lion-headed Goddess' below.
37. Eleven-headed 'Glancing Eye'.
38. The 'One Mother'.
39. Lama 'Merit Intellect'.
40. Lama 'Religious Protector Glorious and Good'.
41. Detail of Pl. 40.
42. Lama 'Glorious Intellect'.
43. Detail of Pl. 42.
44. Lama 'Merit Intellect'.
45. Detail of Pl. 44.
46. Mystic Circle of the Fierce Divinities.

MAPS

Map I: Dolpo and Surrounding Regions
Map II: Western and Central Tibet, 15th – 18th Centuries

PREFACE TO THE SECOND EDITION

This earlier work of mine is now being reprinted with only one essential change. The dates of the first three of these four Dolpo lamas have been moved on by 60 years, *viz.* into the next 60 year cycle. I am grateful to Dr David P. Jackson (now of the University of Vienna) for drawing my attention to this necessary change in two of his subsequent publications, namely "Notes on the history of *Se-rib* and nearby places in the Upper Kali Gandaki Valley" (in *Kailash*, vol. VI, pp. 195-227, Kathmandu 1978) and *The Mollas of Mustang* (Dharamsala LTWA 1984). It should be noted that these two works of his provide a most useful general historical background for the lives of these four Dolpo lamas. My second volume, containing the Tibetan texts in manuscript form is not now being reprinted. Any scholar of Tibetan interested in checking the original texts on which my translation is based, will easily find Volume II of the first edition in almost any library of oriental books.†

Torre Pellice, David Snellgrove
31st March 1992

† PUBLISHER'S NOTE :

With the publication of the present third edition of *Four Lamas of Dolpo* Volume I, we are pleased to advise that a new edition of *Four Lamas of Dolpo* Volume II – *Tibetan Texts and Commentaries* will be published simultaneously (Orchid Press, Bangkok, 2011; ISBN 978-974-524-143-5).

PREFACE TO THE FIRST EDITION

I first drew attention to Dolpo as a geographical and cultural entity in 1956.[1] The names *Dol-po*, *Dol-pa* and *Dol-po-pa* were already known to Tibetan scholars from Tibetan historical sources, but previously no one seems to have identified the region to which the name refers.[2] Between March and September 1956 together with my Sherpa assistant, Pasang Khambache, I made a long journey on foot through the remote north-western regions of Nepal which border on Tibet proper. An account of this journey was published in 1961 with the title *Himalayan Pilgrimage*, and the longest chapter in this book is devoted to 'The Land of Dolpo' (pp. 70-162).

Thanks as always to the interested support of the School of Oriental & African Studies in the University of London, I was able to make a second visit to Dolpo during 1960 and 1961. My own interests tend to be primarily literary and I was anxious to have with me an anthropologist, who would be able to take a closer interest in the basic economy and everyday activities of the people of this extraordinary land.

I was also intending to spend the winter in Dolpo, and I knew that having once crossed the great passes into the heart of this remote region, we would be completely cut off until the following spring. The tracks leading northwards and eastwards from Dolpo remain open most of the year, but they lead down to the nomad regions of Tibet proper, where the Chinese were then still trying to suppress the determined resistance of groups of 'free' Tibetans. If we had trespassed in that direction, we would probably not have emerged even by the next spring. With the prospect of such a long winter of self-imprisonment before one, it would be reassuring at least to have a fellow European within reach. I found a willing companion in Monsieur Corneille Jest of the *Musée de l'Homme* in Paris, who was planning to visit Nepal during the same period. As well as having made anthropological studies in France and North Africa, he already had

---

[1] In an article in the *Manchester Guardian* of 4th November 1956.
[2] See p. 11 fn.

some experience of working amongst Himalayan peoples in the Kalimpong area. The only condition I made to his accompanying me was that he should learn enough Tibetan to be able to collect his material through the medium of the local Tibetan dialect that is spoken in Dolpo and this he readily agreed to do.

Our journey into Dolpo just before the onset of winter and our subsequent experiences there are described in the third part of the Introduction. For three months I was snowed up in *Nang-khong* in inner Dolpo, where I was staying all the time with a local lama in his riverside hermitage, named pleasingly 'The Residence of Great Happiness'. I spent most of my time there working with his assistance on some local biographies from his private collection of Tibetan block-prints and manuscripts. I have since worked through them again in England, solving a number of remaining difficulties with the help of two Tibetan scholars, *Geshey* Tenzin Namdak and *Geshey* Samten Gyaltsen Karmay, who accompanied me to London from India as my research-assistants. Their help in understanding the 'spirit' of these texts has been invaluable. I have now prepared a complete translation of four selected biographies and added an explanatory introduction. It seems to me that such a presentation of local literature provides a far more intimate description of the ways of life and of thought of these people of Dolpo, than I could ever achieve myself by direct analytical means.

The biographies are those of four Dolpo lamas, two of whom lived during the 16th century, one during the 16th and early 17th centuries and one during the end of the 17th and the beginning of the 18th centuries. Since Tibetan civilization became permeated by Indian Buddhism, all Tibetan historical writings have been religious in character. Only the lives of lamas and yogins have been considered worth the telling, and the Tibetan term (*rNam-thar*) which we translate as biography really means 'salvation', for it is assumed that it is the function of biography to tell of the works of salvation.

This religious bias does not however falsify unduly the impressions of Dolpo society that we receive from these works, for life in Dolpo was as much pervaded by religion as was life in Tibet itself up to 1959. Moreover these lamas spend much of their time and energy in trying to satisfy the insatiable demands of their faithful lay followers, and many references to lay life occur in these narratives.

Much of the information given in the Introduction has already been touched upon in *Buddhist Himalaya* and in *Himalayan Pilgrimage*, and I would like to regard *Four Lamas of Dolpo* as the last volume of a trilogy. The first of these three resumes the origins and development of Buddhism in India, and describes how this religion spread through Nepal and Kashmir to Tibet, how it established itself there, and how it began to penetrate certain Himalayan regions. The second provides a general survey of all the Tibetan-speaking Buddhist regions of north-western Nepal, and draws attention to Dolpo in particular. This last book concentrates upon Dolpo, and through the medium of my travels there and the interpretation of local narrative literature, attempts to give a realistic description of the religious life and the strange beliefs of these people.

As these biographies simply tell of the experiences of lamas who lived quite ordinary Dolpo lives, they may not seem at first quite as exciting and extraordinary as that notorious autobiography of the bogus Tibetan lama, Lobsang Rampa. But on his terms I have no wish to compete.

I hope my readers will be satisfied with the quite valid descriptions of meditative practices, the details of the ritual methods employed for counteracting diseases and epidemics, and the accounts of visionary struggles with the local mountain-gods, whose displeasure was usually accounted the cause of illness and untimely death. I hope that with my assistance they will be able to envisage the social conditions in these lands, the feuds between local chieftains, the quarrels between lamas, the villagers' persistence in hunting, however often they promise their lamas that they will renounce the taking of life, their simple fear of death combined with trust in their lamas' power to save them from unhappy rebirths, and their insatiable demands for consecrations and benedictions. There is sometimes a certain monotony in these routine activities, and all these lamas lament the time spent on serving others in trivial ways. They know well themselves that it is more important to practise true religion oneself than to put one's trust in the charms and the amulets that the simple-minded demand of them. Their relations with the ruling families of Lo (Mustangbhot) and the kings of Jumla are of considerable historical interest, but all these matters we will consider in more detail in the first part of the Introduction.

The second part of the Introduction 'Philosophy and Religion' gives a succinct account of Tibetan Buddhism as immediately relevant to these four biographies. It is primarily intended as a ready means of reference, to which the reader, guided by the footnotes, may refer when he is reading the biographies themselves.

I express my thanks to Mr. Philip Denwood for the help he has given me in the checking of proofs and of references and in the preparation of the maps. I am also very grateful to Miss Winifred Large who has taken so much interest and care in preparing my photographs for the illustrations in this book.

Among friends who have given us help and encouragement in Nepal, I would like to mention in particular Ambassador and Mrs. Henry Stebbins, Lynndon and Elizabeth Clough and Ralph and Lora Redford, to whom Corneille and I owe so much.

Berkhamsted,   David Snellgrove
29th November 1965

NOTE

The use of italics for individual words and phrases indicates:
1. correctly transliterated spellings for Tibetan (and sometimes Sanskrit) names and terms, which are thus distinguished from 'phonetic' spellings normally appearing in Roman type;
2. my own English translations, many newly devised, of Tibetan names and terms, e.g. *would-be Buddha, Powerbolt-Holder.*

The manner of these special spellings and translations is explained on pp. 71-74.

INTRODUCTION

I

THE LAND AND ITS PEOPLE

As may be seen from the map (end of book) the inner part of Dolpo is enclosed by a horse-shoe of high ranges consisting of the Sisne Himal (of over 22,500 feet above sea-level), the Kanjiroba Himal (of over 22,000 feet) and its southern extension which swings round to join with the most northerly range of the Himalayas (over 21,000 feet), nowadays the political frontier between Nepal and Tibet.[1] This horse-shoe opens to the north-west, and the whole internal river system drains through the gap and forms the head-waters of the Karnāli River. From the south-west side of the horse-shoe two subsidiary ranges, rising to about 20,000 feet, jut out into the centre of the horse-shoe. The inner part of Dolpo consists just of the inhabitable parts of the three intervening valleys. According to the Survey of India they would appear to be about 15,000 feet above sea-level, and in relationship to the general structure of the whole region, this height does not seem excessive. The whole area is a high table-land dipping towards the north-east between massive ranges, of which the heights are not in doubt. (See the cross-section, end map.) The main inner valleys of Dolpo are not deep troughs in these mountains, and they cannot be more than 4–5,000 feet below the summits.

The valleys are generally V-shaped, and the bottom is usually cut by a deep gorge of anything from 50 to 200 feet deep, except for the gorge below Shey which is a cleft between mountain-sides of sheer rock rising 2,000 feet to their summits. In some places the gorges become less pronounced and the valley-bottoms open into level stretches which are suitable for human habitation. Apart from these limited stretches of valley-bottom, villages have occasionally developed high above the gorges where there is an adequate water-supply from a tributary stream and some land suitable for cultivation (pl. 15).

[1] According to Mr. John Tyson's surveys of 1961 and 1964 the highest point of the entire Sisne Himal and Kanjiroba massif lies somewhere between 22,550 and 22,600 feet above sea-level.

Of the three main valleys the one below Shey is almost completely uninhabitable for its whole length. Shey itself is a remote monastic settlement, deserted during the long winter, at the foot of the pass leading over from Phoksumdo.[1] The village of *Bi-cher* (spelt Phijor on Survey of India maps) is the only large village in this valley and it has developed a long way back from the gorge along the banks of a gentle tributary stream. The important monastery of Samling and the nearly 'hamlet' of Trä, which are both dependencies of *Bi-cher*, are built on 'alps' in an isolated position high above the precipitous gorge. Being practically uninhabited, this most westerly of the three main internal valleys, has no local name at all.[2]

The centre one of these three valleys is known as *Nang-khong*, the 'Inner Recess', and the eastern valley is known as *Ban-tshang* which may be an old family name.[3] These two valleys are the scene of most of the events described in the biographies of the four lamas. Their waters meet at a place called Do-ra-sum-do, the 'stone enclosure where three waters meet', just below Yang-tsher Monastery.[4] There is a bridge at Do-ra-sum-do, strong enough to take pack-animals, and this bridge and the stupas at the junction of the two rivers were constructed and kept in repair by the lamas of Yang-tsher from the 16th century onwards.

Ascending the *Nang-khong* valley from Do-ra-sum-do, one travels along a gorge for five miles with the villages of *Kyi* and *Ka-rang* high above on the western side of the valley. From Saldang onwards (pl. 9) the gorge opens out for six or seven miles, making way along the river bank for the straggling village of Namdo and lastly for the village of Tsa (*rTsa*). At the head of a steep gorge just opposite Tsa is the little monastery of Hrap, which was founded by the Lama *Glorious Intellect* (pl. 24). Beyond Tsa the track leads up into uninhabited mountains and over the head of the horse-shoe to Tarap, two days journey distant.

[1] Concerning the route from Phoksumdo to Shey see *Himalayan Pilgrimage*, pp. 70–3, for the route from Phijor (*Bi-cher*) to Shey, pp. 134–5, and concerning Samling and Trä, pp. 110–33.
[2] The Survey of India name 'Sibu Khola' is an interesting example of how new names may be invented in the conviction that one is reproducing a genuine local name. The Indian surveyors must have pointed to the river valley above Shey and asked its name through the medium of a Nepali speaking interpreter. They must have been told 'Shey phu', which simply means the 'head of the valley above Shey'. They heard the reply as 'Sibu' and assumed it was the name of the whole river. In fact these rivers have no names locally.
[3] I have unsatisfactory spellings for both these names in *Himalayan Pilgrimage*. Although pronounced the same, *Nang-khong* should not have been confused with *gNam-gung*, which is the name of a village high above Namdo. For both places I used the spelling Namgung, *op. cit.*, p. 77. The Survey of India does not mark the village and spells *Nang-khong* as Nangung. The correct spelling *Ban-tshang* should replace my earlier phonetic spelling 'Panzang' and the Survey of India spelling 'Panjang'. Although it is quite reasonable to apply these names to the rivers (khola) as the Survey of India has done, it is worth recording that locally these names apply only to the very limited inhabitable stretches of these two valleys.
[4] The correct Tibetan spelling is *rDo-ra gsum-mdo*. As explained on p. 72 I have used 'phonetic' spellings for well known names and for those that occur frequently in the present book. All these geographical names are listed in the index. *gSum-mdo*, literally 'lower valley of three (waters)', is the regular Tibetan term for a junction of two rivers, for they count the united waters of the two rivers as a third one.

Starting again from Do-ra-sum-do a two hours climb up the right bank of the river which flows down from *Ban-tshang*, brings one to Yang-tsher Monastery, founded by *Religious Protector Glorious and Good* (pl. 14), and to the near-by village of Nyisal. Margom, the hermitage founded by *Merit Intellect*, can be seen high up on the cliffs above Yang-tsher.

Beyond Nyisal the way along the gorge is blocked, but judging by the ease with which Yang-tsher was reached from *Ban-tshang* in earlier times, one might assume that there used to be a route that way. Nowadays in order to reach the upper *Ban-tshang* valley (and it is really only this small territory to which the name properly applies), one must make a long detour through the village of Mö (*dMos*).[1]

Shimen (*Shi-min*) and *Ting-khyu*, each with more than thirty houses, are now the only villages of any size in this upper valley, but in former times T'ha-kar (*mTha'-dkar*) Monastery and the linked villages of *Phal* and *rTar* lay between them. These places are now ruins. Beyond *Ting-khyu* the track ascends through *Po-ldad* to the *Bin-du* Pass, and so out of the horse-shoe and down to the Tibetan 'steppes'. This was the route to Mustang and thence to Central Tibet. Until the end of the 18th century there was no political frontier to be crossed. Other tracks lead southwards out of the horse-shoe to Tarap and to Tsharka.

The two valleys of *Nang-khong* and *Ban-tshang* are linked by a route across the watershed from Shimen to Namdo. Half way across on a tributary that drains into the *Ban-tshang* river is the village of Koma (*Ko-mangs*).

From *Nang-khong* one can reach *Bi-cher* in the western valley by a choice of routes, either across the watershed from *Ka-rang* or from *gNam-gung*, which is the highest permanently inhabited site in Dolpo. The latter route leads also to Shey, which like *gNam-gung* is a dependency of Saldang.

From Do-ra-sum-do down to *Phod* (*S of I:* Phopāgaon) at the open end of the horse-shoe the gorge is practically uninhabited, as is also the whole area to the north. High above the left bank of the gorge are the villages of *lHo-ri*, a two to three hours' climb from Do-ra-sum-do, and *Ku* (*S of I:* Kuwāgaon) which I have not visited.

This completes a brief survey of the three valleys of 'inner Dolpo'. Lying outside the horse-shoe to the south are Tarap, Tsharka and Barbung, all of which drain westwards into the Bheri river. Routes remain open between Tarap and Tichurong the whole year, although in winter travel can be very difficult.[2] This southern part

[1] Concerning this route see *Himalayan Pilgrimage*, pp. 94–5.
[2] M. Corneille Jest spent the whole of the winter of 1960–1 in Tarap, and a description of this southern part of Dolpo is best left to him. Professor von Fürer-Haimendorf and Mr. John Tyson made brief visits there in 1962. Jest has made further visits in 1963 and 1965.

of Dolpo is enclosed to the south by the Dhaulagiri massif, which effectively cuts off all Dolpo from the Kāli Gandaki valley for almost half the year (p. 2). The inner part of Dolpo is thus doubly barricaded on this side during the winter months (pl. 7). To get from *Nang-khong* to *Ban-tshang* to Tarap or Tsharka one must cross the watershed between the head-waters of the Karnāli and the Bheri, and these routes are quite impossible in winter as we learned in 1960–1, when I was inside the horse-shoe at Namdo and effectively imprisoned in a stretch of valley twelve miles long. There is a route north-westwards beyond *Phod* which takes one out of the 'open end' of the horse-shoe and down through *Karma-rong* to Jumla or to Mugu (*Mu-gum*). This was the route used by *Merit Intellect* who stayed some time in Mugu, but it seems to be little used nowadays, for the people of inner Dolpo have lost the social contacts that they once had in that direction.[1]

Except in bad weather the routes on the Tibetan side seem to be possible most of the year. It is to these Tibetan 'steppe-lands', known in Dolpo simply as the 'North' (*byang*) that the Dolpo villagers send their herds and flocks in winter. The Tibetan nomad herdsmen who inhabit these regions, are the closest neighbours of the people of inner Dolpo. The route connecting Dolpo with Mustang which was so much more used in earlier times, crosses a southern projecting tongue of nomad territory. Unfortunately these border areas on the Tibetan side are practically unmapped, and since I could not cross the political frontier myself, it has not been possible to fix some of the place-names that occur in the biographies. The lamas of Dolpo were certainly much in demand among the nomads of the north right up to the Tsangpo throughout the region known as *Gro-shod* and as far east as *rDzong-kha* (*S of I:* Jongkha Dzong). They went on quite frequent visits to Kyirong, and Lama *Lord of Merit* was even invited (in A.D. 1699) to Sikkim, but he did not go. Monks from Dolpo were well known in Central Tibet and in the great *Ngor-pa* monastery of *Thub-bstan rNam-rgyal* they even had a 'Dolpo College' of their own. All this will be sufficiently illustrated by the events described in the biographies.

The people who occupy the remote Dolpo uplands are exclusively of Tibetan stock. They probably penetrated the northern flanks of the Himalayas in the early centuries of the Christian era. Their dialects, which vary appreciably from one valley to another, are akin to the speech of the Tibetan nomads to the north, but I would not assume that they belong to exactly the same racial strain originally. One

[1] John Tyson who led a small well equipped mountaineering party up a very difficult section of the higher reaches of the Karnāli (the Langu gorge) in 1964, boggles at my use of the expression 'open end' of the horse-shoe. Could any thing be less 'open' than this gorge, he asks. However, he assures me that although this route through to Dolpo is extremely difficult and little used, it is none the less quite practicable in autumn and early winter. Our lama *Merit Intellect* and others may perhaps have used a high level route of which we so far know nothing.

learns to recognize certain facial differences, and one can often distinguish the more recent nomad settlers. There is still much social contact, and intermarriage is not infrequent. However there is considerable difference between the nomads' way of life and that of the Dolpo villagers, and if for no other reason, this difference is imposed by the very different geographical conditions. As is well known, the nomads (Tibetan *'brog-pa* pronounced 'drokpa') live a vagrant life in their black tents and their whole economy is based upon their flocks and herds. The only buildings in their lands are the occasional monasteries, and some of the place-names in our biographies will apply not to villages but to nomad camping sites which are occupied regularly in certain seasons. By contrast the people of Dolpo live in settled communities, in villages of sturdily built stone houses, surrounded by the fields which produce their barley, buckwheat and occasionally wheat (as at *Bi-cher*). They can maintain their herds of yak and flocks of sheep only in close co-operation with their northern neighbours, for during the six desolate months of the Dolpo winter they have to farm out their animals on the Tibetan plains, making a fixed payment in grain for each head of livestock to the nomad custodians. Likewise their main trade consists in receiving the wool and salt of their nomad neighbours in exchange for their own grain as well as that which is traded up from the lower Nepalese valleys. The women of Dolpo are also good weavers (pl. 21), and their plain homespun cloth and their bright coloured blankets find a ready market in the lower valleys of Phoksumdo, Tichu-rong and Tibrikot.

As in all other Tibetan lands their staple food comprises barley-meal (tsamba), flat buckwheat cakes, meat, butter, curds and the large Tibetan radish (*la-phug*). Potatoes are grown very little. The only supply we found in the whole of *Nang-khong* came from a villager in *Ka-rang*. In 1960–1 the only chickens in inner Dolpo were two that were kept by a Tibetan refugee monk at Hrap Monastery. Sugar is very rare indeed, although on special occasions the sacrificial cakes, which are later eaten, are sweetened with molasses. Tibetan tea is drunk, but it has become very expensive, as supplies are no longer available through Tibet, and the tea-bricks that reach Dolpo now come up from Kathmandu among the loads of some enterprising small trader. Like all Tibetans, the men of Dolpo delight in travel and in small trading ventures, and during the long winter many of them leave Dolpo to earn their livelihood elsewhere, for only the comparatively wealthy can afford to stay at home consuming quite unproductively their accumulated supplies of food and fuel.

Dolpo lies at the same latitude as Cairo, but there the similarity ends. It may well appear as inhospitable a land as any human beings could choose to settle in. It lies across no route from anywhere to anywhere else. It can have attracted few invaders despite battles and conflicts around its borders.[1] A villager of *Bi-cher* says to the Lama *Religious Protector Glorious and Good* (p. 158): 'Generally speaking we have nothing else here in Dolpo, and so we are very fortunate when good lamas come duly to see us'. But in fact it is difficult enough even for a devoted lama to make the journey to *Bi-cher* during much of the year. The Dolpo winter is long and severe, lasting effectively from October until April. Although the weather is often fine during these months with clear blue sky and blazing sun, the whole land remains snow-bound. We ourselves travelled about as late as December, and started moving again as early as March, but with very little co-operation from the villagers who did not doubt that we were courting disaster. In *Nang-khong* the night temperature drops to $-27°$ C (more than $50°$ of frost F), and one learns to welcome the rising sun in his full dignity of life-giver. Even on a winter's day the direct rays of the sun produce a localized temperature of $30°$ C, but they have no penetrating power and in the shade the temperature will remain all day below freezing point. Winter storms lasting several days at a time may blot out the sun altogether, and then there is no ready relief from the bitter cold. Like the people of Dolpo we dressed in gowns of sheep-skin, locally made with the wool turned inwards. A way must be kept open through deep snow to one's water-supply, usually just a hole hacked in the frozen river (pl. 11), but for several days at a time even neighbours may be beyond reach. On days of good weather, and fortunately these are the majority, one is free to travel within the limits of the valley where one lives. The frozen river provides a far easier route than the tortuous rocky track that connects the villages in summer. Thus living in Namdo during the winter of 1960–1 I had all *Nang-khong* from Tsa to Do-ra-sum-do as my play-ground with Yang-tsher and Nyisal added as it were to give good measure. But we were completely cut off from *Ban-tshang* to the east, Shey and *Bi-cher* to the west, Tarap to the south, and by the uninhabited Karnāli gorge to the north.

During this long period from early October to late May the whole land is completely barren, and any livestock kept in the villages must be fed entirely with fodder stored from the last harvest. We fed our horse on a ration — generous for Dolpo — of dry barley-stalks, buckwheat and occasionally fermented barley as a special treat, but he was unusually favoured, for many of the domestic animals that stay in Dolpo can barely be kept alive.

It is not until May that the fields can be ploughed and hoed. The first green barley shoots appear in June, and quite suddenly it seems, the summer covering of grass and alpine flowers spreads over the mountains. The few clumps of willows in the villages, the only trees in Dolpo, burst into foliage. The snow retreats up the

[1] In the biography of the Lama *Good Deliverance* (*rNam-grol bzang-po*), which I have not included in the present volume there is a stray reference (folio 35a) to a Mongol incursion into *Ban-tshang*. Unfortunately exact dates cannot be given, but this lama lived in the 14th century.

mountain-sides and wild roses bloom in the valleys. Dolpo is at its best in June. The yaks[1] and sheep are brought back from their winter pasturage in the north. The villagers are busy cleaning out the irrigation channels which bring water to their fields from the mountains above, and the rivers are boisterous and turbid with their flood of melted snow and ice. The weather is like that of England in an unusually fine and warm spring.

From July onwards the monsoon clouds begin to force their way over the main Himalayan range, and although they have already let fall the bulk of their load on the southern flanks, the skies over Dolpo become overcast, and showers and short storms are frequent. Without the sun it becomes chilly, and one is reminded of an English summer at its worst. In September the skies clear again and Dolpo rapidly becomes dry. The harvest begins and thrashing and winnowing — all done by hand — continue into October. The animals are led off to the north. The mountains become brown and lifeless, and the long winter begins again.

During the better months Dolpo can be approached from three directions on the Nepalese side, up the Karnāli from the west (a route now seemingly little used by the people of Dolpo), up the Bheri from the south (the route we followed in 1956) and from the east across the north-eastern flanks of Dhaulagiri (the route we used in 1960 and 1961). This last route passes through the village of Sangdak (a day's climbing above Kāgbeni) and then crosses the great watershed between the Kāli Gandaki and the head-waters of the Bheri. From the top of this long pass one has a choice of routes, passing either through Tsharka or Barbung. The route from Sangdak to Tsharka and Barbung is closed during the winter, and so the southern part of Dolpo, although usually open to the south down the Bheri, is cut off for quite half the year from the Kāli Gandaki valley, to which it formally belongs for administrative purposes. This is the result of an unusual combination of historical and geographical factors.

Up to the end of the 18th century Mustang (Tibetan *sMon-thang*) was the chief town of a provincial district known as Lo, which extended down the valley of the Kāli Gandaki as far south as Kāgbeni.[2] Dolpo, a dependency of Lo, could be

[1] We seem to have accepted the term 'yak' as a general term for all animals of this species (*bos grunniens*), whether male or female. In Tibetan however the term yak (*g Yag*) applies only to the male, and our usage of the term never ceases to amuse the few Tibetans who read what we write, e.g. our term 'yak-butter' is analogous to 'bull-butter'. Thus I note in passing that the female is really called *'bri* (pronounced in Central Tibetan rather like 'Dee' as for the English river of that name). The 'dzo', which is a common Tibetan cross-breed of a *'bri* and an ox (*glang*) is also often wrongly referred to as a 'yak' in travellers' tales.

[2] The name Lo survives on the Survey of India maps (spelt Lho) in 'Lho Mantang', a 'phonetic' spelling of the local Tibetan name of Mustang. The Gorkhas invented the new district name 'Mustangbhot', but Lo is still used locally as the name of the whole region. See *Himalayan Pilgrimage*, pp. 188–99.

reached in three days during most of the year across what is now an intervening tongue of Tibetan territory. In former days no political frontier was involved, and as is clear from the biographies, the provincial governor of Lo was in constant contact with Dolpo. He himself or members of his family or his officials would come to ask for consecrations and blessings of Dolpo lamas, while their followers meanwhile collected the taxes.

Lo itself was a dependency of Nga-ri (Western Tibet), which in the 10th and 11th centuries consisted of three kingdoms, *Mar-yul*, *Gu-ge* and *sPu-hrangs*. The frontiers of these kingdoms remain undefined, but *sPu-hrangs* certainly bordered on what is now the NW corner of Nepal.[1] We learn from the first of the biographies (p. 84) that Mustang belonged to the kingdom of *bKra-shis-mgon*, king of Purang, who seems to have gained control over the other two kingdoms and established his capital in *Gung-thang*. The ruler of Lo is usually referred to in the Dolpo biographies as *sDe-pa* (provincial governor), but very little authority can have been exercised over Lo in the period with which we are concerned, and the office of 'provincial governor' had already become hereditary. In one of the earlier biographies he is referred to as 'enthroned' (*khri thog-pa*) and in the last of them (16th to 17th century) as 'king' (*rgyal-po*). But whatever his title, he seems to have had little local power.[2] There was a chain of strongholds (all now in ruins) the whole length of the Kāli Gandaki valley from Kāgbeni to Mustang, and the 'lords' of these castles seem to have ruled as absolute masters in their own small domains. They were fighting continually amongst themselves. In contrast to Dolpo, which is completely off the beaten track, Lo lay along one of the main trade-routes between Tibet and India.

At the end of the 18th century the Gorkhas, who had gained possession of the Kathmandu Valley in 1769, extended their control over the whole Kāli Gandaki valley, and Dolpo as a dependency of the old province of Lo, became theirs without their having to fight a blow on its account. But they failed to secure and indeed probably never thought of securing the piece of nomad territory connecting the two regions, for this lies beyond the most northerly range of the Himalayas which makes a loop to the south between Mustang and Dolpo. Thus it has come about that a perfectly good geographical frontier has effectively disrupted a long-standing historical relationship, for nowadays in order to travel from Mustang to Dolpo one must make a long detour south almost as far as Kāgbeni and then make the arduous journey across the two great watersheds between the Kāli Gandaki and the Bheri and between the Bheri and the Karnāli. However until quite recently there was

[1] Concerning these western Tibetan kingdoms, see Tucci, *Indo-Tibetica* II, p. 14 ff. and his *Preliminary Report on Two Scientific Journeys in Nepal*, p. 51 ff.
[2] The Mustang 'dynasty' has continued under present Nepalese administration with the title of Mustang Rāja. The family continues to seek brides from aristocratic Tibetan families.

nothing to prevent the simple villagers of Dolpo travelling freely across what had suddenly become a new political frontier, for the old routes to the north remained freely open to them and they could still travel to Central Tibet if they wished. But the new political changes gradually influenced the earlier cultural relationships. Religious life in Dolpo had always received encouragement and financial support from the leading families of Lo, and Mustang had been the primary stage in the journey of Dolpo lamas to Central Tibet. But now the castles of Lo were destroyed and their 'lords' either killed or impoverished. Moreover these new Gorkha rulers of Nepal proceeded to make war on Tibet in 1788 and 1789, and Mustang was committed to the Gorkha side in all the ensuing troubles. As a result Dolpo became politically and culturally more isolated than it had ever been before. Its people certainly gained in local independence under the Gorkha régime, for the yearly visits of the Nepalese tax-collector from Tukucha were less onerous than their earlier liabilities to the ruler of Mustang.[1] But since they received nothing in return for the little that they paid to their new rulers, their loss has been far greater than their gain. Religious life has certainly deteriorated in Dolpo during the last 150 years, and one must remember that their religion provided all their cultural and educational needs. Judging by the deserted sites that one sees, one would assume that there has been economic decline as well.

Dolpo's chief neighbour to the west was the kingdom of Jumla, and this too was absorbed into the new Gorkha domains. Jumla was the chief town of a people known as Khasa, whose language Khaskura had been spreading steadily eastwards, so that before the 18th century it had already become the *lingua franca* throughout the valleys south of the main Himalayan range at least as far as the Kathmandu Valley. The Khasa were a vigorous and aggressive people, and they certainly made their presence felt in the Kāli Gandaki valley. One of our biographies refers to an occasion (p. 153) when the King of *Mon* asked a lama of Dolpo to come and act as intermediary at a reconciliation that he and his ministers were arranging between quarrelling clan-leaders in Lo. The term *Mon* is still used in Dolpo to refer generally to the lower valleys to the west and the south, and since until the end of the 18th century these regions were all more or less subject to the king of Jumla, he is usually referred to in the biographies as the King of *Mon*.[2] There is no suggestion that he ever exercized any control over Dolpo, but the Tibetan-speaking areas to the NW of Dolpo clearly belonged to his domains. We have the interesting story (pp. 117–8)

---

[1] The Dolpo communities still make small nominal offerings to the Mustang Rāja, and they are still willing to accord suitable respect to any member of his family who may happen to visit them.
[2] The only names of these kings that occur in our texts are *'Byid-ras* and his successor variously spelt *Dza-li-phan* (p. 202) and *'Dza'i-'phan* (p. 174) who must both have lived in the 15th century. It seems impossible to relate them to the names which occur in the genealogies quoted by Tucci in his *Preliminary Report*, p. 116 ff.

of the meeting of Lama *Merit Intellect* with the Queen of Jumla in Mugu (*Mu-gum*). The Jumla royal-family was Hindu, but they were clearly tolerant towards their Tibetan Buddhist subjects, and always ready it seems to ask the advice and the help of Dolpo lamas, in whose special powers of prognosis they were quite willing to believe.

When *Merit Intellect* came to Dolpo from Lo in the 1540s, Tibetan religion, both Buddhist and *Bon*, was firmly established there. His teacher, *Sher mKhan-po* of Lo, advised him to go, saying: 'If you go to Dolpo, the people there are well based in their faith and well disposed to religion. Thus conditions are favourable and there will be an increase of benefits to others, so it would be good if you went there'. So far as 'professional' religious practice was concerned, Dolpo seems to have been primarily a land for the solitary meditation of lama-sages, assisted by one or two chosen disciples. Near *Ting-khyu* there were three small monasteries (*dGon-pa*), *Ba-lung*, *sPang-ri* and *Grva-lung*, which had been founded by a lama from *Gro-shod*, named *rTogs-ldan Rin-po-che*.[1] Higher up the valley was the village and monastery of *Po-ldad*. *Ban-tshang* was more accessible to Lo than any other part of Dolpo, and the religious traditions there were *Ngor-pa*, a branch of the Sa-kya tradition, just as they were in Lo.

There was another small monastery at *Zho-gam* above the gorge beyond *Do-ra-sum-do*, and yet another near *Bi-cher*, where a lama known as the 'Cave-Hermit' was living. Also near *Bi-cher* was the important *bon* monastery of Samling, which had been founded by *rGyal-mtshan rin-chen* in the first half of the 13th century.[2] Although Buddhism and *Bon* flourished together in Dolpo, they usually ignore quite deliberately one another's existence, for although the villagers must always have had recourse to both forms of religion, the 'professional' practisers were very careful to keep apart, and it is they who have produced all the available literary material.

Up to this time (the 15th century) the Dolpo monasteries (*dGon-pa*) were all very small and might really better be referred to as hermitages. Usually there was just a meditating lama there, assisted by one or two chosen disciples. Thus when *Merit Intellect* arrived in *Ting-khyu*, the Lama *Good Deliverance* had just completed one year of a three years' strict retreat at *Grva-lung* Monastery, so all he could do was to continue his journey and look for another lama to help him.

From the start Dolpo must have been in contact (through Lo) with some of the main religious centres in Central Tibet, and it is likely that many young men of

---

[1] This lama, of whose biography I have a MS copy, founded monasteries in Tarap as well. I have not yet sufficient cross-references for fixing his dates.
[2] Concerning this approximate date, see my *Nine Ways of Bon*, Oxford 1967, pp. 4–5 fn.

THE LAND AND ITS PEOPLE 11

Dolpo who went there for religious studies, spent the rest of their lives in Tibet proper.[1] Perhaps only those of an ascetic and contemplative disposition returned to live the life of hermits in their own country.

Merit Intellect (1516–1581) founded the monasteries of Margom and T'ha-kar. Margom is built high up on the cliffs above Nyisal, and as there was not sufficient room there for a growing community, *Merit Intellect's* successor, *Religious Protector Glorious and Good* (1536–1625) founded Yang-tsher Monastery down below on an 'alp' overhanging the gorge. Thereafter Yang-tsher and T'ha-kar developed as full-scale monastic communities under the authority of a single abbot.

Glorious Intellect (1527–1596) was also a disciple of *Merit Intellect*, but being better suited to the life of a meditating sage, he established himself in a small monastery at Hrap about half an hour's climb above the village of Tsa at the upper end of *Nang-khong*. This place was occupied by a refugee Tibetan monk from Drepung in 1960–1. T'ha-kar is now in ruins, but the line of 'abbots' still continues at Yang-tsher, where the present incumbent *bSod-nams chos-rgyal* is 17th in succession from *Religious Protector Glorious and Good*. Lama *Lord of Merit* (1660–1731), whose biography completes my translated set of four, was 9th in this succession.

As far as I know, there are no other biographies of lamas of this succession. That of *Merit Intellect's* teacher, *Good Deliverance*, might have been included, but it is concerned almost entirely with lists of works studied and meditations practised, and so contains little information of general local interest. There is a 'Book of Songs' (*mgur-'bum*) of Lama *Ngag-dbang rNam-rgyal* of *gNam-gung*, and an interesting biography together with a song-book and other writings of Lama *bsTan-'dzin ras-pa* ('Cotton-clad Comprehender of the Doctrine') of Shey. Both these lamas were contemporaries of Lama *Lord of Merit*. *bsTan-'dzin ras-pa* followed Ka-gyü-pa tradition and I hope to devote a separate work to him in due course. He was a friend of *Lord of Merit*, who visited him several times at Shey (see pp. 267–9), but his life really lies outside the context of this present work, which is concerned with four lamas all of the same *Ngor-pa* tradition and their activities in *Ban-tshang* and *Nang-khong*.

---

[1] *Dol-pa* occurs as the 'clan-name' of several Tibetan lamas and yogins. The most famous of these was the great scholar *Shes-rab rGyal-mtshan* (1292–1361), founder of *Jo-nang*, who was nicknamed *Dol-po-pa* and was certainly a native of Dolpo. He is still remembered locally and the Lama of *bDe-chen bla-brang* kindly wrote me quite spontaneously a short note about him, quoting the date of his birth quite correctly and giving as his birth-place Pu of *Ban-tshang*. Roerich mistranslates slightly the relevant passage in the *Blue Annals* (p. 776) as 'he was born in the family known as Ban-tshang of Dolpo'. There is no word for family in the Tibetan text. Also mentioned in the *Blue Annals* (p. 353) is a certain 'Great Hermit of Dolpo' (*Dol-po sGom-chen*), who being a contemporary of *Rin-chen bZang-po*, must have lived in the 10th and 11th centuries. It is likely that Buddhism came to Dolpo in the 10th century, that is to say during the reign of King *bKra-shis-mgon* of Purang, who is remembered traditionally as their 'religious king'.

Their biographies represent these four lamas as of four different types. *Merit Intellect* seems to be primarily a hermit, *Religious Protector* a teacher and organizer, *Glorious Intellect* a dreamer and exorcist, and *Lord of Merit* a scholar and traveller. But reading more carefully, one realizes that with the possible exception of *Lord of Merit* their activities embraced all these various pursuits and practices. From his biography *Merit Intellect* may appear as a hermit, but from the biography of his pupil *Religious Protector* we learn that he must have done a great deal of teaching. Also, like *Glorious Intellect*, he roamed around in his dreams, visiting his previous lamas and quelling local gods, but in his case we are simply informed of this briefly without any illustrative stories, whereas *Glorious Intellect* or possibly his biographer delighted in such tales. *Religious Protector*'s powers of clairvoyance are described as a kind of supplement to his biography, and *Lord of Merit* for all his urbanity spent several periods in contemplative retreat. He alone is not credited with magical powers of any kind. Thus the seeming differences probably reflect the predilections of the lamas themselves, for although these biographies were composed by devoted disciples, the material used was all explicitly autobiographical. It is this that makes them so unusually interesting. *Glorious Intellect* for example certainly believes in his own extraordinary powers, but when he is defeated by a local god, he does not hesitate to say so. A devoted disciple writing up the events afterwards could not have failed to present his master as triumphant throughout.

These biographies provide us with the means of comparing a worthy lama's own estimate of his nature and powers with his followers' presentation of their teacher as a predestined and perfected buddha. In *Buddhist Himālaya* (p. 279) I quoted the observation of M. Mircea Éliade that 'at a certain "popular" level every master in the spiritual life comes to join the archtype of the Great Magician, who has obtained release in this very life and is thus possessor of all powers' (*Le Yoga*, p. 294). This would suggest that magical powers are a simple attribution of his credulous followers and originally unclaimed by the master himself. I doubt on present evidence if such an assumption is justified. There certainly is a marked difference between these lamas' opinions of themselves and their disciples reinterpretation of their lives, but it seems that the possession of magical powers is one of the few attributes on which all are agreed. The disciples merely extend the scope of these powers so as to include those which are traditionally associated with the perfection of buddhahood.

It is assumed by all concerned that a good lama can diagnose the cause of sickness and trouble and that there is a good chance of his effecting a remedy. If a man's life-force (*bla*) is carried off by a disgruntled local god, the lama may be capable of redeeming it and wresting it back by force. The layfolk believe that a competent lama may be able to guide a man's consciousness after death to a happy state of rebirth. His success in this task will depend to a large extent upon the merits of the deceased, but neither he nor his clients doubt his ability to improve upon any given situation. All are agreed that a competent lama can produce rain. Lamas and layfolk alike believe in the effectiveness of charms and amulets and especially of the auspicious verses and gifts that the lamas themselves send to one another. One only marks a greater deference on the part of the lama in the use of all these external means. Perhaps I should add that we are not concerned here with the quackeries of self-seeking and unqualified lamas who cynically dispose of charms and cures for their own material gain. Our use of the term 'magical powers' is really misleading, since for a qualified lama it is rather a matter of manipulating the complex relationships of causes and their effects, much as a qualified medical practitioner (in an entirely different context it is true) relates his cure to the known condition of his patient. For both men success depends upon accurate diagnosis and professional knowledge, and in some cases, by the very nature of the circumstances, there can be very little or even no hope of success. Thus *Merit Intellect*, using tried methods appropriate to the whole tradititional Tibetan setting, fights single-handed against an outbreak of small-pox in *Mu-gum* with just the same determination as a good physician, alone amongst ignorant and frightened people, might set to work nowadays.

The extra powers attributed to these lamas, which they do not claim for themselves, relate to their predestined perfection, their omniscience and their power over their own time of death. The first they deny implicitly by their own accounts of their struggles towards their present state, and the rest they deny explicitly whenever the occasion may arise. Thus *Religious Protector* is asked by one of his faithful attendants who is on the point of death, if he will promise that they will always be born together in their future lives. He replies: 'Since there was some connection from our former lives, we have met in this one. So by the combination of these circumstances it would seem certain that we shall meet in other lives. Apart from this I am not a sage who can promise such things, but it would be alright to say a prayer' (p. 169). When he himself is about to die, the monks and the villagers beg him to remain, urging their request with the promise that the monks will spend three years in retreat and the villagers will give up hunting for five years. *Religious Protector* replies: 'As for your asking me to stay, you need someone who has power over birth and death. I am not such a person.' Maybe these requests to the lamas to prolong their lives are just pious make-believe, like the descriptions of flowers raining down from the skies, rainbow colours in the shape of a tent and the spontaneous sounds of religious music, which regularly accompany the cremation of these holy men. The expectation of relics in the form of bones shaped like divinities or embossed with mystic syllables never goes disappointed, and in this respect I might mention that in 1961 I was shown a bone curiously embossed with the Tibetan letter A as a relic from the funeral urn of Lama Sherap of Samling, who was so helpful to me during my stay at his monastery in 1956 and who died in 1958. The conditions of life in Dolpo have changed hardly at all.

In Dolpo there were no chieftains ruling from fortified strongholds, as in Lo, and unlike some other Tibetan territories Dolpo never belonged to any kind of feudal system.[1] The villages, often by their very remoteness from one another, have remained responsible for their own affairs. Local authority is vested in a village headman, usually the senior member of a locally respected family, whose long ancestry is generally acknowledged. Some of their names clearly suggest the origin of the family concerned, e.g. *sPu-rang* (the old western Tibetan kingdom of that name), *Khyung-po* (from *Khyung-lung*, the old capital of western Tibet), or *bKag-ga* (from *bKag* that is Kāgbeni in the Kāli Gandaki valley). Others such as *lDong*, *Se*, *rMu*, *mDza'*, are probably derived from old Tibetan families who came to Dolpo from Lo. *Ya-ngal* is the family-name of the lamas of Samling and of the chief family of *Bi-cher* nearby. According to the genealogy of the lamas of Samling, this family came to Dolpo in the 12th century from *Klu-brag* (*S of I:* Lubra) in lower Lo. Another important family-name is *Phyug-'khor*, to which the Yang-tsher lamas and the leading family of Nyisal belong.

As in Tibet itself, it seems to be generally assumed that pre-eminence in worldly and religious affairs are simply different sides of the same coin, and all our four lamas (or their biographers) are at pains to trace their lineage back to royal connections. In the period covered by these four biographies the lamas of Yang-tsher and T'ha-kar were either designated by their predecessors or elected on their personal merits. But such a system can only survive in a well organized religious community where scholarly attainments and teaching ability receive due recognition. With any serious deterioration in monastic standards the monastery becomes drawn inevitably into dependence upon the nearby village, where the leading family will soon provide for lamas as well as for headmen. This is the system to which Yang-tsher has now reverted, and it is the one that was always followed at Samling and *Bi-cher*, for in the case of celibate lamas the succession passes from uncle to nephew. There is nothing rigid about such a system, for as is well known, Tibetan family relations tend to be vague and all-embracing. No distinction need be made between one's own children, those of one's brothers', those of a second wife, or even those adopted. Thus a family line is kept going fairly easily and there may

[1] The name of the local god of *Zel*, namely 'King of the *Zel* Fort' (*Zel-rdzong rGyal-po*) might suggest that there was a fort there originally, but it is possible that the name was suggested by the rock itself, which towers above Namdo. There is a small monastery there now. The only fort now standing in Dolpo is a small defence-work, never used for human habitation, just above *Ting-khyu*.

even be quite a wide choice of suitable 'candidates'. The office of headman is hereditary in just this kind of free and easy way. A resolute son will naturally follow in the steps of his father, but the office may equally well pass to a nephew or a son-in-law. Until his death two years ago the 'chief man' of all Dolpo was *Nyi-ma Tshe-ring* of Saldang, about whom I have already written in *Himalayan Pilgrimage* (p. 81 ff.). He was recognized as such quite informally on account of his personal wealth and prestige (pl. 32).

Our texts refer often to the 'inner and outer corners' (*gru phyi nang*) of Dolpo. The 'inner corners' were the five villages around the monasteries of *Zho-gam*, Margom and Yang-tsher, namely Nyisal, Mö, *Ka-rang*, *Ti-ling* and *Ku*, and the 'outer corners' were the rest of *Nang-khong* and *Ban-tshang*. In this context Tarap, Bi-cher and Phod are listed separately as outlying places. The expression 'four corners' (*gru bzhi*) of Dolpo was used to refer to the whole of *Nang-khong* and *Ban-tshang*. These expressions were used without any special administrative significance, and nowadays the expression 'four corners' of Dolpo is used to include Tarap, Tsharka and Barbung as well.

Every village and monastery has its own local god, such as 'Our Lord the Local God' (*Jo-bo Yul-lha*) of Namdo, *Wa-la-wa* of Yang-tsher, 'Refuge of All Joy' (*Kun-dga'-skyabs*) of T'ha-kar and the 'King of the Fort' at *Zel*. They are conceived of as living in lordly style in palaces inside the mountains. They appear dressed in fine white clothes with turbans of coloured silk and jewelry of all kinds, sometimes riding on horseback with a large horse-borne following. It is important that the villagers should not offend the local gods in any way, e.g. by polluting his domains or by disturbing the soil for building operations without his consent. When a villager is clearly in the wrong, there is little a competent lama can do against the power of a local god, and unless a ransom can be arranged, the offending villager will fall sick and die. When the local god's attack is merely malicious, the lama is in a much stronger position and he can be reasonably sure of winning the contest through the power of his own (Buddhist) tutelary divinities.

Nothing happens in an arbitrary way. There are reasons for everything if only one is clever enough to work them out. A misfortune of any kind is always capable of explanation, and if it is undeserved, it can be the more easily averted. A strong moral sense is present the whole time, coupled with the conviction that one should never expect something for nothing. Bargaining plays as important part in the religious life as it does in everyday buying and selling. Ransom offerings compensate a divinity for his favours. One's accumulated merits compensate for one's accumulated demerits. Sometimes religious bargaining comes very close to blackmail. Thus the villagers sometimes bargain in the bluntest possible way with their lamas, as when the people of *Ting-khyu* want Lama *Religious Protector* to come and solve a local quarrel with the neighbouring nomads. He protests quite truthfully that he is really not well enough to travel, but they force him to come by saying that they will only give up hunting if he will visit them. Hunting is the chief abomination in the eyes of the lamas of Dolpo, but despite continual promises, it is clearly never given up except for short periods. Lama *Merit Intellect* makes use of it as a method of coercion to gain his own ends. He wants as his own disciple *Religious Protector*, who is then a young monk attached to the Abbot of *Zho-gam*, and he is not content that this pupil of his should spend some time at *Zho-gam* and some time at Margom. Thus on one occasion when *Religious Protector* delays his return from *Zho-gam*, *Merit Intellect* sends a message all around saying that he is so displeased at the way the villagers persist in hunting around Margom, that he has resolved to go to *Lab-phyi*, one of the places a long way eastwards on the northern slopes of the Himalayas, where *Mi-la ras-pa* used to meditate. The monks and villagers gather around begging him not to go, and when the Abbot of *Zho-gam* joins his entreaties to theirs, *Merit Intellect* says in effect: 'I may not be moved by the others, but I am moved by you. Just let *Religious Protector* stay here with me, and I will not go away'. In the general state of anxiety that *Merit Intellect* will really carry out his threat and go, the Abbot of *Zho-gam* has no choice but to accept the bargain, although he is expected to provide for *Religious Protector's* maintenance as well. I hope my readers will not miss in these biographies such pleasing subtleties as these.

The villagers are presented throughout as being rather tiresome with their unsatiable demands and their overwhelming attentions, but also as equally generous in their offerings. One remains impressed by the great accumulations of gifts and the continual return distributions to all and sundry. Their religion was clearly a vital force in the life of these people, and except for the troublesome *Khang-dkar-ba* family of Lo, there seem to be none who could not be finally urged to attend to its precepts. The story of Chief Olo, brother of the Ruler of Lo, who is forced to return to political problems at home, when all he really wants is to go into religious retreat in Dolpo, seems to typify all the inner yearning of these people towards the religious life as their final ideal. At the same time their moral code, which outwardly resembles ours so closely, operates as part of a set of entirely different philosophical and religious beliefs, and thus all kinds of different human values emerge.

II

PHILOSOPHY AND RELIGION

The elements arise from causes and it was their cause the Buddha told,
And the way to bring them to a stop, that too the Great Ascetic told.

These ancient verses, engraved on shrines and written at the ends of manuscripts, have been quoted from early times as the quintessence of Buddhist teaching. I have argued elsewhere that although there have been considerable developments in the forms and methods of practice, the ideal life of a Buddhist has continued to follow much the same patterns,[1] and religious attitudes in Dolpo have been in many respects no different from those in other Buddhist lands.

The Elements of Existence

The fundamental 'world view' of Buddhism is expressed in the doctrine that phenomenal elements, comprising the whole of existence, arise as a complex causal nexus. Everything in all its parts is causally related with everything else. Partial knowledge of these causes enables one to manipulate phenomenal events to some extent, and perfect knowledge of the causes enables one to bring the whole process to a stop. (By his power to change the course of events, the 'manipulator' may appear to be outside the causal nexus to some extent at least, and I shall refer to this apparent contradiction in the system later on.) Now most people in Dolpo, as elsewhere, are interested in the uses to which partial knowledge can be applied, for this can be of help to them in their everyday affairs. Only a minority (the true ascetics) have been concerned to gain perfect knowledge in the Buddhist sense, and it is only they who know why they have wanted to bring the whole process to a stop. It is they who have taught that all the elements of existence are causally related, that they are all essentially impermanent and so ultimately unreal. This fundamental impermanence, they have argued, results in universal suffering, for no sentient being can ever retain in the phenomenal sphere the objects of its desires. Phenomenal life progresses by selfishness and discontent. The primary Buddhist truth, the 'truth' of the sages, is universal suffering. Ordinary Buddhists every-

[1] See *Buddhist Himalāya*, pp. 279–80.

where have subscribed to these views without necessarily accepting them as practical propositions, as they are usually all too concerned with the problems of their daily lives. They have no hope and perhaps no wish to bring the whole process to a stop. All they can do is to live their lives as best they may, asking the help of their 'spiritual superiors' in times of special need, and hoping that in their next lives they will be born in no worse circumstances.

The Doctrine of Rebirth

The belief in rebirth belongs to the general conception of existence as one great causal nexus. Sentient beings, together with all the surrounding circumstances of their existence, are causally produced by previous states of existence. Although Buddhist philosophers have continued to deny the existence in formal terms of a 'soul' or 'inner self' or 'person' which transmigrates from one life to another, the idea of personal survival in the sense that one sentient being is reborn as another and yet another sentient being in what is in effect a kind of personal series of existences, has always been implied in Buddhist teachings. Apart from the idea of universal ignorance (as opposed to perfect knowledge which brings the process to a stop) no beginning in time for these series of existences is ever suggested, and we are often told that it has by now gone on for so long that all sentient beings everywhere have been (or at least might well have been) our own mother in some other state of existence. This is one of the main arguments advanced for exercising kindness to all beings. This general Buddhist belief in rebirth as a series of personal existences gives special point to the warnings of the sages that amidst the myriads of different kinds of life throughout the universe, human life is rare and so hard to obtain. Yet it is human life alone that provides a possible way towards the perfect knowledge of buddhahood and an escape from the revolving circle of rebirth and universal suffering. Thus the least one can do, they argue, is to perform good deeds in one's present life, so that the accumulated merits of these good deeds may result in rebirth in a well endowed human body, for if the conditions of life are adverse, even a human body will be of little use. The necessary conditions for the practice of a satisfactory religious life are listed conventionally as ten blessings and eight disablements. The ten blessings are arranged as two groups of five, one group referring specifically to oneself, and one group to outside circumstances:

1. one must be a male,
2. one must be born in a Buddhist country,
3. one must be complete in one's senses and physical parts,
4. one must not be of perverse intentions,

5. one must know how to direct one's faith aright,
6. a Buddha must have appeared in the world,
7. he must have taught the doctrine,
8. the doctrine he has taught must have remained intact,
9. one must be willing to follow his doctrine,
10. one must have a good religious guide.

The eight disablements are the following:

1. to be disturbed by the Five Evils (stupidity, wrath, desire, malignity and envy),
2. to be a fool,
3. to be taught by an heretical teacher,
4. to be lazy,
5. to be overwhelmed by the effects of one's former evil acts,
6. to be in another's power,
7. to be concerned for the needs of one's present life,
8. to practise religion only for the sake of outward appearance.

As with other Buddhist 'sets of propositions', one could find fault with the logical coherence of these eighteen conditions, and this is because they have developed in a haphazard manner and afterwards have gained conventional acceptance.[1] They are interesting however in the importance that they attach to human life as such, for despite its continuously expressed concern for 'sentient beings' everywhere, Buddhism for all practical purposes is primarily concerned, like all other religions, with the lives of human beings.

Forms of the Universe

Having diagnosed to their own satisfaction the causal nature of all existence, Buddhist teachers are far less concerned about the actual forms of the world or worlds in which we live. They have usually been content to accept the forms suggested by other thinkers, for forms are all relative and impermanent anyway. They often refer to existence as the 'threefold world', that is to say the 'world of desire' (the ordinary phenomenal world), the 'world of form' (the world of divine beings) and the 'formless world' (the pure realms leading to the perfect knowledge of enlightenment). Thus conceived as a series of higher states of existence, the universe is represented physically as a central mountain (known as *Kailāsa*, *Meru* or

[1] In the present case these lists are taken from an important 19th-century work, *The Teachings of Lama All-Good* (*Kun-bzang bla-ma'i zhal-lung*), folio 14a onwards and folio 20a onwards.

Ti-se), surrounded by four major continents, of which the southern one is occupied by human beings. The gods dwell on the higher reaches of the central mountain, whose very summit represents the supreme enlightenment of perfect knowledge. This general lay-out is repeated in the symbolism of the 'mystic circle' (*maṇḍala*), which will be described below.

The phenomenal world is also described as the 'wheel of existence' (*srid-pa'i 'khor-lo*). This consists of six segments, representing the six possible realms of rebirth, the realms of the gods, of the titans, of men, of animals, of tormented spirits, and of the hells.[1]

As a kind of poetic cliché existence is sometimes described as the outer vessel and the inner elixir (*phyi snod nang bcud*), the lifeless parts that form a kind of basis being the 'vessel', and all sentient beings, gods, men and the rest, being the 'elixir'. It is interesting to note that in Tibetan rituals an actual vase containing consecrated water, symbolizes the whole of existence in its perfected state, but this need not concern us here. It is enough that the reader should be familiar with the term 'the vessel and its elixir'.

Tibetan Buddhists have been content to conceive of the universe on the pattern of a central mountain and four major continents, and they have otherwise given little thought to the whole subject. Since phenomenal existence consists of constantly fluctuating elements, which by their very impermanence lack all essential reality, the whole show presents itself, so far as their philosophers are concerned, as one great illusion, and through perfect knowledge of the causes, their sages are intent on bringing this illusion to a stop. Illusion and suffering are the two concepts that they strive to transcend. This transcendence manifests itself to them as 'universal sameness' (*mnyam-pa-nyid*), as the 'sameness of flavour' (*ro mnyam-pa*). They have realized that there is no essential difference between phenomenal existence and its transcendence, between the physical and the metaphysical. These twin concepts are expressed in Tibetan by a concise abbreviated term '*khor-'das*, which means in full the 'wheel of existence' and 'suffering transcended', representing the Sanskrit Buddhist terms *saṃsāra and nirvāṇa*. It is the satisfactory translation of terms such as these, so concise in their form, yet so complex in meaning, which makes the translation of Buddhist works rather difficult. A translation such as 'physical and metaphysical', however satisfactory as a readable translation, inevitably represents Buddhist philosophical concepts in a western garb, and this may be misleading. But perhaps it is enough if the reader is warned against this in advance. Another Tibetan term used for these same twin concepts in *srid-zhi*, meaning literally the 'emergence' of the phenomenal world and the 'calm' that is effected when the illusion is brought to a stop.

[1] For a description of the Wheel of Existence see *Buddhist Himālaya*, pp. 13–17.

Formalized Conceptions of Buddhahood

The concept of the 'universal sameness' of the physical and metaphysical spheres allows for the conception of a Buddha as a saviour who has the power to manifest himself at the various levels of existence. Thus a Buddha is simply a manifestation of the supreme enlightenment of perfect knowledge at any level of existence that suits the needs of religious practisers.[1]

Parallel with the three stages of the threefold world, the world of desire, the world of form and the formless world, buddhahood is conceived of conventionally as possessing *Three Bodies*, an *Absolute Body* which corresponds to the formless world, a *Glorious Body* which is manifest in the heavens to meditating sages, and a *Physical Body* which appears on earth usually as a human teacher. These *Three Bodies* may be represented by Buddhas of different names. Among the older orders of Tibetan Buddhism with which we are concerned in this present book,

the *Absolute Body* is represented by the Buddha *All Good* or the Buddha *Boundless Light*,
the *Glorious Body* by the *would-be buddha Glancing Eye* or *Powerbolt-Being*,
the *Physical Body* by *Lotus-Born*, Teacher from Urgyan and all the perfected lamas of his tradition.

Thus since they are regarded by their followers as perfected buddhas manifest in the world of men, the four lamas of Dolpo with whom we are concerned here, are identified as manifestations of *Lotus-Born (Padmasambhava)*.[2]

In accordance with another conception of buddhahood as manifesting itself throughout space in all four directions, there exists a set of five buddhas, one for the centre and one for each of the four main directions. A sixth buddha, the *Powerbolt-Holder*, is sometimes added as representing the supreme and essential unity of the more usual set of five.

Buddhas are also frequently praised under their three aspects, physical, verbal and mental, as Body, Speech and Mind. This set of three is sometimes increased to five by the addition of their Qualities and their Acts.

As a set of five, whether as five in a special sense, or five in a psychophysical sense

[1] See below pp. 82, 186–7.
[2] For an account of his miraculous activities see W. Y. Evans-Wentz, *The Tibetan Book of the Great Liberation*, pp. 105–92, 'The Epitome of the Great Guru's Biography'. 'Lotus-Born' holds this pre-eminent position among the followers of the older orders of Tibetan Buddhism, the Nying-ma (Old Order), the Sa-kya (the Order of the great monastery of Sa-kya and its daughter monasteries) and the Ka-gyü (Order of the Transmitted Word), and it is to the teachings of these three orders that Buddhism in Dolpo adheres. These orders possess mystical (more or less secret) teachings concerning yoga and meditation, which are referred to in our texts as the *Great Perfection* (*rDzogs-chen*), which is primarily Nying-ma, and the *Great Symbol* (*Phyag-chen*), which is primarily Ka-gyü. See below.

(*viz.* Body, Speech, Mind, Qualities and Acts), they are regarded as the purifiers or neutralizers of the Five Evils (*viz.* stupidity, wrath, desire, malignity and envy).[1] This set of Five Evils is however an extension of an original set of just Three Evils (stupidity, wrath and desire), and thus the evils of phenomenal existence may be referred to collectively as the 'Three Evils' or the 'Five Evils'.

These different overlapping sets of conventionalized terms may appear a little bewildering and sometimes even contradictory, but one must remember that despite the efforts at precision of Buddhist philosophers during certain periods of the doctrine, the actual practisers of the religion have usually set no great store by precise philosophical definition.

Meditation and the Mystic Circle

While they owe their conception of existence to philosophical speculation, it is by means of meditation that they validate their ideas. Hence they are far less concerned with arguing (although this is certainly part of their training), than with asserting what they themselves now know to be the truth.[2] Truth itself is regarded under two aspects, as absolute (*viz.* the known truth of universal sameness), and as relative (*viz.* philosophical, doctrinal and moral truths as may be necessary for one's advance towards the absolute truth). All conventional sets of philosophical and religious terms belong to relative truth, and in so far as they may be drawn up to suit the needs of different types of religious practisers, they may quite understandably appear contradictory sometimes. It is only essential that they should all lead to the same goal. The training of a qualified monk or yogin[3] is devised to lead him beyond relative truths to the supreme and absolute truth, or in other words from the outward appearances of things to a realization of their inner essential non-reality, which is actually experienced as blissful fulfilment.

One of the chief means to this end is the mystic circle (*maṇḍala*), which is a physical representation, either painted on cloth or marked out on the ground, of the whole of existence as Buddhist sages conceive it. The mystic circle is thus primarily the symbolic representation of all the psychophysical conceptions that fit into the fivefold scheme of a centre and four main directions, namely:

---

[1] Concerning the sets of Five Buddhas and of Five Evils and their development from earlier sets of three, see *Buddhist Himālaya*, pp. 64–7.

[2] The activities of an academically qualified lama are defined as threefold: 'expounding' ('*chad-pa*) refers to his teaching ability, 'confounding' (*rtsod-pa*) refers to his skill in debate, and 'propounding' (*brtsom-pa*) refers to his literary activities.

[3] Just as for Hinduism, so for Buddhism, the term 'yogin' refers to a religious practiser who achieves his aims by means of strict bodily and mental training and control, whether he lives inside a monastery, or as a solitary hermit, or as a married man. There are practices to suit all these ways of life.

the Five Elements (earth, water, fire, air and space),
the Five Components of Personality (body, feelings, perception, impulses and consciousness),
the Five Evils and the Five Buddhas (who purify the evils).

Thus representing at one and the same time the physical world, human personality, the evils of existence and the supreme enlightenment of perfect knowledge (further defined for this purpose as a set of Five Wisdoms), the mystic circle serves as means to the reintegration of refractive relative truths.[1] It is the supreme symbol of universal sameness.

Like all symbols, it is useless in itself, and its practisers must first be educated in the relative truths that it represents. Thus all our lamas in these biographies begin their serious education with the study of philosophical and doctrinal works. This part of their education is not so very different — at least in its outward forms — from some of our university education today, although learning texts by heart no longer forms an essential part of our training. But learning texts is not enough in itself. Learning is defined as a dual process, first of 'listening and thinking' (*thos-bsam*) and secondly of 'absorbing', literally 'receiving into one's spirit' (*nyams-su len-pa*). Merit Intellect's father says to him: 'Now you have completed your studies, but that is of no benefit if you do not absorb what you have learned and practise meditation now that you are still young' (p. 87). This fits our own experience, for we can distinguish perfectly well between knowledge that we have simply acquired, and knowledge that we have absorbed and can thus reproduce spontaneously as our own ideas. Time and experience as well as quiet musing can transform 'acquired knowledge' into 'spontaneous knowledge'. Thus the relative truths symbolized by a mystic circle should first be absorbed by the practisers, for only then can they expect to recognize the supreme truth spontaneously.

Nevertheless the enactment of a properly performed consecration in a mystic circle by a fully prepared celebrant, is conceived of as conferring power in its own right. It can thus be a means of 'grace' (*byin-rlabs*) even to layfolk who have been prepared in no special way, for it is a valid assertion by means of ritual of the supreme truth as this is taught by sages and lamas. But it is only those qualified by their initial training who see the divinities face to face and are conscious of the descending power of grace.

Tutelary Divinities

For this to happen the mystic circle must be enlivened by divinities who are known to the celebrants. These divinities are their tutelary divinities whom they

[1] For a detailed study of the significance of the mystic circle, see my *Hevajra-Tantra*, especially pages 29–33.

have learned to know by means of concentrated and persistent meditation. The Tibetan Buddhist pantheon offers a vast variety of divinities, some tranquil, some fierce, to suit all tastes and needs. The only ones useful for this special purpose are those who are referred to as 'gods of knowledge' (*ye-shes-kyi lha*) and are regarded as consubstantial with buddhahood. These divinities are ordered according to the 'families' of the Five Buddhas, so each has his proper place in the mystic circle. Any one set of divinities will serve the same purpose as any other. Thus the mystic circle of *Hevajra* is no more or less effective than that of *Supreme Bliss* (*bDe-mchog*) or *Boundless Life* (*Tshe-dpag-med*) or the *Saviouress* (*sGrol-ma*).

By reciting their individual spells and envisaging their forms a yogin will strive to get to know as many of these divinities as possible, just as a man of the world, striving towards some objective of his own, might seek the support of as many powerful friends as possible. Thus although in theory any one set of tutelary divinities will do, in practice most monks seem to go for as many as possible. Lesser mortals just try to get as many consecrations as they can, perhaps without understanding any of them properly. In any case it is generally assumed that one gains merit and grace simply by being present at a consecration, in much the same way perhaps that an uninstructed Christian may believe that he gains merit and grace simply by being present at mass. This explains why the layfolk in these biographies always seem to be clamouring for consecrations and blessings.

To get to know one's tutelary divinities is a long and hard process. First a qualified lama who already 'possesses' that particular divinity, must initiate one in the relevant liturgy (the description, the praises, the spells of the gods, etc.) and perform the consecration in the relevant mystic circle. One is then introduced as it were, and taken into the protection of the divinity. Then one must go into solitary meditation and concentrate upon the chosen divinity, reciting his spell hundreds of thousands of times.

As a means towards stilling the mind and concentrating the thought, rhythmic control of the breath is a well known feature of Indian and Tibetan yoga, and needs no special explanations here.[1] This practice is used to slow down the breathing processes. Thus *Merit Intellect* reduces the number of 'full vases' (periods during which the breath is held down in the body) from 500 to 100 in the course of his early morning practices (p. 108).

Rather more difficult to explain is the process of the actual 'coercing' of one's chosen divinity. We really have no satisfactory western term for this practice, since western mystics have never tried to do quite this kind of thing despite the variety of their meditative practices. The Tibetan term (*bsNyen-sGrub*) is another of the concise compound terms which Tibetans seem to like so much. The first part of the

[1] See Evans-Wentz, *Tibetan Yoga and Secret Doctrines*, especially pp. 125–7 and pp. 187–9.

term means literally 'bringing near' and the second part means 'achieving' or 'effecting'. (It corresponds with the Indian Buddhist term *sādhana*.) The nearest concise English translation for the whole idea is probably 'coercing', for in effect one 'coerces' the divinity by concentrating upon his imagined form and by repeating his spell. This translation is only unsuitable in that it suggests a lack of respect for the divinity, who is revered and worshipped as well as being 'coerced'. I have therefore translated the term as 'invocation' or even as 'concentrated meditative practice', assuming that the reader will now have some idea of what is actually involved in this particular performance.

'Life-denying' Practices

Most monks seem to have remained content with practices such as these. Others have used more violent means of self-preparation. Lack of food is clearly recognized as assisting towards clarity of thought. Thus as a special privation *Merit Intellect* mixes sand with his meagre ration of tsamba during his early training. Solitude is also conducive to mystic states. The whole art consists in cutting oneself off as much as possible from the world and even from life itself (short of actual suicide)[1]. One might describe it as a kind of psychophysical 'brinkmanship', which produces sickness and even insanity if it fails, and extraordinary clarity of intellect if it succeeds. The Tibetan yogin may practise a special rite of ritual self-sacrifice, known as 'Cutting Off' (*gCod*). By an imagined ritual offering of his own flesh and bones to assembled gods and demons, he makes a total abnegation of himself.[2] All these 'life-denying' practices may seem incomprehensible and even objectionable to most people nowadays, but it must be allowed that they are in accordance with the conviction of Buddhist sages of all periods that the best thing to do with life is to bring its illusions to a stop. This is not the same as bleak pessimism that would bring life itself to a stop, for having gained the perfect knowledge of existence as it really is, the true yogin should apply his knowledge and powers to benefitting others. This results in the conception of a buddha (which simply means originally an enlightened yogin) as a teacher and a saviour, of which more will be said below. One can certainly describe many of the techniques that are used as forms of self-hypnotism, but this detracts in no way from their effectiveness, for the practisers themselves regard them as no more than means to an end. Thus the chosen divinity

---

[1] Although it was prohibited, suicide seems to have been practised in some exceptional cases during the early period of the doctrine. See E. J. Thomas, *Early Buddhist Scriptures*, London 1935, pp. 113-16, and *A Record of Buddhistic Kingdoms*, being the account by the Chinese Monk Fa-Hien of his travels in India and Ceylon, translated by James Legge, New York 1965, p. 86.

[2] See Evans-Wentz, *op. cit.*, pp. 277-334, 'The Path of the Mystic Sacrifice: the Yoga of subduing the lower self'.

will appear to the yogin who invokes him long and well enough, and it is really meaningless to ask whether the divine forms are real or imagined, as one of the main purposes of the practice is to train the yogin towards the realization that all seemingly real forms are but imagined. By power of his meditation a yogin places himself as it were at the very centre of the mystic circle, which represents the whole of existence in its idealized state. He has power to invoke any set of divinities of which he now has control thanks to his concentrated meditative practice. The ordered calling forth of the divinities (which is conceived of as corresponding on an idealized plane with the emanation of the whole universe) is known as the 'Process of Emanation'. The recognition of the essential non-reality of the divinities (the elixir) and the mystic circle that serves as their support (the vessel) is known as the 'Process of Realization'. The experience of this dual process, referred to as the coalescing of 'two-in-one', represents the enlightenment of perfect knowledge.

Religious Succession

Tutelary divinities, their liturgies and rituals, are passed on in a continual succession of masters and pupils. Thus a Tibetan who wants to practise religion seriously will choose in the first place (or be chosen by) a teacher who is willing to receive him. His tutelary divinities will therefore normally be those of his teacher. On his teacher's advice, he may request other special rituals from other lamas, but in general a religious practiser chooses his teacher first, and his gods afterwards. Knowledge, like any other commodity, is normally obtained by payment. *Sher mKhan-po*, *Merit Intellect*'s teacher in Lo, speaks quite frankly on this subject: 'You have been to Central Tibet, but previously thanks to the wealth of worthy parents you had whatever you wanted, and so lamas received you compassionately and your companions in the schools were well disposed to you. But now you have nothing to take, and you cannot go begging. So if on this later occasion you possess nothing, it will be difficult for lamas to receive you compassionately, as they did previously, and it will be difficult for others to behave as they did before' (p. 92). Even when a lama takes on a pupil because of a personal interest in him, it is the pupil who must supply all the offerings necessary for a consecration if he wants one. Tibetans would assume that it is just common sense never to expect something of value for nothing. *Merit Intellect* later shows himself unwilling to impart some special knowledge to another lama, until he is sure just what he wants to ask in return (p. 102). Such a mercenary attitude towards 'higher truths' might seem to conflict with the conception of a *would-be buddha* whose generosity is available to all and sundry, but it quite clearly applies in so far as lamas are conceived of as 'sage-magicians' disposing of special powers. It applies especially to secret teachings such as those of the 'Six Doctrines' of *Nāropa* and of his sister *Nai-gu* (or *Ne-gu*).[1] These doctrines make use not only of breath-control but also of control of the seminal fluid, which is supposedly impelled through the body of the trained yogin along 'vital channels' which go from the groin to the top of the head. A feminine partner may be used in the course of his practice, and she is referred to simply as the *yoginī*, or in secret terms as the 'spell' or the 'symbol'. Thus these teachings are often referred to collectively as the 'Great Symbol'.

The most interesting of this special set of 'Six Doctrines' is probably that of the 'transfer of consciousness'. It is believed that a yogin who has perfected this power, can transfer his consciousness at the moment of death into the state of buddhahood. It was also believed that while still alive, he could transfer his consciousness into other bodies, but there is no reference to this practice in our texts.[2]

The 'Soul' and the 'Intermediate State'

The Tibetans seem to have developed some special doctrines on the subject of death, and their origin remains uncertain. Some connection with ancient Egyptian beliefs, which might gradually have reached western Tibet by way of pre-Muslim Iran, is by no means impossible. As it is, we are presented with non-Buddhist ideas in Tibetan Buddhist garb. The terminology and the names of the divinities involved are all Buddhist of a kind, but the idea of the survival of a person from one life to another with an intervening period of 49 days in an 'Intermediate State' (*bar-do*) is scarcely Buddhist, although it can easily be brought into relationship with the Buddhist doctrine of rebirth as a continual process of causal relationships. According to early Buddhist teachings 'consciousness' was just one of the 'five components' of personality and as impermanent as all the rest. Now according to these developed Tibetan beliefs 'consciousness' is regarded in effect as a kind of 'soul' that goes from one body to another in accordance with the laws of cause and effect. It is regarded in this way by most Tibetans and by the lamas of the older orders of Tibetan religion without there being any formal change in the accepted philosophical teachings. The philosophical basis of all orders of Tibetan religion is provided by the 'Perfection of Wisdom' texts with their teachings of universal relativity.[3] The term for a series of lives is the perfectly orthodox word 'succession' (*rgyud* corresponding to Sanskrit *santāna*) which commits itself in no way to what

[1] See Evans-Wentz, *op. cit.*, pp. 155–276, 'The Yoga of the Six Doctrines'. See also my edition of the *Hevajra-Tantra*, especially vol. I, pp. 33–9.
[2] See J. Bacot, *La vie de Marpa, le traducteur*, Paris 1937, p. 3–5, 39–44, 55–57.
[3] Concerning the 'Perfection of Wisdom' literature, see Edward Conze '*The Prajñāpāramitā Literature*, Mouton & Co., The Hague, 1960. For examples of the texts themselves in English translation, see his *Buddhist Wisdom Books*, Allen & Unwin, London, 1957, and his *Large Sutra on Perfect Wisdom*, Luzac & Co., London, 1961.

actually passes from one life to the next. In English translation the word 'succession' would have little meaning, and so I have translated it as 'inner-disposition' and sometimes as 'soul-series'. 'Inner disposition' probably comes near enough to what a well read Tibetan would understand by the term, for he would take for granted the idea of continuity. 'Soul-series' expresses what most Tibetans really believe, but it commits them to a term the validity of which any well instructed Tibetan would have to deny.

There exists another term for 'soul' or 'life-force', namely *bla*, and this term is manifestly non-Buddhist although it has been introduced into Tibetan Buddhist doctrine.[1] It is this kind of 'soul' which is at the mercy of local divinities, if they are offended in any way, and *Glorious Intellect* in particular makes it his business to gain the release of such abducted 'souls'. On two occasions when he manages to regain them, they are handed over in the form of a sheep with a brown face. Whatever formal Buddhist philosophy may say on the subject, it is clear that villagers and lamas alike all take for granted belief in a 'life-force' (*bla*) and in a 'consciousness' (*rnam-shes*) which passes in succession (*rgyud*) from one body to another, taking with it 'subtle influences' (*bag-chags* representing Sanskrit *vāsanā*) accumulated from its former states. Generally speaking, past 'accumulations' of merit and knowledge result in happy rebirths, and past moral and mental 'obscurations' result in unhappy rebirths. Thus such terms as the 'two accumulations' and the 'two obscurations' can be used by our biographers in the knowledge that any Tibetan who reads their works will know what they are referring to. In English translation one must resort to paraphrase, and the significant technical nature of the terms may be obscured. There is little help for this, if a translation is to be readable.

Interfering with Laws of Cause and Effect

According to Buddhist philosophical theory, whatever happens in this life or another comes about as the result of a complex combination of preceeding and attendant causes. In theory everything should be predestined. There is thus an apparent conflict with Buddhist moral teachings, which assume that a man is capable of a free decision to do right or wrong, and promise various rewards and punishments in future lives. One can also make life unpleasant for oneself by offending local gods, and in this case one's sufferings are not caused so much by one's own evil acts, as by the deliberate spitefulness of some non-Buddhist divinity. Thus affairs in this life are controlled not only by the laws of cause and effect with

---

[1] See *Himalayan Pilgrimage*, pp. 141–5 for a description of the 'Life-Consecration', the purpose of which is to nourish the 'life-force' (*bla*) of living beings.

all their moral implications, but also by the seemingly arbitrary reactions of others.

'Fertile fields and good harvests,
Spread of royal power and extent of dominion,
Just half is predestined by one's former deeds,
But half comes from the powerful local gods.
If you do not know how to act methodically in this matter,
A root cause of evil and harm comes from this,
So you must attend to the local gods, to the serpents and the furies.'

This quotation comes from a *bon-po* work and not a Buddhist one,[1] but it expresses very well what most Tibetans believe, whether they call themselves Buddhist or *bon*. Whatever kind of evil befalls them, they must have recourse to their lamas who are often able to explain the causes of seemingly undeserved misfortune. The powers of the lamas too often appear to work in an arbitrary manner. They can overpower local gods and force them against their will to relinquish their hold on other people. It is also assumed that they can obtain for others a happier state of rebirth than they would otherwise have gained. It is assumed that they can produce rain, when rain would not otherwise have fallen. It is assumed that they can produce auspicious circumstances artificially by giving certain kinds of presents and pronouncing valedictory verses. The charms and amulets they distribute are supposed to protect the wearers against harms of various kinds that would otherwise have befallen them. At the same time lamas who possess all these special powers (like these four lamas of Dolpo) are regarded as perfected buddhas, possessing all the traditional attributes of buddhahood. They represent in effect not only the supreme ideal of Buddhist sages and philosophers, but also the popular conception of a sage-magician.

Popular Conceptions of a Buddha and a Would-be Buddha

One may well ask whether the reactions of simple Buddhist followers in India from the earliest Buddhist times onward, were really very different from the reactions of the people of Dolpo. The cult of relics (together with the faith and devotion that this cult implies) was fostered assiduously throughout all periods. Has a buddha, who was not at the same time something of a sage-magician, ever existed except in certain philosophical texts? These are interesting questions, and although there is no need to try and resolve them here, I remain persuaded that the great changes that have taken place in Buddhism throughout 2,500 years are often more apparent than real. While outwards forms have often changed, the range of

[1] See my *Nine Ways of Bon*, p. 199.

psychological reactions have remained very much the same in any given period of the doctrine.

Thus a buddha may be regarded by his followers under several different aspects:

as a great religious teacher,
as an enlightened sage,
as a great wonder-worker,
as a predestined saviour of the world,
as a great hero intent on others' welfare.

Buddhas seem to have been regarded under all these different aspects throughout the whole recorded history of Buddhism. At times some aspects have been emphasized to accord with certain preferred forms of religious life, and sometimes it is possible to trace lines of historical development. Thus the development in early centuries of the Christian era of the ideal of the *would-be buddha* (*bodhisattva*) as the highest of human aspirations was closely associated with the much earlier conception of a buddha as a great hero intent on others' welfare. The extraordinary development of the whole *would-be buddha* theory is instructive in itself. The theory was first enunciated as a kind of programme for sainthood, and a candidate who had taken the necessary vow should strive to accomplish the ten great perfections of generosity, morality, forbearance, energy, meditation, wisdom, skill in means, resolution, strength and knowledge.[1] More concisely his activities were defined as a combination of the wisdom of a sage and the zealous compassion of a divine hero. His compassion was extolled as the means towards enlightenment, and thus the terms *Means* and *Wisdom* came to represent the twin co-efficients of his perfection, while it was the *thought of enlightenment*, eventually conceived of as a kind of subtle essence, that impelled him towards his goal. The career of the *would-be buddha* remains one of the noblest aspirations of man, and during the early centuries of the Christian era Buddhism achieved amongst some of its followers its most lofty conception of a saintly and heroic perfection which man by his own efforts might achieve. But by most followers of the doctrine such perfection was felt to be entirely superhuman, and the term *would-be buddha* with all its heroic associations was applied to the great Indian gods who under changed names now began to enter the Buddhist fold. The progressive stages of a *would-be buddha* (variously numbered from ten to thirteen), originally evolved to mark his progress towards enlightenment through myriads of self-sacrificing rebirths, were later scarcely mentioned except as a laudatory invocation of revered lamas, who may be extolled as having reached the

---

[1] For a most useful general work on the whole subject see Har Dayal, *The Bodhisattva Doctrine in Buddhist Sanskrit Literature*, Kegan Paul, London, 1932. The ten perfections are discussed on pp. 165–269.

13th stage. *Would-be buddhas* are no longer generally conceived of as human beings who are slowly progressing towards enlightenment, but as special manifestations of the buddhas themselves, and they figure in the scheme of the Three Bodies of buddhahood (see above p. 21) as the *Glorious Body*, the divine emanation whose proper place is in the heavens.[1]

Likewise the term *thought of enlightenment* changes its meaning, for as a kind of subtle essence it becomes identified with the seminal fluid which the expert yogin imagines he can impel from his groin to the top of his head. Thus the expression 'raise the thought of enlightenment', once a summons to heroic striving in the phenomenal world of impermanence and suffering, becomes in later Indian Buddhism and hence in Tibetan Buddhism a euphemistic reference to secret practices of yoga.[2]

Yoga and Meditation as primary concerns of the religious life

In its essential practices Buddhism seems always to revert to yoga and meditation. Despite the enunciation of the doctrine of the *would-be buddha* and his heroic struggles in the phenomenal world on others' behalf, Buddhist religious practice in India remained primarily concerned with the gaining of perfect knowledge for oneself, and it was this form of Buddhism that the Tibetans received. There is often much talk about saving all sentient beings, but it seems to be assumed that the best way of saving them is through the practice of one's own meditation. One returns to the world to help them in another life after one has gained enlightenment for oneself. All our four lamas of Dolpo are regarded by their followers as returning buddhas of just such a kind. It is significant therefore that when a worthy lama such as *Merit Intellect* is involved in an outbreak of smallpox at Mugu, he clearly does not envisage his efforts on others' behalf as a means towards enlightenment, but rather as an unwelcome interruption of his own practice of meditation. His own lama points out to him that such actions will be of great benefit to sentient beings and that is more meritorious than his own religious practice, but even this advice does not raise such actions to the level of a *would-be buddha* who should devote himself to others while expecting nothing in return. Thus the main motive for the religious life is not so much the *thought of enlightenment* with its spontaneous religious fervour, as the calculated accumulating of merit and knowledge.

---

[1] The Dalai Lama is supposed to be an emanation of just such a *would-be buddha*, namely 'Glancing Eye' (*Avalokiteśvara*), a god of Indian origin who as 'Lord of the World' (*Lokeśvara*) bears a close relationship to the great god *Śiva*. The original meaning of the term *would-be buddha* is not entirely lost. See pp. 89 and 245.

[2] The original meaning of the term is however occasionally preserved. See pp. 93 and 245.

The twin terms *Means* and *Wisdom* continue to be used in reference to the two co-efficients of enlightenment, but *Means* no longer refers to the compassionate zeal of a *would-be buddha*, but to one's own skill in yoga as means towards one's own perfection. As far as its actual religious practices are concerned, Buddhism would seem to be far more concerned with saving oneself than with helping others. Men of a kind and generous disposition certainly often help others in need, but once a man begins to practise the religious life seriously, he seems to expect to be a receiver rather than a giver. Thus it comes about that most Buddhist monks appear to be less generous than Buddhist layfolk. There are happily notable exceptions, but these are often those who have made such a success (in a worldly sense) of their religious practice, that they can afford to be generous with their property in just the same way as a wealthy layman may be generous. But they may not be so generous when it comes to imparting to others their accumulated knowledge, for this is usually reserved for those who will pay for it and sometimes for a favourite disciple who gives his devoted services in return. It seems that in practice the Great Vehicle is not as much concerned with the salvation of all sentient beings, as it continually professes to be.

The Tibetans have had no occasion to compare their religious practice with that of the followers of the Lesser Vehicle, whom they know of only from their own texts.[1] Whenever they refer to them it is always to contrast their selfishness in seeking salvation for themselves alone, with the vast magnanimity of the followers of the Great Vehicle. The term 'Great Vehicle' implies little more to them than the unquestioned excellence of their own religious teachings, and they have remained generally unaware of their kinship with the Buddhists of China and Japan who have also been followers of the Great Vehicle. Approaching their religion from outside, we are bound to see it in an entirely different perspective from the way in which they see it themselves. What they may take for granted, we often find anomalous and even contradictory.

[1] Although one part (the *Vinaya*) of the Tibetan Canon consists of translations of texts of the old Mūlasarvāstivāda Order of Indian Buddhism (which presumably would be judged as belonging to the 'Lesser Vehicle'), by accepting the 'Perfection of Wisdom' texts as the basis of their religious philosophy, the Tibetans have always considered themselves followers of the 'Great Vehicle'. The term however has lost all its real comparative significance, and even the *bon-pos*, who have never had a 'Lesser Vehicle' in the Buddhist sense of the term, consider themselves followers of the 'Great Vehicle'. Tibetans have long since ceased to wonder what the term really means. Since Islam put an end to organized Buddhism in India in the 12th century, Tibet has been effectively cut off from followers of the 'Lesser Vehicle', namely monks from Ceylon, Burma and Siam and Indochina, who have existed outside their known world.

The Powerbolt Vehicle

Some of the practices which have been described briefly in this introduction, especially the rite of consecration in the mystic circle and the yoga which involves control of the seminal fluid, are referred to collectively as the 'Powerbolt Vehicle'. The term 'powerbolt' is my newly coined term for the Tibetan word *rDo-rje* (Sanskrit *vajra*), for which there exists no satisfactory translation in any European language. It is sometimes translated as 'thunderbolt' or 'diamond', but both these translations are unsatisfactory, and in any case the Tibetans usually employ different terms for these particular meanings. *rDo-rje* is used in Tibetan in the sense of the ritual instrument (see p. 273) which symbolizes divine power in its absolute indestructible form, and also in the sense of penis, specifically that of the yogin who unites ritually with his feminine partner. In this particular context, she is referred to as the 'lotus'. Thus for this kind of Buddhism the two co-efficients of enlightenment are the powerbolt and the lotus, and these are equated with the Means and Wisdom of the *would-be buddha*, for this kind of yogin claims to be a *would-be buddha* too. The ritual instrument known as 'powerbolt' thus symbolizes Means, while Wisdom is symbolized by a small hand bell, representing the pure sound of the doctrine. But since the powerbolt alone represents divine power in its absolute indestructible form, it is identified in this kind of Buddhism with the supreme and absolute truth. Thus the sixth buddha, the supreme one, who unites all the others, is known as the *Powerbolt-Holder*, and for the same reason the term is prefixed to the names of several divinities of *buddha* and *would-be buddha* rank.

The Divine Realms of Buddhahood

From what has been already written it should be clear that a *would-be buddha* should be either a human being (or in theory any other living creature) who is gradually progressing towards buddhahood, or a divine being who is an emanation of a buddha and has come to help all 'sentient beings'. Thus in the scheme of the *Three Bodies* of buddhahood, the *Absolute Body* is represented by a buddha, the *Glorious Body* by a *would-be buddha*, and the *Physical Body* by a human teacher. But at the same time they are all considered to be of buddha rank. When our four lamas leave this world, they go to the divine realms of *Boundless Light* (a buddha), of *Glancing Eye* (a *would-be buddha*) or *Lotus Born* (once a human teacher), and there is really no difference between them. They are all regarded as the antechambers (if I may use such a word in this context) of buddhahood, and it is from those realms that buddhas may return to the suffering phenomenal world.

Tibetan religion, even if one leaves aside the originally indigenous non-Buddhist elements, is bound to appear complex and diversified, for so many different theories (sometimes even contradictory in themselves) and so many different kinds of religious practice have come within its fold. Most of all this was inherited from mediaeval India and Nepal, where Buddhists had long since ceased to question what might be orthodox or unorthodox. It was enough to attach some recognized Buddhist names and terms to any new divinity or practice to which one happened to be partial oneself, and there was no recognized authority to which others might appeal if they happened to dislike the changes and developments that they saw taking place. Those who did enter into debate on the subject of Buddhist religion were in the later phases of the doctrine primarily concerned with philosophical questions, and not with what we might call 'faith and morals'. A Buddhist is always free (until he has committed himself to a particular teacher or a particular community) to direct his faith where he likes and perform what practices he likes. Looking back on all the heterodox development that has taken place, one finds it difficult to write on so complex a subject without the risk of self-contradiction.

III

LIFE IN DOLPO 1960–61[1]

We flew from Kathmandu to Pokhara in the regular Dakota flight of the Royal Nepalese Airlines on 19th September 1960. This 100 miles journey by air saves eight to ten days of travel on foot, for no road yet links Pokhara with the outside world, and however much luggage one may have, it is cheaper to carry it by air than to pay porters to carry it on their backs. On this occasion we had a great deal of luggage, clothing and camping equipment, films and notebooks, tape-recorders and cameras, special food supplies and heavy bags of coins. Corneille Jest was anxious to see all the seasons through in Dolpo. Having seen Dolpo during the summer of 1956, I was primarily interested in seeing the winter through, and I had already planned to return to India the following April. But as I envisaged the possibility of returning to Dolpo in May, we decided to take a year's supplies of all necessary things for the whole party. Besides us two Europeans, this consisted of Pasang Khambache, who had been with me in England since my return there at

---

[1] For a more detailed description of the author's experiences in Dolpo, the reader is referred to the section "Nepalese Frontier Regions Bordering on Tibet" commencing page 135 in *Asian Commitment: Travels and Studies in the Indian Sub-Continent and South-East Asia*; Orchid Press, Bangkok 2000.

the end of 1956, another Sherpa, also named Pasang but nicknamed 'Jockey', because he used to ride in the races at Lebong (below Darjeeling), a second mountaineering Sherpa called Pemba and lastly Pasang's 'henchman' Prem Bahadur, a Tamang from Solu, who is nicknamed Saila.

We had sent Jockey Pasang in advance to Pokhara so that he might hire the 32 porters we would need and have them ready waiting for us on the airfield, but there were inevitable delays and its was not until the following morning that all the men needed could be assembled and made content with advances of their pay. Thus having spent a night by the airfield, we finally set out on our journey on the 20th. The monsoon was now over and the weather was superb, so we were looking forward to a pleasant three weeks' journey on foot across foothills to the valley of the Kāli Gandaki and thence across the north-eastern flanks of Dhaulagiri into Dolpo. The first part of our journey was no more eventful than other Himalayan 'approach-marches'. The first two nights we camped comfortably on river banks (by the Garbung Khola and the Modi Khola), the third night uncomfortably on muddy terraced fields above the village of Ulleri, and the other nights comfortably enough in village houses (in Sikha, Dana and Lete). Thus on the seventh day of travel we reached Tukucha, the chief township of the Thākāli people.[1] Here twelve of our porters decided to leave us, so we delayed one day and eventually made up their missing numbers by hiring seven mules, which with the remaining twenty porters would come with us as far as Sangdak, two or three days journey further on. I bought a horse in Tukucha of the small Tibetan breed for the equivalent of about £20, and in our next halting place of Jomosom (*rDzong-gsar-pa*) I bought a second one, larger and more sprightly, for about £25. Pasang parted company with us here, and riding our first horse, set out northwards for Mustang, four days journey distant. He was going to find a Tibetan friend of ours, Sonam Panden Trangjun, with whom we had not been able to make contact, although we knew he was staying with the Rāja of Mustang. We had met Sonam as a refugee in the spring of 1960 and he had stayed with us in Kathmandu, where we had helped him with money and letters to make the journey up to Mustang, so that he could visit his elder sister who was the sole surviving member of his family. She is the widow of the eldest son of the Mustang Rāja, and is normally simply known as the Mustang Rāni. The royal family of Mustang has continued to seek brides among the aristocratic families of Lhasa, of which Trangjun (*Brag-'jun*) is one. I was anxious to re-establish contact with Sonam again, for I had already invited him to accompany me to England in the autumn of 1961 and I hoped he would be willing to join me in Dolpo in the meantime, at least for a short while.

[1] Concerning Tukchä (*Survey of India* Tukucha) and the rest of the Thākāli region, see *Himalayan Pilgrimage*, pp. 177 ff. A proper study of whole region still waits to be done.

The rest of us continued our journey up to *Bar-lag*, which lies high above the right bank of the Kāli Gandaki about midway between Jomosom and Kāgbeni. It was the first Tibetan speaking village on our way. From there we had a long and splendid day's journey to Sangdak, following the track that climbs steadily over the flanks of Dhaulagiri. To one's right one looks across the chaotic eroded landscape of Lo (Mustangbhot) and behind one are the massive snow-covered summits of Annapūrna. One climbs to a pass of about 15,000 feet above sea-level, and then the track turns westwards, traversing a whole series of mountain sides and then dropping steeply down to the village of Sangdak, a cluster of some twenty-five houses, which are built precariously on the edge of the Keha Lungpa gorge. Sangdak is the gateway into Dolpo and there is no way of avoiding it on this side.[1] It lies at about 12,500 feet, and beyond it there rises the great pass that leads over to Barbung and Tsharka. One must normally change one's transport here, as porters from the lower valleys will not go any higher, and even if they show willingness, it is wise to discourage them. We agreed however to keep on five of ours, for they were adequately equipped with boots, warm clothes and blankets, and it seemed better to entrust to them such fragile things as tape-recorders, typewriters and photographic equipment, rather than to the yaks whom we hoped to hire at a reasonable rate from the villagers of Sangdak. We began our bargaining from a position of strength, for on the way up we had met four men from Barbung with forty wool-laden yaks on their way to Jomosom, and we knew that they would be returning unladen through Sangdak to Barbung. Thus if we liked to wait for them, they would be able to accommodate us. But our bargaining with the villagers of Sangdak was cut short by a sudden change in the weather. We had reached their village late on the 30th September and established a camp just on the outskirts. The next day the sun shone fierce and brilliant. The villagers were working hard on their wheat-harvest which had already been gathered in. They were sitting on the flat roofs of their houses, cutting the ears off the stalks and throwing them down into their courtyards. When a sufficient quantity was amassed, the women would set to work with their flails in two facing lines of four, threshing rhythmically, now fast, now slow (to ease their muscles perhaps) and then fast again. They are dressed in their own woollen home-spun and are quite dirty like simple Tibetan villagers everywhere. Yet they are all quite well-to-do with their fields for wheat and buckwheat, potatoes and turnips, and adequate grazing for their yaks and sheep. They said they were all too busy to accompany us, and suggested excessive rates for their yaks, and for our part we were content to rest and wait for a day or two.

But on 2nd and 3rd October it rained persistently. The villagers had to give up work on their harvest, and most of them sat quietly in their houses spinning wool.

[1] Concerning the other routes into Dolpo, see above p. 7.

One or two men were sewing cloth boots of the usual Tibetan style. Others just sat talking and drinking *chang* (brewed from fermented barley). But for us life was not so easy. The small field on which we were encamped was soon flooded, and we were busy digging trenches round our tents to keep the water out. With no sun to warm us it became bitterly cold. Corneille and Jockey Pasang and I all caught colds and mine developed into quite a high temperature, and to make matters worse one of the horses pulled free of his cord during the night, tripped over my guy-ropes and brought my tent down in pouring rain. Having released myself from this chaos, I lay in my wet tent feeling very ill indeed. Early next morning Corneille and Jockey Pasang decided to move me into a house, and the only suitable place they could find was a small outhouse, built of uncemented stones and with a floor of damp earth. They hung the walls and ceiling with local blankets, for dirt fell out of the ceiling whenever people walked about overhead. It was like some mediaeval prison cell. My two companions took shelter with me during the day, and returned to their own tent at night. The rest of our party slept in the house upstairs in rather warmer conditions and together with other 'sentient beings', men and fleas and lice.

On the 4th the weather improved and since antibiotics had brought down my temperature, I moved back with the others to our camp-site. Rain at 12,000 feet meant snow higher up, and the pass ahead of us now presented an entirely different aspect. The villagers said that to cross into Dolpo now was out of the question, and leaving us to our own sad reflections, they set to work smoothing the surface of their yards, so as to restart their threshing. Jockey Pasang offered to go down to *Bar-lag* to look for the returning Barbung villagers and their forty yaks and begin negotiations with them. He returned a few hours later with the news that the way we had come was blocked. Since we were now beginning to look forward to Pasang's arrival from Mustang, this news was perturbing, for we wondered how he would be able to get through to us at Sangdak. Matters became worse the next day, for rain began to fall heavily again. During the night it turned to sleet and snow, and my tent collapsed again, this time under the weight of accumulated snow. Sleet was still falling in the morning. We fixed up a sort of 'kitchen' in a shelter by the side of the courtyard, made a fire and sat around it drinking Tibetan tea. There was clearly no hope of leaving Sangdak for several days at least, and so we decided to make a determined effort to find some suitable shelter in one of the houses. But this proved quite impracticable. The courtyard we were using belonged to a villager named Sridar. His house was the largest in the village and served as a kind of 'hotel'. His living-room was therefore a public room, used not only by members of his family, but also by travellers. These consisted of our own porters, a Tibetan from Mustang who had been caught up here in the bad weather, two Tibetan nomads, a dignified and authoritative female and a man who spoke little and seemed to be her husband. These men and women all sat in a large circle round the fire, on which they cooked their food in turns, and sat drinking *chang* (sold to them by Sridar) most of the time. Sridar had already invited us to settle in this room, but it was far too crowded for our use. Across a kind of veranda there was another large room, which he used as his private chapel and store-room. He offered us this, but it was so crowded with articles of all kinds, that it was quite unsuitable. It was also very dark and smelt strongly of *chang* and dried meat and sausages. (The villagers make sausages with tsamba and blood, and when they have boiled them, they hang them up to dry from their smoky ceilings.) The rest of the house (except for the outhouse we already had at our disposal) was reserved for his livestock. One of Sridar's daughters was married to a young man of 21, named Wang-gyel, and in accordance with a well known Tibetan custom, to his younger brother, aged 20, as well. We knew that both his parents were dead, and that he had two small children. But thinking that perhaps he might have room, we went to see him. He was drinking tea by his hearth together with his wife and an old aunt, who seemed also to live with them. He obviously had no room, for his house consisted of just the one living room with store space below. Although the houses of these villagers may look quite large, much of the space is taken up by flat open roofs on the first storey as well as the second. Unable to offer us anything himself, Wang-gyel kindly went to ask on our behalf in neighbouring houses, and returned to say that a villager named Dar-gyä had a room to offer us. Dar-gyä's house was at the eastern end of the village, and part of it had already fallen down the steep slope on the edge of which the whole village is built. He offered us a small room on the first floor with a small window overlooking the precipice below. He seemed not at all perturbed at the perilous position of his house, and merely asked us not to light a fire in the room. We declined the offer with thanks. Later on we heard that his wife often sought refuge in Sridar's house in time of bad weather.

The weather was now certainly at its worst. Rain and sleet fell continuously. Unable to find accommodation anywhere else we returned to Sridar's house and agreed to take over his store-room if the weather showed no sign of improvement by that evening. We laughed at the absurdity of our plight, as we sat in our open shelter with the rain splashing down in the courtyard. When we became too cold and wet, we would go and sit by the fire in Sridar's smoky living-room. This was certainly the most interesting place in the whole village. Sridar's family and the authoritative female and her demure husband were having a meal of *zan* (a thick paste made of tsamba mixed with hot water and salt) and stewed potatoes and turnips spiced with chillies. While the nomad woman was talking of the difficulty of looking after animals in such weather, news arrived that Babuk's house (one of those next to

Dar-gyä's) had collapsed. We ran out to see the calamity. No one had been inside fortunately, for what had once been a house was now a vast heap of stones with lengths of timber sticking out here and there. Babuk and his neighbours were already at work in the pouring rain trying to strengthen the inner wall of the next house, which had now become an outer wall. We had scarcely returned to Sridar's hearth, when there was the alarming sound of more collapsing masonry, very near this time. Looking out of the window, we saw that the whole back had fallen out of the shelter, which had been serving as our kitchen. The surrounding wall of the terraced field above the courtyard collapsed shortly afterwards, and one began to imagine that with a very little more rain the whole village would shoot down into the gorge below. The whole place was now running with water, for since the village is built on a slope, streams of water poured between the houses and even over their roofs into the courtyards of the houses lower down. The villagers were saying to Jockey Pasang that never before had they suffered such a devastating storm, and we began to suspect that they held us responsible in some way.

By the late afternoon the rain began to stop and the sky cleared a little, and we decided after all to sleep in our tents again. By noon the next day (the 7th) all was well again, and our midday meal took the form of a picnic near our tents. The previous day a nomad who was making a skin coat for Sridar, had offered to sell us a sheep for 15 rupees. We now decided to take up this offer, although it was sad to think that our new interest in life should immediately result in the death of this unhappy animal. The five porters who had offered to stay on with us, had now had more than enough of present sufferings and said they wanted to go. We willingly agreed to this, for we still had no idea when we would be able to continue our journey and they had to be maintained and paid all the time whether we were travelling or not. Their fear of the difficult journey back seemed to be less than their fear of remaining with us, and as we paid them off generously they left in good spirits. The sky was now blue again and the sun as fierce as it had been the day after our arrival. The villagers repaired all the lesser damage they had suffered on their properties, smoothed out their courtyards and resumed the work of threshing and winnowing. They called a meeting in the evening of all the thirteen householders present to discuss problems caused by the Tibetan nomads who from fear of the Chinese were coming from the north in such large numbers. The villagers were complaining that they were using up the grazing grounds, and after discussion they decided that the nomads should from then on pay the price of the grass they used. The fact that a nomad had sold us a sheep was also mentioned, and it was ordered that in future nomads must ask the consent of the village-headman before selling animals within the village precincts. Actual relations between the nomads (just then there were only three families encamped above the village) and the villagers seemed to remain quite cordial, and after the meeting they all gathered in Sridar's house and drank *chang* together.

From then on the fine weather continued uninterrupted, although the snow remained thick on the passes. The route we had followed up to Sangdak remained blocked, but an alternative route which ascends the gorge behind Tingri (*S of I:* Tirigaon) in the Kāli Gandaki valley, remained open. The track is precipitous and dangerous and unsuitable for laden animals, but on the 10th October Pasang Khambache arrived by this route travelling with the four men of Barbung and their forty unladen yaks. Pasang's horse had to be temporarily abandoned at one particularly difficult section of the route, but food was left for him and we retrieved him later on. Pasang also brought a new camp-follower, a Tibetan from Kyirong, named Norbu. Such were the difficulties ahead of us, that we were glad of all the help we could get. There now followed two days of hard bargaining with the four men of Barbung. They had already agreed on twenty rupees per load to Tarap, but in Sangdak the villagers hastened to impress upon them the difficulty of our plight. Realizing that if they did not carry our loads, no one else would, they demanded ninety rupees per load. Our position however was equally strong, for they either took our loads and were paid for their return journey, or they went unladen and so earned nothing. Thus they finally agreed to accept 450 rupees for the whole operation, however many yaks we used and however many days the journey lasted. As we had no more than twenty yak loads, this figure was little in excess of the original terms of twenty rupees per load. But we now spread the loads over many more yaks so that they were all lightly laden.

There are two routes up onto the great Dolpo Pass beyond Sangdak. One goes by the gorge along a narrow precipitous track, like the route that ascends the same gorge below Sangdak. The other route leaves the gorge just below the village of Günsa (the winter village of the Sangdak villagers some four hours climb beyond their summer village) and ascends steeply to a high pass, the Kyi-tse La (*c.* 18,000 feet). Beyond this pass there is a long basin-like valley, and having crossed another pass on the far side of this, one descends onto the main Dolpo Pass, which keeps to a fairly level height of 16–17,000 feet for a distance of six to seven miles.[1]

We had descended by way of the gorge when we came out of Dolpo in 1956. It is quicker and easier for men, but quite unsuitable for laden animals and rather unpleasant even for unladen ones. Thus without much discussion, we decided to go by way of the Kyi-tse La, although the villagers of Sangdak continued to prophesy woe. They were quite right, for after the heavy storms of the past few days, the basin beyond the Kyi-tse La proved to be quite impassable. But we went right to the top to find this out. On the 12th we travelled to Günsa and camped just below

[1] For these estimates of heights, I am relying upon the *Survey of India* maps of the area.

the village. A sore throat and a high temperature attacked me again and I lay ill in my tent the next day, while we debated whether to split the party, allowing me to follow on when I was strong enough. But this was too inconvenient to arrange, and since antibiotics had brought my temperature down by the next morning, we decided to make the ascent of the pass and camp that night in the basin beyond. The men of Barbung selected the gentlest of the yaks for me to ride and with one of the horse-saddles tied securely on his back, I rode him quite happily to the top of the pass, about five hours ascent from our camp. It is an exhilarating but a very cold way of travelling at such altitudes. While the two unhappy horses made their way up unladen and with obvious difficulty, the yaks advanced with quiet determination and, when the track was at all difficult, with the nimbleness of goats.

We camped that night in the snow filled basin. The minimum temperature recorded during the night was $-14°C$, about 40 degrees of frost F. The next morning the four men of Barbung seemed unwilling to start. They sat huddled around their little camp fire, eating broth made with mutton and tsamba. Meanwhile our two 'mountaineering' Sherpas, Jockey Pasang and Pemba, set out with ice-axes and long poles to find a way to the top of the snow covered pass that rose above us. They were accompanied by one of the henchmen of a prosperous Tibetan nomad, named Gopala, who had joined our party in Günsa, and also by a Namgung villager who was on his way back to Dolpo, for our caravan was clearly going to be the last one to enter Dolpo that year. Slowly and surely they all advanced to the top of the pass, while the rest of us wasted time watching them. I was still feeling too weak to attempt the climb on foot myself, and so had no choice but to await the yaks. Not until Jockey Pasang and the others had reached the very top of the pass were the four men of Barbung sufficiently reassured. We then loaded the yaks and set off. The leading yaks were sent up with no loads, so that they would be able to force a way through the snow unimpeded, but they found the going very difficult. Then they began to turn back in their ranks, and this caused general confusion. Several loads fell off, and the yak men had to toil through the snow, lead the animals back to their loads and strap them on once more. It was thus impossible to maintain any proper order in the caravan, and when the leading yaks finally refused to advance any further and just stood buried up to their flanks in deep snow on a 30° to 45° slope, the yak men could do nothing but order a general retreat. Thus we plunged back down the steep snow slope, still scattering things by the way, till we reached our old camp site in the snow filled basin. It was now three in the afternoon; the sun was disappearing and bitter cold was setting in upon us again. The four men of Barbung simply relit their fire and sat huddled around it quaffing small cups of raw spirit (arak). Jockey Pasang and Pemba returned disconsolate from the top of the pass, dragging and rolling down as many of our scattered possessions as they could. Pasang Khambache and Norbu went to their assistance, and everything was eventually retrieved. The men of Barbung still sat round their fire, and the yaks wandered off as they pleased. Pasang Khambache was roused to fury at their seeming lack of concern, and angry words were exchanged. But since the animals belonged to these four yak men, it was clearly they who would have to decide what should happen next. It was agreed that in any case we must return to our camp site below Günsa. So we loaded the yaks and set off. Corneille likened our sad discomforted procession to Napoleon's retreat from Moscow. I was able to remain on my yak up to the top of the Kyi-tse La, feeling cold and ill and disheartened. From the top of the pass we descended rapidly on foot, and set up our camp in the dark on the site we had left the morning before.

The next morning the four men of Barbung announced their intention of abandoning us, for they would now have to approach the Dolpo Pass by way of the gorge, and as we already knew, loaded animals could not possibly go by that route. But Pasang Khambache had a counter proposal. Apart from the forty yaks and two horses which would, we all agreed, have to ascend the gorge unloaded, we now had a total of eleven men in our party, so there was no reason why we should not man-handle the loads up the gorge, while the animals waited below. They had agreed on a price of 450 rupees for getting us to Tarap, and if they did not assist us in getting there when there was a practicable means of doing so, they really had no right to any part of the sum. If however they were still willing to help us, we would recompense them for all their extra trouble. Finally they agreed. They were glad to delay in any case, so that their animals would have time to graze.

After a day's rest below Günsa, we set out again on the 17th, and descended to the river which we followed up as far as the spectacular little bridge that spans the gorge and marks the beginning of the difficult part of the route. Just before the bridge there is an overhanging rock, where we established our first camp. The yaks carried the loads a little way beyond the bridge, as far as they could in fact. When they had been unloaded, they returned in the direction of Günsa to graze. The next day we carried our loads farther up the gorge, leaving them here and there, as far as we could carry them that day. Then going on unladen, except for necessary camping equipment and some food supplies, we established a second camp at the top limit of the difficult sections of the route. In the course of the next two days we gradually moved all our loads up to the top camp, and so on the 20th when the yaks arrived unladen, we simply loaded them up in the gorge, and went happily on our way to the top of the Dolpo pass, which we reached by noon. It was as usual now a quite splendid day with a clear blue sky and hard frozen snow under our feet. I had now completely recovered from my illness and was happy to be on the borders of Dolpo at last. It seemed certain that our main difficulties were now over.

By dusk we reached the far side of the pass, where the track branches northwards to Tsharka and westwards towards yet another pass that leads over to Barbung. Here we set up camp and were promptly visited by a servant of the nomad Gopala (who had arrived before us), bringing a present of fire-wood and a joint of mutton. We were especially glad of the wood in a place where there is none except that which one carries oneself. When the sun had disappeared it was, as always, bitterly cold. The next morning Gopala invited us to his tent and served us with buttered tea and raw spirits (arak). He too was on his way to Barbung, where he had left some of his sheep to graze.

The next day, the 21st, we climbed the long gentle ascent towards the pass, which only towards the summit rose steeply through scree to a great crest of frozen snow. On the other side we descended at first gently on the frozen snow with an ever increasing view of the Barbung gorge below us. Then suddenly the track began to descend even more steeply and clusters of houses appeared deep down below us. This track is perhaps the steepest and most tiring that I have ever known in the Himalayas and the descent went on for a long time. It was with great difficulty that we persuaded the horses to follow us, and at last one of them refused to come and had to be temporarily abandoned once more, for one cannot drag a tired and unwilling horse down a steep mountain side. The track led us almost onto the roofs of the village of Trhim-nyer (*S of I:* Darengaon). We settled in the house of Ngö-drup, one of our yak men, whose house happened to be in this village. Several of the Trhim-nyer villagers are 'religious laymen' (*chos-pa*) of the Nying-ma Order, and as sign of their calling they wear a wide circle of twisted hair (*ral-pa*). Ngö-drup's eldest brother was one of these. There were three brothers in all with one wife in common. The second brother was away trading in Tichu-rong during our stay, but their old father was living in the house. They possessed a small collection of books, mainly Nying-ma ritual texts, but among them there was a local manuscript copy of the biography of a local lama, *U-rgyan bsTan-'dzin*, of which I was able to make a microfilm.

After much discussion about the number and weight of our loads, which were decreased by consumption on the journey so far, but increased by local purchases of grain and potatoes, we finally set out towards Tarap, where they had agreed to take us, on the afternoon of the 25th. We had not gone far up the Barbung river, when our four yak owners remembered that they had left all their own food supplies at home, and by the time they had gone back to fetch these, it was already time to set up camp for the night. We continued upstream the next day to a point where the valley begins to turn north-eastwards towards Tsharka. Here we turned westwards towards the pass that leads over to Tarap, and after climbing steadily for the rest of the day, we set up camp on a small wind-swept piece of flat ground just below the pass. It was no colder according to our thermometer than previous nights (namely − 16°C), but the cold was intensified by a fierce wind that blew down from the pass. We built a shelter on the wind-swept mountain side, using our boxes and great stones that lay around. Inside we lit a fire with the wood we had carried up with us and prepared a meal of soup and chopped meat and noodles. Corneille and I and the two Pasangs slept in the tents, but the rest of the party slept in the open shelter by the dead embers. One never ceases to be amazed at their fortitude, for the cold seemed more intense than ever before. The next morning Pasang Khambache was ill and feverish, so he took my place on the gentle yak. The summit of the pass was covered in deep frozen snow, which lay thick and hard all down the far side (pls. 6 & 7). We descended rapidly, digging our heels in the firm snow, to the frozen stream at the foot of the next barren valley. From here we crossed another pass and then descended by a long valley to the eastern end of Tarap. By now the sun had set and the cold gripped one's limbs even as one walked. As I have explained elsewhere, Tarap is not a village, but a whole valley comprising a complex of small villages and monasteries.[1] We passed through the villages of Do-ro and Do and went on to the small cluster of buildings, known as Gä-kar (*Gad-dkar*), built just above the river in a bend in the valley. One of these buildings is the 'All Good Isle of the Doctrine (*kun-bzang chos-gling*), the residence of Lama sKyabs, the senior lama of Tarap, who had befriended us in 1956. It was dark when we arrived, and the yaks were unloaded outside his house in what might well have appeared to be hopeless confusion. But within half an hour our tents were erected together with a Tibetan style tent, which Pasang Khambache had borrowed from the Lama. A fire of twigs and dried yak and sheep dung was soon burning, and Pemba was serving everyone with well buttered tea.

We had originally estimated three weeks for our journey. It had taken us 38 days of travel and enforced delay to reach our main destination, where we intended to establish some kind of headquarters. But we had still not yet reached inner Dolpo. In the course of the next few days we turned ourselves into Dolpo householders. Lama sKyabs lent us one of his houses. Our horses lived on the ground-floor and we installed ourselves in the two rooms on the first storey. One of the rooms we made into a kitchen and the other one into our sleeping and living quarters. Like all Dolpo houses, it had a flat roof, and round the edges of this we stored the supplies of wood and barley-stalks that we now bought up as fast as we could. Brush-wood could be obtained about seven miles away at the far eastern end of the valley and we paid village boys six rupees a load for collecting it for us. Once the winter came in earnest, no more fuel would be available. The villagers were still finishing their

[1] See *Himalayan Pilgrimage*, pp. 154–58.

harvest work, threshing and winnowing the grain, for their seasons are about a month behind those of Sangdak. We bought up large supplies of barley and wheat, while the prices were at their lowest. The barley we turned into tsamba ourselves by first roasting and then grinding the grain. For the horses we bought supplies of buckwheat and the barley-stalks that adorned our roof-top.

When we were in Tarap in 1956, we had wondered what it would be like to live here in winter, and it was largely this simple curiosity that had brought me here now. It was only the beginning of November, but already we had some idea what the winter would be like. The long green valley that I remembered from 1956 was now a valley of dead brown grass. Snow lay on the mountains all around and ice never left the streams. It was warm while the sun shone (normally from about 8.30 a.m. to 3.30 p.m.), but bitterly cold the rest of the time. We heated our living room with a small stove which Pasang had made in Kathmandu from beaten corrugated iron, and this worked quite well except when gales blew the smoke down the chimney.

Soon after our arrival we discovered that we were not the only visitors in Tarap. Staying at the *bon* monastery of Sh'ip-chhok near Do were two *bon* lamas from Tibet, namely the Abbot of *gYung-drung* Monastery in Tsang and a much younger man, named Sangye Tenzin and nicknamed Yam Lama. They were both refugees from their country, and having first fled to India, they had now made this long and difficult journey up to Dolpo in search of *bon* books, which they knew to be available at the old *bon* monastery of Samling near *Bi-cher*. They had already spent more than a month at Samling and were now on their way back to India with three loads of borrowed books which they intended to publish for the use of their co-religionists who were also refugees in India. Sangye Tenzin impressed me at once with his grasp of realities. He had been a refugee in India for just over a year, but it was clear that he had not been wasting his time, for not only had be been collecting books, but he had also raised funds to print them. I begged the Abbot of *gYung-drung* to delay their departure, so that we would have time to talk further, but he insisted that they must leave as soon as possible as they were anxious to return to India and the routes out of Dolpo would soon be closed finally for the winter. But as so often happens, delay was forced upon them by their travelling companions, and so we all met again the following day. Sangye Tenzin now impressed me so much, that I thought of inviting him to England, and with this idea in mind I suggested he met me in Kathmandu at the end of the following March. He drew up a list of books at Samling which he had not been able to bring away, and I agreed to make microfilms of these some time during my stay. This was an unexpected and most successful meeting, for later events worked out just as we planned.

On 4th November Sonam Panden Trangjun arrived from Mustang. He had had to send his own horses back from Sangdak, where he had spent a week in a nomad's tent waiting for the Sangdak villagers to hire him three yaks. This they eventually agreed to do at the exorbitant rate of 17 rupees a day each. He had travelled via Tsharka, where he met friends en route who had kindly lent him horses and a monk-attendant. These friends were a small party from Sera Monastery near Lhasa, who had been in charge of some of the Sera livestock that happened to be grazing in the nomad areas to the north of Dolpo. So they had escaped from Tibet into Nepal, bringing their animals with them. Sonam Panden arrived splendidly dressed in a brocade-silk fur-lined jacket, blue knickerbockers and a long Tibetan gown of fine black serge, also fur-lined. We realized that we might give more thought to our appearances, and Pasang Khambache began to buy up scores of lamb-skins so that we could have fur-lined garments made for our use as well.

Lama *sKyabs* seemed to have grown very old since we had last met him in 1956. Swathed in a fur-lined cloak, he sat most of the day in the sun on his roof, reading texts, saying prayers and receiving a large number of visitors. He asked me one day if we had by chance any '*chang*' made with grapes', for the Teacher from Urgyan, *Lotus-Born*, had mentioned such a drink, and he though it might be good for his health. We happened to have one bottle of sherry, and we opened this and gave him some, which delighted him immensely. He put his small library at our disposal, and with Sonam Panden's help I looked through and made microfilms of some of his books. Meanwhile we had succeeded in making a home of a kind for ourselves, and we now planned a month's journey into inner Dolpo before the winter finally set in.

We set out rather late on 11th November, Sonam Panden and I riding and everyone else on foot. To carry our necessary belongings we had six yaks, which we had hired in Do. The ascent towards the pass was long and gradual and we camped in a pleasant place where there was an adequate supply of brushwood and no wind to make us feel colder than we need. By now we were quite used to night temperatures of $-20°$ C and less, and we had learned that if one got into one's sleeping-bags while the body was still warm, one would usually remain warm most of the night. The worst part of the day was always the early morning before sunrise, and we learned to welcome the sun as the life-giver that he really is. The approach to the pass the next morning led across a gleaming expanse of snow and ice. The view towards the south was superb with the great domed summit of Dhaulagiri framed between the lesser peaks rising above the valley that we had ascended. Having crossed the pass, we made our way down a frozen gully to the head of the valley that leads down to *Nang-khong*. As is so often the case on these travels, the journey down the valley took much longer than the map would suggest, and it was not until after nightfall that we passed the prayer-walls and stupas, sure signs of a nearby village. Thus we reached the bridge below Tsa, only to find that it consisted of just two solid ends, for the connecting arch had collapsed into the torrent. We persuaded the horse to wade backwards and forwards and carry everyone over in relays, and then we climbed up to the village. There was no response to our shouts, for the villagers were too terrified to come out and see who we were. So we set up our tents on a threshing ground and helped ourselves to wood for our fires and grass for the hungry horses. Having drunk some soup, we went straight to sleep. At dawn we were awoken by angry shouts, for the villagers who would not come to our assistance by night, now showed themselves disproportionately brave by light of day, when we in our turn lay sleeping. They demanded an absurd sum for the wood and grass we had used, and threatened to complain to *Nyi-ma Tshe-ring* of Saldang. We invited them to accompany us to his house there and then, for it was in fact our first destination. He is the chief man of Dolpo, and having availed ourselves of his help in 1956, we now intended to call on him and make suitable presents. We made an uneasy peace with the villagers of Tsa, paying them more than was reasonable, while they continued to abuse us. Later on we heard that they thought we were a party of Chinese invaders, and this rumour caused great alarm to a Tibetan monk from Drepung near Lhasa, who was living at that time in Hrap Monastery just above Tsa. It was he who told us the whole story when we made his acquaintance later on. Hrap is visible from the small village of Tsa, but we had no time to visit it that morning, as the boy who was accompanying the yaks now threatened us with new problems. He suddenly said that his father had told him to return to Tarap when he had completed two days journey with us, wherever we might have reached. This was contrary to all normal practice and the boy was so hopelessly outnumbered that he had no choice but to allow his yaks to carry our belongings as far as Saldang, but not wishing to delay him unnecessarily, we set out as soon as possible.

To travel the length of *Nang-khong* is only a short day's journey, and it was a very happy experience to ride along the track that runs the length of this valley. We passed another small group of houses, known as Shugu, and then down by the river we caught sight of the 'Residence of Great Happiness' (*bDe-chen bla-brang*), which I had failed to visit in 1956. The river widens into a small lake in front of it and this was now a sheet of glistening ice. The red painted walls of the buildings cling to the rock face of the gorge, and above it the cliffs rise up towards the great watershed separating *Nang-khong* from *Ban-tshang* (pl. 10). There are a few stone enclosures for animals, a few bare willow trees and a little way down stream a small water mill which in this winter season is quite frozen up. We passed below Sham-tr'ak Monastery without visiting it that day, for it is built high up above the left bank of the gorge, and the track along the valley keeps close under the rocks at this point. Then crossing several frozen streams, we followed the track up to *Zel* Monastery, which is built on a protruding crag dominating the whole valley.[1] Then we hastened on through the straggling village of Namdo, climbed across the mouth of the gorge which leads up to Namgung (*gNam-gung*) and followed the rows of prayer-walls that line the track to the village of Saldang (*Sa-ldang*). Like many other Dolpo villages, Saldang consists of a group of scattered houses built high on an 'alp' well above the gorge. The name probably means just 'Raised Place'.[2] To reach *Nyi-ma Tshering*'s house one clambers round the mountain side above the gorge and below the village, until it suddenly becomes visible standing in the middle of its fields on a small 'alp' of its own.

We were greeted by the laughing girls of the household who were attending to the animals in the courtyard, and then the master himself came out to see who this crowd of visitors might be. Realizing our needs at once, he assigned us some out-houses as a temporary home, and then invited us upstairs to his own dark living-room. We arranged some presents on a large dish, soap and towels, packets of cube sugar, bricks of Tibetan tea, packets of cigarettes, a length of good cloth, and enlargements of photographs we had taken in 1956. A photograph of the 'Precious Lama of Shang', whom we had met in 1956 on his travels in NW Nepal and who died two years later in the nomad country to the north, pleased *Nyi-ma Tshe-ring* most of all, and he placed it at once on the alter in his private chapel.

He seemed pleased to see us again, but could not understand what should bring us to Dolpo in winter when travel was so difficult. He asked about our plans and then made discouraging comments. However he urged us all to accompany him to a ceremony at Sham-tr'ak Monastery that was due to take place in a few days time, and to this we readily agreed. He seemed chiefly concerned to gain some reassurance from us that the Chinese, who were just the other side of the frontier some two days journey away, would not invade his territory. On our side we were relieved to know that no Chinese had yet set foot inside Dolpo. We learned too that *Nyi-ma Tshe-ring* had already sent messengers to a local Chinese commander, asking if it would be safe to send their yaks and sheep across the frontier as usual for winter grazing. He had received an encouraging reply to the effect that Nepalese subjects and their flocks and herds would be welcome. But in practice all was not so well. Many of the nomads who normally cared for these animals during the winter months, had arrived that summer in Dolpo as refugees, bringing their own animals with them. Moreover even when nomad friends were still available to look after the animals, the Chinese, it seemed, were in no position to guarantee their protection.

[1] *Zel* Fort is mentioned in our biographies, and this is undoubtedly the same place. In *Himalayan Pilgrimage* (p. 103) I quoted the name incorrectly as *gSal*.
[2] Once again I must amend the suggested spelling of *gSal-mdangs* which occurs in *Himalayan Pilgrimage* (p. 104).

LIFE IN DOLPO 1960-61   49

Only two months previously the Khambas (those warrior Tibetans from the eastern provinces), who while fighting with the Chinese were always desperately in need of food, had captured over a hundred yaks belonging to the villagers of Tsharka. Thus apart from one village, which had sent its yaks and sheep to the Tibetan plains seemingly under Khamba and not Chinese protection, most Dolpo villagers were sending their animals south that year. Except for limited grazing around Tichu-rong and Phoksumdo, the southern valleys are barely suitable for yaks, and the numbers of animals needing winter grazing were swelled considerably by those of the refugee nomads who had fled to Dolpo during the summer. The resulting loss of livestock that winter was a terrible blow to the people of Dolpo, and the effect on the economy was probably disastrous, although this was only gradually becoming apparent during 1961. In the autumn of 1960 meat was absurdly cheap, as many animals had to be either killed off or allowed to die slowly of starvation. Grain prices were already inflated during the summer because of the demands of the refugee nomads, and although the harvest relieved matters for a while, prices soon rose again even higher than before. Thus we were paying four to five times as much for our wheat and barley as we had paid in 1956. At the same time we could buy slaughtered sheep for a few shillings each, and since the temperature indoors never rose above freezing point throughout the winter, keep them in cold storage as long as one needed.

While Pasang made us a temporary home in *Nyi-ma Tshe-ring*'s outhouses, I looked through the small collection of books in his private temple. Among them was the biography of the Lama *Glorious Intellect* of Hrap, and looking through this I conceived the idea of recovering something of Dolpo's past from this and similar works. The next day I noticed the biography of Lama *Religious Protector Glorious and Good* in the house of *Nyi-ma Tshe-ring*'s brother-in-law, who lives in Saldang village, and I began to make enquiries where I might find other such biographical works.

From 17th to 19th November we stayed at Sham-tr'ak Monastery where *Nyi-ma Tshe-ring* had urged us to accompany him. We intended to stay only one night, but he was clearly so happy there for he was entertained with almost regal honours, that we stayed on with him at his insistence. The young lama's mother supplied us with meat and tsamba and chang throughout our stay, as well as with food for the horses. The ceremony performed on this occasion was the 'Union of the Precious Ones' (*dKon-mchog spyi-'dus*). First came the recitation of the liturgy and the offering of the sacrificial cakes, then the ceremonial dance ('*cham*') which was performed at night, and lastly the 'life-consecration'.[1] The chief celebrant was

[1] The divinities and liturgy of the 'Union of the Precious Ones' are described in *Buddhist Himālaya*, pp. 228 ff. The 'life-consecration' is described in *Himalayan Pilgrimage*, pp. 141 ff.

Karma rGyal-mtshan, the young lama of Sham-tr'ak. We had first met him in 1956 soon after the death of his step-father, the previous lama, and he now seemed quite secure in the succession. He was assisted in the present ceremony by the 'community-members' of Sham-tr'ak, mostly married men, and by two visiting lamas, the Lama of *Zel* and a Khamba lama, renowned for his knowledge of the *Great Perfection* teachings, who was passing through Dolpo.

When the ceremony was over, we made a brief visit to the 'Residence of Great Happiness' down in the gorge below Sham-tr'ak. The lama there was about 36 years old. He showed pleasure at seeing us and expressed his regrets that we had not visited him in 1956. I asked him about the existence of local biographical and historical works and soon discovered that he knew far more about these than anyone else we had met. He showed a copy of the biography of Lama *Lord of Merit* and another copy of that of Lama *Glorious Intellect* (pl. 12). These biographies were local manuscripts and it would help the task of editing them considerably if one could find more than one copy in each case. The small library of the Lama of the 'Residence of Great Happiness' was the largest I had seen in inner Dolpo so far and he himself certainly seemed to be the best local scholar to help me look through this material. I asked him if I could come and stay nearby with a rather smaller party later on, and he said: 'Please come'.

On our return towards Saldang we called on the Lama of *Zel*, who had also been present at the Sham-tr'ak ceremony. He offered us a meal of buttered tea and rice, spiced meats and *chang*. While admiring his collection of painted temple banners (*thanka*), we learned that several of the newer ones had been painted for him by the Lama of the 'Residence of Great Happiness', so it was clear that my future host was an accomplished religious painter as well as a literary scholar. The Lama of *Zel* possessed a manuscript copy of the biography of Lama *Merit Intellect* and also a very old *thanka* illustrating the life of the same lama. We discussed how I might get a copy made of the manuscript and he suggested that his brother-in-law in Karang, who was a good scribe, might help with this. I also had in mind now to ask the Lama of the 'Residence of Great Happiness' if he would produce a new *thanka* for me of *Merit Intellect*, and possibly of other lamas as well. So it was that all the ideas came together which were to form the basis of the studies, of which this book 'Four Lamas of Dolpo' is the first fruits.

Although I would have been well content to settle down to some work on local manuscripts straight away, we were still involved in a series of local visits, and it is never a waste of time to make friends of people amongst whom you intend to live for several months. So we attended the ceremony of setting up new prayer-flags on the house of Rab-gyä, a neighbour of *Nyi-ma Tshe-ring*'s in Saldang. We made a visit to Yang-tsher Monastery, offered a general tea-ceremony to the members of the community, did some photographing and looked around to see what local literature of interest there might be. We found another copy of the biography of Lama *Religious Protector Glorious and Good* and the biography of *Good Deliverance*, one of the first lamas of *Grod-lung* Monastery near *Ting-khyu*.

Our return from Yang-tsher to Saldang was memorable for the near death of my favourite horse Tshering. Sonam Panden and I followed the left bank of the river below Yang-tsher, so as to avoid having to cross it later on, for the bridge had collapsed and the water was very deep. But we were forced by the enclosing cliffs to seek a way up the mountain-side and above the gorge. We followed what seemed to be a track, and I was going first leading Tshering by a guide-rope. I suddenly found myself descending into a steep ravine, which opened out below me into steep scree and then seemed to end in a precipice descending to the gorge below. By descending the scree carefully and keeping to the rocks on the right, one could get a footing on the cliff beside the precipice and so clamber down to the river's edge. But it was obviously no place for a horse. It should have been possible to lead him up again, but he took fright and when Sonam came to help me, he threw Sonam back against the rocks. A long struggle now ensued, and the horse, even more frightened, remained where he was. We climbed up to the top again to consider the problem and to rest, while the horse quietened down. It now seemed quite impossible to persuade him to come up, and so the only hope was to get him to climb down. It would be easy to get him onto the scree, but more difficult to keep him going to the right and so onto the rock ledge. But this seemed to be the only way of saving him in his present predicament. Sonam and I returned to the ravine. I led the horse by the bridle and Sonam held his tail. It was not pleasant to be in front of him, for he moved down the scree far too easily. Although I held him to the right, he failed to get a footing on the ledge, struggled so violently against us that for our own safety we had to let him go, then tumbled with no sense of self-preservation down what remained of the scree-slope and went over the precipice out of sight. There was a sickening thud and then silence. I hoped he was killed outright, for nothing could be done for a horse with broken limbs. As we climbed down to him, he raised his head, and I voiced my first thought to Sonam: 'How shall we kill him?' This question clearly surprised and perturbed Sonam, who would never kill a suffering creature whatever its plight. While most Tibetans kill animals for food (and this too is against their religious teachings) they have all sorts of complex scruples against killing animals for any other reason. In practice, they will kill when killing is socially acceptable, and this includes killing for food and killing in self-defense and in war. But killing an animal to put him out of his suffering is not socially acceptable, and so it remains a serious sin. So Sonam replied: 'He will die very quickly'. But this was not necessarily true, and as is usual in these cases, the vultures would almost certainly start eating him before he was dead. Meanwhile I thought rather feebly of my own clasp knife, and reproached myself for leading a horse into such a place without first investigating it more carefully. Then Sonam raised Tshering's head, and to our amazement he stood up of his own accord and began nosing around in the hope of finding some stray tufts of grass. It seemed impossible that any living creature could have fallen down such a place, a hundred feet at least of uncontrolled fall including quite thirty feet of sheer precipice. Yet there this animal stood, behaving as though nothing unusual had happened. After the agonies suffered on his account, it was like some miracle. We realized that he had fallen on his back and so had been protected by the thick bedding, which we had luckily found no other means of transporting that day and which had been strapped on under the saddle together with a thick foam rubber pad. The wood and leather saddle was smashed and Tshering's hair was torn out in places and his legs and thighs were all bleeding, but otherwise he seemed to be unhurt. While Sonam climbed up to get the other horse, I washed him in the river. Having learned our lesson for the day, we crossed back to the right bank of the river and followed the usual track. Tshering limped a little, but within ten days he was his normal self again.

As a general gesture of good will we had decided to finance a ceremony for as many local religious practisers as could be gathered together. *Nyi-ma Tshe-ring* insisted that it should be held at Tr'a-gyam[1] by Namgung. Tr'a-gyam is a new monastery founded jointly by *Nyi-ma Tshe-ring* himself and the Precious Lama of Shang. When we visited it in 1956 the sole occupant was a monk from Mugu, who was living there in solitary retreat. The only occupants now were the same monk (also named Sonam), a grandson of *Nyi-ma Tshe-ring*'s who had taken to the solitary life, and one or two Khamba lamas. As *Nyi-ma Tshe-ring* was going to supply us (at our cost) with all the butter and tsamba needed for the ceremony, and it was he who would summon those who would take part, we readily agreed to his choice of place and time. As the date we decided upon the 8th day of the 10th Tibetan month, which was sufficiently auspicious. The days leading up to the full moon, the 15th of every Tibetan month, are generally auspicious.

Our journey to Namgung, which can be reached in an easy day's journey from Saldang, was complicated by arrangements we were making to travel on to Samling and *Bi-cher* after the ceremony at Tr'a-gyam Monastery. We would need supplies not only for the ceremony and for a three days' stay in Namgung, but also for the journey to Samling and back and a few days' stay there. *Nyi-ma Tshe-ring* was not

---

[1] The literary spelling of this name is probably *Brag-gyam*, meaning 'craggy grotto', for there is one nearby. Locally I was given the spelling *Phred-rgyam*, meaning 'crossways' and this is also possible.

at all helpful with these further arrangements, for like all Dolpo villagers he considered it was already too late in the year to travel over passes from one Dolpo valley to another. Thus he dissuaded from accompanying us those villagers whom the promise of adequate payment had won as our helpers, and the morning we set out for Namgung we had more loads than men and animals to carry them. I pressed Tshering into service, but he still limped, and so had to be led back. The others went on ahead and late in the day Pasang Khambache and I set out a second time with another horse that we had managed to borrow. Pasang himself was loaded with an extra 20 lbs of butter intended for the sacrificial cakes and butter lamps. Thus we completed our rather cold and fearful journey up to Namgung in the dark. Travelling by night through such wild and stony places makes a journey quite twice as long, and one begins to think that one must have got into the wrong gully somehow and is on one's way into uninhabited mountains. When it is quite dark, thoughts of getting lost in this way can be quite alarming. The silence is complete. The track is unrecognizable sometimes even by the light of a torch. During the daytime the track may disappear under one's feet, but one can usually pick it out somewhere on the mountain-side above. At night such reassurance is entirely lacking. At last we thought we recognized the formation of the mountains above Namgung, well remembered from photographs taken in 1956. Then a torch appeared above us, coming nearer and nearer. It was Norbu, the Tibetan youth from Kyirong, who had come out to look for us.

We were led straight into a large room under the temple. *Nyi-ma Tshe-ring* was presiding over the gathered assembly, and I was shown to a seat next to him. Pemba served us with soup and noodles. The others had already had their fill of buttered tea and tsamba. Then everyone recited together the invocations of the *Saviouress*, after which all retired to sleep in various parts of the building. Corneille and Pasang Khambache and I slept in the temple above, where it was cold, but quiet and comfortable. Before we were awake the next morning our 'religious guests' were busy in the middle of the temple-floor mixing tsamba and moulding sacrificial cakes. Those present included the Lama of Sham-tr'ak, the Lama of *Zel*, Sonam the 'hermit', *Nyi-ma Tshe-ring*'s nephew, and the Khamba lamas. The only lay-folk present consisted of our own large party and *Nyi-ma Tshe-ring* himself, who had come without any attendants and clearly expected to be looked after by Pemba and Norbu, to whom he did not hesitate to give orders.

We performed the ceremony of the General Offerings to the *One Mother*, which lasted all day. Meanwhile Pasang supervised preparations of food for the whole assembly, and everyone seemed well content and at ease. We slept in the temple again that night, happy at having made this gesture of good will to the religion of the people of Dolpo. The next day we should have set out for Samling, but

Nyi-ma Tshe-ring was so discouraging, that in the end only Corneille, Pasang Khambache and Norbu set out with the sole assistance of a nomad herdsman who was encamped at Namgung. No Dolpo villager would go and Pemba was complaining of pains in his stomach, so he accompanied me down to the 'Residence of Great Happiness', where Sonam Panden soon joined us.

I stayed there from 28th November to 9th December, quietly working on the manuscripts that were already available. We visited the Lama of *Zel* again and borrowed his very old *thanka* of *Religious Protector Glorious and Good*, so that the Lama of the 'Residence of Great Happiness' could paint one anew for us. During our stay one of the Khamba lamas came down from Sham-tr'ak for a few days, and he bestowed upon our lama and a few other recipients the textual initiation and the consecration of the *Heart-Drop of the Great Expanse* (*Klong-chen snying-thig*) from the *Great Perfection* teachings. The household was a very pleasant one, and there was now so much work for me to do on these various local biographies, that I decided to make a long stay at the 'Residence of Great Happiness', where we were surrounded by good will and all the materials we needed.

On 3rd December Corneille, Pasang and Norbu returned from their brief tour to Samling and *Bi-cher*, thus proving that it was still possible to make this journey so late in the year. But it had proved difficult and exhausting, for the snow was very deep on the western side of the pass, but not sufficiently frozen for easy movement, so one sank deep into it at every step. I myself had no intention of going there until the following summer.

We decided now that we would all go back to Tarap together, for there was a ceremony at Do-ro that we wanted to attend, and also if I were going to stay longer in Namdo at the 'Residence of Great Happiness' we would need to bring back fresh supplies. It was agreed therefore that we should all spend Christmas together in our house at Gä-kar in Tarap and that I would return to Namdo immediately afterwards for six weeks or more. After the usual difficulties with porters we made our way back over the pass to Tarap. Sonam Panden was now over-anxious to return to Mustang, for there were rumours of troubles on the frontier and he was concerned about his sister. We managed to borrow another horse for him by depositing its value and we lent him Norbu as his only attendant. Two days after he had gone two men and three horses arrived from Mustang by the northern route, for which he must have arranged in advance without having told us. All we could do was to give them food and send them after him. We later heard that they all eventually reached Mustang after a most difficult journey. The horse we had borrowed fell down a ravine and was killed. Sonam and Norbu rescued with difficulty the load it was carrying, which they then had to share between them and carry themselves as far as Barbung, where they fortunately met Jockey Pasang and Saila.

Before setting out on our month's journey into inner Dolpo we had sent Jockey Pasang and Saila back to Kathmandu. There were several reasons. We had spent so much money getting into Dolpo that we feared we would not have enough to last us through the winter. Also one of the tape-recorders was broken, and it was the only one of our two that would work at all under the conditions of intense cold in which we were living. We were also glad to be able to send off mail and films, which would otherwise have had to await my next departure, planned for the coming March. We were now getting anxious about the return of these two travellers and counting the days since they had left Tarap. They arrived on 18th December, the 39th day of their absence, and our joy at seeing them safe was quite unbounded. We gave them some of our scarce sherry and all sat on the roof of our house in the sun listening to their travellers' tales. They had reached Pokhara from Tarap in nine days in quite remarkable speed, for they were lightly laden and had no animals to bother about. In Pokhara there seemed to be so much trouble on account of pilgrims and tourists that they had to wait eight days for a plane to take them to Kathmandu. There they went straight to our good American friends, Ralph and Lora Redford, who did everything possible to help them. The tape-recorder was repaired, the large cheque was cashed, photographs were developed and enlarged and selections sent to England and France together with our mail. After six days' stay they set off on the return journey, only making the mistake of trying to bring too much. They brought one man-load of rice and another of sugar, 50 lb of butter and a whole 25 lb of cheese, spices and pickles, and lastly two bottles of whisky and a load of periodicals that were given us as presents. All went well so long as porters were available, and after delays in Tukucha, they managed to reach Sangdak with their provisions intact. From there on no one would accompany them. The villagers, who were now nearly all settled in Günsa, seemed more afraid of Khambas than of snow and ice. There had probably been a few unfortunate incidents, including the loss of the hundred odd yaks belonging to Tsharka, and these had been so exaggerated by village talk that all Khambas were now regarded as murderers and robbers. But Jockey Pasang was so insistent, that at length with Sridar's help, a young nomad Tibetan was cajoled into accompanying them. Even this meant that all the rice, sugar, butter and half the cheese had to be left in Sridar's house. Then the three of them set out sharing the rest of the loads between them.

In one day they reached our old camping place on the far side of the great Dolpo pass. It was now a terribly desolate place. Two wild dogs were there feeding off the carcasses of dead yaks and sheep. The three of them lay throughout the night huddled together in the snow. The young nomad was lamenting in advance his own death and saying how his parents would sorrow for him. Jockey Pasang and Saila were so concerned on his account that they slept close on either side of him, lest in his fear he should run off into the snow and really be lost for ever. They reached Trhim-nyer in Barbung the next day and going straight to Ngö-drup's house where we had all stayed before, they found Sonam Panden and Norbu already there on their way from Tarap, and listened to their tale of woe. Jockey Pasang was so sorry for them, that he offered them the young nomad as companion when they left the next day. The fellow was overjoyed at being saved from what he feared might be a worse fate if he went on into Dolpo. Thus Jockey Pasang and Saila made the journey from Barbung to Tarap alone. They divided the loads between them with the result that they tried to carry too much. Thus they took nearly three days on the journey involving two nights unprotected on the open mountains, where the temperature must have been less than $-25°$ C. They chose places where there was brushwood available and kept fires burning all night, so they slept very little. They looked remarkably fit, but were very tired indeed. Needless to say perhaps, the villagers of Sangdak and Dolpo were by now quite amazed at these comings and goings. The journey however had served its purpose, for we now had money enough, the tape-recorder was repaired, our films and mail had been despatched, and of course they had brought up incoming mail for us. The supplies they had left in Sangdak all came in useful the following March.

During December two large scale ceremonies took place in Tarap, a performance of the 'Union of the Precious Ones' at Me-kyem Monastery above Do on the 16th of the month, and a 'coming out' feast at Do-ro on the 23rd to celebrate the ending of a strict retreat of three novices. We spent Christmas together in our house in Tarap, and then on the 29th I set out with Pasang Khambache, our servant Saila and the horse Tshering to return to Namdo, as we had already planned. Pasang persuaded two nomads to accompany us as load-carriers and the horse carried our clothes, bedding and a light tent. The northern side of the pass had become much more difficult since we last crossed it, for it was now covered with really hard ice and deep snow. We released the horse of his loads and guided them down ourselves on ropes. The valley we entered the other side of the pass was a dead gorge of solid ice, and travel was fairly easy except when there was not enough snow on the ice for the horse's hoofs to grip, for then we had to cut tracks for him with an ice-axe. We reached the 'Residence of Great Happiness' at dusk on the second day, and after a hot meal for everyone including the horse, we all fell fast asleep.

All the previous days the weather had been fine with the usual clear blue winter skys of Dolpo, but the morning after our arrival in Namdo clouds appeared and it began to snow. We were concerned for the two nomads who had set out early on the return journey to Tarap, but with no loads on their backs they got through quickly and just in time (so we heard later). It now snowed continuously for three days, and all the passes in Dolpo were finally closed to the intrepid members of our party until the end of February. Our enforced retreat had begun, for we were now completely cut off from the outside world. This suited me very well, for my work programme was already arranged. From the 4th until 28th January the weather was superb, and from about nine in the morning until 3.30 in the afternoon we could sit happily on the roof of our house in the full warmth of the sun. The Lama had started on the *thankas* I had asked him to paint, while I worked on my manuscripts, asking his assistance as necessary when words or phrases were obscure.

The 'Residence of Great Happiness' is a complex group of buildings all built up against the cliffs (pl. 10). The lama's own house consists of a ground-floor, reserved as usual for his livestock, a first floor with two quite large rooms, one of which he lent to us, and a second floor which comprised his own small temple, an open-roofed anteroom where he would do his painting and reading, and a small open roof. These various storeys are all connected by ladders made of notched tree-trunks, and from the anteroom on the second floor one can ascend by another such ladder to the flat roof of the temple. Here I would spend much of the day seated under the overhanging cliffs. As the house is on the northern side of the gorge, we enjoyed the maximum amount of sunshine, while the surrounding rock cliffs gave shelter from the wind. The whole landscape was completely snow-bound. Just across the valley was the house of *A-ne* Sonam. (*A-ne* means 'aunt' and is the polite and friendly way of addressing married women, just as one normally addresses men as *A-jo* 'elder brother'.) Her husband was away all the winter with their animals. She was very friendly to us, letting us have brushwood from her own stocks and singing songs for me so that I could record them. Well above her house was that of Karma Lobsang, one of *Nyi-ma Tshe-ring*'s two brothers. He too had quite a good voice and would sing for us sometimes to the accompaniment of a Tibetan guitar, known as a dram-nyen (*sgra-snyan*). Next to his house was that of *Nyi-ma Tshe-ring*'s son, who was also away the whole winter with his animals. As immediate neighbours we had on one side a man and his wife, who were charming and very friendly. Regrettably I have forgotten both their names, as we addressed them always as *A-jo* and *A-ne*. They kept one cow throughout the winter and would always sell us milk when they had it. They also made very good clear *chang*. Their house adjoined that of the Lama's, and the flat roofs were kept separate just by piled up brushwood. On the other side of the Lama's house is a small temple containing a large prayer-wheel. In the loft over this temple there was living a refugee nomad monk named *Phun-tshogs* together with his wife, for he was a renegade monk who had broken his vows. He used to earn fees by reading religious texts and reciting prayers in people's houses, but to the distress of his wife he used to waste much of what he earned by gambling it away. They had this accommodation because of a special family relationship, which may seem remote to us, but is close enough to be of use in Dolpo. The sister of this monk's wife was married to a well-to-do Tibetan nomad named Tshe-den, who was living in his tent just outside the 'Residence of Great Happiness'. This Tshe-den was the sworn friend of *Nyi-ma Tshe-ring*'s son, who was therefore bound to help not only his friend, but his friend's wife's sister as well. So she and her monk husband had been given the room over the temple. She was a very good woman indeed. She would come to help us in the house, grinding our wheat and our tsamba for us, for in winter all this must be done by hand. She asked me several times to try and stop her husband gambling, but this was no easy matter. He befriended me for his own purposes, and suggested one day that we should take ceremonial scarves, visit the lama at Hrap and swear friendship to one another. I neither took up this offer nor his suggestion that he should accompany me to England. He had no more idea than anyone else in Dolpo how far away Europe really was.

    The Lama's household consisted of his wife, whom we also addressed as *A-ne*, and their two nephews who lived in the house like sons. They came from *Shi-min* (Shimen) in *Ban-tshang* where his wife's family lived. Being a lama of the 'Old Order', he was free to live as a married man. When the weather was fine we worked in the anteroom to the temple and on the open roofs. He first of all prepared the 'canvas' for his painting by stretching a length of cotton cloth on a wooden frame, coating it lightly with glue and chalk and rubbing the surface smooth with a flat smooth stone when the coating was dry. Having drawn in the designs and the figures, he then patiently put in the colours, using paints which he mixed for himself in the normal Tibetan way. He had a sufficient stock of mineral colourings which he had obtained from Tibet, and these he mixed with glue according to his immediate requirements. Each of the four paintings which he did for me represented about a month's work, but this was spread over a rather longer period, for during bad weather such work was impossible. From 28th January until 8th February we had twelve terrible days when the sun was never visible. The cold was intense day and night, and we spent most of our time in our sleeping bags with plastic jars as hot water bottles. By moving my camp bed against the window, I had sufficient light to work during daylight hours, and in the evenings I would use two candles, of which we had a good supply. The window, like all windows in Dolpo, had no glass in it. It was just a rectangular trellis-like frame that fitted into a small rectangular hole in the wall, but Pasang had redesigned it with some strong transparent plastic that we had brought with us from England for just this purpose.

Every evening we would sit round the Lama's fire-place in his living-room, which was next to ours, asking him questions and answering his. He was interested to learn about the shape of the world, different peoples and different countries, evolutionary theories and historical events. I came to know him so well that I was soon used to his way of speaking and we conversed fairly easily together. The Dolpo dialects (for they vary slightly from one valley to another) are a form of western Tibetan. An intelligent well travelled man such as this Lama, knows how to accommodate his speech to someone who is more familiar with the speech of central Tibet. Pasang who is well used to these Tibetan frontier dialects was never in any difficulty, but I was never able myself to follow the free flowing conversation of Dolpo villagers. Some days friends would gather in the lama's house, and I would record songs and conversations. They readily agreed to this not only out of friendliness, but because they were so glad to hear everything played back.

Apart from these limited periods of bad weather, the winter in Dolpo was really superb. The snow everywhere was deep but hard frozen, and we could make short excursions up and down the valley. We visited the lama (actually a Tibetan refugee monk from Drepung) who was staying at Hrap, and he lent us sugar and molasses and made us presents of eggs. In the whole of inner Dolpo he alone seemed to have a small supply of sugar and certainly he alone kept chickens. When we visited the Lama of *Zel* one day, he was busy putting up new prayer-flags on his roof. As we floundered through the snow, we heard the sounds of drum and conch-shell and saw flocks of choughs circling and squawking round the temple-roof. Making sure the dog was out of the way, we climbed up through the house to the top roof. The sun was so fierce that the lama was seated under the shade of a stretched out blanket, reading the liturgy and striking the drum. Before him was a small table, loaded with sacrificial cakes, small and large, and with jars of *chang*. He was assisted by his son-in-law, who would stoop down by his side to read on occasions, and then when the right moment came, he would blow the conch-shell and toss a ladleful of *chang* and offer a sacrificial cake to the divinity whose turn it was to receive his share. They were considerate enough not to hurl the cakes into space like the *chang*, for he placed them on a wooden board on the edge of the roof, where they were accumulating faster than the choughs could eat them. They motioned to us to sit down and wait, and when the ceremony was over we joined them in a meal of buttered tea and lumps of sacrificial cake.

The main religious festival of Yang-tsher Monastery takes place during the last four days of the 11th Tibetan month, which corresponded that year with the 13th–16th January. We set out on the 12th, taking a minimum of things, but even these amounted to three or four man-loads. Saila carried one, and a Tibetan nomad youth who was staying in Namdo, another, and Tshering our horse carried the rest. The upper route, a track running precipitously along the side of the valley, is impossible for a horse, so we went by the river route. The river twists its way between precipitous cliffs and in summer a man can go this way only if he is prepared to wade continually through very deep water. But in winter all is frozen — more or less. We soon found that the ice was treacherous in places, and once Tshering got badly stuck, but we were able to pull him out. Arriving after dark, we arranged our bedding in one of the temples, and then went to buy some wood and grass from the monastery steward, whom we had met when we were last there in November. He was away with his animals, and only his wife and grown-up son were there. We were very tired, and we needed wood for our fire and grass (really dried barley-stalks) for our hungry horse, and we had come to a place where we were well known and had several friends. Normally one expects twenty trusses of grass for a half rupee coin, but the son would only give us six. When we protested, he said: 'Well go and buy it in the village, if you want more for your money'. The village of Nyisal is half an hour's walk away, and at that time everyone would be in bed. Pasang said to him: 'If you do not sell us grass at a reasonable rate, we shall just take what we want and leave you this money'. They unwillingly gave us ten trusses, and said 'Pay in the morning'. As it happened the next morning the son cut his left thumb through to the bone while he was chopping meat, and he rushed straight to us, asking for help, as though we were his best friends in the world. I attended to the wound throughout our short stay, and he really was our friend after that.

The long ceremonies followed the same pattern as those that we had witnessed at Shey Monastery in 1956. First came the preparation of the sacrificial cakes, moulded out of tsamba moistened with *chang*. Then came the invocations to the main protective divinities, preceded by libations scattered from the temple-roof. The second day more sacrificial cakes were prepared, this time for the great divinities of the ritual cycle of the *Union of the Precious Ones*. A small model of a yak was also made, which served as a 'ransom-offering'. All adverse influences were impressed by means of ritual, and then the little figure was put up on the temple roof to be eaten by eager choughs (pl. 18). That evening there were masked dances in the main temple, at which crowds of Dolpo villagers and Tibetan nomads were present as spectators. The third day the liturgy of the 'Union of the Precious Ones' was recited and the sacrificial cakes were offered. Masked dancing lasted throughout the night until four the next morning. On the fourth day the 'life-consecration' ceremony was performed, and everyone crowded around the cerebrants to receive consecrated pellets of pressed tsamba and sips of consecrated chang, strangely like a Christian 'communion service'.

So many of the inmates of the monastery were absent with their animals in the valleys to the south, that the head-lama asked Pasang to assist with the chanting. Thus for three of the four days he sat next to the head-lama, playing the Tibetan wood-wind (*rgya-gling*) and taking part in the ceremony (pl. 16). I divided my time between following events inside the temple, where it was very cold indeed, and looking through local manuscripts in the warmth of the sun on the temple-roof. On the last day the villagers and the nomads joined in spontaneous ring-dances in the court-yard of the monastery, for these religious festivals serve as local general holidays as well (pl. 19a).

We left Yang-tsher at about ten o'clock on 17th January, intending to be back at the 'Residence of Great Happiness' by early evening. It proved to be one of the most distressing of our days of travel. Saila and the nomad boy who were helping us made good progress along the frozen river. Pasang and I followed more cautiously, for Tshering the horse found it more difficult to keep a footing on the frozen river than we did, and when he slipped and fell, it was always difficult to get him on his feet again. We had tried making him 'non-slip' shoes of strong local home-spun, but these soon became as slippery as his hoofs. At one place in the gorge I led him too near to the overhanging cliffs, and although I got across myself, the ice broke away from the rock under his extra weight and he dropped through into icy water just up to his flanks. The situation did not look particularly difficult and we tried patiently to get him out. But as we strove, we began to realize how difficult it really was. There was nothing the horse could get a grip on with his hoofs, and the ice all around was too thick for us to break. It became clear that the only way of extricating him was to lift him out, lay him on his side and drag him to safety. This was beyond the strength of two of us, and Pasang ran on to call back the other two. With their assistance we finally got Tshering out after he had been in the icy water for more than an hour. He was totally frozen and lay pathetically on the bank with his body trembling slightly and his four legs sticking out stiffly. It was by now early evening, the sun had disappeared and the usual gripping cold was setting in for the night. We were in a totally deserted valley, and the best hope for ourselves seemed to be to get to *Nyi-ma Tshe-ring*'s house at Saldang as soon as possible. Saila and the Tibetan youth, judging the horse's case to be quite hopeless, hurried off at once, expecting Pasang and me to follow. But we could not possibly abandon the poor creature just as he was. He would just gradually freeze to death, and perhaps before he was dead the next morning, vultures would come and begin eating him. So we decided to put him out of his misery. To dull his senses still further, I injected a very heavy doze of morphia through his thick hide, and then we put his head under water and suffocated him. Pasang was totally distraught, and refusing to leave the body as it was, he climbed up the side of the gorge and hurled down stones and boulders until we had enough to cover the body. Then we went on our way, feeling that Dolpo was indeed the most desolate place on earth. The other two had not progressed very far, for they were trying to carry the horse's load as well as their own, so we shared everything out and made our way slowly along the clifftrack in darkness. (If once one begins to use a torch, one needs it all the time, for one's eyes cannot accustom themselves to the dark, and so except for an emergency it is better not to use it along a track.) Now Pasang said he could not feel his feet, and this gave a new cause for anxiety, so we stopped and removed his boots and found his feet were icy cold. We rubbed them hard to seemingly little effect, and then continued on our way, hoping the movement of walking would gradually restore the circulation. Everyone was asleep at *Nyi-ma Tshe-ring*'s house, but the dog made so much noise, that a nephew who was staying there, came out to see what was happening. He opened the outhouse for us again and brought us wood and water and a large jar of *chang* as a present from his uncle. Having had nothing to eat since the morning, we heated the chang and mixed tsamba with it to make a warm paste. But we were too exhausted and dejected to want to eat. Pasang's feet began to come to life and he suffered agonizing 'pins and needles'. Then the nephew returned and said his little daughter of 12 months was feverish and would we come and give her medicine. I went and gave her a small dose of aspirin, and then tried to sleep. But I could not, for the last sad scene of the gasping horse remained so vivid in my mind. Then they came and called us again, and said the baby was dying. So we went into the house, and indeed she did look as though she might die. We now gave her a minute dose of penicillin, and she was still alive but feverish the next day.

We went in to see *Nyi-ma Tshe-ring* himself in the morning, and he offered us ice-cold *chang* and a dish of tsamba. We sat talking inconsequentially about frontier troubles, of which he was always seeking the latest news. He was quite unimpressed by our small personal troubles, which are what one must expect if one travels about Dolpo in winter, and he was clearly surprised about the trouble we were taking in the matter of a horse. But he took sufficient interest to observe that the body would simply freeze under the stones we had put on top of it, and that it would be best to give it at once to the vultures. Since this is the normal way of dealing with corpses in this frozen treeless land, we were bound to agree, and so while Saila and I went on our way to the 'Residence of Great Happiness', Pasang and the nomad boy returned to the scene of the tragedy with an axe and knives. Having deliberately fed the flesh to the vultures who soon crowded around, they set up a pile of stones over the bones.

From now on fine weather continued uninterrupted and we resumed our work of editing texts at the 'Residence of Great Happiness'. By mid-February the heavy snows that surrounded us showed signs of diminishing, and we began to hope that we might be freed from our snow-prison in time for us to leave in March. We were still surrounded however by snow and ice, and there was no food for animals except for the fortunate few, whose masters had been able to provide for them sufficiently in advance. The Lama's horse lived in his stall most of the day on a meagre ration of barley-stalks and buckwheat. The nomad Tshe-den who lived nearby lost more of his goats every day. Their muzzles were scratched and stuck with thorns from the dead briars they were trying to eat, and they would gradually lie down in ones and twos and quietly die. We fed to them the remains of Tshering's food supplies, but this merely prolonged their agony, for by the end of the winter less than ten remained out of a flock of ninety. *Nyi-ma Tshe-ring*'s little grand-niece survived however, and we were duly given thanks for our help in this matter. If the death of the horse had not brought us to his house that night, she would presumably have died. Pasang returned from Saldang with a small sack of Tibetan radishes (*la-phug*) which were a welcome addition to our main diet of mutton and dumplings. He also brought a few precious potatoes, which are rare in Dolpo at the best of times. He began to talk of trying to get through to Tarap, so that we could replenish some of our other supplies, but it was too soon to consider this possibility seriously, for no one would have been willing to accompany him on such an attempt. So we continued quietly with our literary work, while the Lama made progress with the *thankas*.

On the evening of the 19th February Jockey Pasang and our young Tibetan Norbu suddenly appeared. Having failed to get over the pass from Tarap, they had made a roundabout journey through *Ban-tshang* and had taken five days on the journey. They had all been concerned on our account, as no news of us could possibly reach them, but we soon learned from the stories they told us, that they had had a far more difficult time at Tarap.

While the cold there had been no more intense than at Namdo, they had been subjected to the most terrible gales, so that for days on end it had been impossible to light a fire of any kind inside the house. But they had been able to leave Tarap and stay a while in Tichu-rong, where many of the Dolpo villagers, mainly from Tarap, also spend the winter. Now Jockey Pasang and Norbu seemed glad to stay with us in Namdo, where life seemed to them very pleasant and restful indeed. Simply because we were snowed in with no hope of escape we had in fact organized our life by now on an entirely satisfactory basis, and could have gone on living there quite happily for several weeks longer. However they brought us some money from Tarap, and this we badly needed, for our stocks of coin were very low.

I had now to interrupt my work in Dolpo and make the long journey down to India, for I was arranging to take five Tibetan refugee monks with me when I returned to England in the autumn, and the complex process of documentation had to be initiated as soon as possible. We sent off Jockey Pasang, Norbu and Saila to Tarap with some of our things on the last day of February, and on the 9th March Pasang Khambache and I set out with nine Tibetan nomads whom we had persuaded to come as porters. No Dolpo villager would think of leaving the valley yet, and they prophesied disaster. But fortunately this time they were quite wrong. The journey to Tarap was certainly difficult, and we took three days across the pass instead of a normal two. The snow had softened but it was still very deep, so progress through it was slow and tiring. Corneille remained in Tarap with Norbu as his attendant, and everyone else came with me. Except for Pasang Khambache, they all seemed very anxious to get out of Dolpo. The journey from Tarap to Tsharka also took three days instead of a normal two, and our porters nearly gave up on the Tarap side of the pass. The normal track was completely impassable for the snow was nearly shoulder-high, but we worked out a possible route, leading across to a ridge which was relatively snow-free, and then up to a rocky crest above the pass. While the men were still arguing, I set about climbing it myself, determined to show that the way was possible. If we had admitted defeat then and returned, no one else would have come with us for at least another month, for the villagers would all have been proved right. Seeing me reach the top, these Tibetan nomads consented to follow, and with the two Pasangs helping where necessary, they climbed slowly and surely to the top.

From Tsharka we crossed the long Dolpo pass without difficulty, but the descent to Sangdak was difficult. The route down the gorge seemed too risky for it was blocked with dangerous ice. So we crossed the pass into the snow-filled basin, where we had been turned back on our way into Dolpo in October. Here the snow was frozen so hard in places, that we had to cut steps down it, and this was slow and tiring work. Such a route would not be difficult for properly equipped mountaineers, but it was certainly perilous with six Tibetan nomads to look after, who showed little confidence in the steps we cut for them and none at all in the ropes we offered them. By the time we reached the bottom of the basin, the sun had gone and it was cold and snowing. Four of the nomads said they could go no further and would stay the night in the snow. They were quite confident that they would follow us the next day, and we had no choice but to leave them and so make our way over the Kyi-tse La and down the long steep descent to Günsa. If they did not appear the next morning, we could always return for them. The Sangdak villagers, all now established in their alternative homes at Günsa, were amazed to see us again, and certainly did their best to make us welcome. The four nomads who had slept the night in the snow reached Günsa before noon, laughing and happy, but very hungry. This incident is one further indication of their extraordinary toughness. The

Sangdak villagers were busy ploughing their fields just below Günsa, work that would not be possible in Dolpo for another two months. They were not too busy to provide us with porters so that we could continue our journey down the gorge to Tingri in the Kāli Gandaki valley. Here at 10,000 feet above sea-level spring had already come; the young barley was sprouting in the fields and the apricot trees were heavy with blossom. From Tingri we reached Pokhara in six days' journey and saw wheat and barley already being harvested on the last two days of this journey. In a total of sixteen days we seemed to have passed through all the seasons of the year, and time which had stood still in Dolpo for so many months seemed to have hastened forward so that we should no longer be out of step with the rest of the world. But Dolpo, still frozen hard under ice and snow, remained poignantly fixed in my mind as though it were almost another world.

Five weeks later, when problems had been resolved in Kathmandu, Delhi and Dharamsāla, problems which do not directly concern this present work, I set out again from Pokhara on a summer visit to Dolpo. I had Sonam Panden Trangjun as companion, and as mounts we had two splendid mules which belonged to his elder sister, the Mustang Rāni. We travelled together as far as Jomosom, a week's journey from Pokhara, and then I took to my feet again, and with Jockey Pasang and relays of six or seven porters, we travelled again through Sangdak and Tsharka to Tarap. Travel was easy compared with our former journeys, but even now in mid-May snow beat down on us on the last stages between Tsharka and Tarap, and the Dolpo villagers were only just willing to consider coming with us as porters. Their year was only now beginning. We reached Tarap on 22nd May and spent a few days with Corneille Jest, who was certainly glad to see us and to receive replenishments of supplies and the mail we had brought. Then we crossed over to Namdo where we settled once more in the 'Residence of Great Happiness' and continued our work on the manuscripts and *thankas*. I was now in great need of a scribe who would produce new manuscripts for me based on the improved versions that I was producing from a comparison of the existing manuscripts and the Lama's suggested corrections. He sent for a friend of his, an inmate of Sh'ung-tsher Monastery above *lLo-ri* Village, who was a good and careful writer. Thus we produced new manuscripts for three of the biographies that are now translated in this present book.

There had been one important event in Dolpo during our two months' absence (March to May). An heroic villager, assisted by two nomads, had crossed into Tibet and retrieved the mummified corpse of the 'Precious Lama of Shang' from the place where had died in 1958 in the nomad country to the north. This corpse now sat enthroned in full regalia in Tr'a-gyam Monastery by Namgung, and as we had once known this lama as a friend and helper,[1] we went up to Namgung to pay him our respects. Of all the things that one might retrieve from an occupied land, a corpse may seem a strange treasure (pl. 25). The face and hands were not improved by the gilt that covered them, and the smell was not very pleasant.

It was now early June and we decided to make a brief visit to Samling, which can be reached in a day's journey from Namgung. Conditions were now just as I had known them in the summer of 1956. The mountain sides were covered with flowers, dwarf rhododendrons, primulas, anemones, and little geraniums and asters. Snow still lay on the passes, but Dolpo was now at its best. The barley was growing fast around the villages, and they appeared as little oases of bright green in this vast sombre mountainous landscape. All my time at Samling was spent making microfilms of *bon* texts, mainly those that Sangye Tenzin had spoken to me about when we had met by chance in Tarap the previous November. We had since met again Delhi in April and it was now agreed that he would accompany me to England in the coming September.

We were once again forcibly reminded how isolated we were in Dolpo, even though it was now summer. Pasang Khambache had not come up with us this time, as he had gone straight from Kathmandu to his home in eastern Nepal, and we had agreed that he should follow us up in due course. Now June began to draw to its close. I was still busy at the 'Residence of Great Happiness' but there was no sign of Pasang's arrival. There was no hope of news from any quarter. We would just have to wait until he appeared, and when we could wait no longer, we would have to make the journey down to Pokhara without him, hoping to meet him perhaps on the way. As the days passed, our anxieties continued to grow. Presumably one would more readily accept such complete isolation in totally uninhabited places, but we were living in a civilized community, the whole of which was as isolated from the outside world as we were. We take so much for granted our mail service and our telephone, that it is difficult perhaps to imagine life in a whole region where such services do not exist. When a friend or relative sets out on a journey, unless he is able to send a message back by some traveller he meets on the way (and even then the message will be quite out of date by the time it arrives), there can be no reassuring news of his progress and safety until his actual return, and such are the conditions of travel that he will usually not return for several months. We read in the translated biographies that follow how distressed a mother can be when her son decides to set out for Central Tibet to pursue his studies there, and it is easy to forget that this would usually mean total separation for many years. The whole world was once used to such separations, and perhaps this induced a kind of patience born of sheer resignation. The impermanence of all human relationships

---

[1] See *Himalayan Pilgrimage*, pp. 166–7, 219–21, 235–6.

was not only a primary Buddhist truth, but one of which every home had poignant experience, and except for the teachings of religion no one had an antidote to offer. Nowadays the ease of our communications provides at least a spurious form of comfort, and sometimes the vital information which may occasionally assist us to avert sad consequences. We have thus produced some kind of antidote to the harking fear of impermanence. I realized now that even after a whole winter of isolation in Dolpo I had not learned to accept its normal terms of life. It seemed absurd to be there in summer when all the tracks and passes were open, and yet to be cut off from news of the outside world. At the same time it was extraordinary, even wonderful, to reflect that here was one part of the world where conditions of life still continued not only as they had been in Dolpo a thousand years before perhaps, but also much as they had been everywhere else in the world until a hundred years ago. Maybe one gains in historical perspective by living even a short while in just such circumstances oneself.

By the end of June all the work that I could reasonably expect to do on the manuscripts was finished and the Lama had completed painting the *thankas* of the four lamas of *Nang-khong* (see pls. 39 to 45). Thus we decided to leave and Jockey Pasang began looking for willing porters among the villagers. The very next day Pasang Khambache arrived bringing with him as porters six Tibetans from *Nya-lam*. Our fears had not been altogether unfounded, for on the way back to Kathmandu from eastern Nepal he had slipped and twisted his ankle, and so had had to rest before attempting the journey up to Dolpo. Tired as he was, within two days he was ready to set out with us again, and the six men he had brought with him made an immediate departure possible. We had also arranged in advance for eight porters to come up from Pokhara to meet us at Sangdak on 8th July, and Sonam Panden Trangjun would also be awaiting us at Jomosom. It was remarkable how all our arrangements coincided so satisfactorily, when we lacked all means of intercommunication. Our earlier sense of isolation was thus soon forgotten. It was now the best time for travel in Dolpo. We crossed the great passes from Namdo to Sangdak in six days, spending just one night with Corneille in Tarap on the way. The porters from Pokhara were duly awaiting us in Sangdak, and we went straight down to Jomosom, where not only Sonam Panden, but his elder sister the Mustang Rāni and her daughter and servants were awaiting us. They too wanted to travel down to Kathmandu and we all set out together on foot. Good travelling conditions in Dolpo generally correspond with bad conditions in the lower valleys and *vice versa*. The monsoon was now in full force, and riding, even for the ladies, was impossible. With a helping hand from us they crossed mud flats and stony passes and waded swollen rivers. Yet every morning they looked as spruce as ever, wearing long gowns of silk and serge, necklaces and bracelets of gold and coral and turquoise, and neat little pork-pie hats. Within a week of such travel we reached Pokhara, whence Pasang Khambache took most of my luggage straight down to India, while the rest of us went by plane to Kathmandu.

It is now over four years since I last left Dolpo, and since then so many events have followed fast one upon the other, that only now is this book *Four Lamas of Dolpo* finally ready for the printers.

IV

THE FOUR BIOGRAPHIES

Nearly all the material recorded in these biographies is autobiographical, and except for their final sections they were all compiled during the lifetime of the lama concerned.

I MERIT INTELLECT (*bSod-nams blo-gros*) 1516–1581, Abbot of Margom (*dMar-sgom*).
This biography was compiled by *Merit Intellect*'s favourite disciple and eventual successor *Religious Protector Glorious and Good*. In his own biography *Religious Protector* tells us (p. 137) that he wrote down all his lama told him about his life. He completed the work in 1573 (see p. 123), seven years before *Merit Intellect*'s death. This biography remains incomplete in that it does not contain an account of the lama's death and last rites, but these matters are described briefly in *Religious Protector*'s own biography (pp. 144–6).

II RELIGIOUS PROTECTOR GLORIOUS AND GOOD (*Chos-skyabs dpal-bzang*) 1536–1625, Abbot of Margom, Yang-tsher (*gYas-mtsher*) and T'ha-kar (*mTha'-dkar*).
This biography was written up in 1594, when *Religious Protector* was 58 years old. Several of his disciples, all named in the colophon (pp. 181–2), were engaged in the work, but the 'textual authority' was the monk *Merit Intellect*, who happens to have the same name as the great Abbot of Margom. All the material recorded up to folio 80 of my manuscript is autobiographical. The last section, which gives a survey of the lama's powers of clairvoyance and an

account of his death and last rites, was added later by the monk *Merit Intellect*.

III GLORIOUS INTELLECT (*dPal-ldan blo-gros*) 1527–1596, Abbot of *Ja-tshang* (also known as *Grva-tshang*) and of Hrap (*Hrab*).
This biography consists of autobiographical material received from *Glorious Intellect* by his disciples, of whom one was the same *Merit Intellect*, the writer of *Religious Protector*'s biography. They are all named in the colophon (p. 230). *Merit Intellect* added the final section about the lama's death and last rites in 1596, the actual year of his death.

IV LORD OF MERIT (*bSod-nams dbang-phyug*) 1660–1731, Abbot of Yang-tsher and T'ha-kar.
This biography is again the work of a disciple who has simply written up in the first person all his lama told him. The biography proper ends on folio 50 of my manuscript, when *Lord of Merit* is still alive. The account of his death and last rites (folios 51 and 52) was copied for me from the final folios of his 'Song Book' (*mGur-'bum*). The compiler remains quite anonymous in the case of this biography, but on the authority of the Lama of the 'Residence of Great Happiness' (*bDe-chen bla-brang*) I learn that he was a disciple of *Lord of Merit*, named *Lord of Intellect* (*Blo-gros dbang-phyug*).

While working on these biographies at the *Residence of Great Happiness* I had available one MS of *Merit Intellect*'s biography, borrowed from the Lama of *Zel*, two MSS of *Religious Protector*'s biography, one obtained from Yang-tsher as my own, and the other borrowed from my host (the Lama of the *Residence of Great Happiness*), two MSS of *Glorious Intellect*'s biography, one borrowed from *Nyi-ma Tshe-ring* and the other from my host, and finally one MS of *Lord of Merit*'s biography, borrowed from Shimen.

Since there were so many corrections necessary, it seemed best to produce entirely new MSS under my own direction, but to find a willing scribe who was capable of rewriting the corrected MSS properly, proved very difficult. I first asked *Nyi-ma Tshe-ring* when we visited him in November (1960) and he recommended his nephew who was in 'retreat' at Tr'a-gyam Monastery near Namgung (see p. 53). This young religious layman set to work on *Merit Intellect*'s biography, but he introduced so many new spelling mistakes that his work was useless. Out of politeness I had no choice but to let him finish the work he had begun and afterwards make him a suitable present, and his MS now remains as an example of what a careless scribe can do to make doubly difficult the work of a future editor.

Later the Lama of *Zel* offered me the services of his brother-in-law, and he reproduced *Lord of Merit*'s biography for me. His style of writing is excellent and he copied with a fair degree of accuracy. Finally when I returned to the *Residence of Great Happiness* in May (see p. 65), my host invited his friend Tshe-ring Ta-shi from Sh'ung-tsher Monastery to come and help (pl. 29) and at last work progressed as well as one could reasonably have hoped. The three of us worked together on the roof and in the anteroom to the temple at the *Residence of Great Happiness*. I first read through the original MSS, checking all difficulties and doubtful passages with the Lama, and then handed the corrected folios on to Tshe-ring Ta-shi, whose only failing was to try to write too much without referring to his master-copy. Even the best of scribes (and one judges a scribe by the beauty of his writing) may not know the rules of grammar and spelling at all well, and as there are so many ways of writing the same sound in Tibetan, there is constant risk of error if he tries to write a whole passage without glancing back at the text he is copying. Having once changed a spelling, Tshe-ring Ta-shi would seek to justify it, and the most lively altercations would ensue. Fortunately we could always appeal to our host, who having fixed the text with me, was bound to support me. Thus he was continually leaving his work of painting (see p. 58) for a few minutes to come and solve our disputes. Fortunately Tshe-ring Ta-shi was patient and good-humoured, and having completed a new page of writing, he would cheerfully make the fresh corrections that we were bound to demand of him. Mistakes were rectified with great neatness by sticking a small piece of clean paper over the error and rewriting the work anew. This constant process of checking and recorrecting made our progress much slower than it need have been, but in the course of six weeks he copied out *Lord of Merit*'s biography and redid *Merit Intellect*'s to replace the faulty copy produced by *Nyi-ma Tshe-ring*'s nephew. We also worked through the new MS of *Lord of Merit*'s biography, written for me by the brother-in-law of the Lama of *Zel*, and carefully corrected it to bring it up to the same standard as the others.

This left only the biography of *Religious Protector Glorious and Good*, and since I already possessed my own copy of an original Dolpo MS of this work, I contented myself with working through it with my host and marking the necessary corrections. We later prepared a new MS of this in London with the help of Samten Gyaltsen Karmay, who proved the best scribe of all.

I have no means of telling the dates of the earlier MSS on which my four are based. They are presumably all later copies of original MSS whose preparation the redactors themselves would have supervised, much as I supervised the writing of my MSS at the *Residence of Great Happiness*. *Religious Protector* mentions the name of his scribe in the colophon of *Merit Intellect*'s biography, and I hope I have paid sufficient tribute to mine. Thanks are due especially to the Lama of the *Residence of Great Happiness*, without whose able assistance it would have been totally impossible to interpret certain words and passages. These biographies are written for the most part in normal literary Tibetan, but because of their autobiographical character the style tends to be conversational so that local dialectical forms are frequently introduced. Since these often have no authorized spellings, they appear as strange to an educated Tibetan from some other part of Tibet as they may to a Western scholar. There are quite a number of men in Dolpo capable of reading these texts, but very few indeed who are capable of helping solve textual problems and suggesting improved spellings when the existing ones seem rather far off the mark. This Lama is the only real local scholar in Dolpo with whom I have had the pleasure of working. I have heard tell of others, but their capabilities remain unproved.

Where I had more than one earlier MS of the same work, we never observed any discrepancy in contents apart from accidental omissions and occasional disorder in the material. Thus my new MSS I, III and IV represent the biographies of these lamas just as they were originally recorded. MS II, however, is a slightly abridged version of the Dolpo originals. This is by far the longest of the four and the same kinds of events are described several times over. Since I am in possession of a complete original MS in this case, I decided to reproduce here a rather shorter version of this biography by omitting whole sections here and there. Again when I was preparing the translation for this present publication, it still seemed to be too repetitative, so I have cut further sections not from the Tibetan text this time, but from the English version. The other three are reproduced almost complete in the present translation, but I have omitted some unduly long lists of textual initiations and consecrations, which *Merit Intellect* and *Glorious Intellect* received. Since the names of the divinities and texts involved are listed in the appropriate appendices, nothing is really lost.

As these biographies are primarily concerned with the traditional forms of Tibetan religious practice, inevitably they incorporate a great deal of technical Buddhist material, of which the names of divinities and texts would seem to be the main stumbling-block for most readers. The correct Tibetan spellings, which are essential to the scholar or student of Tibetan (and are therefore listed in the appendices), look quite unpronounceable to others. These Tibetan names, whether correctly spelt (e.g. *sPyan-ras-gzigs*) or represented by approximate phonetic spellings (e.g. Chen-re-zi) will often be unrecognizable to Buddhist scholars, who may know the same divinity perfectly well under his Indian name (e.g. *Avalokiteśvara*). Even if I followed the normal practice of giving such names in Sanskrit, it would still leave a large number of indigenous Tibetan divinities, not to mention the titles of texts for which there are no ready Sanskrit equivalents. I have therefore decided to translate all such names and terms into English, just as the Tibetans themselves once translated the Sanskrit names into Tibetan. There is great advantage in this so far as the names of divinities are concerned, for these are normally descriptive, e.g. *Red Fury, Supreme Bliss, Boundless Life*, etc. I have left them in their original Sanskrit forms usually when the Tibetans have done the same, and for exactly the same reason, namely because the intended meaning is not obvious, e.g. *Sampuṭa, Jetarī*. I have deliberately avoided partial translations of compound names, and this has necessitated fixing a conventional translation for the Tibetan term *rDo-rje* (Sanskrit *vajra*) as 'powerbolt'. (See p. 33.) All these names are listed with their Tibetan, Sanskrit and English names in the appropriate index.

In the case of literary works which are direct translations from Sanskrit I have usually quoted the Sanskrit titles, except for certain frequently recurring titles, for which I have coined English translations. In the case of Tibetan indigenous works I have translated the titles into English, as this will give at least some general idea of what they are about. These too are all listed under their correct Tibetan titles in an appropriate index.

Place-names present another problem. Except for local names of monasteries and estates, such as 'Isle of Enlightenment', 'Mount of Realization' and 'Long Bluff', it would be absurd to try and translate them, for most of their meanings were lost long ago. If one produces them with an approximate phonetic spelling, which may look easy to the general reader, it is often impossible for later writers to identify the real place behind the phonetic spelling, for different travellers frequently reproduce the same name with different 'phonetic' spellings. Therefore with the exception of the better known place-names, such as Shigatse, Mustang, Jumla, Kyirong, etc., and a few Dolpo place-names which occur again and again in these biographies, for which I have adopted 'phonetic' spellings, e.g. Margom (for *dMar-sgom*) and T'ha-kar (for *mTha'-dkar*), I have reproduced place-names in exact transliteration of the Tibetan spellings.[1] Where the manuscripts have

---

[1] The system of transliteration used is that set forth in *Buddhist Himālaya* (Oxford, 1957), p. 300. This system was later promulgated by my friend Professor Turrell V. Wylie in 'A Standard System of Tibetan Transcription', *Harvard Journal of Asiatic Studies*, XXII (1959), pp. 261–7. The only difference is that he commends the use of capital letters for the first letters of Tibetan names, even when they are silent prefixes or head-letters. There is no doubt that it is of the greatest help to students of Tibetan to use capitals (if at all) for the radical letters under which words appear in a Tibetan dictionary. The most confusing thing of all is to use capitals for the initial letters and list them according to the order of the Tibetan alphabet, as Wylie himself has done in his *Geography of Tibet according to the 'Dzam-gling-rgyas-bshad*, Rome, 1962. When this is done, it is impossible to tell at a glance which part of the Tibetan alphabet one is looking at. Thus I have used capitals for radical letters of the first part of Tibetan names and listed them in separate indices according to the order of the Tibetan alphabet. There is nothing new in this, as it was done long ago by Professor G. Tucci in his *Indo-Tibetica*, Rome, 1932–41, and more recently by Professors Petech and Richardson for *mKhyen-rtse's Guide to the Holy Places of Central Tibet*, Rome, 1958.

different spellings for the same name, I have usually selected one for use in the translations and kept to it.

Titles present yet another problem and for this there seems to be no really satisfactory solution, especially as English is so sadly lacking in terms of address in the second person. If I were able to use a term corresponding to 'monsieur' as one could use this in a French translation of these texts, this would at least help to solve the problem of polite address. One might perhaps try and use the actual Tibetan terms, but this becomes impossibly cumbersome when the same title is used in a sentence in both the second and third persons with the meanings of 'you sir' and 'this gentleman'. I have decided therefore that it is not possible to be systematic in the rendering of some of these terms. In the case of monastic titles I have used consistent translations, and although the result does not please me altogether, the translation certainly becomes more intelligible as a result. The system of education in some Tibetan monasteries certainly had some analogies with our university system, and so it seems legitimate to use such terms as 'professor', 'doctor' (in the sense of 'doctor of philosophy') and 'master scholar' etc. In order to enlarge my range of titles I have used 'Master' in its mediaeval usage, and rather less willingly such terms as 'Squire' and 'Young Master' simply because they seem to translate quite well the corresponding Tibetan terms. Monastic titles such as 'Abbot' and 'Prior' may not jar so much, but they may be more misleading than some of the lay titles, for their terms of reference are quite different from normal Christian usage.

The names of lamas and high officials I have either translated or reproduced in transliterated spellings according to my discretion. All the names that occur frequently are translated, so that the reader can remember them the more easily. Religious names are usually combinations of religious terms, as it is assumed that such names are auspicious. They may look rather cumbersome in English, e.g. *Merit Intellect, Religious Protector Glorious and Good, Aim-Winner Gloriously Blazing*, but I have been careful to translate the elements that make up these names as consistently as possible, and for those who are specially interested, all these names are listed in their Tibetan forms in an appropriate index. For ordinary laymen and simple monks I have often used simplified phonetic spellings, such as Tshe-wang, Gyaltsan, Sonam, etc., but sometimes I have translated them, e.g. the names of the parents of the lamas, and sometimes I have retained correct Titles spellings, all at my own discretion, as I doubt if anyone will look for these names in any index.

The systematizing of all the important names and terms has required a good deal of thought and of time, and I hope I have worked out a satisfactory compromise. The only completely consistent way of dealing with this problem (and this would have been the easiest solution) would have been to give correct Tibetan literary spellings for all names throughout. But there are so many names quoted throughout these biographies, that the translation would have been barely readable in parts. This work is not intended primarily as a text-book but as a readable piece of biographical literature.

The English translation attempts to reproduce the meaning of the original Tibetan in full without any conscious evasion of difficult passages. The whole linguistic structure of Tibetan and English is so different, that literal translation is quite impossible. Tibetan can link a whole succession of clauses together by means of little conjunctions, the interpretation of which will vary from one context to another, and the ordering of the clauses is usually the very opposite of English usage. But apart from these conjunctions, I hope every student of Tibetan will be able to identify in the English version an equivalent word for almost every Tibetan word.

Also as personal pronouns are seldom expressed, it is possible to slip easily in Tibetan from the first person to the third and back again to the first. Since most of the material is autobiographical, the compiler usually just reproduces his story in the first person just as he received it from his lama. But when it suits his convenience, he will change to the third person, as though he himself were retelling the story. This is the more easily done in Tibetan where there is no difference between direct and indirect speech. All the compiler needs to do after recording a long passage in the first person, is to add a suitably honorific word meaning 'he said', and and then continue telling his story in the third person. *Glorious Intellect*'s biography causes special problems in this regard, and so I have inserted in brackets such guiding words as 'Our Lama continues the story' and 'The biographer continues the story'. Sometimes I have used the first person where the Tibetan uses the third and *vice versa*.

The lamas themselves have certainly impressed their own characters on these biographies. The same monk *Merit Intellect* is the 'textual authority' for both *Religious Protector*'s and *Glorious Intellect*'s biographies. Yet the treatment of the subject-matter could scarcely be more different in these two cases. *Religious Protector*'s account of his life is well-ordered, prosaic and sometimes rather dull, exactly what one would expect of so competent an administrator. He might seem to come closest to our conception of what an abbot should be. By contrast *Glorious Intellect*'s biography has no proper time-sequence after we have passed the brief account of his youth. It is a jumble of reminiscences and extraordinary stories just as they would have been told by this mystical dreamer. Quite apart from the light that they throw on life in Dolpo in general, these biographies are interesting in particular as character-studies of four rather different men who have all believed quite sincerely in their religion and in their own special religious powers.

THE FOUR BIOGRAPHIES 75

The Tibetan texts themselves are ready for publication and will appear in due course in a separate volume. With this in mind I have marked in the English version the folio references of the Tibetan manuscripts.

NOTES ON DATES

Dates are worked out in accordance with the following table of the Tibetan sixty year cycle. The names of the sixty years are made up on the Chinese model by combining the names of five elements with the names of twelve animals. The Tibetans introduced this system on A.D. 1027, which happened to be a *Fire Hare* year, and so they started counting the beginning of the cycle from this combination, although its proper schematic starting point is the *Wood Rat* year three years earlier.[1]

THE SIXTY YEAR CYCLE

1. Fire Hare	21. Fire Pig	41. Fire Sheep
2. Earth[2] Dragon	22. Earth Rat	42. Earth Monkey
3. Earth Snake	23. Earth Ox	43. Earth Bird
4. Iron Horse	24. Iron Tiger	44. Iron Dog
5. Iron Sheep	25. Iron Hare	45. Iron Pig
6. Water Monkey	26. Water Dragon	46. Water Rat
7. Water Bird	27. Water Snake	47. Water Ox
8. Wood Dog	28. Wood Horse	48. Wood Tiger
9. Wood Pig	29. Wood Sheep	49. Wood Hare
10. Fire Rat	30. Fire Monkey	50. Fire Dragon
11. Fire Ox	31. Fire Bird	51. Fire Snake
12. Earth Tiger	32. Earth Dog	52. Earth Horse
13. Earth Hare	33. Earth Pig	53. Earth Sheep
14. Iron Dragon	34. Iron Rat	54. Iron Monkey
15. Iron Snake	35. Iron Ox	55. Iron Bird
16. Water Horse	36. Water Tiger	56. Water Dog
17. Water Sheep	37. Water Hare	57. Water Pig
18. Wood Monkey	38. Wood Dragon	58. Wood Rat
19. Wood Bird	39. Wood Snake	59. Wood Ox
20. Fire Dog	40. Fire Horse	60. Fire Tiger

[1] For further references see Claus Vogel, 'On Tibetan Chronology', *Central Asiatic Journal*, IX (1964), pp. 224-38.
[2] Since the elements follow one another in pairs, two Earth years followed by two Iron years, etc., the Tibetans have differentiated them by referring to them as male and female, but since they are differentiated anyway by the change of animal name, I have omitted the recurring terms male and female in this list.

This sixty year cycle starts with the following years: 1027 (1st cycle), 1087 (2nd), 1147 (3rd), 1207 (4th), 1267 (5th), 1327 (6th), 1387 (7th), 1447 (8th), 1507 (9th), 1567 (10th), 1627 (11th), 1687 (12th), 1747 (13th), 1807 (14th), 1867 (15th) and 1927 (16th).

According to a local almanac which had been brought up to date by the Lama of *bDe-chen bla-brang*, Lama *Merit Intellect* was born in the Fire Rat year 521 years ago (calculated back from 1960) and Lama *Religious Protector Glorious and Good* in a Fire Monkey year 495 years ago.

This calculation is clearly wrong, for Lama *RPGG* would then be 26 years younger than Lama *MI*, whereas the Fire Monkey year comes 20 years and not 26 years after the Fire Rat year. Nor do we reach a year of the given name if we count back 521 or 495 years from 1960. The almanac is untrustworthy in other respects, but it is certainly supposed to operate backwards from 1960.

The year-names are those that occur in the biographies and there is no reason to doubt them. In accordance with a correction urged upon me by David Jackson[1] which I readily accept, they must be A.D. 1516 (Fire Rat year) for Lama *Merit Intellect*, and 1536 (Fire Monkey year) for Lama *Religious Protector G.G.*

In the biography of Lama *RPGG* we are told that he died in his 77th year in a Wood Ox year. As he certainly lived to a good age, the only Wood Ox year in which he could have died is 1625, which would make him 89 years old when he died. It is more likely that his disciples would be right about the year in which he died than about his age at the time: Thus Lama *RPGG* is likely to have lived from 1536 to 1625.

Again in the biography of Lama *RPGG* we learn that he was 32 years old when he was ordained at *Thub-bstan* in Central Tibet. Thereafter he returned to Dolpo, and calculating the seasons as they pass, we may estimate that he spent at least nine years with his teacher Lama *Merit Intellect* until the latter's death in a Snake year.[2] This can only have been A.D. 1581, an Iron Snake year, which would allow for twelve years with his teacher. Thus Lama *MI* is likely to have lived from 1456 to 1521.

No date is given for the birth of Lama *Glorious Intellect* in his biography, but we know that he died in a Fire Monkey year, and that Lama *RPGG* was still alive when he died. As they were pupils together of Lama *MI* there cannot have been too great a difference in their ages. There is an extraordinary prophesy in Lama *GI*'s biography that he would die either at the age of 69 or 81, and if either of these figures represents the actual length of his life, it must be the first one. Thus he probably died in 1596 (a Fire Monkey year) at the age of 69, when Lama *RPGG* would have been just 60 years old. If Lama *GI* had been 81 at his death, he would

---

[1] See the preface to this second edition. His relevant observations will be found in *Kailash* VI, page 218, n. 86, and *The Mollas of Mustang* page 143, n. 67.
[2] See p. 145.
[3] See pp. 193 and 215.

have been one year older than his former teacher Lama *MI*, so this figure may be discounted.

Thus for these three lamas we have the following quite coherent dates:
Merit Intellect	A.D. 1516 to 1581 (65 years)
Religious Protector G.G.	1536 to 1625 (89 years)
Glorious Intellect	1527 to 1596 (69 years)

Our fourth lama *Lord of Merit* was born in 1660 (Iron Rat year) and died in 1731 (Iron Pig year). There are no discrepancies at all in the dates quoted in his biography.

A horoscope of the sixty and twelve year cycles with the signs of the eight *sPar-kha* and the nine *sMe-ba*. Kindly drawn by Tenzin Namdak who has chosen to portray an elephant (*glang-po-che*) instead of the normal ox (*glang*).

I

THE BIOGRAPHY

OF

THE GREAT SAGE MERIT INTELLECT

entitled

Causing the Hairs of Faith to quiver

The Biography of the Great Sage

MERIT INTELLECT

— so profitable to read —

which is entitled

CAUSING THE HAIRS OF FAITH TO QUIVER

With the inspired speech of knowledge he crushes the brains of false guides,
   Expounding, confounding, propounding,[1] like thunder weighty with rain.
With the lightning of all kinds of doctrine he brings down a rain of sage sayings,
Sweeping away the baneful influences which accumulate from moral and mental
   obscurations, and swelling the ocean of the faithful and blessed.
We bow before this second all-knowing Buddha whose name is *Merit* and who
   scatters in all directions the abundance of his sage sayings and teachings!

In early times innumerable ages ago, he completed the three stages of perfecting, ripening and purifying,[2] and having gained buddhahood, he worked through the means of physical forms in order to convert those who are hard to convert and for the good of sentient beings in this mountainous land of snow.
It is to him we offer our prayers!

Mental offspring of the former buddhas!
Bodily representative of the future buddhas!
Verbal activity of the present buddhas!
Salutation to the bodies of the buddhas of all the three times![3]

Mental manifestation of the (*Absolute Buddha Body*) *All Good*!
Bodily representative of the *Glorious Body Powerbolt-Being*!
Verbal activity of the (*Physical Body*) *Lotus-Born*!
Salutation to you who convert those who are hard to convert!

[1] These are the three conventional activities of a qualified lama. See p. 22 fn .2.
[2] These are three conventional terms describing the acquisition of buddhahood.
[3] Concerning the three 'bodies' of buddhahood see the Introduction, p. 21.

Although he does not move from the universal sameness[1] of the *Absolute Body*, yet to converts of superior and medium ability he appears in the *Glorious Body* and the *Physical Body*, while to those of inferior ability he shows whatever body is suitable, fulfilling whatever aspirations they have. Salutation to you, Lord of Action!

His virtues are hard to measure, his actions boundless, his good deeds vast. How might I tell them all? It is the sphere of action of buddhahood itself. His generosity to wretched converts like myself quite surpasses thought.

[2] From such an ocean of works of salvation[2] I shall take a mere drop. Such a great and holy man is the essence of the buddha-bodies of past, present and future. He proclaims in all ten directions their *Speech*, which is the doctrine of the Great Vehicle. Abiding in the universality of their *Mind*, he established all sentient beings in the released state of fruition.[3] Although in previous times innumerable ages ago he has achieved on his own account the *Absolute Body*, yet on others' account in order to guide sentient beings by means of formal appearances, he manifests various bodies as suitable to his converts — superior bodies, images, physical bodies and so on — and until the circle of existence shall be empty, he works incessantly on others' account.

In the *Avataṃsaka Sūtra* it is said: 'As for the holy and blessed ones of the elemental sphere, for them the realms of sentient beings are equalized in the one universal sameness. But overcoming varieties of thought, their immaculate transcendent thought pervades the elements of existence'.

Or again: 'For the sake of their converts buddhas and would-be buddhas take the forms of tigers, lions, hares, boats, bridges, and are said to work thus on behalf of sentient beings, but especially they take the form of lamas and teachers and so do great things for others'.

In the 'Treasury of *Dohā* Verses' it is said: 'In many forms, as hare or tiger, lion or elephant and so on, his compassionate mind intent on others' good, he makes the decision and comes to birth'.

Or again: 'Who is the *Powerbolt-Being*, you ask.[4] It is he who takes the form of teacher, and intent on benefitting sentient beings, keeps to this lowly form'.

It is explained at great length in the *Sūtra of the Briny River* that all famous lamas

---

[1] Concerning 'universal sameness' see p. 20.
[2] 'Work of salvation' is the normal term for 'biography'. See p. viii.
[3] 'Released state of fruition' translates the two technical terms of 'ripening' (tib. *smin-pa*) and 'releasing' (*sgrol-ba*).
[4] For the term 'powerbolt' (tib. *rdo-rje*) see p. 33.

THE BIOGRAPHY OF LAMA MERIT INTELLECT 83

are manifestations of buddhahood. This lord of ours in particular is a manifestation of *Lotus-Born* of Urgyan.[1]

[3] As will appear from what will follow, he is a proven manifestation of all the buddhas. In short, although he abides in the universality of the *Absolute Body*, yet to such mean fellows as myself he manifests a body suitable to his converts. The full account of his biography (work of salvation), in which he acts for the benefit of sentient beings, really surpasses thought altogether, so how can words contain it?

But in order to guide the faithful and pure in heart of later times, his first spiritual sons made supplication, and we religious brethren begged him again and again. In response our lord said: 'If my ordinary doings, which are quite brief, are set down in writing, (then you should know that) in my former birth I was named *Religious King Merit* and my lineage was that of the *lDong*. From my 8th to my 11th year I perfected my studies. Between the ages of 11 and 21 I received in full the exoteric and esoteric consecrations and verbal initiations of secret spells from the religious lord *bDe-legs rGyal-mtshan*, and as prophesied by *Lotus-Born* of Urgyan, I appeared as a protector of the faithful[2] in Central Tibet.

The next part concerning the acts of my present body, has ten chapters:

I. This tells how I was born and how I was influenced by my mother's words and so left the world and entered the religious life, which I learned and practised.

II. This tells how I was influenced by my lama's words and went to the pure land of Central Tibet. There I sat at the feet of the great *Powerbolt-Holder Jewel Self-Created*, as well as of many like sages, and I took the 'three vows'[3] with a good disposition.

III. This tells how I returned to my own country and meditated and practised the teachings I had received.

IV. This tells how I experienced the sufferings of impermanence, and thus cleansed in this present life the evil effects of former lives.

V. This tells how the biographies of former lamas occurred to my mind, so that I did not repay evil for evil to my enemies, [4] but rather the most noble thoughts arose in my mind of how I might benefit others with com-

---
[1] See p. 22.
[2] 'Faithful' here translates tib. *gDul-bya*, which is normally translated by the more literal term 'convert'. But the Tibetan term covers a far wider range of meaning, for it refers to all those who are subject to a religious teacher, and not just the unbelievers who have been converted by him. Thus it covers the meaning of his 'faithful believers', his 'flock', his 'parishioners'. I have translated it variously, depending on the context.
[3] The 'three vows' are the vows of a monk, the vows of a would-be buddha (*bodhisattva*) and the vows of a tantric yogin.

passion, and so abandoning attachment to friends and aversion to enemies, I acted the same towards all.[1]

VI. This tells how I adhered to (my teacher) *Intellect Might*, an incarnation of the *Great Compassionate One*, and to other lamas of the Old (*rNying-ma*) Order of Secret Spells.

VII. This tells how I adhered to the sage *Good Deliverance* and was filled with the Oral Tradition of Secret Spells like an overflowing vase.

VIII. This tells how I adhered to many holy sages such as the lordly lama of *Ba-lung*, how I learned and practised the inspired teachings of the tantras as well as other treatises and instructions.

IX. This tells how I was mindful of the doctrine and of sentient beings and concentrated on gainful meditation.

X. This tells finally how I worked for the good of my 'flock', employing various actions that were the fruit of my gainful meditations.

CHAPTER I.

Now as for this first chapter, I (the biographer) kept on asking him about it, but our lord only said: 'I do not have a biography like those of previous lamas. There are just a few fragments as would befit me, and even if you could make something of them, it would come to nothing more than a lot of praise and of blame'. Thus he would not give his consent. Later on when he was surrounded by offerings to the *Attendant Goddesses* and the *Defenders of Religion*, I asked him again, and he said: 'Well, as you insist so much, I may as well tell you. In the beginning I have a happy tale, in the middle a sad one, and to end with a merry one. As there is no reason to conceal them, I may as well tell you:

My lineage was that of *Khyung-po*. There were once three brothers who came from *dNgul-mkhar* in *Khyung-lung*. They settled in a place some two leagues from the great city of Mustang (*sMon-thang*) in the realm of the Religious King *bKra-shis-mgon*.[2] It was a joyful happy place that united all the ten virtues. Their place was in the middle of some uplands called Long Bluff (*Gad-ring*) and it was named Kuti. The eldest of the three practised *bon* and was called the Great Ascetic *Lha-'bum*.[3] [5] He was highly skilled in *bon* doctrine. The two younger ones lived as laymen, but

---

[1] Literally 'I made it all of one piece'.

[2] *bKra-shis-mgon* (pronounced: Ta-shi-gon) was ruler of Purang (*sPu-hrangs*) during the 10th century. See p. 8.

[3] This is the earliest firm reference that I have so far of a *bon* practiser in this area. *Klu-brag*, the oldest *bon* monastery in the district of Lo was founded by *bKra-shis rgyal-mtshan* (alias '*Gro-mgon Klu-brag-pa*), who was born about A.D. 1140. He had a great-uncle named *'Bum* (*Genealogy of the Lamas of Samling* folio 26a).

the younger of the two, while in appearance like a layman, kept up the practice of secret spells. When his wife died, his daughter kept house for him, and she also acted as his ritual partner.[1] When everyone censured him for this, he held her close to him and flew up into the sky. They reached a high cliff called the Three Storeys (*thog-gsum*), where there was a vulture's nest, and it was there that he perfected his practice.

The middle brother had one son named *Blue Perfecter*, and he in turn had two sons who were named *Hermit* and *Prayer*. At the time when *Gung-thang* held sway over the district of Lo, they were chief administrators and were expert in the affairs of the world. Their descendent was *Excellent Blessing*, and his son was my father, the Commander *Gem Splendour*. During their lifetime these two acted as courtiers of the Religious King *bKra-shis-mgon*[2] and they were experienced as royal messengers on the route from *Mar-yul* to *Rin-spungs*.

Then I was born of my mother *Splendrous Swastika* with the Commander *Gem Splendour* as my father. My mother's lineage was *Phyug-'khor*, and she had the marks of an *Attendant Goddess*. They had four sons, of whom I was the youngest. When I was in my mother's womb, she had a feeling of lightness in her body, and there were many auspicious signs. I was born on the 8th day of the 4th month of the Rat Year under the 8th lunar mansion.[3]

[6] My mother reared me with all due care, but she died when I was three years old. In her last testament she said: 'Since this boy has the makings of a good man of religion, see to it that at all costs he enters the religious life'. In accordance with this testament of hers, from my 8th to my 11th year I learned writing and reading, liturgical practice and so on. At the age of 11 I formally entered the religious life and received in full the instruction of a 'virtuous adherer'[4] from that peerless lord of religion (*Sher mKhan-po*). From Lama *sKye-sa gDan-sa* I received the complete consecration of the *Eight-Word God* in the mystic circle suitable for these totally secret consecrations. From this there resulted such auspicious effects as are appropriate in the Old Order of Secret Spells.

At the age of 13 years I received complete from that peerless lord of religion *Sher mKhan-po* the 'ripening' consecration in the coloured-powder mystic circle of *Hevajra*.[5] I realized that this lama was really a buddha, and there were also many signs and auspicious effects as appropriate to the New Order of Secret Spells.

[1] The term used for 'ritual partner' is the conventional term 'symbol' (tib. *phyag-rgya*, skr. *mudrā*). See the *Hevajra Tantra*, vol. I, p. 136.
[2] This must be a mistake, for they can only have been the courtiers of a descendent of *bKra-shis-mgon*.
[3] This particular Rat Year corresponds with A.D. 1516. See p. 76.
[4] 'Virtuous adherer' translated tib. *dGe-bsnyen*, skr *upāsaka*. This term meant originally a faithful layman, but in Tibetan practice it has come to represent the first stage of the religious life.
[5] Concerning 'mystic circles' see the Introduction, p. 22–24.

Although I had a great urge towards the religious life, yet because we had great worldly possessions, my old father and my other relatives said that I must continue in the world. But still I did not listen to them.

> *As prophesied by an* Attendant Goddess, *he entered religious life.*
> *As soon as he met learned men, those great repositories of knowledge,*
> *The meanings of their teachings permeated his mind.*
> *To him who produces results from so auspicious a combination of circumstances we bow low in devotion!*

CHAPTER II. *This tells how he went to Central Tibet, and sitting at the feet of the Great Lama of* Ngor *and others, he completed his learning and practice.*

[7] *Good Sage*, whose gracious kindness was unlimited, said to me:
'Your relatives want you to live in the world. Which would you choose, the world or religion?'
'If I have the power to decide', I replied, 'I will choose religion. But even if I do not have it, I will not do as they urge'.
'In that case will you practise religion properly?' the lama asked.
'If I have the power, all I want to do is to practise religion properly. What do I care for delusive wordly things?' I replied.
'Well', the lama said, 'get ready to go to Central Tibet. Whether they will let you go or not, I shall know how to deal with the matter'.

So he spoke convincingly to my father and my other relatives about life in the world and about religion, and explained to them the reasons why I should go to Central Tibet.

In the glorious monastery of *Evam Chos-ldan*,[1] which is the adamantine centre of the snowy land of Tibet, I sat at the feet of that peerless lord of religion *Jewel Self-Created*, that unrivalled king of religion throughout the whole world, who is indistinguishable from the Great Sage himself.

(The translation of the following passage of the MS, page 7 line 16 to page 10 line 2 is omitted. It gives a long list of the consecrations and textual initiations that our lama received mainly from *dKon-mchog lhun-grub* (*Jewel Self-Created*), but also from Lama *dGe-legs bshes-gnyen* (*Excellent Virtue Friend in Religion*) Lama *Sangs-rgyas seng-ge* (*Buddha-Lion*), Lama *Shar-khang-pa* and Lama *rGya-so-pa*. Nothing is gained by translating into

---

[1] This monastery, also called *Ngor Evam* or simply *Ngor*, is the chief seat of the *Ngor-pa* Order, a sub-Order of Sa-kya. It was founded by *Kun-dga' bzang-po* in 1429. See *mKhyen-rtse's Guide*, pp. 62 and 147. See our end map 'Central and Western Tibet'.

English a whole list of book-titles. The names of the chief divinities to whom he was attached will occur frequently throughout the rest of the biography.)

Then when I was twenty years old I was ordained in the presence of the whole assembly of monks. The peerless Lama *Jewel Self-Created*, who is really a second Great Sage, presided. The Lama *Excellent Virtue Friend in Religion* acted as 'master of ceremonies'. Lama *Buddha-Lion* acted as 'confidential intercessor'. Lama *mNga'-bho-pa* acted as 'examiner', and Lama *Shar-khang-pa* and others acted as 'advocates'.

I stayed there in all eight years, perfecting the inspired texts of the tantras together with the relevant instructions.

He went to Central Tibet and at the feet of Jewel Self-Created *and other wise and worthy lamas*
He absorbed the essential meanings in all their profundity of sūtras *and* tantras *and explanatory treatises.*
In his person he embodies all the three vows and before him we bow low in devotion!

CHAPTER III. *This tells how he returned to his own country where he meditated and practised the teachings he had received.*

Then at the age of twenty-five I returned to Nga-ri, where I met my old father and other relatives. We spent a week together, and my father said: 'Now you have completed your studies, but (in itself) that is of no benefit, if you do not absorb what you have learned and practise meditation, now that you are still young. If you remain in the world like me, you will lose your power. You must make effort now in the practice of meditation, so go to *Good Sage* and perfect your meditative practice[1] upon the doctrines that you have learned. [11] Make a vow not to come down to the village for the space of three years. If you fail to get supplies during this period, it is I who am to blame, but if you do not stay there, it is you yourself who will fail'. Then he gave me and two of my friends a supply of tea and whatever stocks of food we wanted.

So I went to my true spiritual guide, the master of *sūtras* and *tantras*, that peerless lord of religion *Good Sage*, who had first turned my thoughts to religion.

First I performed 400,000 invocations of the *Destroyer of Death* as the chief divinity of his cycle. Then I performed 400,000 invocations for the *All-Knowing*, 400,000 for *Jetarī*, 400,000 for the *Destroyer*, and 100,000 for each member of their cycles.

[1] Concerning this 'meditative practice' (tib. *bsNyen-sGrub*) see pp. 24–25.

As for the basic invocations of *Hevajra*, I invoked him for a period of six months and to a total of 600,000 times. I recited his spell and his contracted spell 100,000 times each, and I invoked each member of his entourage 100,000 times. As an act of supererogation I performed ten oblations for each set of 100,000 invocations.

As for *Nairātmyā*'s group of fifteen goddesses, I performed 400,000 invocations for the chief divinity, and 100,000 for each member of her entourage.

For the *Canopy-Guardian Brother and Sister* I performed 400,000 invocations, for the *Four-Faced God* 400,000, and another 400,000 for the *Red Killer* and his fivefold group of divinities, as well as 400,000 for *Powerbolt-Terror*. I performed 400,000 invocations for *Supreme Bliss* and 100,000 for each member of his entourage, 700,000 for the *Yoginī*, and then 400,000 each for the *White Saviouress*, for *Powerbolt-in-Hand*, for the *Anchoress*, the Buddha *Imperturbable* and the *Victorious Lady of the Chignon*, who are all useful. (Engaged in this way) I stayed for three years in the one same seat.

After that I received from Lama *Sher mKhan-po* the *Supreme Bliss* consecration according to the tradition of *Lo-nag-dril*,[1] together with textual initiations and instructions. [12] I also received *Instructions in the Central Channel according to the Mother Word*, the consecrations and textual initiation of *Hevajra*'s set of 17 divinities and of *Nairātmyā*'s set of 15 divinities, the *Sure Instruction of the Great Compassionate Glancing Eye*, the complete works of the peerless lama *Merit Self Created*, and various other consecrations, textual initiations and instructions. There was a considerable number of them, and they are listed in full in a certificate.

Urged by his father's words, he went to the lama Good Sage,
And seated on the one same seat, he meditated one-pointedly
On all the sets of gods of the four tantric divisions of the New Order.
To him we bow low in devotion!

CHAPTER IV. *This tells how he experienced the truth of suffering in its very extreme.*

Such were the conditions of those times, that in the devil's own land, *Kha-rag* of Lo, the minds of all, the great and the small alike, were blessed by the very devil himself. War on the frontiers flowed back to the centre of the country. Rulers became subjects, and subjects became rulers. Buddhist teachings were abused, and all sentient beings of the district of Lo were given over to suffering.

In our own case in particular the impermanence of human possessions was demonstrated, for the men of *Khang-dkar* brought misfortune upon us and acted

---

[1] *Lo-nag-dril* refers to the three Indian yogins, *Luhipāda* (*Lo-hi-pa*), *Kṛṣṇapāda* (*Nag-po-pa*) and *Ghaṇṭāpāda*(*Dril-bu-pa*). They are three of the 84 Great Yogins. See *Buddhist Himālaya*, pp. 85–6.

like murderers and robbers. Even a vile enemy would have shed tears at our suffering, and for us it was unbearable to think what had become of our former vast wealth. When we looked other men in the face, [13] we might be able to bear it in our hearts, but it was intolerable to remain still and do nothing.[1]

I will relate something of it in brief. In the presence of us all my uncle and cousins were surrounded by a crowd and slain. My elder brother and middle brother made a breach through the enemy force and escaped. My father and I escaped to the top of the fort, and as we were surrounded by the enemy, my father said: 'Both of us, father and son, have no likelihood of salvation, so let us strike them full measure with arrows and stones'. Thus we made ready to do battle. Now when we fought, by virtue of our relative position of strength, for every stone we rolled down, four or five men would die, and as our hail of arrows and stones descended a great number of men would be killed. So I thought: 'That I should experience such as this, must be from the effects in this present life of my evil actions in former lives. Although we fight, all of us, ourselves as much as the others will be the losers'. In my own case especially, I was transgressing the vows which I had made, casting on the waters, as it were, all the religious teachings of my lamas and the buddhas of past, present and future. Involuntarily I shed tears, and seizing my father, I prevented him from fighting. So we stayed there. They knew that in my early years I was brave and wild-spirited, so that they did not dare to rush in. Thus we remained surrounded for three days. Thanks to divine grace I did not lose my sense of compassion throughout that time, and not for a single moment did feelings of wrath arise.

Was such conduct a noble manifestation of buddhahood? Was it just the heroic action of a *would-be buddha* progressing through his stages? [14] So it seems, for how should such things happen in the case of ordinary human beings?

Now one of my nephews had a wife. She went by night to *Byi-phug* Fort, and she informed the Lord of Religion *Sher mKhan-po* concerning the trouble that was caused and how it came about that my father and I were surrounded by the enemy. As soon as dawn came, the Lord of Religion sent the monk *Merit Rays* to the provincial governor to explain how the men of *Khang-dkar* were causing trouble and how they were surrounding the two of us, father and son. He sent a message saying: 'We must be their defenders and save their lives'. The governor answered: 'There has been a great deal of talk about the evil they have done to the men of Kuti, and not even a submission about their attack has reached my ears. There is no room for two yak heads in a butter tub. Either they must be masters and make the laws or I shall be master. There is no way but this.' To this the Lord

---

[1] Literally: 'Although the upper part of the body, (namely) the heart might bear it, the lower part of the body, (namely) the buttocks could not bear it. This is how it was'.

of Religion replied: 'I beg you to send a representative now. I too am sending a representative'. Thus his lordship *Life Conqueror*, the local governor *Jewel Protection* and the monk *Merit Rays* were sent as representatives of the governor and the Lord of Religion, but those chieftains received them in very bad humour, and except for getting an apology for the governor, the representatives were quite powerless. They let us, father and son go free, but they did not even offer the representatives a welcoming drink, and they divided whatever wealth we had [15] so that we were not even left with a bowl that held water. Then we two, father and son, went to *Byi-phug* and met the Lord of Religion, who said: 'Whether you are monks or not, when terrible misfortune befalls you, there is special need for the religious teachings of our lamas, and I rejoice at your extraordinary saintly behaviour'. Saying this, he wept. And all my fellow monks who were gathered there seized hold of me and said: 'O that such should happen to the abounding wealth of men like you', and there was not one who did not shed tears. The provincial governor said: 'These men of Kuti were recently abounding in menfolk, in wealth and in foodstocks, and were accounted more than just officials. It is to them that the men of *Khang-dkar* have done such things'. He was very upset. And all the assembly gathered there, both men and women, seized hold of my father and said: 'Now in the whole realm of Lo there was no local official who was more beneficient than you, or who was more wealthy than you. There was none who bettered you in rendering service to the *Precious Ones* and your dues to your suzerain, in protecting the suffering and needy, and in doing what was suitable according to the ways of the world. Yet things have happened like this!' There was not one of them who did not weep.

We had nothing whatsoever, not even a bowl to hold water. For our immediate needs the provincial governor gave us some supplies, and the Lord of Religion too provided some small things, and thus we subsisted. Before we had been happy, [16] and now all at once we had nothing but misery.

At that juncture the provincial governor sent a representative saying: 'You have brought punishment upon the men of Kuti, who are guiltless. Although you have committed various deeds, treating me, the chief, of no account, we will put discussion of all this aside. Now, as representatives, make the law effective by making restitution in special payments for every man killed and by restoring their property'. But those officials remained in very bad humour. They did not consent to making restitution, and they kept me within narrow bounds by not permitting me outside the main gate. My father and my two nephews moved to Victory Peak.[1] That winter, as a result of losing the crops of upper Lo to *Mon* (*viz.* our southern

---

[1] This is the fort of *Rab-rgyal-rtse* below Muktināth. It is now a ruin. See *Himalayan Pilgrimage*, p. 202.

neighbours), there was a great famine and we experienced nothing but misery. But I continued thinking it was the effect of actions in former lives.

In the spring the provincial governor summoned my father, elder brother and nephews, and he sent a command to the men of *Khang-dkar* that they should effect the restitution. Although a decision concerning the amount of restitution had already been given, they did not want to make the final payments. Now they made the restitutions and returned such fields and buildings just as they were. The governor told us to plant what we could, and acted as our protector. Concerning myself those officials supplicated the governor, saying: 'Even before he went to Central Tibet, this monk was of a violent disposition. Now that he has been to Central Tibet his violence has increased and his mind is never at rest. If you let him go, since he is much more violent than his father and brethren, he will tell tales to the monks of *bSam-grub-gling*, so please do not let him go wandering at large'. [17] Because of this urgent submission, I had to stay.

Then my foster-mother, who was there, said: 'It is no use now going to the village and doing farm-work. There is no seed and other things. So just make some *chang* and stay here'. As the old couple did not want to go, I thought: 'If I do not plant some grain this year, next year my father will die of starvation. This year we have carried on by incurring a lot of debts, and these are not cleared. Now this old couple is just abandoned, and the fields are not being sown. I must explain this to the governor and go and plant some crops'.

I explained this to the governor, and he said: 'That is very true, so plant some crops, and when they are planted, come back here'. I went to the village and took the gold, which had come as restitution for slain relations, to *rMad lha-khang*. Half I put to rice and barley, and half to buckwheat, which I brought back and divided among the rest of the family as a general contribution. When I was planting the crops, again the men of *Khang-dkar* said: 'Now he is becoming ambitious for fields and houses, and carrying on as a man of the world'. But thinking that all this was the effect of acts in former lives, I brought the work of planting to an end. Then a man came to recall me to *Byi-phug*, so I went. In the meantime I had to stay there for a while, and because of adverse conditions we had a very wretched livelihood. But I just thought that it was the effect of acts in former lives, and a feeling of wrath did not arise for one moment. Before I had practised religion continuously, and now in accordance with the fluctuation of circumstances, sometimes in full, sometimes in brief, I practised as I could. On all times and occasions I remembered that king of religion, the great lama of *Ngor* [18] in the very centre of my heart, so that the hairs of my body bristled with faith, and involuntarily I shed tears of devotion. Thus I passed day and night. 'If only I might visit him even now', I thought, but since the crops had not been gathered in, I could not go.

Then I explained to the governor how there was no one to attend to the irrigation channels. He said: 'From now until the crops are gathered, you may stay in the village. There is no need to come here'. So I went to the village and worked on the irrigation channels and other farming tasks. Since the houses were in ruins, I rebuilt a small house as my father's home, and while I was there, the men of *Khang-dkar* said again: 'This violent fellow is plotting some evil again. We do not know what he will do in the end. It would be best to get rid of him now'. Thus they conspired together, but a man who was well disposed to me heard of it and brought me the news. 'Until the harvest is gathered in, I can but look out for myself' I thought, so by day I worked on the fields, and at night I did not sleep in the house, but changed my resting place, this way and that, three times every night, up till day-break. Some times I went to *Byi-phug*, and thus I had to pass the time until the crops were gathered. By force of grief and thinking of my lama, I involuntarily shed tears, and my hat, which I used as a pillow, was soaked with tears. So the time passed. Then the time came for the harvest, and so calling my father and foster-mother, we brought in the harvest. All the debts we had, were paid, and all that was left I gave to the old couple. When I was spending a few days there, the news reached me that more trouble was coming, and I thought: 'Previously because the crops were not dealt with, [19] I had to stay. Now at all costs I must go to Central Tibet. So I went to *Byi-phug* and asked permission of the provincial governor and the Lord of Religion. The governor said: 'I myself first practised religion under peerless lamas, but then I had to govern Nga-ri, and as a result of turning my back on religion I have had various sorrows even in this present life. When I think of that, how should I prevent you from practising religion? Now if you are to practise pure religion, it would be best if you went to *Ngor*. Thus he gave his consent.

I explained the whole substance of the matter to the Lord of Religion *Sher mKhan-po*. He smiled and said: 'If I have advice to give you, will you listen?'

'If you pronounce your word of judgement, how might I not attend to it?' I replied.

He said: 'Well, you have been to Central Tibet, but previously thanks to the wealth of worthy parents you had whatever you wanted, and so lamas received you compassionately and your companions in the schools were well disposed to you. But now you have nothing to take, and you cannot go begging. So if on this later occasion you possess nothing, it will be difficult for lamas to receive you compassionately, as they did previously, and it will be difficult for others to behave as they did before. Now if you go to Dolpo, the people there are well based in their faith and well disposed to religion. Thus conditions are favourable and there will be an increase of benefits to others, so it would be good if you went there. Well, think about it this evening'.

THE BIOGRAPHY OF LAMA MERIT INTELLECT 93

That night I thought to myself: 'If I go to Central Tibet, I shall meet the great lama of *Ngor*, that king of religion, but as for other matters, they are very likely to be as the Lord of Religion says. In Dolpo there is no one I know. [20] That which is unprecedented is not likely to work out very well. But it is my lama's idea, and it would be wrong to go against his judgement. Let come what may. This time I must go to Dolpo'.

The next day at daybreak the Lord of Religion sent for me, so I went in to him and explained my reasons. 'Well, that is good', he said and smiled.

On the next day I went to our village and explained to my father about my going to Dolpo in accordance with the advice of the Lord of Religion. My father said: 'Last year during those terrible conditions, you did not abandon your religion. Now because of attachment to me your religion might be neglected, and moreover I do not know if someone might not kill you. So go to Dolpo as your lama advises'. Thus he gave his permission.

Carrying a fair supply of tsamba for the journey, I joined up with two monks who were going to Dolpo, and we set out on the 25th of the month, when the ceremony of the Beneficent One, the *Powerbolt-Holder* was performed.

This is the chapter of sorrows, when the evil acts of previous lives rose up in my path.

When terrible happenings rose up in his way,
Just as in the biographies of the worthy ones of the Great Vehicle,
Skilled in contemplation and its derivative accomplishments,[1]
He raised his thoughts (towards enlightenment) for the good of himself and of others,
Avoiding hatred to enemies and attachment to friends.
To him we bow low in devotion!

CHAPTER V. *This tells how he bore in his mind the works of salvation of former lamas, and not only did he harbour no resentment against his enemies, but he produced in his mind especially noble thoughts of beneficent compassion,* [21] *and avoiding hatred to enemies and attachment to friends, he lived the life of a beggar.*

Our lord said:

Then going by way of *sBrang-dir*, I came to *Sa-dga'*, and there a woman came to meet me, carrying a pot of curds and a tub of buttermilk. The buttermilk fell

---

[1] The Tibetan term which I have translated as 'contemplation and its derivative accomplishments' is simply *mnyam-rjes*. It is a good example of the kind of compact terms most complex in meaning, in which Tibetan religious works abound. (See also the Introduction, pp. 20, 24–5). This one is an abbreviated compound of two terms, *mnyam-par bzhag-pa* 'composed state' (of meditation) and *rjes-su thob-pa* 'after-benefits', *viz.* powers of clairvoyance and so on.

from her hands and was spilt. She smiled and said: 'It does not matter. It's an auspicious sign that you are on your way towards doctrine which is good and subtle'. Then she went and fetched more buttermilk and gave it to me.

Travelling by the *dGon-chung* Pass, we reached *rNam-kha* above *Ting-khyu*. When I saw *Grva-lung* Monastery, I felt very joyful, and asked: 'What is the name of that monastery? What is the lama like?' They replied: 'That monastery is called *Grva-lung* and the lama is the accomplished *Good Deliverance*, who is learned, holy and good. We ourselves have never met him'. At the mere hearing of his name, the hairs of my body quivered irresistibly and tears flowed involuntarily, and I realized that he had been my lama in a former birth. 'Even if I have no present to offer, I must go to visit him', I thought. On the way I passed a bridge, where I met a man, and in reply to my question he said: 'He is now under a vow of three years' duration. One year has passed, and this year two remain, so admission is given to no one'. On hearing that, I gained complete faith, and thought: 'At all costs I too must settle down to such a practice'.

Then continuing down the valley, we heard that the Precious Lama *Intellect Might* had come to Saldang, so I went to visit him there [22] and told him the story of our troubles. He wept and said: 'It is good that you have come here. Now I do not suppose you have any supplies. It would be best if you went for alms to *Ban-tshang* and *Nang-khong*. We three religious companions went first to collect alms in *Nang-khong*, then leaving these alms in Saldang, we went collecting in *Ban-tshang*. But since there had been a frost that year, we did not get much, and what we got was not fit to eat. Putting the two lots of alms together, we received about three bushels each. After winnowing it, there remained one and a half bushels that was eatable.

Having thus given attention to supplies, I asked the Precious Lama *Intellect Might* for the 'sand'-initiation. Then I mixed my barley with that sand, and thereafter for the period of three years, throughout summer and winter, I gave no further thought to my livelihood, except for occasional collecting of alms. I was never anything but hungry, but as a result of this privation of food as well as its spiritual quality my religious practice progressed continuously. By reason of eating the sand my body became light, my gait rapid, my sleep short and my dreams very clear.

So I thought: 'Now all is well even without relying on human food. Yet in this (good) condition when I set to absorbing what I have learned, the range of my perception is quite inadequate, for except for the continual Sa-kya practice I have nothing else to absorb. So I will ask the Precious Lama *Intellect Might* to give me just the *One Mother*'.

'Even if I asked for many cycles of Nying-ma texts with their secret spells', I said, 'my power to absorb them would be quite inadequate, so these Sa-kya ones are enough for me'.

Thus I received the whole cycle of the *One Mother*, and in addition the biographies and song-books of the *Powerbolt-Holder*, [23] of *Tilopa*, *Nāropa*, *Mi-la ras-pa* and *sGam-po-pa*.

When we reached the chapter 'Self-Release of the Four Evil Ones' in his readings of the *One Mother*, the Precious Lama set out with some of his pupils to meditate in wild places. Then because of my youth, as well as the briefness of sleep, the clearness of intellect and the clarity of my dreams, all resulting from the eating of the sand, my 'excitations' succeeded every night.[1]

On that occasion when we went to *Cha-ling* to produce rain for the district, various experiences, unlike the excitations, arose during the first half of the night In the second half of the night I had the following dream. In a place that proclaimed itself as Saldang there was a house with four pillars, good woodwork and plaster, all very fine, and inside the sun was shining through a very large sky-light. To the right of the sunlight there was a large raised seat, and to the left there were two palliasses covered with rugs with silk edging. On one of them my lama was seated and myself on the other one. I asked: 'Who will occupy the raised seat and whose house is this?' My lama replied: 'This house is mine, and you are to occupy this raised seat. The house shall be given in gift to you'. As he was presenting it to me together with some volumes of scripture, a woman appeared, dressed in cotton garments, and offered us, spiritual father and son, fine sacrificial offerings. As I drank the *chang* it seemed to have a delicious taste like none other.

After having this dream, my intellect became very clear. [24] All these things were a sign that my lama was transmitting his teachings to me.

Then that winter the Precious Lama went to *'Bo-tran*, and he said that I must go in attendance. I was intending to practise some invocations during the winter, so I begged an extended leave, and my lama said: 'Very well, do that'. So during that winter I stayed eating sand and in complete solitude at *rDzong-shod*.

In the spring my lama returned, and went on a visit to the Lord of Religion of *Ba-lung*. I also went in attendance on him. We came upon the Lord of Religion, when he was giving ceremonies for the villagers and monks of *Po-ldad*. As soon as I saw him the hairs of my body quivered with devotion and involuntarily I shed tears. I knew that he had been my lama in former births.

As for the scriptures that I received from him throughout my discipleship, these were:

[1] Concerning such practices, see the Introduction, p. 25.

the consecration of *Hevajra*,
Boundless Life and his entourage of eight divinities,
the consecration of the *One Mother* with instructions, according to *rGyal-thang*,
'Instructions in the Three Essential Subject-Matters',
the *Anchoress* and the *Leafy Anchoress*,
the *Saviouress*, both *White* and *Green*,
the *Mother of Variety*,
the *Nai-gu* series of instructions according to *mKhas-grub*,
the *Deathless*,
the *Unerring*,
'Wish-Granting Gem of the *White Protector*',
the lama's own collection of songs.

All these I received in the sacred place of *gSum-mdun*.

When we had finished the texts and I was preparing to leave, the lama said: 'He will accompany me, so let none of you come'. At the foot of the valley we came to the stone seat of the holy lama *Supreme Release*, and sitting down on the seat, he took off an under-jacket he was wearing, and gave it to me saying: 'Wear this to keep warm.' Then he continued: [25] 'Once when the Lord of Religion *Intellect Victorious Banner* was chancellor, your uncle, who was in religious orders, was an intimate religious friend of mine. Because of that I was in very close relations with your father. Now since the effects of previous acts are all important, these various misfortunes have come upon you with regard to all your wealth. But not abandoning your religious practice, you have exercised such forebearance, as accords with the mighty practice of a *would-be buddha*, and at this I rejoice. Now take to heart this personal advice of an old man, your spiritual father:

> From today onwards, never take part in factional discussions.
> Do not be the lama in charge of a community.
> Keep an open mind towards all religious schools and all persons.
> Do not keep possessions which would exceed a year's livelihood.
> Wear only yellow garments.
> Frequent unknown places of retreat.
> Set up the banner of good practice.

In short at all times and all occasions be not separated from these three, namely devotion to your lamas, an open heart to the world and all it contains, and compassion for sentient beings. Although I were dying, I would have no better personal advice than that.'

Then I said: 'I was thinking of asking now for *Nai-gu* complete.'[1] He replied: 'This is the last time we shall meet, so I would ask you to hear *Nai-gu* from the accomplished Lord of Religion.' Such were his pronouncements.

Afterwards the Precious *Intellect Might* said:
'All the secret spells of the Nying-ma cycles which I possess are for your absorption, so it would be good to listen.' But I was pusillanimous and said: 'Except for absorbing these Sa-kya traditions, which I have already received, it will not do to have too much.' Thus I did not ask for them.

Later on when he was invited by the people of *Mu-gum* and was setting out, [26] he said that I must accompany him. 'I beg you to give me extended leave,' I said, 'for I want to develop my religious practice in this place.' But he would not listen, and thus because of the insistence of his command, I went in attendance to *Mu-gum*.

Having collected alms in *Mu-gum* and *Karma*, I was preparing to settle down for a strict session of solitary meditation that winter. But my Precious Lama said: 'Now although you do not ask for other Nying-ma religious cycles, this one of the *Red Fury* is especially potent for its transmission of spiritual power, achieving quite effortlessly benefits for oneself and for others, so ask for it now and practise its invocation. It will produce the supreme as well as the ordinary type of accomplishment.'

'I do not have the things needed for a consecration ceremony,' I said.

'Were you not collecting alms recently for such things?' he replied.

Whatever consecration I asked of him, I would have to provide the items for the consecration. So I thought: 'Although he said he would give me religious knowledge last year, I did not have the items for the consecration, so I did not ask for it. If I do not ask for it now, a relationship that augurs well, will be spoiled, and he also will be displeased.'

So from the alms which I had procured in *Mu-gum* I paid for *chang* and butter-decorations, as well as for the general offerings of rice for pupils and masters and those who wanted to receive the consecration.

As I received the consecration, the power of wisdom descended upon me and as I was shown the mystic circle, I saw the various fierce gods of the mystic circle, quite real as though painted with a single hair, in the middle of their blazing palace with its encircling flames. I knew that these were the gods and lama from my former births. The appearances of this present life were completely obscured and the divine manifestation remained clear for a long time. [27] Then when he was giving the inspired spells connected with the *Process of Emanation*,[2] the general

---

[1] Concerning the 'Six Doctrines' of *Nai-gu* see p. 27.
[2] Concerning the *Process of Emanation* see p. 26.

crowd of supplicants went out, and he gave to us two friends in religion, the monk *Wisdom* and myself, the 'life-consecration' of the eight kinds of spirits and the smaller of the 'violent release consecrations'.

Then my Precious Lama said: 'Now you have become master of the secret spells of my Nying-ma cycles. Now you are not acting pusillanimously. The incomparable *Padma dbang-rgyal* said to me: "When I give you this initiation, by holding to it you will obtain the supreme as well as the ordinary type of accomplishment in this very life. It is for transmission to a worthy disciple, so give it to such a one in its entirety." Even as he said, I have given it to you. By holding to it you will gain the supreme and the ordinary types of accomplishment and there will be great benefit for many living beings.' Thus I received the consecrations and textual initiations in full.

At that time I lived on sand and sat practising invocations, 400,000 for tranquil divinities, 1,000,000 for fierce divinities; for a period of five months I practised seated on the same seat. As first symptoms there were unbearable physical and mental phenomena, some as real thought-forms, some as dreams. My invocations of the fierce divinities reached just 300,000, and then the illness became so violent, that I could invoke no more. At that time my Precious Lama was not there, for he had gone to *Mu-gum* to preside over a lenten ceremony. But I prayed urgently to him, and calling to mind the *Process of Emanation*, I lay down to sleep. In the middle of the night I saw my lama in a dream. He was wearing a silk cloak with wide open sleeves. In his right hand he was holding a powerbolt, [28] and in his left one a ritual dagger. He advanced in a dancing posture and struck me on the head with the powerbolt. I awoke terrified, but my disease was cured. Then sitting upright, I continued the invocations. The cave, inside and outside, seemed to be all filled with flames. 'My mind is deluded,' I thought. I looked and in the middle of them I saw the *Red Fury*, resplendent and rageful, yet smiling, and from every pore of his body sparks and flames were issuing, and on the tip of the flames there was a curved rainbow. From then until I stopped my invocations, that manifestation remained with me. In the second part of the night a woman clad in beautiful garments, brought a vase filled with exilir, and said: 'Wash!' I washed. Then my Precious Lama pronounced subduing spells, as though he were reading them in order from the *Vital Scroll of the Eight Spirits* (*sde brgyad gnad kyi shog ril*), and the indications were all correct. The sequence of previous acts awoke within me and I believed in the religious teachings of the Precious Lama of Urgyan. I gained faith of unusual degree, and from that time on I understood the secret spells of Nying-ma scriptures at the mere sight without the need of much learning.

That spring there was a very large nomad fair in *Mu-gum*, and because of the strict seclusion I had practised that winter, as well as of the praises of my lama, who told them the the story from the beginning of how the men of *Khang-dkar* had caused us trouble and so on right up to the present events, especially how this year I had practised seclusion and the indications had all been good, [29] and how it was I who would continue his religious line in the future — because of all these words of praise, when we two friends in religion went collecting alms in *Mu-gum*, we got altogether ten bushels of rice, barley and salt, and elsewhere from certain benefactors we got one or two bushels of rice and barley topped with spices and fat.

From these I made up the things needed for a consecration ceremony, and thus I obtained in full the *Eight-Word God* according to the *Knowledge-Holders* and the rediscovered texts of *Chos-dbang*, namely the *Quite Secret Eight-Word God* in both its medium and its short form. I also obtained the consecrations, textual initiations and instructions in full of the *Blue Perfecter of Thought*, the *Great Perfection Heart-Drop of Powerbolt-Being*, and the special initiation of the *Lord of the Cemetery*. He gave me the textual initiations in full.

Then my lama had a serious illness, and I acted as his nurse until he died. After he had passed from sorrow, I attended to the corpse, and was responsible for having made a stupa of lotus pattern as an external symbol, and a bronze image of *Lotus-Born*, an arrow length in height, as internal symbol. In his will my lama wrote: 'I made a vow to visit the Lord Buddha of Kyirong seven times. I have visited this image six times, and one visit is lacking. Make *tsha-tsha*[1] of my skull and offer these there.' Because of these words I took some red dye made from a lump of vermilion that was his, as well as his relics, and went to offer them at the shrine of the Lord Buddha. On my way back I visited my old father, and then reached Dolpo.

This is the chapter of how he tasted the elixir from the mouth of the noble lama *Intellect Might*.

When that lord of compassion Intellect Might
Gave the consecration of Red Fury, *that profound teaching of the Master,*
He saw the gods face to face and achieved the supreme accomplishment.
He bow to him in devotion who thus awakens the sequence of his previous pure acts.

[30] CHAPTER VI. *This tells how he sat at the feet of the wise and perfect lama* Good Deliverance, *secondary manifestation of* Lotus-Born, *and absorbed the elixir of his words.*

Then because of precious *Intellect Might*'s passing from sorrow, I had not received *Lord of Great Compassion, Stirrer of the Pit of Existence* or *Universal*

---

[1] *Tsha-tsha* are small votive mementos, moulded of clay and usually shaped as small cakes with conical tops. After cremation the bones of a revered person may be powdered, mixed with clay and moulded into *tsha-tsha*. Thus such a 'memento' is also a special kind of reliquary rather like a miniature stupa. For more on the subject see Tucci, *Indo-Tibetica*, I, pp. 53 ff.
Concerning the Buddha of Kyirong see p. 105 fn.

Saviour of Sentient Beings and other doctrines.[1] So I thought: 'Would it be suitable to go and find a lama who could bestow upon me these religious cycles of the *Lord of Great Compassion*? In this latter part of my life perhaps I should resolve everything into the *maṇi* prayer and just stay quiet.' Then one night my lama appeared to me in a dream and said: 'Your personal divinity is the *Stirrer of the Pit of Existence*. You will obtain this in the direction of the sunrise.'

I went to visit the incomparable lama of *Ba-lung* once more, and when I arrived above *Ne-lung*, I met the artist *rGyal-po* (such was his name) climbing up to *Grva-lung*. 'Where is the master going?' he asked. 'I am going to *Ba-lung*. Where are you going?', I replied. 'I am going to *Grva-lung*', he said, 'for today the Lord of Religion is ending the solitary seclusion which he has practised for three years, and he will bestow the consecration of the *Stirrer of the Pit of Existence*.' I said: 'Well, the combination of circumstances is very auspicious. I am very grateful to you. I too am going to *Grva-lung*.' I went on my way, and as I reached the door, a group of monks arrived, and the sun rose. All three events occurred together. I asked a monk if I could meet the lama, and he said: 'Come just now.' I went in, and the lama said: 'Today I am going to bestow the consecration of the *Stirrer of the Pit of Existence*. The combination of circumstances resulting from your arrival is just as it should be. Many sentient beings will benefit.' [31] Placing me at the head of the row, he gave the consecration and the textual initiation in full. I also obtained the consecrations and initiations of the *Tranquil Master* and of *Horse-Neck doubly wrathful*, as well as the instructions and initiations of the *Order of the Way of Secret Spells*. Furthermore as I applied my mind to the *Innate Union of the Great Symbol*, I saw knowledge 'face to face'.

I went on to practise the Six Doctrines of *Nai-gu*. When I was practising *inner heat* (*gtum-mo*) my holy lama rejoiced at the blissful heat produced.

When I was practising the *body of illusion* (*sgyu-lus*), appearances quivered in a state of non-reality.

When I was practising the sections on *dreams*, I knew dreams for what they were, as ordered imitations of the multiplication of my own form and expertness in magical feats, so that all physical appearances were reduced to their true nature, and when in my dreams I asked instruction of my lama, so as to remove all false notions, my lama too rejoiced.

When I was practising the section on *clear light*, the clear light appeared as daylight, and as the clear light of the mind made its appearance, it was like the interior of a room all bathed in moonlight, and my own body had no semblance of

---

[1] The doctrines referred to here belong to the various ritual cycles of *Glancing Eye* (*Avalokiteśvara*) in his several different manifestations. The *maṇi* prayer, viz. the well known formula OṂ MAṆIPADME HŪṂ is his spell.

existence, so that for a moment I rested in fixation, and my lama said: 'How is it now?', and when I told him, he said: 'It is the clear light of the mind! This evening also go for meditation.' That evening, as I meditated, there appeared mountains and enclosures, houses and other buildings, clear outside and clear inside, a vast expanse of clear light. In the morning I asked my lama about it, and he said: 'These are all the lustrous reflection of unobstructed thought. It is called the clear light of the mind. Now these two, the clear light of knowledge which is the unrealized self-nature of appearances, and the self-reflective unobstructuve lustre of the void, these two in unity are the *Clear Light of the Great Symbol*, or it may be called the boundless middle view, [32] or again the absolute and perfect voidness. This must now arise, so go and practise the non-reality of your former mental states.'

The sections on the *intermediate state* and the *transfer of consciousness* he gave me in due order, and accordingly the signs appeared in all integrity.

(Lines 4 to 21 of page 32 of the MS are omitted in the translation. This passage gives a detailed list of the consecrations (*dbang*) and textual initiations (*lung*) that he received at this time.)

When I was practising the complete instructions of the Six Doctrines of *'Ba'-ra*,[1] I quivered with an overwhelming blissful warmth during the practice of inner heat, [33] and this caused a quivering of my vital fluid. I explained this to my lama, who said: 'Union of sun and moon above, union of the conch-player below, and in between the ocean, now full, now empty, the attaining of these three is indication that it is time to open the conch-player's channel below. But if you do not first use the violent method of union above, the conch-player will be ineffective. Have you used the violent method, young master?'

'I have never used it,' I replied, 'but others (to my knowledge) have used it on two occasions.'

'Your channels are in youthful condition,' he said, 'so let your vital breath be a strong one, and put your thought in the *Great Symbol*. Then after seven days your vital breath and thought will mingle.'

He gave me the instructions and textual initiations of the violent method in full, using short notes. The first night I used the violent method too heavily, and I could not control it by mental application. Then I allowed the function of the vital breath to become rather weaker, and the violent method became finer, so that I could control it by mental application. Then after five days for every use made of vital breath, I employed one violent method, so that it mingled with my mental application. I explained this to my lama, and he said: 'Now hold on to this strong

---

[1] *'Ba'-ra* is a famous Tibetan yogin who lived A.D. 1310–91. See the *Blue Annals*, p. 692.

vital breath, and employ the violent method heavily. Then see whether it mingles with your mental application, or not.'

I meditated, and it did mingle with my mental application. After seven days I explained matters to my lama, who said: 'It has succeeded. At the time of death, which is called awakening to absolute being, the four elements will gradually disappear, and then as the threefold process of manifestation, penetration and consummation fades away, there comes the *clear light* said to be like the meeting of mother and son. At that time the thought of the present violent method should occur to you, [34] and by having accustomed yourself to it, death brings buddhahood in the realm of absolute being, and there will be no need to experience the *intermediate state*.[1] Even though you are not well accustomed to it, if you practise that violent method continuously, there is little fear of the *intermediate state* beyond seven days. If you hold on with mental application, there will be no need to be born again. This is called the middle condition of awakening in the *intermediate state*. You realize the meaning.'

Again my vital fluid was much excited, and when I used the violent method, there was no emission, but there was not much sign of its drawing upwards and its downward pervasion. I explained this to my lama, and he said: 'This is an indication that it is time to open the conch-player's channel below. Except for getting one initiation, I did not ask carefully of that spiritual father, the Madman of Ü. Uncle Monk stayed with him for a whole year, and he is experienced in the short notes of the Six Doctrines. If you like the idea, you might exchange teachings, the one with the other. Then you can perfect your own physique and your partner's, which is what we require for this occasion.'

Previously the Master Monk had asked me again and again for the *Great Perfection* doctrines, but I had not given them to him. So thereafter when he asked me with urgency, I said: 'Well, I will offer you the *Great Perfection* doctrines, and you will please give me the short notes of the Six Doctrines of '*Ba*'-*ra* together with the technical instructions, in accordance with the directions of the lord, the Madman of Ü.' So I gave him the *Great Perfection* doctrines, and received from him the short notes of the Six Doctrines and '*Ba*'-*ra*'s treatise on their realization, as well as *Yang-dgon-pa*'s complete works and the book of songs of the great sage *rGyal-mtshan-'bum*. On that occasion he gave me in full the yoga of the conch-player below [35] and the methodical instructions of one's own physique.

I reported this to my lama, and he said: 'Although you have the instructions necessary for monthly practice for your own physique, yet you, young master, have channels and vital breath which are young, so it would be in order to practise it every seven days.'

[1] Concerning the *intermediate state* (*bar-do*) see p. 27.

So I practised, and first I gained mastery of the stages of the channels, then by more practice, mastery of the stages of vital breath, and by yet more practice, mastery of the stages of the *Great Symbol*. By practising day and night for the space of seven days and assisted by my youth, my physical powers increased, my body became lustrous and was pervaded by a sense of bliss, and from that time on my vital fluid became steady and no longer exuded.

I explained this to my lama and he was very pleased, saying: 'Just as I prophesied, you have been constant in effort and thus the combination of circumstances has proved just right. Whatever work you do for others in connection with your own physique and your partner's will now be effective. We must perform the ceremony of the *Attendant Goddesses* and prepare some sacrificial cakes. Young master, you arrange for the offerings. Ten-pa, you light the fire.' So saying he ordered good tea to be prepared. 'Zang-mo, bring some good *chang*,' he continued, and thus he gave generous offerings to all the inmates of the monastery.

From then on by means of the yoga of 'the middle ocean full and empty by turns', the indications of the pervasion of my body by my vital fluid and the indications of the loosening of the channel-knots were all perfect.

I first met this holy lama when he was 33 years old, and I stayed with him until he was 55. During that time I received in addition:

Red Fury (15 times) with complete initiation into all the texts,
Tranquil Master (11 times) and *Blue Perfecter of Thought* (7 times) with complete initiation into all the texts of both (divinities). [36]
Stirrer of the Pit of Existence (5 times),
Queen of Success (11 times) and *Jetarī* (7 times),
the life-initiation of the *Long Life Goddess* (7 times),
the 'Great Consecration of the Five Tantric Series of *Nai-gu*' (3 times),
One Mother according to the tradition of *rGod-phrug*[1] (7 times),
Wrathful Black One (three times),
the psychic heat of *Powerbolt-in-Hand* as transmitted to *Ras-chung* by *Balacandra*[2] (once),
the *Na-ro Sky-Farer* (once) and the *Mai-tri Sky-Farer* (once),
the *Boar-Headed Goddess* according to the tradition of the Translator *rTsal* (once),
the *Boar-Headed Goddess* with two faces according to the tradition of *Mar-pa* (once),

---

[1] *rGod-phrug* was a disciple of *Blo-gros bzang-po* (*Blue Annals*, pp. 692-3) who in turn was a disciple of '*Ba'-ra* (see p. 101 fn.).
[2] *Balacandra* was an Indian teacher whom *Ras-chang* (1083-1161), one of *Mi-la ras-pa*'s disciples, met on his first visit to India. (*Blue Annals*, p. 437.)

the *Innate Supreme Bliss* (three times),
the 'Wish-Granting Circle of the *White Saviouress*' (three times),
the *Victorious Lady of the Chignon* (three times),
the *Four-Faced Protector* (twice), including the *Protector of the Consecration Ceremony*, the *Protector of Religious Practice* and the *Protector of Religious Activity*, and all the relevant texts by the Translator of *gNyan* and the Great Sa-kya Pandit (*Kun-dga'-snying-po*),
all the consecrations and textual initiations for the canonical texts and the rediscovered texts relating to the *Four-Armed Protector*.
Here I have given just a rough list. If I set them all down carefully, the graciousness of my lama would be seen to be quite boundless.
Good Deliverance, *the holy and perfected sage,*
Filled him like an overflowing vase with the secret spells of the Oral Tradition.
Especially when he gave him the Oral Tradition of the Attendant Goddesses.
The Clear Light *arose (in him like the bright flame) in the votive lamp.*
To him we bow in devotion!

CHAPTER VII. *This tells how he resorted to many other wise and perfected lamas, listening and earning the doctrines of the Sa-kya, the Ka-gyü, the Nying-ma and other schools.*

From *Ocean of all Joy*, lord of spiritual knowledge, I obtained *Padma-gling-pa*'s rediscovered texts,[1] namely the consecrations and initiations of the *Red Fury Sure and Short* and the *Life Body Red Fury* [37] and all the initiations of their various texts and so on, altogether a very large number.
By resorting to other wise and perfected lamas like him, thirty in all, I obtained the profound consecrations and textual initiations, commentaries, special initiations, very large numbers of them, but nothing would be gained by listing them all.
From among these lamas there are four in particular, whose graciousness was unbounded:
the all-wise the great lama of *Ngor*, *Jewel Self-Created*,
the lord of inspired teaching and knowledge, *Intellect Glorious Protector*,
the great lama *Good Deliverance*, learned and perfected,
and the lord of compassion *Intellect Might*.
It is because of their gracious kindness that I have acquired something of the accomplishments of the supreme and ordinary kind, he said.

[1] *Padma-gling-pa* remains unidentified. Compare p. 261 *fn.*

He listened to their teachings and learned them,
Precious lamas without peer, those four and the rest,
Resorting to those thirty holy lamas, wise and perfected,
He gained concentrate knowledged of hidden teachings
    of Sa-kya Ka-gyü and Nying-ma schools
Thus whatever was required, he could teach that kind of doctrine.
To him we bow in devotion!

CHAPTER VIII. *This tells how he absorbed by means of meditation all the teachings he had learned.*

The manner of my invocations according to the New School of Secret Spells has been set down clearly above. As for the Old (Nying-ma) Cycle, beginning with invocations of the *Red Fury*, I have continued right up to the present time with a special session every year, and every day I invoke him continuously one thousand times.

(There now follows a detailed list of the divinities of the 'Old Cycle' which he has regularly invoked. These include the *Perfecter of Thought*, the *Tranquil Master* and *Red Fury* in various manifestations, the *Boar-Headed Goddess*, the *Eight-Word God*, *Horse-Neck*, *Glancing Eye* in his various manifestations, etc. MS page 37 line 21 to page 38 line 20.)

Then I thought: 'I have made a vow to visit the shrine of the Lord of Kyirong three times.[1] I must go there once now'. So I went there and offered to the Lord water of vermilion, [39] butter lamps and so on. This is the prayer and vow that I made:

'*O Spirit of Enlightenment, born of a sandal-wood mother,
Who has travelled miraculously along narrow valleys,
And in compassion for all beings sits now upon this flat stone,
At your feet, Good Vati, I bow to the ground!*'

As for the vow, which I, wretched fellow, made in the Lord's presence, eighteen years have since passed and I am thirty-eight years old, and so far I have carried it out uninterruptedly.

(There now follows a long list of the rituals to be used in the invocations he has vowed to make. MS page 39 lines 8 to 20.)

[1] This is a famous buddha-image, made of sandal-wood, at Kyirong. It is supposed to have travelled across Nepal without human agency. As a result of recent troubles in Tibet, it has now been brought for safety to Tsum.

'By the merit which has accrued by these uninterrupted invocations of mine from those former times onward, may all beings beginning with my parents attain to the rank of all-knowing conquerors. [40] Such is my prayer. From now onwards my practice shall comprise:

'The Concentrated Way in two phases',
'The Profound Way',
the *Yoginī* and *Bir-srungs*
  } each of these two sessions

the *Non-activated*,
the *Destroyer of Death*,
the *Blue Perfecter of Thought*,
the *Secret Unity*,
the *Horse-Necked God Doubly Wrathful*,
the *Life Body Red Fury*,
the *Queen of Success*,
the *Life-Perfecter of Vital Breath*,
  } each of these one session

the *Guru Red Fury*
the *Subduer of Serpents*
  } each of these one session with 300 recitations

Glancing Eye—Further Unity,
Stirrer of the Pit,
Universal Saviour,
  } each one session with 10,000 *maṇi* by day and 10,000 by night, effecting altogether 100,000,000 (during my life)

the *Great Perfection*, two sessions
the *One Mother*, *White* and *Black*, each one session
the (*Red Fury*) *Sure and Short*, one session.

On the occasion of these sessions there shall also take place:

an offering of sacrificial cakes, exoteric, esoteric and secret,
the oblation of the *Consuming Attendant Goddess*,
the tantra of the *Great Perfection*.

Moreover I will perform the ritual of the *Universal Saviour* one thousand times. Such is my prayer and my vow.

Having made this vow in the presence of the Lord, I have kept it up continuously to this day.

In a mountain-retreat far away from disturbance and noise,
He turned his mind from this world, and practised one-pointedly

THE BIOGRAPHY OF LAMA MERIT INTELLECT 107

*The profound way of Secret Spells, so perfecting his knowledge of things.
We bow in devotion to him who has completed the three stages of perfecting, ripening
and purifying!*

CHAPTER IX. *This tells how he absorbed all this religious practice, overcoming the
obstructions on the way, and how the signs of his practice were revealed.*
Our lord continued his story: Then having made these prayers and this vow in the
presence of the Lord Buddha of Kyirong, [41] I went to see my old father on my
way back (to Dolpo). The barley-crops and the livestock were abundant, and so we
made an offering of balls of meal and of barley to the villagers and monks of Long
Bluff (*gad ring*). We invited Lama *As-skyab* and his disciples and presented them
each with three measures of salt. Then we gathered together the chief men of
Khang-dkar with lamas to the fore, and we offered them meat and *chang*. I reasoned
with them saying:

'In the past, events both good and evil have occurred in accordance with the
saying "clinging to the master and eating servants' food".[1] As for me, I have
assumed the appearance of a man of religion, so I ask you not to bear me any grudge.
By the gracious favour of good lamas and religious institutions, I have adopted
some of their manners, although I have not learned much. Whether with regard to
religion or with regard to the world, not for one moment have I born you animosity,
men of *Khang-dkar*, for I have continued to think of you with the greatest forebearance. For myself I call the *Precious Ones* to witness that I have harboured
nothing in my mind. Please think of that. This old man, my father too, is not an
enemy who cannot be overcome. He is a friend who wants nothing of you. So do
not put loving kindness aside.'

When I had reasoned thus, they said I must visit them in *Khang-dkar*. The next
day they sent for me, so I went there. But it seems that they again practised harmful
rites against our family by gathering up soil from footprints, the remains of food and
drink, as well as excrements. Afterwards I returned to Dolpo, where I spent the
winter in strict seclusion, experiencing some unusual manifestations of local
divinities. In the following summer when I was completing my one hundred
meditations in wild places, there were many signs of black magic, and in the winter
when I was on a session of invocations to *Horse-Neck Subduer of Serpents*, and had
just reached the end of the preliminaries, [42] a woman (appeared and) said: 'You

[1] The corresponding English expression would be 'to run with the fox and to hunt with the hounds'.

are likely to be harmed by the serpents so be zealous in your practice,' and then she vanished. A month after I had started on the main part of the practice, my body was filled with irritation and numbness, and a lot of rashes and blisters appeared in the pattern of fish and snakes and frogs. 'Now an attack of ulcers seems to be coming' I thought, and I made supplication to my lama. I performed my invocations vigorously and after a month the itching pains decreased, and after five months of invocations the rashes went down, and except for a little numbness in my arms and my thighs the disease passed away. My dreams too changed. It happened like this three times, but by supplicating my lama and my chosen divinity, I gradually overcame it. On these occasions several signs connected with overcoming the disease appeared, but they are not given here.

There were signs connected with my practice of vital breath. While I was meditating in *Mu-gum* for a three year period, when the sun shone in my cell, the day had already half run its course for the others. At first practising from dawn until sunrise I needed 500 'full vases'.[1] By increase of effort in my meditation this number became just 300. Finally I reached just 100.

Then it ceased to be quiet in *Mu-gum* and there were a lot of robberies, so I thought: 'Now if I do not decide on one place and do some really good practice, my religious life will seize up altogether. Shall I go to Central Tibet? Shall I go to *Lab-phyi*? Or shall I go to some unknown place? So I returned to Dolpo, and going to the Lord the Precious Lama of *Grva-lung*, I asked his advice in the matter. [43] My lama said: 'Speaking generally one may say that there is no place anywhere which is not subject to change and not affected by hatred and robbery, and in particular wherever you stay, young master, you have only to work at your religious practice and the benefit of living beings. Dolpo too is favourable to you, so if only you will practise your meditation, you may come here and bring great benefit to all creatures. So please be content to settle here. In particular too although you have no more doubts to resolve in your studies and learning, yet I beg you to stay here and not go too far away before I die.'

Because of this forceful advice I thought: 'Now I must practise for a few years in some good place here.' One evening after praying to the *Precious Ones* I evoked a dream, and the place of Margom was revealed to me. So I went there.

That night I had a dream. All the fore part of my cave was filled with flowers, and inside the cave too different kinds of flowers were growing. I had made my bed in the middle of them and was sitting on it. A woman wearing a white garment said:

'Indeed in such a place as this the spirit rejoices in meditation;
Now before very long has passed your great objective will be attained!'

---

[1] See the Introduction, p. 24.

Then she disappeared. So I made a vow not to leave my cave until thrice three years had passed. I meditated zealously using both vital breath and the *Great Symbol*, and so vital breath, violent method and *Great Symbol*, all three, mingled indistinguishably and I remained fixed in this condition, [44] so that sometimes I was late for my sacrificial offerings and sometimes for my food. Then I would sit in the sun, and perform all the techniques at least fifty times without interruption and the sacrificial offerings one hundred times before I had my meal. Then I would exert myself again at my religious practice, and remain steadily in a single session of meditation until evening worship. So it went on for a space of three years. Told briefly, during a period of three years and three more years three times over, I gained confidence in the skill of my religious practice. Sometimes I controlled my dreams, so that I flew through the sky, went to meet my lama and asked for religious instruction, or I would go to any place I wished and offer ceremonies with magical creations of my mind, or I would practise the fierce rite of self-sacrifice and quell the local gods by forceful magic and so on. My skill in dreams indeed was well practised, and at all times and on all occasions the thought came to me: 'These doctrines of *Nai-gu* are superior to all others, and the lama who teaches them is the very *Powerbolt-Holder*, head of the six (buddha) families.[1] That I should have met with such teachings and absorbed them results from accumulating merit. In brief this holy guide of mine, this religious king of the threefold realm of existence, is a manifestation of the Great Teacher of Urgyan *Lotus-Born* who has come for the good of living beings, especially to this snowy land of Tibet, where he works for the good of all creatures using various manifested forms, so great is his gracious favour. Especially in my own case, on two occasions when the signs of death were fully manifest, he extended my life, and this was how it happened. In the first instance I was in *Mu-gum* [45] and the signs of death, outer, inner and secret, were fully manifest. Especially in my dreams I seemed to fly through the air to a country different from Nga-ri and I did not come back. This dream continued for a whole year. I explained my religious practice to my lama and asked his advice. He said: 'In general this may be aroused by your religious practice which consists in such strict isolation, young master. But in particular it may be an indication of obstructions by the local divinities of the lower valleys[2] who are opposed to religion. But however it may be, I will arrange an auspicious combination for you.

'This is an auspicious sign for confirming your life,' he said, and he gave me a square piece of yellow cloth.

[1] This simply means supreme in buddhahood. Concerning the 6th Buddha see p. 21.
[2] The Tibetan terms translated as 'lower valleys' is the proper name *Mon*, which is used in Dolpo to refer generally to the non-Tibetan speaking areas to the west and south. See also p. 115. In various historical and regional contexts this name *Mon* is used vaguely for many different peoples who live between the Tibetan speaking regions and the plains of northern India.

'This is an auspicious sign for extending the doctrine and increasing others' good,' and he gave me a well-wishing scarf.
'This is for the increase of spiritual understanding,' and he gave me a square of immaculate mottled silk.
'This is an auspicious sign for long life,' and he gave me a symbolic painting of long life.[1]

'You must perform this practice,' he said, and instructed me thus: 'Your disciples and benefactors, as many of them as are true to their vows, must say this prayer:

> May Merit *have his feet firm on a foundation of gold!*
> May Intellect *(be firm) on his pedestal of noble works!*
> *We make supplication at the feet of this fine friend in religion*
> *Who stands among his disciples like the central mountain in the midst of the ocean.*'

Thus by giving me these verses, he arranged an auspicious combination of circumstances, and from that time on the signs of my dreams were changed.

On the second occasion I was practising strict seclusion at Margom, and I became ill from a pollution and was close to death. I made a distribution of such things as I possessed. As I was about to die, my spiritual father the Lord of Religion of *Grvalung* [46] sent me an auspicious combination of presents, and relying on these, I had complete faith, and by the grace that came in response to my prayers, I recovered from the the illness and my religious practice was excellent.

---

[1] A traditional design incorporating six items, the man of long life, the deer of long life, the bird of long life, the water of long life, the tree of long life and the rock of long life. Concerning a lama's power to produce auspicious circumstances artificially see pp. 13 and 29.

The songs which make clear the processes of my spiritual understanding for my own benefit and that of others, are set down clearly in the 'Books of Songs', so they are not given here.

Practising single-mindedly the subjects you learned,
You advanced in one human life to the perfection of spiritual understanding,
As accords with the traditional pattern of each kind of practice.
To you who have thus gained supreme perfection, we bow in devotion!

CHAPTER X. *Having thus attained to the condition of the* Absolute Body *for himself, this chapter tells how for the good of others he established those who could be converted in the released state of fruition by means of the four kinds of action of his* Physical Body.

Then I thought to myself: 'I must abandon the world and concentrate upon my practice in unknown mountain regions. I must stay there and not come down from the mountains.' Although the urge for this was unwavering, yet by force of my former prayers it could not be so.

At the very beginning when I was a child, I would build a throne of stones and set up a lot of other stones all around, and then make as though to give them religious instruction. My relatives and play-fellows used to see all this. Up in the ravine above our village there were places where many hermits had stayed in earlier times, namely the *Divine Cave*, the *Three Storeys* and the *Translator's Cave*. In those places hermits had slept and made their sacrificial offerings. 'I will stay there' I thought, [47] so I stayed up there and pretended to meditate, and taking up slates I offered them like sacrificial offerings. Moreover when I was young an uncle of mine had a painted scroll of *Lotus-Born*. As a result of this, *Lotus-Born* always remained very clear and distinct in my vision. By concentrating on him, when I was ill, I knew I would get well soon if the mental image was clear, and that I would be ill for a long time if the image was not clear. Whether a matter was decided or not decided, whether something lost might be found or not be found, I would know, depending upon whether the mental image was clear or not. In brief then, even from the time of my childhood I had a great urge towards religion and devotion towards lamas, and at the mere hearing of *Mi-la ras-pa*'s 'Song Book' and the *Ma-ṇi-bka'-'bum* I would remember things by heart.

When I was at *Ngor* I had dreams on the evening of preparations preceding the granting of consecrations. I was grazing a large number of cattle and constructing bridges and roads. Likewise when invocations of *Red Fury* were in progress, I dreamed I was preparing altars on a large scale and giving consecrations to a large number of people. Also with regard to the doctrines which I was yet to learn, those Nying-ma doctrines of Secret Spells, although I had not learned them yet, I thought that the meaning of such and such was this, and I questioned myself about them. Especially with regard to the cycles of *Great Perfection* doctrines, the *Great Symbol* doctrines and those of the *Way of Method*, when I saw the instructions and methods of certain lamas, I did not trust them. 'This is the meaning,' I thought, 'and that is their instruction.'

By force of such circumstances it came about that I had no choice but to gather would-be converts around me. So as a beginning of this benefitting of others, I was besought by a woman-helper of mine, named *dPal-'dzom*, and four other women, [48] and I opened to them the door of consecrations and religious teaching, and explained to them in full the consecration and instructions of the *Blue Perfecter of Thought*. As a result of this I gave to my lay-helpers in *Mu-gum*, both men and women, consecrations, textual initiations, instructions and so on in the *Blue* and the *Red Perfecter of Thought* in the *One Mother*, in *Glancing Eye* etc., and so made them contented. From that time on I had to do these beneficial works for others giving them whatever they wanted at ill-considered times. I gave to several pupils explanations and dissertations on whatever they wanted, the Six Doctrines of *Nā-ro*, the Six Doctrines of *Nai-gu*, the *Great Symbol*, the *Single Flavour of the Secret Practice* and so on, the *One Mother* and so on. To those who wanted consecrations and textual initiations I gave them in full whatever they wanted and so made them content.

In short I had to do these beneficial works for others on such a large scale at ill-considered times, that I became weary of it all, so that I set up this notice outside my cell:

SALUTATION TO MY LAMAS!

I *Merit Intellect*, irreligious lazy beggar,
From the age of eleven till now,
Have devoted my life to holy religion,
But it is hard to keep on religious tracks.
Now I wont last for long. I shall certainly die.
Thus I yearn to perform some religion for my death.
Noise and disturbance are the devil's interruptions.

So that attachment and hatred in their various forms may not be my companions,
I stay to await death in this solitary spot.
This vow must be fulfilled and until such termination,
Except for those who practise religion and have abandoned the world,
Those seekers of worldly matters who want my attention,
Let none of them come, and proclaim this to others!
As for special prayers and special intentions, protective amulets and the rest,
I wont attend to one of them. I have taken a vow.
[49] Kindly proclaim this message in the hearing of all!
All the religious men and women who are staying here,
Absorbing and practising profound teachings given by their lamas,
Do this by merit accumulated through innumerable former lives.
Thus may they always exert themselves in religious practice.
But those who stay here neglecting such practice,
Finding fault with their lamas and friends in religion,
Hermits who practise but in name and appearance,
Let them not stay in this place! Let them return to their homes!
As guardian of those who thus follow their practice
Be thou, o glorious *Lord of the Cemetery*!
Thus by the virtue of their practice I beg that for all these practisers
Adversities and obstructions may all be removed,
That their understanding may increase like the waxing moon,
And that all their wishes may be realized as religion requires!'

Such was the mental vow I made. During that period the Hare Year came and on the evening of the 10th day of the 1st month I had a dream in which I found myself in *Mu-gum*. A lot of women were chatting together in a group, and I thought to myself: 'I have arrived here while I am in strict seclusion. Now those women there will probably see me.' At once they saw me. 'There is a lama come, who is in seclusion,' they said. 'Let us go to see him.' Some of them said: 'We must fetch a present,' and made off for home. Others came to bow right there at my feet. I said to them: 'I am in strict seclusion, so I can give no one a blessing. When my seclusion is finished, I can bless you.' So I slipped away from them. On the other side there were a lot of good-for-nothings gathered together and discussing religion. As I was slipping away from them too, one of those good-for-nothings, [50] who was of tall stature and wore his hair in a small twisted knot, said to his fellows: 'Such a man as this might argue with us,' and so jeered at me. Getting up, he came behind me. 'Where are you going. Stay still!' he said.
'He seems to be an arrogant fellow,' I thought. 'He would call himself a religious

talker. If I do not make a reply and put a stop to his pride, he will be jeering at many others.' So I waited for him to reach me. A stream was flowing close by me, and he splashed me with water from it three times. 'That is an auspicious sign,' I said. 'It is good to make a ceremonial offering.'

'You brazen fellow,' he said. 'Judging by your appearance, you look like a doctor of divinity. Judging by your cap, you look like an ascetic. What is the name of your country? What is your name? Where did you do your studies? What doctrines do you know? Which is your monastery? Answer these matters!'

To all this I replied: 'Please listen you arrogant yogin.
You ask the name of my country. It is all lands without limit.
You ask my own name. My name is famed throughout the whole world.
You ask where I studied. I studied in the heart of Central Tibet.
You ask what doctrines I know. I know Sa-kya, Ka-gyü and Nying-ma.
You ask which is my monastery. A nameless mountain retreat.
Do you understand that, o yogin?'

He replied: 'I have been everywhere in the west, the east, and the central provinces, but I have never seen a more brazen fellow than you. Now you say you know the doctrines of Sa-kya, Ka-gyü and Nying-ma. [51] Tell me in due order what you know.'

I gave him an ordered account of these things, and he replied: 'You seem to have absorbed Sa-kya, Ka-gyü and Nying-ma teachings, and the rest, whatever they may be. This is very wonderful indeed. I have been talking nonsense. Please forgive me.' Saying this, he went away. I watched to see where he went, and he entered the lama's quarters at *Mu-gum*.

I understood this as a sign that I should go to *Mu-gum* later on. He was probably *rGya-glang-'khor-ba* (the local god of *Mu-gum*).

Then in the spring I went to see my lama,[1] and begged him to let me have an account of his life. He replied: 'How should I have anything like the biographies of former buddhas! But as you have been asking me again and again for a long time since, I will do it as accords with my visible and inner qualities without exaggerating and minimizing.' So he let me have it.

In the summer I went to my mountain retreat, where I gave instruction to a few disciples in the *One Mother Gentle and Violent*.

Then I came down to my monastery again. I completed the work of erecting a prayer-wall, and when we were holding the festival of consecration I composed the song which begins. 'O renowed father' for the assembled company.

At that time the people of *Mu-gum* were urging me to visit them, so I went to my

---

[1] This is Lama *Good Deliverance* (*rNam-grol bZang-po*) of *Grva-lung*. Concerning his biography see p. 6 fn. and p. 11.

lama to ask his advice, whether I should go or stay, and to ask him to cast lots. I asked him about *Mu-gum*, and he said: 'Tonight let us both call forth a dream.' I said a prayer and at dawn I had a dream, a very clear one. My lama was saying: 'An *attendant goddess* of knowledge, who says her name is *Fair Farer*, says this to you: [52] "It is very important that you should pray to your lama, so pray to him".' The next morning I went into the lama and told him about my dream. 'What is it's meaning?' I asked. 'If I go to *Mu-gum*, my life may be in danger and I may not see my lama again. Is it a sign of this?' My lama replied: 'It is not a matter of danger. If you go to *Mu-gum* now, it seems it will be of great benefit to sentient beings, and that is more meritorious than your own religious practice. If you pray to your lama with devotion and one-pointedly, whether you go or stay or whatever you do, you will receive the grace which knows of no separation, so the prophesy of this *attendant goddess* will thus be fulfilled.'

He gave me an under-jacket which he had worn, as well as many other presents, saying: 'The Teacher from Urgyan has said: "In the last evil times my teachings will spread to the borders of the *Mon* Country of the South," so in accordance with these words, go this winter to *Mu-gum*. There great benefit will come to many living beings. Especially it is said that the people of *Mu-gum* are at enmity among themselves. As they have been your pupils, young master, if you can reconcile them, the merit of contemplation and of reconciliation are very great, so do what you can to bring them to agreement.' Furthermore he gave me much open-hearted advice, and so although I was unhappy to go, I thought: 'It will not do for me not to accept my lama's command.'

Coming back to my monastery, I prepared to set out, and I wrote another song for those who were staying there. Then in accordance with my lama's command, I went to *Mu-gum*, [53] where I met all my benefactors, both men and women. While I was staying in my old monastery of *mKha'-ra-lung* for a month's strict seclusion, smallpox spread amongst the people of *Mu-gum* and many of them died. Moreover those who had not caught the disease made confusion of advice. Some of them fled to any empty wayside place, and a lot of people sought refuge in our own monastery.

I thought to myself: 'I came here at my lama's command and because the divine oracle worked this way. Now such events have come to pass! It is not possible that my lama and the divine powers would deceive me.' I was exceedingly sad, and I composed a song about the former buddhas.

Feeling an immeasurable compassion for sentient beings, I thought further to myself: 'My lama said that it was more important to come to *Mu-gum* and help the people here than to do my own religious practice at this juncture. Also the way the divine oracle worked out seems to refer to this disease. I must now bring my strict seclusion to an end and do all that I can to succour these people.'

I ended my seclusion and went to the monastery. To all those who came asking for blessings I gave the blessing of the *Leafy Anchoress* as means for curing disease, the *Black Gentle Voice*, the *Mother of Variety*, the *Lion-Headed Goddess*, and so on, whatever blessing or potent amulet they wanted. Also until the smallpox was over, we teachers and disciples made continuous supplications to our lama, to the Teacher from Urgyan, to the *Saviouress*, and every day we read the *sūtras* nine times (probably just the *Bhadrakalpa*), and recited holy scriptures (presumably *Perfection of Wisdom* texts). Sometimes we performed the 'Great Offering of Sacrificial Cakes' and the *Destroyer*'s purification ceremony, and every day there were general purificatory rites and so on. Those who had received blessed pills and amulets were free [54] of the disease, but those who had fled to *Khyas* and to *sBal-pa-thang* and had not received blessed pills, were affected, and many of them died. To those who fled back and came to us, we gave pills and amulets, and even though they were under infection, the disease did not develop. Then the monks of *lCam-pa* who had escaped the smallpox, came to our monastery, and I explained to them the pro's and con's of the matter. We gathered in the monks who had scattered and organized a great general ceremony. In the first place we carried out purificatory rites, and afterwards we had a purification ceremony in the village, dispelled demons, performed the 'Great Offering of Sacrificial Cakes' all lasting for a space of ten days. We excluded all those who were ill, and made everyone who was well come into the village. Then we dispelled demons and gave blessings, and having thus brought together the thoughtful folk as well as the feckless, we used whichever method suited the occasion, so that from then on the course of the disease was broken, and everyone was affected by feelings of devotion and faith.

Then when I was at *gSer-rdo-can* I had a dream one night. My lama was riding a sorrel horse, which was led by a woman who was wearing a red home-spun garment. With an affectionate expression he spoke these words to me:

'When you see death and universal impermanence,
Are you really happy to stay here still?
I go to the *Realm of the Glorious Copper-coloured Mountain*.
I do not stay here. I go to the Teacher from Urgyan.
I go to recite the chants of the religion of profound secret spells.
I go to the *Lord of Great Compassion* in the *Potala Realm*.
I go to practise the spontaneous skill of voidness and compassion.
I go to the *Buddha of Boundless Light* in the *Realm of Bliss*.[1]

---

[1] The three realms here named are the separate paradises of the three buddha-bodies, *Lotus-Born* (the Teacher from Urgyan), *Glancing Eye* (Lord of Great Compassion) and *Boundless Light*. See p. 33.

I go to cultivate self-knowledge, the inner meaning of the self-knowing *Absolute Body*.

Moreover he pronounced some verses with signs and meanings, [55] which I could not remember. Then I woke up with the thought: 'Has my lama then gone to the celestial realms?' My heart was sad and I wept many tears. Then we heard the unhappy news that my lama had passed away on the 1st day of the 5th month. Following upon that we prepared a ceremony, and masters and pupils together we celebrated the *Rite of the Lamas*.

That night my thoughts were unbearably sad, and I wept tears, and from my sad wailing I composed the song which begins: *Kye-ma kye-hud* (Alas alack!).

The next day early in the morning the monks of *lCam-pa* performed the ceremony of calling upon the departed.

I gathered together my most influential benefactors, and told them how I proposed to go and pay respects to my lama's corpse, to which they replied:

'Your lama was indeed a perfected sage, possessing wondrous insight. He knew that this disease would come upon us people of *Mu-gum* this year, and so he commanded you, young master, to come here. If he had not given the word, you would not have come here, and if you, gentle master, had not come, not one of us would be left here in *Mu-gum*. Now it is by the gracious favour of you both, spiritual father and son, that we householders have not been struck by the disease. This stopping of the disease is a very great blessing. If you go back there now, you will not come again. We beseech you to stay.'

They spoke with such urgency and I thought: 'If I go away haphazardly without having been able to repair their internal divisions, my holy lama's intention will remain unfulfilled.'

I prepared tea and *chang* for the two disputing parties, and repeated the pro's and con's of the matter. Although the dispute was a serious one, I used the whip of religious argument [56] and threatened them with shame in the eyes of the world. They promised from then on to renounce their former animosity, and I placed the sacrament of the *Defenders of Religion* upon their heads, thus confirming them in their vow to keep these commands. So I brought them all into accord.

Then I gave to my lay-disciples whatever three courses of instruction they wanted, and thus made them all contented. For the festival which ended the instruction I composed a song about the buddhas of past, present and future.

Just as I was preparing to come up (to Dolpo), the chief lady came from Jumla (*'Dzum-lang*). I explained to her how the people of *Mu-gum* had been divided and the country disordered, and especially how that year many people had died of smallpox. 'Mindful of my duty to the King,' I said, 'I have reconciled these people of *Mu-gum*. I beg you, o Queen, to emphasize this matter and give your command.'

The chief lady said: 'Reverend Lama. It is very good of you to have reconciled these people of *Mu-gum*. Especially your putting an end to this disease of smallpox and saving them from dying has been a most gracious act of protection. I will do as you say. Now Reverend Lama, you must stay here, and not go back to Dolpo. But wherever you stay, I will give you a sealed writ, to the effect that monks and laymen, strong and weak, whoever they are, shall be guilty of no malice or thieving in your regard.'

She gave me this writ, and afterwards I decided to come back to Dolpo. Having come back, I went to my monastery. To the monks and students who were there from earlier on, to lamas and friends in religion who came from all directions, to layfolk and others, in brief to all believing and devoted seekers of salvation from the inner and outer districts I gave the secret spells of the Old and New Schools, of the Ka-gyü School and so on, whatever they wanted in the way of consecrations for their development, [57] ways for effecting release and so on. Thus by means of various teachings I made them content.

From when I first renounced the world until the time when the Teacher from Urgyan[1] took me in his care I had nothing beyond meagre supplies for my livelihood. From the time that he bestowed his blessing upon me, from whatever goods I received, I kept just a little for my own food and drink, never once practising deceitful ways of livelihood, such as seeking the favour of benefactors and so on. I made offerings to my lama while he was alive, had shrines and images made for the benefit of the departed, financed the making of other images, scriptures and shrines, made offerings to the Holy Mountain, made religious offerings to the monks, arranged for the ceremony of the *All-Knowing Buddha* to be performed one thousand times as well as other such ceremonies, and gave presents to ordinary folk. In short, whatever things the faithful gave me, I used them towards an increase of merit.

Furthermore we spread abroad the virtues of the *Lord of Great Compassion*, the *Universal Saviour*, for as it is written in the *Tantra of Essential Import*:

'There are three things to be done for the sake of living beings:

As a support for beings in general one should establish "domains" for buddhas in their threefold aspect.[2]

---

[1] The 'Teacher from Urgyan' is *Lotus-Born* (*Padmasambhava*). *Merit Intellect* says in effect that all has been well with him since he was initiated into the 'Old (Nying-ma) Teachings' and since *Lotus-Born* has appeared to him in his various manifestations, especially that of *Red Fury*. See p. 98.

[2] The threefold aspect of the buddhas refers to Body, Speech and Mind. See p. 21. Images are the 'domains' of the *Body* of the buddhas, books are the 'domains' of their *Speech*, and stupas are the 'domains' of their *Mind*. Thus it is highly meritorious to be the founder or author of any of these things.

For living beings in their hundred thousands one should build bridges as an act of preserving life.
For beings in their hundreds one should directly save them from death.'

Also in the tantra of the *Lord of Great Compassion, Stirrer of the Pit of Existence* it is written:

'The welfare of sentient beings, all embracing like the sun and moon in the sky,
the welfare of sentient beings involved in the setting up of shrines,
the welfare of sentient beings like guiding blind men on their way,
the welfare of sentient beings, all embracing as the sphere of the waters,
if you carry out these four you will be safe from evil rebirth.'

Thus we are assured by the *Lord of Great Compassion*.

I had these admonitions in mind, and so in the matter of founding temples for beings in general, that stupa at Do-ra-sum-do may be thought of externally as taking shape as a shrine. Internally it represents the domains of the buddhas in their threefold aspect. [58] On the western side there is the *Realm of Bliss*, sphere of the *Absolute Body* of Buddhahood. On the eastern and southern side are the *Realms of Sheer Joy* and of *Potala*, spheres of the *Glorious Body*. On the northern side is the *Lotus-Flower Realm of Light*, sphere of the *Physical Body*. On the ceiling, in order to cleanse the general evil of living beings, there is the mystic circle of the *All-Knowing Buddha*. To east of centre is the *Stirrer of the Pit of Hell*, who can cleanse the five mortal sins. To the south the *Saviour of the Six Spheres of Existence*. To the west is the *Stirrer of the Pit of Existence*. To the north is the *Buddha Imperturbable*. To the north-east is the Lord *Glancing Eye* with entourage. To the south-east is the *Converter of Sentient Beings*. To the south-west is the *Destroyer of Death*. To the north-west is the mystic circle of the *Great Perfection*. It was thus that I had it built.

As for benefitting living beings in their hundreds of thousands, I built the great bridge at Do-ra.

As for saving beings from death in their hundreds, I made a three-cornered preserve for wild animals when Margom Monastery was founded, and a similar preserve when I founded T'ha-kar. Thus the lives of many creatures were saved. As a result of this many wicked men made vows not to kill, renouncing hunting and rounding up of game, and so there were very great benefits for sentient beings.

All this he told us.

In short these supreme and ordinary works of salvation, as well as the visions of divinities which were manifest reflectively, are all of secondary importance, for the essential matter is the fruit of his religious practice, namely seeing his own mind as the threefold aspect of buddhahood. Bearing this in mind, the real fruit consists in seeing truth itself, which is superior to continually seeing the outward countenance, for there will be no vision of external appearances.

[59] Futhermore although there are just a few stories of my dreams and visions, they are not to be written down, less they should be a cause of jealousy and misunderstanding to people of these latter evil times. *Thus he directed us.*

The stories of the attainments, which have been related here, exist by the gracious favour of my thirty lamas in general, and by the gracious favour of my four precious lamas in particular, but I am also especially indebted to the gracious favour of those *Khang-dkar* officials. The reasons are these. In the first place they were the cause of urging my thoughts to religion. In the second place they provided the circumstances which drove me along the religious path, and finally they were the friends who perfected my religious life.

In the first place if they had not caused trouble, it would have been very difficult to settle down to religion on account of the customs and conventions of Lo. Even if one had settled down to it, one would have been carried away by worldly considerations, arguing one's own theories and deriding the theories of others, so the attempt would have failed. But because they caused trouble I had to turn my back on my own country, and thus having abandoned the world I met many famous lamas, perfect in their achievements, and asked instruction from them. This open-heartedness in which I am practised nowadays, with impartiality towards all religious schools and all persons, has thus come about by the gracious favour of the men of *Khang-dkar*, who thereby have become my lamas.

In the second place I would argue that from then on I had little desire for land or possessions, and having aroused in my spirit a sense of the impermanence of all things, I desired the things of religion. Thus I obtained the doctrines of Secret Spells of the Old and New Schools, of the Ka-gyü and others, and especially of the *Great Perfection*, the *Great Symbol*, and the profound doctrines of *Nā-ro* and *Nai-gu*, which I absorbed in large numbers, thus gaining the spiritual understanding related above. This came by their gracious favour, [60] so it is for these reasons that they appear as my lamas.

In the third place I consider what was done for my own sake as well as for the sake of others. My faith in the signs of progress in my own religious practice on the one hand, and on the other the very great benefit for other people, involved in the various types of teaching depending on whatever each would-be learner wanted, all this came about by the gracious favour of those men of *Khang-dkar*. In short those *Khang-dkar* officials really were my most gracious lamas, and this is the really true story that I have to tell.

THE BIOGRAPHY OF LAMA MERIT INTELLECT   121

Such were our lama's words.

He emanated from the Absolute Body, *motionless in its self-knowledge,*
Infinite and self-reflecting, and manifesting such form as suited his hearers,
He instructed the people of this degenerate age, skilfully employing the four kinds of
   action.
To him we bow down in devotion!

It may be said in brief that he is the essence of buddhahood in all its four aspects and of wisdom in all its five aspects, for he is indistinguishable from the Sixth Buddha, the Great *Powerbolt-Holder*. For his own sake he practised complete renunciation and perfected his understanding and all the other virtues pertaining to the course of a would-be buddha. Thus he triumphed in the overlordship of the 13th (and last) stage, which is that of the *Powerbolt-Holder*.[1]

To the noble *would-be buddhas* who have reached the 10th stage, he emerges in the *Glorious Body*. For the three grades of worthy disciples he appears in the perfect *Physical Body*, and to mean fellows like myself he shows whatever form is suitable for their conversion. He establishes worthy converts in the released state of fruition. He benefits unworthy folk by means of the four kinds of action, in so far as he makes contact with them all by sight and hearing, thought and touch. How could one write such a biography in full even in the age-span of the Buddhas of Past, Present and Future!

In these present times he has taught us, mean disciples that we are, in this snowy land, [61] using various teachings, Sa-kya, Ka-gyü, Nying-ma and so on, as suited our aspirations. Thus in these times when the religion of the Great Sage approaches its eclipse, he set up the foundation pillar of the precious and unchanging doctrine together with the banner of victory which never droops. Sitting in the unchanging posture of buddhahood upon the fearless lion-throne at the very centre whence the doctrine extended and spread, throughout all times and all seasons his spirit never moves from tranquillity and bliss. Yet by means of various kinds of teachings he establishes beings in the released state of fruition, and becomes the one gateway for all the blessings and happiness of the worlds of living beings and gods, and even nowadays he remains firm like the unchanging Mountain King.

---

[1] Concerning the stages of a *would-be buddha* see p. 33. All these titles are simply clichés indicating the attainment of buddhahood. The 'four aspects' of buddhahood refer here to the buddhas of the four directions, indicating the universality of buddhahood. The five aspects of wisdom, corresponding with the fivefold pattern of the mystic circle (see pp. 21-22) are mirror-like wisdom, the wisdom of sameness, discriminating wisdom, active wisdom and the wisdom of the pure absolute. See *Buddhist Himālaya*, p. 67.

May the victorious emblem of his body remain steadfast as the holy and glorious protector of living beings, from now on until the wheel of existence is void!

For his own sake he has realized buddhahood in the perfection of its three aspects.
For the sake of others he has taken up the victorious banner of the doctrine which never droops.
To this Precious Lama who achieves both his own good and that of others,
Benefitting wherever he made contact, to him we bow in devotion!

From the seeming ocean of stories of this holy leader of ours, I have taken a mere drop and set it down here as a guide to the integrity of the faithful. The master scholar *Buddha Spontaneous Achievement* and the master of *gSer-phug* and others of his leading disciples asked him again and again, and I and my friends in religion [62] joined in again and again with our entreaties. As a result our lama gave this account of his inner and outer life in a rather sketchy manner, and I have put this together without any deliberate falsifications. If there are many mistakes, I beg my lamas and the *attendant goddesses* to forgive me.

By the immaculate virtue of this pure aspiration may all living beings, as close to us as parents, be cleansed from mental and moral obscurations, and having rapidly perfected accumulations of merit and knowledge, may our glorious lama, lord and buddha, take them in charge and may they abide in great bliss.

We bow in devotion to him who in his wondrous knowledge,
As with the magical movements of a hundred dances,
Establishes on the path towards salvation and bliss
The many creatures of the three spheres of the world,
And who reveals to us in clarity and completeness
Such boundless works of salvation like a rosary of faith!

Men who possess some small virtue in one particular direction, or those who show some slight signs of having perfected revelation and understanding, are praised in their arrogance by thousands, just as atoms might be noted by very small creatures. So how can anyone not have faith in this lama of ours, who is lord of both the emergence and calm of the uncreate,[1] the *Powerbolt-Holder* himself, who completed for his own sake his own perfection in the past, and now, as with the dancing movements of magical knowledge, acts as the protector of sentient beings? He is the one eye which sees truth in its essence.

Thus all beings, I myself and all others, worship him, our lord in religion, from the very core of our hearts.

Henceforward throughout my whole series of lives, having first obtained a

---

[1] Concerning the expression 'emergence and calm' see the Introduction, p. 20.

powerbolt-body replete with the six elements, may I be born as the foremost of your pupils, holy one, and be enabled to establish all beings in the released state of fruition.

Having gained complete faith in this master of inspired teaching and knowledge, this second *Powerbolt-Holder* of our degenerate age, [63] it was I, irreligious and lazy, the least of his disciples, despite my name *Religious Protector Glorious and Good*, who composed this biography. The scribe's name is *Kun-dga'-'phan-dar* and we completed the work during the first half of the ninth month of the Female Water Bird year (A.D. 1573).

May the merit derived from the virtue of this composition flow like rivers of nectar from the sacred snow mountain, and assuage such heat and cold, such hunger and thirst as afflict all sentient beings!

May there be great benefit for the doctrine and for many living beings!
May the *Five Sisters of Long Life* be our religious protectors!
May the bodies of us flies become fat with the joyous feast of honey, which that bee named *Merit* has gathered from the pistils of the four precious (flowers)!

Leader of the doctrine in this snowy land!
Foremost of guides for the three spheres of the world!
Single eye of the whole world! Self-reflecting mirror!
The crest jewel of men like us!
Stay firm and unchanging! Grant us supreme attainment!
Save us from all hostile obstructions!

May you take care, holy one, of all beings, as close to us as parents, and establish them soon in the state of omniscience!

II

THE BIOGRAPHY

OF

RELIGIOUS PROTECTOR

GLORIOUS AND GOOD

Hail to our teacher whose name is

RELIGIOUS PROTECTOR GLORIOUS AND GOOD!

King of religion who has won the jewel-treasury of doctrine full with the seven kinds of precious gems,
Who in his love and compassion knows how to spread for all men a joyous feast of the gifts of four kinds, fearlessness, protection and the others,
Who for his own sake has realized the *Absolute Body* in its perfection of renunciation and knowledge,
And who, for the sake of others, using physical forms, has turned the Wheel of Religion for the three grades of those who are fit,
Defeater of the four Evil Ones, *Devadatta* and the heretics!
Glorious Protector of the Doctrine, fearful and good!
At your feet we bow!

The *Absolute Body*, begotten of pure merit and knowledge, is realized as the motionless celestial expanse,
Where that physical orb which is the splendour of sentient beings, emerges,
Concentrating the loving wisdom of all buddhas, those protectors of many diverse kinds,
And spreading in the ten directions warm rays of pure actions, which nourish like so many clusters of lotuses the various beings who are fit for conversion.
Omniscient Sun, most excellent, you who lead in the day of the buddhas' doctrine,
From birth to birth we bow in devotion to you with our body, our speech and our mind!

Like the lion of the snows, dwelling on the mountain-summit of the buddhas' pure doctrine,
You have fully developed your physical powers of accumulated merit and knowledge.
You are resplendent with the mane of expounding, confounding, propounding,
And the roar of truth resounds from your wide open jaws.
[2] With the sharp fangs and claws of inspiration and learning you rout the wild animals of false doctrines.

Your most secret and excellent name is *Lion of Speech*, and in the midst of many learned men you succour those of clear intellect.
To you we bow down!

As for the oceans of stories concerning such a guide as this, even if all buddhas and would-be buddhas related them throughout a whole world-age, their number would still be unmeasured, so what can be expected of petty minds like our own!
But in order to guide the pure and faithful, as well as to arouse the devotion of future converts, I will take just a drop and set it down here, begging our lamas and *attendant goddesses* to grant their approval.

Now it is certain that the very essence of buddhahood will become manifest in this age when the five evils are on the increase, and take the form of a friend in religion. Quoting from the *Ornament of Comprehension*: 'It is the *Physical Body* of the Sage, continuing uninterruptedly, which bestows various benefits upon all living beings equally, as long as existence lasts.'
[3] Thus our holy guide is just such a friend in religion as this. Now the very essence of the buddhas of past, present and future, and of their spiritual sons, is the Teacher of Urgyan, *Lotus-Born*. His direct reincarnation was the Master of Spells, *Religious King Merit*. The reincarnation of this lama was *Merit Intellect*, that great leader of men in this depraved age, who clearly prophesied in his secret biography concerning this chief of his disciples who would be even greater than himself.
In short this lord of ours is a buddha-manifestation, who has taken the form of a friend in religion and worked for the benefit of living beings. That I should have extracted a small part of his inconceivable works of salvation and set it down here came about in this way. We religious brethren kept on beseeching him, and he replied: 'How can an ordinary fettered mortal like myself have a religious biography to relate? Please just perform your several religious practices.' We asked again with insistence, urging that we wanted just a little. He said: 'Well if it seems so important, there is nothing to conceal, for there is nothing to write about except my eating and drinking, so I beg you to write just a little.'
When I was committing his doings to writing, he said:

'Having been born of good family
And awakened connections with good acts from the past,
I entered holy orders and practised religion a little.
I drank the water of life at the feet of holy teachers,
And absorbing a little of what I had learned,
I experienced in a small way the clarity of truth.

BIOGRAPHY OF LAMA RELIGIOUS PROTECTOR GLORIOUS AND GOOD 129

[4] And brought some small benefit to the doctrine and living beings. Such is my story, poor beggar that I am!'

In this work there are five main subjects, and a sixth one concerning his passing from sorrow.

I He is born from his mother's womb, awakes connections with effects from his past lives, and performs wondrous acts.
II He realizes the non-substantiality of phenomenal existence, enters the door of religion and pursues his studies.
III He stays with famous lamas and tastes the elixir from their mouths.
IV He absorbs the substance of his studies and extraordinary perception results.
V As the final fruit of his perfection he brings benefit to the doctrine and to living beings.
VI He completes his works of conversion in this world, and thinking of work to be done in other spheres, he passes from sorrow.

CHAPTER I *We supplicate him who was born as the glory of mankind*
In a body which concentrates the loving wisdom of all buddhas,
And issuing from the womb of his noble mother,
Performed auspicious signs of great wonder!

[5] Our lord himself told the story thus:
My lineage was that of the *Mung*. As for the meaning of *Mung*, there was a certain King *Mung-ston-gtsug-tor* who was a manifestation of the *Glorious Gentle Lord*, and his lineage, using just the *Mung* part of the name, seems to have been known as *Mung*.

Moreover his mother, who was called the Royal Lady *Mung-sa*, became one of the wives of the Protector of Religion, King Song-tsan-gam-po, and the royal family of today probably represents her descendants.

Thus the *Mung* family came westwards from Central Tibet, and as feudatories of the King of Mustang, they spread throughout various districts of Dolpo. In particular my ancestors settled in the lower part of *Nang-khong* on prominent uplands, known as Lion Vale (*Seng-ge lung*), where they gradually acquired more and more territory. Among them there seem to have been several religious teachers, active in the affairs of the doctrine. The laymen too were straight-forward and honest, devout and faithful to the *Precious Ones*, zealous in religion, yet modest. One might list their virtues further, but in brief let it be said that they understood the laws of cause and effect, and so all knew how to avoid evil and encourage good.

One such was my father, named *Magnificence Renown*, who possessed those good qualities listed above. My mother was named Lady *Glorious Gladness*. Possessing all womanly good qualities, she was spotless, as well as of good family, and lamas had made prophesies on her account. Having entered her womb, I was born on a favourable day in the 11th month of the Male Fire Monkey year.[1] Auspicious signs accompanied my birth, but being very discreet, my mother said nothing of these. Later on an aunt of mine, who was a nun, acted as my nurse, [6] and when I was sleeping, she saw my eyes wide open and staring. She said to my mother: 'What kind of child is this, who thus sleeps without closing his eyes?' 'From early on he acted like this, but do not tell anyone,' my mother replied.

On another occasion my aunt scolded me a little, and my mother said: 'Do not be angry with him like that. It wont do to accumulate demerit in his regard.' Thus she made matters quite clear.

As far back as I can remember, it seemed as though subtle influences from my former lives had awoken a little, for even in my games, I would set up pretty stones, white ones and red ones, on a board, and then make as though to worship them as if they were images. Or I would turn a basket upside down, sit on it, and make as though to instruct my play-fellows. Furthermore I felt myself markedly different from others. I passed the time thinking about religion, and at night in my dreams fearful phantoms and suchlike caused me to fly away through the sky, and there were other such signs of magical powers. I thought with great longing: 'If only I could abandon this life in the world, and practise meditation one-pointedly in a lonely mountain place.'

CHAPTER II. *He realizes the non-substantiality of phenomenal existence, enters the door of religion and pursues his studies.*

Seeing the elements of existence as non-substantial,
Handsome in conduct, he entered the door of religion.
At the mere sight of a text he absorbed its whole meaning.
We supplicate him, who thus studied and practised!

As for the meaning of this, our lord himself told the story:

Then by the time I was three or four years old, [7] I had learned to read and write without difficulty. When I read a Ka-dam-pa book which was in my possession, I had a feeling of its absolute truth.[2] Tears ran down to the end of my nose, and I thought: 'If only I might go to the mountains! I must do something of this sort.'

[1] This corresponds to A.D. 1536. See p. 76. [2] See p. 188 fn 1.

BIOGRAPHY OF LAMA RELIGIOUS PROTECTOR GLORIOUS AND GOOD 131

From the exalted and excellent Intellect Might *at the age of three years
He received consecration and really saw the* Red Fury,
*Understanding the ritual and the whole meaning of the consecration.
We supplicate him, who thus gained perfection of both (the supreme and ordinary)
kinds!*

As for the meaning of this, our lord himself told the story: When I was about three years old, I was taken in my parents' arms, and we asked the exalted lama *Intellect Might* to bestow upon us the consecration of the *Red Fury*. As the consecrating power of knowledge descended, I was bathed in the grace of that noble and precious god, so fearful in appearance with red round wide open eyes. Thus as a result the main substance of this consecration, as well as the manner of its giving, the ritual items and the whole operation remained very clear in my mind for a long time. From that same lama I received the *Perfecter of Thought*, both *Blue* and *Red*, the *Queen of Success* and other consecrations. At the age of ten I was taken by my parents and in the presence of the aged scholar *Sky-King* I received the vows of a 'virtuous adherer', I learned without any difficulty the liturgies of immediate use, such as the *All-Knowing One* and others. After a while my parents and relatives argued that being the eldest son, I should remain in a worldly calling, but I remained firm in what I had already understood, namely that phenomenal life consists of suffering by its very nature, and so I did not listen to them at all. After that decision of mine [8] I practised the rites of *Supreme Bliss*, *Hevajra* and *Secret Unity* from the new set of tantras, and those of the *Tranquil and Fierce Divinities*, the *Eight-Word God*, the *Perfecter of Thought*, both *Blue* and *Red*, *Secret Unity* and others from the old set of tantras. I did not have to make great exertions in these studies. Also in village rites I became quite skilful, so that I could remove material troubles by the three means of suppressing demons, performing oblations, hurling spells, and other methods. Whatever was necessary in whatever case, I understood merely by looking, and others benefitted by all this. Also I knew very well the Indian and Chinese systems of astronomy, the five periods of the *Wheel of Time* and so on.

When he heard from the lama named 'Good' (bZang-po), *the topmost gem among sages,
The secret and profound religious doctrine of* 'Bir-ba,[1]
*In the assembly of many wise men he was foremost in recitation.
We supplicate him who fulfilled all his teachers foretold!*

[1] This is the Tibetan spelling of the Indian name *Virūpa*, one of the 84 Great Yogins, who are regarded as being the main propagators of the Buddhist tantric traditions. (See *Buddhist Himālaya*, pp. 85–6.) In Tibet *Virūpa* is especially revered by the Sa-kya Order, for it was from his followers that the teachings of the *Way and its Fruits* and other doctrines were received. See the *Blue Annals*, p. 206. See also Tucci, Indo-Tibetica IV, part 1, pp. 94–5.

As for the meaning of this, at the age of twelve I obtained in full from the precious abbot *bZang-po Dar-dar* the teachings of the *Way and its Fruits* together with consecrations, guiding instructions, admonitions and textual initiations. I was foremost in recitation at the fixed sessions, and so my lama was very pleased. He gave to my parents and relatives *chang* and meat and various things, and said to them meanwhile: 'Whatever happens this young monk must remain in the religious life.' He really made such statements as these. At that time too I received from that great tantric sage, the Hermit of *Bi-cher*,[1] the full consecration of the *Illusion of the Tranquil and Fierce Divinities* and also *Boundless Life* of the *Lady Tradition*, and he was very pleased with me.

From the great abbot *Intellect Victorious* I received *Jetarī* three times over. From the lord of religion *Powerbolt Saviouress* [9] I received the consecration of *Hevajra*, and the consecrations and textual initiations of *Jetarī*, of the *All-Knowing*, of the *Hawk King of Birds* in the form of *Powerbolt-in-Hand*, and of the *Fierce One with the Up-turned Moustache*.

Frequenting the presence of many holy sages,
Such as Spontaneous Achievement *and others who have reached the supreme attainment,*
He culled the essence of the profound doctrines of Sa-kya, Ka-gyü and Nying-ma,
Thus possessing the know-how of inspiration and knowledge.
To him we make supplication!

As for the meaning of this, from *Spontaneous Achievement Glorious and Good* I obtained the consecration, instructions and textual initiation of the Six Doctrines of *Nai-gu* in the manner of *Shangs-pa*, also the seven part work *Purifying the Mind*, a dissertation on the *All-Knowing*, the consecrations together with textual initiations of *Powerbolt-in-Hand*, the *Lion-Headed Goddess, Eleven-Headed Glancing Eye, Secret Unity, Gentle Powerbolt*,[2] *Hevajra*, as well as the *Volume of Precepts*, the *Ma-ṇi bka'-'bum* and the *Padma thang-yig*. He gave me in full the 'single-session' consecration of the *One Mother* and the relevant instructions, and I went in attendance on him. When we went out on the mountains, the clarity and insight of my excitations and animations and all the rest came off very well, and it would not be possible to write about it all. In brief that holy lama was very kind to me indeed both from the religious and the worldly point of view. At that time I thought to myself: 'Since human life seems to be quite worthless, I will make for a place in lonely mountains where no one knows about me and stay there.' But that peerless

---

[1] Spelt as *Byi-cher* or *Bi-cher*, this is *Survey of India* 'Phijorgāon'. See *Himalayan Pilgrimage*, pp. 129–31.
[2] Combined name for *Gentle Voice* and *Powerbolt-in-Hand*.

BIOGRAPHY OF LAMA RELIGIOUS PROTECTOR GLORIOUS AND GOOD 133

lama *Spontaneous Achievement Glorious and Good* said: 'Since you are so wise, at all costs you should go once to Central Tibet.'

[10] *Studying in the great monastery,*
He absorbed the whole meaning of the texts,
And that king of religion whose name is Intellect
Ordained him with the threefold vow.
  To him we make supplication!

So I went to the great monastery of Victorious *Thub-bstan*,[1] where I frequented the presence of that lord of religion *Intellect-Born*, and remaining there five years, I received the whole meaning of the interpretation of various books in the field of philosophical definition, and I came to know them unerringly.

As for the manner of his ordination:

Having gone to that excellent place,
He cleared his mind of all error throughout the range of his studies,
And frequenting the presence of many wise men of religion,
He received ordination which was performed in full conformity with the rule.
  To him we make supplication!

As for the meaning of this, our lama said: Then when I was 32 years old I was ordained in the temple at Victorious *Thub-bstan* in the midst of the full correct number of monks, so worthy they atoned for my own shortcomings. The 'officiating abbot' was that master of inspired teaching and knowledge *Loving Firmness*. The 'master of ceremonies' was the prelate *Lion of Compassion* and the 'confidential intercessor' was the teacher from *Byang-sgo* who recites with such eloquence. Moreover from that same lord of religion (*Loving Firmness*) I received the doctrinal cycle of *Powerbolt Terror* in the Sa-kya manner as well as other consecrations and textual initiations.

[11] From the great lama of *Ngor*, *Buddha-Lion*, I obtained the white *Boundless Life* and other consecrations. From the *Great Translator Incarnate* I obtained the initiation of the *maṇi* spell and other things. When I went to visit the *Great Text-Revealer Incarnate* and asked at his feet for a blessing, I prayed that we might meet yet once more. He replied prophetically: 'We shall meet only on this occasion, but at all times and in all circumstances you will remain inseparable from me.' I went to visit many holy places including the images of *Buddha the Prince* and *Buddha the Sage* at Lhasa. Then I returned to my own land of Dolpo, paid respects to my lama and went to see my old mother and other relatives.

[1] This is *Thub-bstan rNam-rgyal*, a famous *Ngor-pa* (subsect of Sa-kya) monastery, founded in 1478 about 25 miles NW of Shigatse. See *mKhyen-rtse*'s Guide, pp. 68 and 158.

CHAPTER III *He visits many famous lamas and relishes the essence of their teaching.*

He frequented the presence of many holy sages,
Including the lama named Merit *who is* Lotus-Born *Incarnate,*
And gathering together the essence of their profound teachings, Sa-kya, Ka-gyü *and* Nying-ma,
He possessed the techniques of inspired teaching and knowledge.
   To him we make supplication.
When the lama named Merit *who is* Lotus-Born *Incarnate*
Was instructing him in Nai-gu,[1] *those profound* ḍākinī *doctrines,*
He remained a long time in the state of true being,
And so recognized the clear light.
   To him we make supplication.

As for the meaning of this, our lama said:
Then at the beginning of summer while I was staying at *Ku*, [12] my lord and father in religion, who had been invited by the people of *Mu-gum*, where he had put an end to an attack of smallpox that had afflicted them, and had also taught them a lot of religion, was now said to be on his way back.[2] Since many people went out to meet him, I too went to meet him quite a long way off and pay my respects, for he had been my former teacher. When we met, he dismounted from his horse and returning my greetings, spoke many words with me in a very joyful frame of mind. The Abbot of *Zho-gam* invited him to his monastery, and while he was making returns for the libations of welcome, he said to me: 'Tomorrow or the next day you should come to Margom.' Following upon this, I went to pay him my respects there together with two companions, and we asked him for the Six Doctrines of *Nai-gu*, which he gave us. During this instruction we were one day in the religious enclosure where he was getting us to envisage the *clear light*, when I perceived my own mind quite clearly. My thought was quite untrammelled and all was still for a moment. Then when the others who had come to attend the instruction had left, I told him what had occurred. 'How wonderful!' my lama replied, 'that is the real inner thought of the *Absolute Body* of buddhahood, which is called *Recognition of the Selfhood of Mind*. Now I must give you instructions in the *Great Symbol*, and we will see how matters go hereafter. But there is really nothing for you to learn beyond this, so guard it well.' Then I received from him the Six Doctrines together with

---

[1] *Nai-gu* or *Ne-gu* was *Nāropa*'s sister. See p. 27. A *ḍākinī* is a special kind of 'attendant goddess', the companion of a yogin in his quest for secret doctrines.
[2] See pp. 115–118.

BIOGRAPHY OF LAMA RELIGIOUS PROTECTOR GLORIOUS AND GOOD 135

subsidiary works, the *Fifteen Admonitions of the Indian Attendant Goddesses* and other items.

That winter I practised invocations of the *All-Knowing, Boundless Life* and other divinities at *Zho-gam*, and when this was finished I helped the Abbot of *Zho-gam* who was building a stupa at Do-ra-sum-do in honour of the precious Cave Hermit (*of Bi-cher*). [13]

That summer I went to meditate in wild places in the region of *Ko-yol*. Then the Abbot of *Zho-gam* said to me: 'While you were in the mountains recently, I had some incense and a piece of crystal here ready. I want to send these for the tea ceremony which is being held for the perfecting of the intentions of the peerless Cave Hermit. If you would interrupt your meditation and go there, (it would help)'. I went to ask the consent of my lord and father in religion, and he said: 'Young master, your accomplishments certainly exceed those of others who have worked at these things for many years. It would really be better if someone else were burdened with this tea ceremony.' Although he looked rather displeased, I urged the matter a little, for this peerless Cave Hermit had been very kind to me. 'So be it,' he replied, 'you will interrupt your meditation, but all you say seems to be true. However do not stay there at the monastery and return here quickly.' So he let me go. I set out with nine new novices, ten of us in all, carrying the things for the tea ceremony. We had no difficulties on the way, so we reached the great monastery,[1] where we greeted the abbot and our monk-colleagues, and then got the tea ceremony ready. Previously when I set out (*viz.* from Margom) my lord and father in religion had been very anxious that I should return, and because of the urgency of his request, I got ready to return and make the journey back. The abbot and the master of ceremonies as well as my monk friends were all very affectionate to me, urging me very strongly to stay. But I did not give in, and begging their leave, I made the journey back. [14] I reached *Zho-gam* and greeted everyone there. I intended to go on to Margom, but everyone said that I should rest a few days. While I was staying there, my lord and father in religion sent the young squire *Intellect* with the message that I should come at once. I got ready to leave, and the two of us went in to see the great *Zho-gam* Abbot. He told us that my lama was angry and was said to be getting ready to leave for *Lab-phyi*, because that winter the people of the lower village (near Margom) had been hunting. 'We must go and beseech him (not to go),' he said. So four of us, the lama himself and we monks, made the journey there. At the same time the householder *Tshe-ring* came from *Kyi* with a (similar) submission. But although all householders and religious begged him urgently to stay, he remained displeased. Then the Abbot of *Zho-gam* said: 'As you are so very displeased,

[1] This is presumably Lang Monastery which is about one mile below *Bi-cher*. See *Himalayan Pilgrimage*, p. 130.

you yourself should make the whole matter clear to all the householders and monks who are here.'

My lama replied: 'Well, as you press me with such urgency, I may not be moved by others, but I am moved by you. So I will not allow your words to come to nothing. You yourself have said that this master scholar will profit the doctrine wherever he is, so please let him remain here, and I beg you to give what is necessary for his upkeep. I will give him all the consecrations, textual initiations, instructions and so on, all that I possess, so that he will be like a vessel filled to overflowing.'

The Abbot of *Zho-gam* gave his consent to this, and all the householders and religious made obeisance and were very pleased. My lord and father in religion then filled up with water the vase which he used every day for purification ceremonies, and gave it to me [15] in order to make the auspices come right.

That summer I went to the 'Isle of Enlightenment' at *Ze-phug* in attendance on him, and for my special instruction he gave me instruction in the *Innate Yoga* of the *Great Symbol*. He also gave me the Ka-gyü work *The Golden Rosary* in its full and condensed forms as well as other works. Then we went to *dGung-khung*, where I received from him in full the consecrations, textual initiations and instructions in the *One Mother, Gentle and Violent*, and several other rituals. Sometimes we went meditating in wild places. Then I thought to myself: 'All these things which I have received from my lama, I should absorb by meditating one-pointedly in some lonely place, for it is uncertain when one will die.'

So I went and asked my lama, addressing him words such as these: 'You have given me all these profound teachings so that I am like a vessel filled to overflowing. Thus you have taught me in your great kindness. But I cannot contain so much, and so there is no very great use in it. I have in mind to stay in some deserted place where I shall live on sand for my food. I beg you to give me leave for something of this kind.'

'Do not be so faint-hearted,' he replied, 'if you carry on, you will become the master of all the knowledge that I possess. So in that case I beg you to stay just this summer and winter.' Thus in order not to break his command, I stayed on.

While practising concentrated invocations in his place of meditation,
As foretold by attendant goddesses, *he performed special ablutions.*
In the midst of rainbow hues he beheld the countenances of Hevajra *and his consort,*
So gaining the realization of perfection.
To him we make supplication!

As for the meaning of this, that winter I started upon concentrated invocations of *Hevajra*, [16] and when all was going well, my lord and father in religion came to my meditation room, bringing all the things necessary for the offering of sacrificial libations as well as for the offering of tea. The sacrificial libations of atonement lasted for five days, and when my period of meditation was completed, my lama gave considerable offerings to all who were in the monastery towards the festivities of my coming out of meditation.

In the spring we pupils all went with our lama to *rDzing-phu*, where as general instruction he gave us the Six Doctrines of Nāropa together with the mystic cycle and other technical matters. He also gave to me the *Small Book of Precepts*, the complete set of instructions for control of the vital breath and other works including the complete set of Six Doctrines together with the mystic cycle and other technical matters.

Then in mid-summer the people of *dPon-spang-lung* invited my lama for the consecrating of the 'Sun Cave' Temple, and at the same time the people of *Ban-tshang* asked him to come and found the monastery of T'ha-kar, which he agreed to do. Then he went to *rDzing-phu* again. I returned to the monastery and practised invocations of *Boundless Life* and the *Queen of Success*. The lama and his pupils returned to the monastery just as I finished this period of meditation. From then on he gave me instruction for close on 15 days, the Six Doctrines of *'Ba-ra*, the *Small Book of Oral Teachings* and other works.

In the autumn my lord and father in religion was invited by the people of *Ban-tshang*, and so he went there. I was involved in invocations of the *Perfecter of Thought*, the *Blue* and the *Red*, which I performed for five and a half months.

In the spring my father in religion returned to our monastery and performed the rite of the *All-Knowing* one thousand times. Then the people of *Ban-tshang* said that I must come in attendance on my lama, and those of *Phal* and *rTar* especially insisted on this. They all asked the lama to order me to go. [17] So having received the command that I should go, I went in attendance on my lama when he went there.

In the first part of summer the lama and his pupils all went to the mountains by T'ha-kar and he gave instructions in the *One Mother* together with consecrations and textual initiations according to the tradition of *rGod-phrug*.[1] As he was giving all this to a large number of listeners, I received it all in full. Furthermore I had already previously asked my lama again and again for his biography, and I was able to write down then all that he had told me.

In the latter part of summer I went meditating in wild places, and from that winter onwards for the space of nine years I had to remain as head of T'ha-kar Monastery. Except that I became rather weary of this, I was fulfilling my lama's intentions and my religious life certainly prospered. Moreover I frequented this holy lama's

[1] See p. 103 fn.

presence for the space of eleven years, receiving from him all the works mentioned above, and especially the consecrations, instructions, textual initiations of the *Great Perfection* and many other things. If one thinks properly, there can be no way of repaying his kindness. Everything is written down clearly in a list of received consecrations.

In short I wretched fellow had thirteen famous teachers, of whom the foremost were:

> my gracious lord and father in religion whose name was *Merit*,
> the lord of perfect inspiration and knowledge *Spontaneous Achievement Glorious and Good*,
> the wise and perfect abbot *bZang-po Dar-dar*.

Because of their compassion and kindness and especially of the crest-gem called *Merit*, I am not poor in religion, since they in their great compassion have not abandoned me, for my mind is still in association with theirs. So now there are no defects of transmission in these teachings, and whoever absorbs them, will receive benefit. This makes me very happy.

[18] CHAPTER IV. *Having absorbed such things as he had learned, he experienced a very special state of self-realization.*

> *When concentrating his mind one-pointedly in a lonely place,*
> *He meditated upon this essence of the sages' teachings,*
> *He beheld the countenance of the tutelary divinities and gained supreme realization.*
> *At the feet of this lord of yogins we make supplication.*

As for the meaning of this, our lama explains:
Thus having left off studying for a while, I had to fix (all I had studied) in my mind and absorb it by means of meditation, and I will now tell something of this process. As for the cycle (of study) relating to descriptive definitions, I performed sometimes three, or sometimes two or four full sets of invocations for the chief of the tutelary divinities who are really important. As for the other more ordinary ones, in no case did I not do one complete set. This is the source of their continuance with me nowadays.
As for the cycle of methodical instruction in the *Process of Realization*,[1] in the matter of the *vital channels*, the *vital fluid* and the *vital breath*, I did not achieve proficiency in impelling them into the crucial place, but I received in several ways a total

---

[1] For the meaning of this term see p. 26. References to the channels, the vital fluid and the breath will be found on p. 27.

experience within my intellectual understanding. In short it was by this way that I came to recognize that one's mental tendencies can be controlled. That is the cause of my not offending against proprieties in the course of the lesser manifestations (of religious life) such as sacrificial offerings and daily religious practice.

As for the cycle of metaphysical thought, it was as though there were some connection with former lives, for even as explanations were being given for the first time, it all came to me with very great ease. My lord and father in religion used to praise me, saying: 'I have a disciple who understands without explanations.'

[19] Once when he was explaining *crossing the crest*[1] to a lot of pupils at T'ha-kar, he was telling them how to absorb (their learning) by fixing their vision on the absolute. I was in solitary meditation in a hut, and pointing in my direction, he said: 'Over there is a man who knows how to absorb (what he has learned).' But although he used to praise me a lot in this way, I do not possess understanding of such a kind. For with regard to precise thoughts my mind was vague, and especially when I seemed to understand well, I suppose I had little knowledge in regard to particulars. When I saw the way some treatises were written, when I saw the techniques some used, or when I saw how some absorbed (their learning), I would think: 'The meaning is not like that, but like this,' or 'If one is working for the good both of oneself and of others, by doing it in this way one will succeed,' or again 'If one establishes the relationship of the outer (form) and the inner (meaning) in this way, it will not do.' With thoughts such as these I seemed to understand things spontaneously without reference to verbal expression. In short if you consider the magnitude of the occasion for this mental instability, a fiendish seduction for one of little merit, it is not likely that anything great would emerge. No great effort was required for all this. If I have not failed in the circumstances of this present life, it is because of what was said above (about my kind lamas).

In the process of absorbing what I had learned, I experienced some clarity amidst such vague mental states. The way it happened was like this. While I was first performing a concentrated set of invocations at Margom, I had a dream one night, in which a woman appeared dressed in white clothes and saying she was my mother. 'Wash, son!' she said. 'Where?' I asked. 'In the pool for ablutions' she replied. Looking to one side, [20] I saw a very small pool filled with water.

I went there, and the water was pure and clear, neither too hot nor too cold. I stipped naked and bathed. When I came out, there was a delightful palace to one side, and I thought to myself: 'My lamas and tutelary divinities must live here. It

---

[1] This is my conventional translation for tib. *thod-rgal*, a term used in the 'Great Perfection' (*rDzogs-chen*) teachings to refer to gaining of supreme enlightenment.

wont do to burst in all at once. First I must worship them and give some sign (of my presence).' In my hands were a powerbolt and a bell. I rang (the bell) and it made such a great noise that I awoke.

A few days later just after the middle watch of the night I had the impression that I saw the round orb of the sun in a very clear sky. Concentrating upon it, I realized the *clear light* of the *crest-crossing*, and I saw there in the midst of rainbow colours the dark blue form of *Hevajra*, his face and his arms all perfectly formed, as he embraced the light blue body of (his partner) *Nairātmyā*.

When I was making invocations to the Red Fury, I dreamed one night, that a paunch filled with dung came out of my buttocks, and it divided into two parts. Although I could throw one part away, I had the other by my side, and at that moment I awoke. Now if I could have thrown both away, it would have been alright. But that one should be left behind accords with all the material wealth that has come to me, these various enjoyable things of life. So it seems that I shall remain in the circle of existence for a while.

Another night I dreamed of a prayer-wall at the end of a great wide bridge, and I was erecting beside it a large piece of coloured cloth as a prayer-flag. Then I heard a bodiless voice saying: 'Establish the Buddhist religion.' Another day I seemed to see in the sky before me a small image of the Teacher, the Lion of the Shākyas, standing out very clear. [21] Furthermore during that period when I was performing invocations of other tutelary divinities and suchlike practices, I used to have some kind of insight portending the purification of evil I had done and so on. But (telling of this) would be just a lot of words and embarrassment to others.

When I was practising meditation in wild places, I was once at the place called Namgung of Saldang, where there are a lot of streams and a place for meditation. I had passed one night there, and at dawn there protruded from under my couch what seemed to be three spear-heads. I was raised up on these points and so transported to the summit of the heavens. Looking down, I saw they were three great snakes. Now this was achieved by my religious practice, and as these beneficient yet unreal appearances came upon me, I composed a small song beginning:
'*The yogin who understands appearances as halucination.*'
So I awoke in a happy state of mind. Appearances floated vaguely around me, and I looked on everything in this blissful and tranquil state, the day was already breaking.

Another evening I had gone with some religious friends to the temple of Shey monastery. Having said our prayers properly, we were preparing to go and spend the night up on top, when I felt myself trembling, so I said: 'You go on up. I will sleep here tonight.' At dusk a strong wind arose, and at dawn a man appeared to me showing a respectful manner. He was dressed in pure white clothes, with a turban of white silk and wearing jewelry. 'If you go round the mountains today,' he said, 'no harm will come from snow and rain.' Then he disappeared. He was probably the local god of Shey. It was the time of the heavy summer rains, and as it had been raining quite hard, everyone said: 'You are not going to make the round of the mountains? Even if you go round, the mist will be so thick that there will be nothing to see.' [22] So we too were thinking that it would be quite unsuitable, and that (previous) morning we had been very doubtful about going round the mountains. But now as this day broke I woke my companions up, saying: 'We must get ready to go today, so get up and come!' We set out, and in accordance with the morning's prophesy, the sky was clear and we saw sights unseen before. The people of Shey believed in us more devotedly than ever. We continued our meditations in the wilds for the space of forty days, but we moved on without staying long anywhere, usually one day in each place. Although I experienced many indefinable states of the spirit, it would not do to write about it all. Briefly told, there was great benefit to our religious practice, and we had good experiences of universal non-substantiality. The feeling that I was not competent at anything, that I was not capable, the hankering after a fair measure of success, all such worldly attitudes meant little to me. Finally in my dreams I had no impressions of dread or fear at the sight of fierce animals and other creatures, or of deceptive appearances of fire and water and so on. I had overwhelming confidence with regard to all states of non-substantial being.

At the turn of that autumn
as he practised meditation at T'ha-kar,
One day at dawn in a cone-shaped projection of rainbow rays,
he beheld the countenances of the Buddhas of the Good Age
and experienced universal non-substantiality.
  To him we make supplication!

As for the meaning of this, at T'ha-kar one dawn a vision appeared in the sky, and looking at it I saw in the sky before me [23] in a complexity of rainbow rays a lot of buddhas in simple unadorned style.[1] I saw only the lower part of the body of some, the upper part of others, the right side of some, the left side of others, and still many more quite complete. At the same time I reached out to them in my meditation and for a moment I was united with them. As they finally disappeared, someone dressed as a layman but who seemed to be the local god of T'ha-kar, came and saluted me

---

[1] Literally: 'buddhas with the appearance of the *Physical Body (sprul-pa'i sku)*.' This buddha-body (concerning all three see the Introduction, p. 21) is represented unadorned, whereas the *Glorious Body (longs-spyod-kyi sku)* is portrayed adorned with crown, necklace, bracelets, etc.

in a respectful manner and said: 'You must please always give me a sacrificial cake of my own, and I will do for you whatever service there may be.' Then he disappeared. It may have been in connection with this, that however long I stayed at T'ha-kar, I was never ill and circumstances were always favourable.

That winter our lama and all his disciples went into retreat. After a month had passed, our lama said to me: 'As you are proficient in dreams, take note (through your dreams) of what I am doing during the next seven days.'
'That being so,' I thought, 'I must see this very night.'
I willed to have a dream, and mastering it, I went to see how things were. All around my lama there were a lot of women adorned with jewelry, the sight of whom caused such distraction, that I could not approach him. In that state I awoke. Again I went to sleep and set out to see him. My lama was seated on his throne but around the outside there were two overlapping curtains. As I could not remove them, I made obeisance from outside. In this state I awoke. Again I went to sleep and exercised all my will to see him. I came to a place which was not our monastery. There was a soft green luscious expanse of grass with all kinds of flowers around. A woman there made some sort of sign, and looking towards the east, I saw a long rainbow [24] shining with five different colours. Again I looked towards the west and a similar one appeared there. 'Is this the *clear light* of the Absolute?' I wondered, and as soon as this thought crossed my mind, the whole place with its expanse of grass lost all form of substantiality and changed into the nature of a rainbow. As I tarried there in a joyful state of mind, again I thought: 'As I must go and see my lama, what is the use of all this?' No sooner had I thought this, than my lord and father in religion appeared before me in the middle of a rainbow. His throne, his garments, his body were all non-substantial, but they shone clearly with the form of a rainbow. All around there were tutelary divinities, attendant goddesses, defenders of the doctrine, so many images, some of which I recognized, others which I could not, all seated there like open seed-pods. They were all non-substantial, as though formed of light. They moved in their seated posture and their course went up to the heavens. I was in such a happy frame of mind, that I performed dancing gestures, and meanwhile I made obeisance and sang these verses:

> *All void forms of mere seeming,*
> *Ocean-like divine concourse of buddhas,*
> *They are all one in the* Absolute Buddha Body.
> *To these void seeming forms I bow low!*

I went on with such verses and referred in turn to their *Speech* and their *Mind*, and as I tarried there, bowed down before them, I suddenly awoke. Everything was scintillating before my eyes, and I was in a joyful state of mind, just looking on blissfully. Then as I performed my morning devotions and made the sacrificial offering of water, [25] I thought: 'It is not good to be so joyfully attached to those things of this morning. They are a cause of bondage and there is no substance in them. Because of them I could not meet my lama, and so did not gain my intended objective. But I went and told my lama how I had thought that there were two overlapping curtains around the outside of his couch, and he said: 'As I feared there would be a storm, those two overlapping curtains were there, and there was no illusion about all the rest.' My holy lama had produced that whole visionary display.

That spring he gave instruction in the Six Doctrines of *Nai-gu* to several advanced scholars, headed by the *Po-ldad* Lama, and to a large number of disciples. I asked leave to remain in retreat. At the conclusion of the instruction there was a great feast of rejoicing, and since master and pupils all demanded my presence, I also went.

(The following passage, MS page 25 line 11 to page 28 line 14, is omitted from this translation. Our lama is asked to sing a song, and he produces spontaneously some rather didactic verses.)

From then on for three years I remained under vows. I passed most of the time in solitary retreat, and during that period I experienced various psychic states and verses burst from my lips with unimpeded spontaneity, but it would not do to write about all this. One night towards dawn I had a vision in which the Lord of our Religion appeared with quite enormous stature. His hands were placed together in the gesture of meditation and I was on them. I got off and found myself in a large market place where I was giving the consecration of the *maṇi* prayer, and at that moment I awoke. A few days after that the people of T'ha-kar [29] asked me to go there, and since my lord and father in religion commanded me to do so, I gave them instruction in the Six Doctrines of *Nai-gu*. As complimentary works I gave them the large version of the *Golden Rosary* of the Ka-gyü Order, the treatise entitled *Seven Kinds of Gems* and other biographical works. I gave them textual initiations in full, guiding instructions and so on.

Then until summer turned into autumn I remained in retreat and my religious practice benefitted greatly. In the autumn my lord and father in religion came up (to T'ha-kar). When the people of *Ban-tshang*, lay and religious, men and women, had been to see him, he went into retreat. From the latter part of winter until the first part of summer he gave instruction in the tantric work *The Way and its Fruits*, and I received in full all that he gave us. In the latter part of the summer he returned to Margom. I and the others at T'ha-kar stayed in retreat. After about nine months had passed, we sent a request to our holy lama, and the people of T'ha-kar went to Margom to invite him and beg him to lead just one ceremony. We did one thousand performances of the *All-Knowing* and very good offerings were made. We came up again and spent the end of the summer in T'ha-kar. I gave consecrations, initiations and whatever they wanted to the many monks and layfolk, both men and women, who gathered there.

At the turn of autumn our holy lama sent a message saying: 'I am going to give here the consecration of the *Eight-Word God*, so as I need an audience and someone to act for me, come down here (to Margom).' So we went to Margom and receiving the consecration, stayed a few days in attendance on him. Then I returned to T'ha-kar in attendance on our holy lama, and so we arrived up there.

I had been in retreat for just about a month, when I heard that my mother was rather ill. 'She is very advanced in years,' I thought, 'This time she may well leave us.'

[30] I sent the monk *Ocean of Intellect* to see her, and when he returned, he said: 'She is not so bad, but your noble mother asks you to make her one visit.' I went to ask leave of my lama, and he said: 'It is likely that your mother will depart now, so at all costs you must go there once. Perform some consecrations a few times, but do not stay there, for you must return here. This year all my own portents, both mental and physical, have been bad, so do as I have said.' Following on this, I went to Zho-gam and saw everyone there. Although my mother was not very ill, she was really very old, and thinking of what my lama had said, for there was no harm that he had not foretold, I performed a lot of consecrations, the *Heart Drop of the Great Perfection* seven times, the *All-Knowing* and the *Buddha Imperturbable* both seven times each and various others. I had the form of a funeral ceremony for a person still living performed both at *Rva-lding* and *Zho-gam* for my mother's intention, and then I got ready to return.

The Abbot of *Zho-gam* asked me urgently to stay, saying: 'Stay this winter here. Our monastery will give both you and your monk-attendant everything you need to make your stay comfortable, food and all the rest.' But I remembered what my lama had said, so I made my way back and reached T'ha-kar. I went to see my lama and then went into retreat once more. When about one month had passed, he sent a message saying: 'Come to this monastery for the sacrificial offering of the 29th. There will also be some technical instructions for you.' So on the 27th I went to see him and he drew up for me a whole set of technical instructions which I had not seen before, 'quittances'.[1] placatory ceremonies, sacrificial ceremonies of

---

[1] 'Quittances' is my translation of tib. *mDos*, a technical term referring to certain kinds of ransom-rites, performed in order to stave off the attacks of gods and demons. *mDos* is usually translated as 'thread-cross', an implement commonly used in such rites. See my *Nine Ways of Bon*, p. 257.

atonement, sets of special intentions together with technical instructions and the rest. 'If you have to perform them some time in the future', he said, [31] 'they are just so.' So he gave me these series of technical instructions together with the various necessary sections of internal subdivisions. 'The doctrines which are not included in the ones I have now already given you, I will give you today. There is probably still something in the way of technical instructions relating to these Six Doctrines.' 'If it is so,' I replied, 'you should give guidance in these matters to the whole community.' 'It is rather early for this,' he said, 'but I will do it.'

We performed the sacrificial offering of the 29th, and on the 30th he rested. On the 1st everyone came out of retreat and I started instructions in the Six Doctrines, and for the space of forty days I contented everyone with general instruction, private instruction, giving them whatever they wanted. About then our lama was intending to return to Margom, but the people of *Phal* and *rTar* were so insistent, that he had to go there. As a result of some ailment, his health was affected. I went in attendance on him and gave a general consecration to the people of *Phal* and *rTar*. Still in attendance on him, I accompanied him to *mTshams*, and I thought: 'In such a state of health as this it is not likely that he will recover. On the way down (to Margom) our benefactors will invite him here and there, and as he is so humble, he will go wherever they ask him. There is a risk of anything happening. It seems it would be best if I requested him to come to T'ha-kar. I asked him and he said: 'Well, I will do that.' He was pleased about this arrangement, for as I explained to him, if we did otherwise, I myself with my monks would go to T'ha-kar, and he with his monks would go to Margom. [32] So he came to T'ha-kar.

From then on whatever ceremonies and general distributions we performed, his health certainly grew no better. For the forty days that he remained ill I attended on him very carefully. Except for tea things, we distributed as offerings all his possessions from religious articles downwards. Then on the 21st day of the 4th month of the Snake Year[1] his physical frame was absorbed into the celestial sphere. Thereafter the monks of both the lower and the upper monastery gathered at T'ha-kar, where they offered worship to his corpse and built a shrine. Then except for two monks who remained on watch at T'ha-kar, everyone accompanied the corpse to Margom. We performed the lama-worship, and all along the route, at Shimen, *Ko-mangs, Ja-tshang*[2] and so on we received a large number of gifts of all kinds which we also brought with us. Afterwards we went to *Zho-tshal* where we summoned artists from all around. For inside the monastery they made an image of the Precious Teacher of Urgyan and another of our lord and father in

---

[1] This must correspond to A.D. 1581. See p. 76.
[2] Concerning this monastery, see p. 201 fn.

religion, each a cubit high. On the four sides of the entrance-stupa they painted murals, to the east the *Realm of Sheer Joy*, to the south the *Potala Realm*, to the west the *Realm of Bliss*, and to the north the *Realm of the Glorious Copper-coloured Mountain*. The spaces between the painting were filled with images of the 1,000 buddhas and so on. For outside the monastery we built a stupa three fathoms across each side, and for the space of 49 days the monks of the upper and lower monasteries and various other places performed funeral ceremonies without a break.

Finally many of the faithful of the upper and lower monasteries and of other places begged me (to take over) and I remembered how my lord and father in religion had said: 'From early on you have been good at everything else, but when it has been a matter of teaching, you have not been at all attentive. From now on [33] do not be so hesitant as you have been before. Do not exclude these two monasteries from your compassion, but do benefit to sentient beings by means of both teaching and the practice of meditation. That will complete my intentions.'

So for the space of a month I gave instruction to about 70 pupils in the Heart Drop of the *Powerbolt-Being*. It was then that I came to Margom.

CHAPTER V. *As the final result of such perfection he served the cause of living beings.*

His teaching and practice are like a banner of victory,
Surmounted by the wish-granting gem of the profound Powerbolt Vehicle.
We make supplication to the blessed one who works for the perfect state of release,
Showering upon us like rain the coveted treasures of his profound doctrine.

As for the meaning of this, from that time on I had to do much which to others seemed to be benefitting sentient beings, although I was not ready for such work.

To begin with when I was a child I had acted as though I was teaching the doctrine, and on all occasions I used to wonder if I was not greatly different from other people. Although I lacked accomplishments, my hold on the doctrine certainly increased. On several occasions I wrestled with my own doubts, wondering how it would be. Then in my dreams I would be teaching many doctrines which I had not known before, and on several occasions I was looking after a lot of cattle. Then on another occasion many people were bowing down before me and taking my feet on their heads. On another occasion I flew through the air and obtained from the serpents the hidden meanings of *sūtras* and *tantras*, which I made known in songs.

[34] On another occasion I was making a bridge and the head-stones of the bridge and everything this way and that began to turn into the forms of the six letters of the *maṇi* prayer. I often dreamed on another occasion of a large prayer-flag on which were written the six *maṇi* syllables, and as it fluttered in the sky the sound of the prayer was heard.

Also once when I was preparing tea for my lord and father in religion at T'ha-kar, he said to me: 'I was thinking that I should transmit to you the responsibility of teaching together with the accompanying wisdom, and that the responsibility for the practice of meditation I would transmit to the master scholar *Buddha Spontaneous Achievement*, but as the result of various combinations of circumstances and of the manifestation of the effects of former vows and so on, I am transmitting the responsibility both for teaching and for meditation to you, so I ask you to think well of it.' It seems to be in accordance with this, that when I was giving instruction in the *Great Perfection* at *Zho-tshal* on one particular occasion, one night towards dawn a white man appeared to me and said: 'From today onwards it will be your turn to be herdsman,' and at once a lot of sheep and goats came round me in my dreams.

Also I saw portents and signs in the way in which the local gods of various places and villages acted with devotion and faith in my regard, meeting me and escorting me on my way.

Especially when the body of my lord and father in religion was passing to the elemental sphere there were many auspicious portents in my dreams. I dreamed the elder monks were replastering my room and several other such dreams. Without any manifest cause or reason thirteen hollyhocks sprang up in one place in the *Wa-la-wa* Gorge.[1] All these things seem to hang together, and so from the time I was very small I had no wish for anything except to practise meditation with all zeal.

(The translation of pp. 35-37 of the MS is omitted. Our lama receives offerings from the people of *Ban-tshang*. He gives them general consecrations. In the spring he gives instructions at T'ha-kar in *Release on the Path through the Intermediate State*. At the terminating feast he sings a song, which is not one of his best.)

[38] About that time I went to Margom, and at the monastery near the village below they paid me the greatest honour and the Abbot of *Ja-tshang* took the lead in this. I gave instructions in the *Universal Saviour* as well as a lot of consecrations and initiations to the monks and nuns on that occasion. Then the *lHo-ri* villagers invited me, and I went onto their fields where a lot of faithful believers including some learned men were gathered together from all over the place. I gave them the

[1] This is just near Yang-tsher.

'Special Instructions' of the *Great Compassionate Lord*, and as subsidiary teachings the *Ma-ṇi bka'-'bum* and whatever consecrations and initiations they wanted, and so I made them quite content. I gave general consecrations to the people of *lHo-ri* and of *Kyi*, and then I returned to Margom. When a day or two had passed, the monks of Margom said: 'These quarters are much too small, and they are very inconvenient for you, reverend lama, and for the images, books and reliquaries. In other ways they are unsuitable. We will put another storey on top.' They did not listen to my objections, and so by their building another storey, the images, shrines and books were well housed, and I had a small room on top, all very pleasant and agreeable.

'Now I shall not travel about much,' I thought, 'I have this pleasant well built room, and here I will practise my meditation undisturbed.' In this happy frame of mind I said:

> *O joy! In such a place as this*
> *to meditate! My heart is glad!*
> *The floor's made solid on the crags.* [39]
> *The walls are firm and strong above.*
> *The roof's been built in good design.*
> *A lofty stance where the mind is fresh!*
> *A solid stance whence views are clear!*
> *Most blessed and auspicious place*
> *Where happy circumstances are at their best!*
> *This place was consecrated by a former buddha.*
> *A place where hero-gods and attendant goddesses forgather,*
> *A place where meditation prospers.*
> *So fine a place! My heart is glad!*
> *To meditate! My mind delights!*
> *O King of Sages, Margom Sage,*
> *That I may keep to your tradition*
> *I beg you grant your blessing!*

Then the cave replied:

> *Just listen to me Yogin!*
> *I am made of rock and clay.*
> *Built some time, destroyed some time.*
> *Delight in me as much you may,*
> *I'm just a deceiving transient thing,*
> *So if you have no place but me,*
> *It's better not to trust in me.*

BIOGRAPHY OF LAMA RELIGIOUS PROTECTOR GLORIOUS AND GOOD

To this I replied: [40]

> *O you are but brute matter,*
> *Yet you explain our holy teachings!*
> *What wonder then is here!*
> *My resting-place is of this kind:*
> *The Voidness of the elemental sphere*
> *Such is the turret of my house.*
> *Concentration never wavering*
> *Such is the nature of my couch.*
> *A sage of self-manifesting knowledge*
> *Wears as robes* Means and Wisdom Two-in-One[1]
> *Decked with the jewelry of various states of trance,*
> *As entourage he has the six self-freed sense-perceptions.*
> *The treasures he enjoys inexhaustibly are the* Three Buddha Bodies.
> *A yogin, thus equipped, is happy.*

The cave replied:

> *This is just what I was hoping.*
> *It's grand indeed if things are so.*
> *I beg you please excuse my chatter.*

I passed the winter there and my religious practice benefitted greatly. At the end of winter I went to T'ha-kar and gave them instruction in the (*Great Symbol* work referred to as the) *Fiver*. Also I gave them whatever other instructions they wanted, the *Great Perfection,* the *Universal Saviour* and so on. At the feast of offerings that terminated this event, I recited these verses:

[41] *I bow at the feet of my lama, prince of two-footed creatures,*
Who unites in his person the knowledge and love of the buddhas of past, present and future,
Cutting through the tangle of doubts in my mind
With the sword of the knowledge of the vanity of all things.

Listen worthy people, gathered here together.
Being an unreligious fellow of no real importance,
I have no ambition for the honour you do me,
But you urge me so strongly and I would not counter your words,
So I offer with pure intention these odd verses. Please listen!

[1] Concerning these terms, see the Introduction, p. 26 and 30.

*For this present time you have gained the blessings of a good (human) frame, so hard
   to obtain.*[1]
*Even if you cannot achieve buddhahood in this one single life,
Would it not be good to turn your thoughts to religion?
Be mindful that the time of death is uncertain, for this fact is sure!*

*The root of suffering is the demon of selfishness.
If you wish to achieve the great reality of personal happiness,
Would it not be good to keep thoughts free of wantings
And at all costs to cleave to contentment of soul?*

*The various joys and sorrows that we suffer now
Are the fruits of good and evil amassed from former lives.
Would it not be good if you acted so as to accept (the good) and reject (the evil),
Convinced that the law of cause and effect cannot be cheated.*

[42] *Present sufferings seem intolerable enough.
If you should experience the sufferings of evil states of rebirth,
Consider how long you would stay there and how intolerable that would be.
Would it not be good to make effort so as not to be born there?*

*The source of all virtues is the code of monastic rule.
If you wish to reach the true way of liberty and release,
Would it not be good to cleave in your soul to the realization of the vanities of life,
Possessing the wisdom that distinguishes defect from virtue and emergence from calm?*[2]

*These sentient beings of the threefold sphere of existence
Have all been our kind parents (some time or another) throughout beginningless time.
Would it not be good to concentrate on supreme enlightenment
So as to gain buddhahood for the sake of these mothers?*[3]

The Process of Emanation — *translucent with divinities who are the ambrosial
   contents of the heavenly vessel,
The* Process of Realization — *unchanging as the elemental sphere,
Their* Coalescence — *self-nature spontaneously realized,
Would it not be good if you concentrated on these three which are the supreme
   tantric way?*[4]

---

[1] Concerning the blessings of a good human body, see the Introduction, pp. 18–19.
[2] Concerning the terms 'emergence and calm', see p. 20.
[3] As for all creatures having been our mothers, see p. 18.
[4] Concerning these two 'processes' and their 'coalescence', see p. 26.

Insight — *cutting off at the roots both the physical world and the metaphysical*,
Concentration — *holding unwavering to its objective*,
Results — *free of hoping and fearing, of preventing and effecting*,
Would it not be good to gaze on these three, for they are the countenance of things as they ultimately are?

Away with all the activities of this ordinary life!
[43] *However things appear, consider all as unreal illusion.*
Whatever occurs, commit it in thought to your lama's compassion.
Would it not be good if one were well practised in so impartial and so pure a disposition?

O Lord and Lama, I present this song as an offering.
O guests from the physical and metaphysical spheres,
  relish this sacrificial offering of sounds!
O Defenders of Religion, remove adverse circumstances!
Make circumstances propitious, O Refuge of All Joy.[1]

I stayed in T'ha-kar for the summer, and at the end of this season went to Margom, where I gave thorough instruction to those staying in the monastery in the *Universal Saviour* and the *Blue Perfecter of Thought*. At the board of offerings of the festival which closed this session, I recited the verses:

'Powerbolt-Holder, *in form fourfold, fivefold in wisdom*' etc.

In the autumn a lot of nomads came to visit me, and I made them contented by giving them whatever consecrations and initiations they wanted. Using the large quantities of butter which resulted from this, I sponsored a thousand performances of the rite of the *All-Knowing*. During the winter I remained in strict retreat and my religious practice prospered greatly.

In the spring I gave instructions in the 'Six Doctrines' to a large number of listeners, but chiefly to those resident in the monastery. At the board of offerings of the festival closing this session, I recited some verses about absorbing the 'Six Doctrines' reduced to their essentials.

Then I went to T'ha-kar, and as we had so much barley that harvest, I sponsored a thousand performances of ritual. At the end of winter I gave instruction in the *One Mother Gentle and Violent*, and when that was over I wondered whether to go and visit the precious image of Buddha the Prince at Kyirong. So I sought a decision (by prognosis) before the *Precious Ones*, asking whether to do or not do as I wished,

[1] *Refuge of All Joy* (*Kun-dga'-skyabs*) is the name of the local god of Margom.

and it was not granted. That summer I stayed in T'ha-kar, [44] and made the residents of the monastery and a large number of the faithful who came from all quarters, contented with consecrations, instructions, initiations and so on. At the turn of autumn I again sought a decision (by prognosis) whether I should carry out my wishes or not in the matter of visiting the 'Self-Moving Image'.[1] I lay down to sleep and at break of day a bodiless voice said:

> By the grace of the Three Precious Ones who are our Refuge,
> By the grace of the unchanging absolute truth,
> By the power of the uncheatable law of cause and effect,
> Blessings on the performance of your religious intention!

Hearing this, I reflected that this matter would probably work out well now, so at the end of autumn I set out. I left together with more than 200 pilgrims from the districts of *Nang-khong* and *Ban-tshang*. When we first set out, we did not give much thought to butter for the lamps, but through the compassion of the *Precious Ones* many people gave us gold, copper, cloth and so on on the way through *Phal, rTar, Ting-khyu, Po-ldad* and other places. On the far side of the *Bin-du* Pass representatives of our great benefactors Kunga and his brother, as well as many other nomads, all gave us presents. Then at *mTsho-bar* the two chief bursars of the people of Mustang with a host of officials and many servants, all gave us gold, cotton cloth, silk, butter *etcetera*. Putting this together, we amassed fifteen loads of butter to offer in the butter-lamps, and in the presence of the Precious Prince we offered prayers on a vast scale.

On the way back from Kyirong up to the crossing of the *rDzong-kha* Pass we received all kinds of good things in the various villages, and I distributed sacraments to many faithful believers and foodstuffs to the poor and needy.

[45] The local governor too showed a very happy disposition towards us and insisted that we must come again, so I promised to do so. On this side of the pass and onwards on our journey many other important nomads gave us gold, butter, curds, cheese and so on, and I distributed sacraments and blessings here and there. In particular the Abbot of *dBu-legs* called us to his monastery in a very cordial way, and all of us, teachers and disciples, received tea, meat, butter and other things. In short there were no difficulties on this journey and all circumstances were entirely favourable. In addition we were able to make circumstances comfortable for all the (other) pilgrims, and so we reached Dolpo.

I spent the winter in T'ha-kar and my religious practice went well. In spring I gave as general instructions the 'Special Instructions' of the *Great Compassionate*

---
[1] See p. 105.

Lord together with the *Ma-ṇi bka'-'bum*, and as private instructions I gave everyone whatever consecrations, instructions and initiations they wanted, so contenting them all. I went to Margom and gave them instructions in the 'Six Doctrines' of Nāropa, and then having inaugurated the recitation of the buddha-names, I spent one month in retreat. Thereafter I gave consecrations, instructions, initiations and the rest to some wise yogins who had come from all over the place and to many other faithful believers, making them all well content. I spent the winter there, and returned in the spring to T'ha-kar, where I gave to a large number of disciples the *Release on the Path through the Intermediary State*, the *Hermit Teachings* in their three parts, and also a lot of consecrations. I had started instructions in the *One Mother Gentle and Violent*, when the people of *Ban-tshang* became so insistent, that I went and gave instructions to ninety odd pupils at the *Ting-khyu* Hermitage in the *Self-Release of the Four Evil Ones* as far as the *Gentle and Violent*. On my way over the mountains I gave general consecrations in *Phal*, *rTar*, *Ting-khyu* and *dGon-chung*, and I made everyone contented by giving them whatever consecrations and initiations they wanted.

About that time the clan-leaders of *Khang-dkar* were quarrelling, and the King of *Mon*[1] kept on sending word that I should come and act as witness at the reconciliation that he and his ministers were arranging. [46] After a whole succession of such messages from Lo, the Abbot *Lion of Merit* came with some monk-attendants, and as a result of this I returned to T'ha-kar and then set out for *dGe-lung*. On the way I gave sacraments to several faithful believers in Tsharka, and many people gave me small presents, meat, butter and other things. So I made the journey there. The *Khang-dkar* leaders came to meet me and led me in procession to *dGe-lung*. I taught in the monastery there to the monks and others, giving them the instructions in the *Innate Yoga of the Great Symbol*. The abbot and Chief *Sri-dar* himself were present. The leaders were all reconciliated, and I made everyone content in one way and another by giving them whatever consecrations and initiations they wanted.

The chiefs, who were related as cousins, said: 'Now the reason for your coming here is this. Since there is not one of us, leaders and servants, householders and monks, who is not devout, we all want to be able to receive the sacraments of religion and we need a monastery for those who (as monks) become the living witnesses of the doctrine. Especially in the case of the womenfolk, who are wont to be living witnesses of worldly matters, but not of religious activities, you must please give a lot of them the tonsure and establish a nunnery.' 'If matters are like this,' I said, 'it is

---

[1] *Mon* in Dolpo usage refers to the non-Tibetan speaking areas to the west and south of Dolpo. 'The King of *Mon*' refers therefore in local Dolpo usage to the King of Jumla, whose power in these areas seemed to have been unopposed. It is interesting that at this time he should have extended his control into Lo, where the clan-leaders of *Khang-dkar* were still giving trouble. See above, pp. 88–92.

very good that I have come. I beg you to lay out the meditation huts and all the rest.'

This was done properly while I was away visiting Upper Lo. For at that time the ruler and his family sent word from Mustang that I should go there. Since a whole procession of messengers came and finally the ruler's own personal representative, I had to go up there. I was met by my benefactor Kunga and others, by the chief bursars and by the inmates of the *Ngor-pa* monastery, and we went in procession to the palace. The ruler and his people said: 'The reason for you coming here is this. We want ablutions, [47] consecrations, initiations and all the rest.' I submitted that it would be suitable to give ablutions, but not to perform consecrations, initiations and the rest. However they would not listen to me. So first I gave them the ablution of the *Destroyer* and others, then the consecration of the *Guru Red Fury*, the *Buddha Boundless Life* and many other different ones. Thus I did all they wanted. Furthermore I gave consecrations and sacraments to a large number of faithful believers including special representatives designated by the chiefs. I gave a general consecration in Mustang, and to my benefactor Kunga and many other faithful believers I gave whatever consecrations, initiations and blessings they wanted, so they were all well content. A lot of evil-doers came to renounce every evil they had done.

Then an urgent message came from Tsarang from the chief and his ministers that I should go there. Following upon this a special representative also came, so I set out with an escort of rows of horses. A procession came out to meet me from Tsarang and we went up to the fort. The governor said: 'We want consecrations, initiations and so on.' Although I submitted that there were too many people, they would not listen, so I gave to the governor and his ministers the consecrations of the *Universal Saviour*, the *Lord of the Cemetery*, the *Yellow Protector* and so on. To the officials I gave whatever consecrations or initiations they wanted, and for the ordinary people I gave a general consecration with blessings and sacraments and so on, and everyone was contented.

Then I went with an escort of a lot of horsemen to *dGa'-mi*, where I performed a general consecration twice, and then went to the monastery, where I stayed a few days, giving consecrations, initiations and so on to the brothers who were the local lords and other important representatives, as well as to officials and their attendants, to householders and monks, to the chief and his son from the Red Crag, and to faithful believers gathered from all around. [48] So I made them happy in different ways. I received some into the religious life and I consecrated others as 'virtuous adherers', so many people entered the door of religion. Many girls too took the tonsure and entered religious life. I set up monasteries and nunneries in various places, establishing monastic discipline with its ordering of technical matters. Having thus placed them upon an isle of salvation, I returned to *dGe-lung*.

BIOGRAPHY OF LAMA RELIGIOUS PROTECTOR GLORIOUS AND GOOD 155

There had been no lama at the monastery there, so I raised the distinguished teacher *Lion of Merit* to the chair. In their gatherings they had no meat or *chang*, and with monastic discipline such as this, I placed them too on an isle of salvation. I gave gesture-presents of small things to the ruling brothers first of all, and then to those of official rank, while to all the others I gave tea-ceremonies, distributions of cloth, all performed very nicely. Many evil-doers took vows not to take life and gave up such evils as hunting, and we made reserves (where animals might not be killed) in the mountains around. In short up to this present day the very name of hunting and the like is unknown in that district.

At that time I received material goods on a very large scale from the district of Lo, from the ruler, the governors, the lamas and monks in the first place, from religious communities, lay communities and from all the faithful. (In return) I gave tea-ceremonies and distributions of gifts to the three main monasteries of Lo itself (the city of Mustang) as well as religious communities of all kinds. Thus the things which were given to me were never put to a wrong purpose. Such was our way, and we shall write clearly of this below. Then they said that I must stay there the winter and give them religious teachings. I put the matter (for prognosis) to the *Three Precious Ones*, but an answer was not granted for the signs in my dreams were confused. So I explained the pro's and con's of the matter to them, and then came back to Dolpo. From the village of *dGon-chung* onwards the leaders and people of *Ban-tshang*, householders and religious, all came to meet me, and so I reached T'ha-kar. I passed the winter there [49] and stayed in retreat. Then I had a serious disease of the tongue, and feeling unhappy about this, I thought I should go to Margom.

(The translation of MS page 49 line 3 to page 50 line 15 is omitted. One of our lama's benefactors asks for religious advice in an easy style and he receives a set of didactic verses.)

Then I came to Margom, but after a few days I thought: 'Since this disease has afflicted my tongue, it is not likely I shall be of any use to others. So as I do not count on living very long, it would be best to go to some solitary place in order to wait for death.' So I went to the 'Isle of Enlightenment' at *Ze-phug* and stayed there alone. My religious practice was prospering in really good form, when one day the monk *Ocean of Intellect* came along and said:

'Those who are close in our affection, those who are perspicacious [51] and those who effect cures are agreed that the water of this place affects the blood, and as a result you will not get better. So at all costs you must go somewhere where the water is good.'

I thought to myself: 'It would be good to stay here awhile, but so that they do not take offence, I had better seek a decision with the *Three Precious Ones*.' I did this, and the answer came that it would be best if I went to *Char-chab*. So I went there without anyone knowing. While I was spending a few days there, I thought: 'Now I shall not remain (in the world) for long and it will be quite alright to die, but how if I who have abandoned everything were to disgrace the Ka-gyü Order by leaving wealth behind me.' So I sent for some artists and ordered some painted scrolls to be made. Then at the turn of autumn I went to my monastery and stayed in strict retreat. As I wanted to die in the course of this winter, I maintained a vow of silence. At the end of winter there were no signs or indications of my getting any better, but I had no thought of ending my retreat, and this was by the compassion of the *Precious Ones*. I stayed there rejoicing that I was thus cleansing away sin and benefiting my religious practice in a good way.

Then in summer I went to *Phyi-mo*, where I was afflicted with a kind of 'watersickness' which had the form of cramp. I myself did not make such a serious matter of it, but my attendants would not listen to me, so I interrupted my retreat. Thinking that I should wander over the mountains alone in order to get the right balance of water, I set out. But they ran after me, and as they would not listen to me, about twelve of them went across the mountains with me in the direction of *Khung*. At the turn of autumn I returned to the monastery, and while I was there, the people of *Ban-tshang* provoked a lot of discussion. 'We are very glad you are better,' they said, 'now you must come to T'ha-kar.' 'I am not very well,' I replied, [52] 'and I cannot get there now, so do not be offended.' But the matter was raised again and they would not listen (to my objections). 'Last year the nomads did violence to the people of *Ban-tshang*, and as reprisals we have decided to beat up the nomad traders,' they said, '(moreover) there are now a lot of hunters who use the method of firing the undergrowth.'

Hearing this, I thought to myself: 'If I go there, there is a good chance of stopping this hunting, and in particular if they beat up the nomads, many people will be landed in difficulty. If I can prevail upon them, it seems better that I go.'

I put the matter clearly to them, and they said: 'As for the hunting, if you come, holy lama, they will be content to give it up. But as for the nomads, last year's fight caused all sorts of animosities and no one has forgotten them. If you come up there, we will refer the matter to you then.'

'If it is like that,' I replied, 'I may come up there, but there will be nothing but shame for both you and for me, so please excuse me.' 'Generally speaking, it would be so,' they said, 'but we beg you to come now in any case, most holy lama. We will give up hunting in *Ban-tshang* for this year and we will promise to do no harm to traders.' As a result of this, I went there and saw all the people of *Ban-tshang*. They carried out everything just as they had promised and everyone was happy.

That winter I stayed in retreat, and in the spring I gave instruction in the *Great Perfection* work *The Heart-Drop of the Powerbolt-Being*. In the summer I went to Margom, where I gave the complete initiations and instructions in the whole cycle of the *Hermit Teachings* to some qualified monks, led by two lamas, and to yogins who had come from all around, to the inmates of the monastery and many other pupils.

[53] In the winter I went to T'ha-kar and stayed in complete seclusion. When that was over I returned to Margom. While I was giving instructions to a lot of disciples in the *Innate Yoga*, a messenger came from the north, sent by the ruler (of Mustang) and his wife, saying that I must go there. 'Although last year you promised that you would come to Lo again, you have not been pleased to come. Now you really must come,' they said. Their message was very urgent, and according to reports I heard, it was said that if I did not go there, they would come to Dolpo. For this reason I promised to go. A little later their representative arrived with horses and baggage yaks, and we set off northwards. On the way I made the people of Dolpo and the nomads contented with general consecrations and whatever else they wanted. The ruler and his ministers, all the five heads of monasteries and others came out to meet me from the 'Victorious Divine Peak' (*rNam-rgyal lha-rtse*) and we went in procession to the palace. From the time I arrived for the space of a whole month I gave the ruler and whomever represented him a major consecration ceremony every day, two lesser ones every day and three small special initiations and various other things every day. This went on continuously. Also I gave him instructions in the *One Mother* and in technical matters. Thus I fulfilled his wishes. In addition I gave instruction to a lot of yogins who had gathered from all around, in the *Innate Yoga* and whatever else they wanted. To the many monks who were in the capital and to a large number of layfolk, both men and women, who had gathered together from all directions, the people from *'Phan-byi*, I gave consecrations, textual initiations, special initiations, blessings and the rest, making them all content in different ways. As well as giving tea-ceremonies at the five main monasteries, I was doing things in all kinds of ways. Then I returned to T'ha-kar.

(The translation of pages 54 to 57 line 13 is omitted. It refers to the ceremonies and initiations which he now gives at T'ha-kar and Margom.)

At that time there came some people from the three villages of *Phod*, *Bi-cher* and *Ku*, who said: 'Since last year we have asked you again and again, now at all costs you must come to the "Isle of Gems".' So I went there, and to the people of the three villages and to many others who had gathered from all around I gave as general teaching, instructions in the *Great Symbol* work called the *Fiver*, and as special teaching, the *One Mother Gentle and Violent* and the *Single Flavour*, and the *Great Perfection* work *Unobstructed Intentions*. I gave a general consecration for *Ku* and *Phod* together, and apart from this I made everyone contented with consecrations, initiations and whatever they wanted. They said to me speaking for all three villages: 'Generally speaking we have nothing else here in Dolpo, and so we are very fortunate when good lamas come duly to see us. You especially [58] are working everywhere for the good of living beings, but we who live in these distant parts and who are getting old cannot come to see you. In particular this "Isle of Gems" is a place that was consecrated by an earlier lama, but now there is no lama in charge. As a result of this the very many wild deer that we have here are being killed by evil men. We beg you at all costs to establish a community.' They insisted on this with such urgency, that I promised to do something to suit the place.

Then some important people of Saldang arrived, saying: 'Although we have asked you again and again since last year, you have not been pleased (to come). This place of Shey is a very special place, not like others. It is a place much visited and blessed by former lamas. At all events you must come this time on your way.' I would not give way to them, but they were so insistent, that I went to Shey. On the way I gave a general consecration to the people of *Bi-cher*, and in particular cases I contented people with whatever they wanted. I reached Shey, where I stayed for the space of eight days, contenting everyone, the Saldang people and also a lot of pilgrims, with whatever consecrations and initiations they wanted, summaries of instructions in religious practice and so on. Then some important people of Karang arrived saying: 'In accordance with the request which we have already made to you previously at *Gung-bu* and the "Isle of Gems", you must promise to come and stay with us at Karang and *sPang-phu*, at best for one month, or if not that then for twenty days, but at the very least for a half month.' As they would not listen to my protests, I said: 'As you will not listen to me at all, there is no help for me but to come once. But I have not time to stay so long, so do not be offended.' So on the way I went to Karang and *sPang-phu*. [59] I stayed there seven days and gave them a general consecration with a ceremony performed seven times, and in special cases I contented them with whatever they wanted. At the same time taking into account that I had already made a promise to the people of the Lower Valley, I spent three days up at *Kyi*, making them happy with a general consecration.

At Shey, *gSer-phug, dPal-sdings*, these (three) religious communities as well as at various other places I provided good sacrificial offerings, general presentations, tea-ceremonies and so on. But on this whole occasion there was so much confusion with so many people. Between the villages a lot of horsemen would come and meet me and there were so many presents, that as a result of all this I became very weary and so quickly returned to my own monastery. While I was spending a few days there the son of Squire Norbu was anxious to apply himself to religion and he said he wanted a song to spur him on. So I wrote this:

Knower of past, present and future, your compassion
Guides on the way such people as us.
At your feet, O Yogin Lord of Religion,
In devotion we make supplication.

Now listen, you who would practise religion.
When you obtain the advantages, so hard to obtain, (of a well-endowed human body)
It is best to accumulate merit
By practising religion and so put all to good use.

The results of good and evil actions
Cannot be cheated, however small.
[60] Since they ripen into joy and misery,
Act so as to accept (the one) and reject (the other).

Drinking the hot salty broth
Of desirable things, your thirst will never be sated.
Cut off this attachment to desirable things!
Put an end to the conceits of learning!

Turning present advantages to no account,
Useless are the activities of everyday life.
If your thoughts rest on them, they are obstructions,
So throw behind you the false values that pertain to this life!

People of these evil degenerate times
Are companions ill-suited to religion.
They are a cause of obscurations and of the three basic evils,[1]
So avoid association with such evil friends!

Fame and the rest of the eight worldly concepts
Are all a cause for future misery.
So always take the antidote,
Do what accords with religion!

[1] Concerning these basic evils, see the Introduction, p. 22.

*If you think of pleasures and ease
Now that you are doing your studies,
You will ever (hereafter) be hungry
From famine of attainments and doctrine.*

[61] *Wine and women, these two
Are the robbers who steal away your good conduct.
Keeping far off from loved ones like poison
Let this be your protective armour!*

*The best way to good rebirths and salvation
Is purity of personal conduct.
So never demean it. Hold to it
As dearly as the apple of your eye!*

*When you are carried along by the demon of Ease,
It is impossible to achieve anything at all.
Give up the idea there will be time later on
And arouse your effort just now!*

*In short — our holy religion
Never deceives, that's certain.
So with staunch effort of body, speech and mind
Bring your studies to completion!*

*Usually a clever man's attainments
Follow in the tracks of his effort.
So abandon pleasures and ease
And work with patient determination!*

[62] *Those worthy of everyone's regard
Are men of good education.
But this comes about by hard work,
So let your gaze be directed upwards!*

*Our Teacher and the other buddhas,
All the former conquering ones,
Were ordinary folk to begin with.
If you practise as in their stories,
You too will be like them.*

Faithful son, to you I offer
With thoughts full of affection
This little spur to effort.
Do not forget it. Keep it well in mind!

While I was spending a few days there, the people of *Ban-tshang* invited me, so I went to T'ha-kar and met the members of the community and all the lay and religious people of *Ban-tshang*. I spent the winter there and remained in retreat, so that my religious practice prospered greatly. In the spring I explained a large number of religious works, *Release on the Path through the Intermediate State* and other texts, and I gave in full the consecrations and initiations of the *Universal Saviour* as well as other such works.

At the end of winter I went to *Zho-tshal* and sent for the artists. On the way back I commissioned the entrance-stupa by the Do-ra bridge. After that the Chief Olo came from Lo with a large following, [63] and I fulfilled all their wishes with consecrations, initiations and so on. For the space of more than a month I gave consecrations, special initiations and so on, whatever would be of benefit to different people. Meanwhile his general following completed the work of (collecting) the 'gifts of welcome'. Then most of them went back to Lo. The Chief himself with about ten attendants went with our lay and religious people to *Khung*, where I gave to a whole host of people the special instructions of the *Great Compassionate Lord*. Most important of all I performed for the special intention of the Chief the fierce rite of self-sacrifice, and so his health improved and the signs (of recovery) were not bad. At that time the Chief Olo and his ministers said they wanted a song that would give advice in actions and their effects and in rejecting (evil) and accepting (good), so I sang them this:

Salutation to our Teacher!
Precious source of all blessings!
O Lama of Margom! O wish-granting gem!
Inseparable from you, from the core of my heart I beseech you.
With your compassion, so limitless, so vast, I beg you protect us!

Now listen my Lords, Ruler and Ministers!
Your command to me is so weighty,
That wretched though I be, I would offer these few verses of chatter.
It is best you should be attentive and keep these matters in mind.

You have obtained well-endowed human bodies, that good support (for the religious life), which is so hard to obtain.
[64] Such high rank and noble birth, so worthy of everyone's regard,
Are gained from the stocks of merit accumulated in former lives.
For this reason it will be best if you always strive to do good.

Death lies before all embodied creatures
And nothing avails then except holy religion.
All the pleasures and fame of this life
Are like dreams. It is best to renounce their pursuit.

Food, wealth, possessions, relatives, servants,
Clinging to these, you are like an elephant sinking in mud.
Sinking in the mud of phenomenal things is the cause of all misery.
If you want release, it would be best to exert yourselves in religion.

Things accumulated, things guarded, things lost, are all conducive to misery.
As final effect, they cause your rebirth in the haunts of tormented spirits.
If you abandon the pursuit of possessions
And cleave to contentment of soul, that will be best.

Now you bring both yourselves and others in misery.
As final effect you will roast and burn in the places of hell.
If you give up the idea of subduing sentient beings
And subdue the enemy of obscurations and wrath, that will be best.

To be the leader of many is of the very nature of misery.
However much you look after them, discontented they deceive you one day.
[65] So avoid the responsibility for helpers and servants.
To look after your own affairs is the best.

The best of riches are the seven noble gems (of virtue).
The best of helpers is your friend 'self-born knowledge'.
If you always cleave inseparably to such inexhaustible riches and to so foe-free a helper, that will be the very best.

The chief of enemies is the demon of selfishness
For he destroys all happiness in this world and the next.
He continually impels your actions towards nothing but misery.
If you overcome this enemy of self-interest, that will be the very best.

How ever much you strive for the good things of this life,
Of gaining them there's no certainty, and if you gain them you're not contented.
Like adding wood to fire, even so lust increases.
It is best to abandon this salty water which is a cause for (fresh) desire.

An evil man gives no thought to death's approach.
For advantages in this life he commits evils of all kinds.
He is a fool who acts in such a way.
If you raise your thoughts to enlightenment, that is best.

The miseries of hell, of tormented spirits and of animals,
If you consider rightly, are really hard to bear.
Yet such are the results of evil conduct.
[66] It's best to make effort in religion if you want release.

Brahmā, Indra and the Universal Monarch,
Though overwhelmed with happiness and honoured by all,
At some time must taste the miseries of hell, we are told.
So it is best to exert yourselves in holy religion.

If you think rightly, for high and low alike
There is no way left us except holy religion.
'I will do it tomorrow, the day after, some time.'
It's best to arouse your effort and renounce such easy-going ways.

The Three Precious Ones are the refuge
In which you may trust and never be deceived.
Since you know what trust and confidence achieve,
Throughout day and night and all the six periods it is best to go to them for refuge.

This vessel with its exilir,[1] appearing as it does in such varied forms,
Abides from all eternity as the circle of phenomenal existence (in the relationship) of support and supported.
By that sure knowledge which knows vessel and elixir as divine,
If you purify your own disposition and the spheres (of manifestation) that is best.

From all eternity one's own mind is the motionless Absolute Body,
Transcending the realms of distinguishing marks to the state where subject and object are one.

[1] Concerning the 'vessel and its elixir', see the Introduction, p. 20.

*Reposing in unaffected 'freshness', you see things 'face to face'.
To keep attentively and thoughtfully to this, is really the very best.*

[67] *Thus whatever merits you have gained
And all merits accumulated in past, present and future besides,
If you set your seal on these as unspecified blessings
For the general benefit of all beings who are (in effect) your mothers, this will be best.*

*Now I, the worthless fellow of the Margom Crag
Offer this little song of the twenty-one best things
In order to fulfil the intentions of my Lord and his Ministers.
By the merit (of its recital) may all sentient beings act as these words advise!*

At that time as I went back to my place of meditation, the Chief said: 'In general there is no substance in worldly activities. In particular my brother stays on in occupation of the throne and that is enough. And now this illness too has the appearance of doing me a really serious turn. This is already well known to you, holy lama. Now for this latter part of my life I should perform some religious meditation. In particular this winter I will make a strict retreat.'
'I beg you to do just that,' I replied, 'for the others it will be all right if they do as suits their intentions, but I beg you to make at all costs a strict retreat of three months at best, if not two, or at the very least one month. Now your health seems to be better. But it will not be difficult for this to go in reverse. Now you must bring this matter to its final conclusion.' While we were making preparations for this, two messengers were sent from Lo by the great lady herself with the message: 'The news from the *Mon* side is not pleasant, so at all costs you must come here now for this once.'
As a result of this he had to leave in a hurry, [68] and meanwhile I said to him: 'Now a really serious thing has happened. What can have caused this, I don't know. To beg you to stay would be impossibly difficult for you. But as soon as you arrive home, do not meet anyone. I beg you at all costs to spend a month or two in strict retreat. Otherwise there is danger of things getting bad again.' So the Chief and his attendants returned to Lo.

A few days later some important villagers came from Tarap and said: 'As you promised us earlier last year, at all costs you must come to Tarap this year.' As they would not listen to my protests, I promised to go. I set out at the beginning of autumn and all along the way, at Tiling, at Saldang and through Upper Nam, I received all kinds of things as presents, and I contented everyone with consecrations and sacraments. When I arrived in Tarap where there were whole series of formal meetings with all the lay and religious folk at the monasteries and other places, the lay and religious leaders said to me: 'You must give us the consecrations, instructions and initiations so as to make up two whole treatises.'

'It is all right for me to give you this now,' I said, 'but what with your autumn trade with the nomads and the valley-men's fair, you will be so busy that you will not have time to listen. As I am going back home for the winter, this time it wont do to have the instructions as well. I will give you whatever consecrations you want as this will not conflict with your lack of time.' There were a lot of nomads, Central Tibetans and valley-men there, and I contented everyone in different ways, giving general consecrations at Tak-kyu, Do and other places,[1] and in special cases giving consecrations, special initiations, the *maṇi* initiation and other sacraments, blessings and so on, in fact whatever each person wanted in the way of religion. I received all sorts of things (as presents), and for the religious communities in general I performed ceremonies in accordance with the customs of the region, and in special cases [69] I gave a dram of gold and good offerings to each of the monks, and to the laymen a measure of salt and of barley. The poor people I made contented with food and drink and so on. Then they said: 'If only you would stay over the winter, and at the end of winter give us a set of instructions.' When I pointed out the arguments for and against this, they said: 'If you really go now, you must promise that when we invite you later on, you will come whatever happens.' 'Although I promise that,' I said, 'not only is the time of our death uncertain, but in a special way a yogin's promise is like a dream. But do as you say.' When I came away a large number of people accompanied me as far as the top of the pass. We shed a lot of tears, and I felt such unbounded feelings of affection, that I composed some auspicious verses to bring blessings on the people of Tarap in general and on the people who were gathered there in particular. The opening words were:

Lama of Margom, father most wise, king of religion
By the power of your wisdom and love which I have by direct transmission, etc.

Then as I came on my way I made people content at *dGon-chung, Ting-khyu* and *Phal-rTar* with general consecrations and so on. So I reached T'ha-kar, where I spent the winter. At the end of winter I gave instruction in the *Release on the Path through the Intermediate State* to the inmates of the monastery together with a large number of people of *Ban-tshang*, both lay and religious. I inaugurated a ceremony. Then I went to Margom, and having inaugurated a ceremony there, I gave instruction

[1] Tak-kyu (spelt in our texts both as *rTag-rgyus* and *rTag-kyus*) is a hamlet at the northern end of Tarap. I must amend my earlier spelling 'Tok-khyu' (*Himalayan Pilgrimage*, p. 154). The *Survey of India* spelling 'Atāli' seems to have no justification. Do (*mDo*) is the largest village in Tarap, marked as Tarapgāon on *Survey of India* maps.

in the *Great Perfection* work *Unobstructed Intentions*. At that time a succession of messengers came from Lo, and since I heard from them that times were very bad just then and that all sentient beings were in misery, [70] I asked the *Precious Ones* for a decision of the matter, and as a result of the answer I received, I set out for Lo. I went to *dGa'-bar*, the place that was blessed by the Precious Teacher of Urgyan, and for about a month, working together with the people of this middle territory, I arranged the clearing and exchange of property (which had been displaced in the disturbances) between Upper and Lower (Lo). I started and kept going instruction in the *Rite of Self-Sacrifice*, and between whiles I offered advice to the leading men of Upper and Lower Lo. Although there were great disputes at the beginning, the guardian-goddess of *dGa'-bar* seemed to have a very powerful effect and the local gods of Lo appeared to produce favourable influences, so although there was great disagreement, the ruler first gathered together there all the leading men of Upper, Lower and Central Lo, and though they met in this way, not one spoke a single ill word to another, chatting and laughing in a boisterous manner, they were all very happy together and a basis for agreement was established. The fact that things have so remained up to the present day and that everyone is so happy there, manifestly comes through the compassion of the *Precious Ones* who never deceive. Although I had to go on this occasion to Tsarang in Upper Lo, to *dGa'-mi*, *dGe-lung* and *Se-rib*, I did not stay more than one or two days (in each place), I contented people generally with general public consecrations, and the leading people with whatever consecrations and special initiations they wanted, or at the very least blessings and sacraments and so on, so fulfilling their wishes in various ways. Many evil men too gave up for ever the evils of hunting and so on, and many people came taking one vow or two vows and so on.

[71] Furthermore I received on this occasion gifts of all kinds, and in various places I did (return-)services, a benefaction for the temple of the Great Sage of Mustang, a benefaction for the assembly hall at Tsarang, benefactions for meditation and ceremonies at *dGa'-mi*, *dGe-lung* and *Se-rib*, and furthermore I offered tea-ceremonies to the religious communities throughout all Upper and Lower Lo. Even down to the very beggars I satisfied the wants of each one.

Then taking into account that our benefactor *'Phan-byi* had previously sent a whole series of messengers, saying that I must come to the north, and yet I had not gone there, on my way back now I went to *Gro-shod*. I made the nomads along the way happy with sacraments and blessings and so on. When I reached the place where the benefactor *'Phan-byi* was staying, he said to me: 'This year I have reached one of my unlucky years. That southerner[1] *Great Teacher* cast lots for me

---

[1] 'Southerner' (*lho-pa*) means here a man from the southern valleys, *viz.* those south of Dolpo. In this context *lho* (south) corresponds with *Mon*. See p. 109.

on a chance occasion, and I am wondering if I shall die. Now that I have you here as my guest, you must stay at all events for several days, at the least for three.' He added: 'I wonder if you would give sacraments to the many people here, especially to the old folk who cannot travel.'

'I have been such a long time in Lo,' I replied, 'that I have no time to stay as long as that. But whatever consecrations you have in mind, I will give you in the course of one day and one night.' Following upon this we prepared the offerings, and by dawn I completed *Boundless Life*, *Jetarī*, also three general consecrations, as well as some nine consecrations and special initiations. The next day as the sun was touching the mountains, we set out on our way. [72] In a short time we reached our monastery.

After a few days the Chief Olo with his attendants arrived from Lo. 'Now last year you had recovered your health,' I said, 'and because of her ladyship things went wrong. Now I can do you no service in this matter.'

'I have not come now hoping for help in this. Now by your compassion, holy lama, my elder brother has taken over the throne and is governor. I have come here with the intention of doing a really good retreat for this last part of my life and with the intention of dying here.'

'If matters are so,' I said, 'it is all right to do that,' and so he went to the 'Isle of Enlightenment' at Margom.

At the same time five lamas including the two chief teachers from *Ja-tshang*, and also a large number of scholars who had gathered from all around, came and said they wanted the text of the *Way and its Fruits*, so because of this I gave instruction in the *Way and its Fruits* that winter.

In the spring the Chief (Olo) lost his hold on life, and I performed his last rites properly so as to fulfil his intentions.

In the summer a messenger came saying that the Chief *Aim-Winner Powerbolt* with a large number of attendants would be coming from Tsarang. I thought to myself: 'If they came here, it would be pleasant for me, but there is the risk that with so large a number of followers, food will be short for our people.' So I went there and met them at *Gang-tsher*, where I fulfilled the intentions of the master himself and all his attendants with consecrations, special initiations, blessings, and everything else relevant.

Then at that time a nomad came from the north with the message that in accordance with an earlier conversation with our benefactor '*Phan-byi*, he had now come to *Khung*. As a result of this [73] and because of a serious quarrel between the southerners and the nomads, I set out on my return journey and went to *Khung*, for I thought that it would be good if the quarrel could be settled. Although it was a serious quarrel with a lot of tussling on both sides, I satisfied their wishes in different ways by whatever means were suitable and everyone was happy.

At that time there were so many of us at Margom that I feared there would be disputes, so I gave religious instruction at the 'Isle of Enlightenment' at Yang-tsher. My students said: 'This confusion of people is not likely to get any less. Margom is an uncomfortably precipitous place. If all is to be well, we must make extensions here (at Yang-tsher). We consider that we need in particular a room for you at all costs.' They did not listen to my objections, and so they built this priory. Just as they finished the roof, an invitation came from the people of Tarap and there had already been a whole succession of such invitations, so I went to Tarap and saw everyone, householders and lamas, lay and religious, the chief men and the simple villagers. Then on my way back I could not withstand the urgent requests of the villagers of Upper Nam, so I stayed seven days at *sMan-rdzing* Monastery,[1] where I gave the special instructions of the *Great Compassionate Lord* to a large number of disciples, and I made everyone happy by giving a general consecration for everyone, and consecrations, special initiations *etcetera* in particular cases. Then the Squire of *rDzong-lung* and all the householders and lamas and especially the two brothers *Bu-chung* who took a leading part, established an enclosure to prevent hunting and so on, and so the names of such practices as the 'trap of stakes' and all the rest were no longer heard.

Then making my way back, I gave a general consecration for the villagers of Saldang, and although they had put an end to most hunting on my previous visit to Shey, they put an end to all the rest of it. Then we continued on our way and reached our own monastery. From the spring onwards [74] I gave detailed lessons in the 'Six Doctrines' to the inmates of the monastery and to a large number of disciples who had come from all around. In the winter I gave detailed instructions in the text of the *Way and its Fruits* to a large number, mostly (monks from) *Grva* and *'Dul*.

That spring while I was at *Khung*, the Great Lady (of Mustang) came with a large number of followers, and I made them content by giving them the consecrations, initiations and so on, just as they intended. At that time I gave instruction in the *Heart Drop of the Powerbolt-Being*. Then that winter Squire Chamba came with his friends from *Se-rib*, and a large number of monks came from the north, from Central Tibet and from all around, and I gave them all instructions in the Six Doctrines of *Nai-gu* and the *Innate Yoga*.

In the spring the Ruler (of Mustang) sent a message saying: 'As I have made a vow to meet you three times, I shall come to see you but my attention will be directed to consecrations, so do not collect official presents from the people.' So when they

[1] Situated in the mountains above Namdo and now a ruin.

came I contented the Ruler and his attendants with consecrations, special initiations and suchlike.

Then in the summer I gave instructions in the *Hermit Teachings* in three parts mainly for the monks. In autumn on the occasion of the alms-collecting I gave instructions in meditation upon one's lamas. In the winter I gave three courses in the *Great Compassionate Lord*. Then many people came from Barbung including the squire of *dGon-gsar*, and I satisfied the wishes of each one of them and made them all happy.

Then in the spring the Lady *Sems-ma-lha-lha* with a large number of attendants came from *Se-rib* and I made them content with instructions, consecrations, special initiations, and blessings.

Then the Lord of Religion *Shākya rNam-sgrol* came with his disciples from the north, and I gave him the consecrations and initiations that he wanted and so made him happy.

[75] At that time the Ruler (of Mustang) came with a large number of attendants, and I fulfilled their wishes with the *Innate Yoga*, consecrations, special initiations and so on. Then the Great Lady herself came also with many attendants, and I contented her with whatever consecrations, initiations *etcetera* that she wanted. Then the Governor *Thought-Perfecting Powerbolt* and his lordship *Wrathful Prosperity* and other lords and ministers, masters and servants, so many of them came, and I fulfilled their wishes with the special instructions of the *Great Compassionate Lord* and with consecrations, textual initiations, special initiations and all the rest.

At that time the Monk *Ocean of Intellect* was seized by a severe illness, and as it became worse, he said to me: 'I do not know whether I have fulfilled my function or not, but I have been in your service for such a long time. You must please promise that we shall not be parted throughout all the series of our (future) lives.'

'Since there was some connection from our former lives, we have met in this one,' I replied, 'so by the combination of these circumstances it would seem certain that we shall meet in other lives. Apart from this I am not a sage who can promise such things, but it would be all right to say a prayer.' Then I recited this:

> By the compassion of the lamas of our own tradition,
> By the grace of the *Three Precious Ones* who can never deceive,
> By the force of events that develop by combination of circumstances,
> May you, faithful believer *Ocean of Intellect*
> Be born together with me through all our lives' series,

And having schooled your 'life-series' by learning and education,
May you do great things for the doctrine and living beings!

[76] He rested with his wishes fulfilled.

Moreover on many other occasions many people came from all directions, lamas and teachers, qualified scholars, officials from Lo, *'Phan-byi*'s representative, men and women, small people and important people. In accordance with their individual wishes I satisfied their wants with various kinds of religious activity, but how would it be possible to write about it all?

On many other occasions brahmans and other high ranking people would often come from Jumla and the King of *Mon*. I satisfied the wants of all of them in various ways, with amulets, blessed kerchiefs, blessings and so on, and all of them seemed to be devout and believing. As for these matters, perhaps these blessed kerchiefs and other blessings were of some use against the non-human beings of the *Mon* regions, for on many occasions, wherever I went, the gods and serpents and even the mountain-divinities seemed to meet me and accompany me in a devout and trusting manner, but others have more (to say about this) than I have. For example the Abbot of *Zho-gam* said to his friends: 'My own guardian divinity goes to meet the Master-Scholar.' All other stories of such a kind were also heard. Although I know some of them, to write about them would only be a matter of embarrassment to holy men.

So as explained above, I wretched fellow, frequented the presence of many famous lamas, drank the elixir of their teachings and applied myself to absorbing it. I developed my own 'soul-series'[1] but I could not gain release. However because of their unerring instructions and my undivided faith, and because their thoughts and mine were mingled, the sign being the way in which I was held in their great love by these holy guides, it is certain that I was blessed with their compassion, and so I did much prematurely that seemed to be for the good of living beings.

(The translation of pages 77 to 80 of the MS is omitted. This passage contains a summary of our lama's activities under the threefold heading of 'expounding, confounding and propounding'. 'Expounding' refers to all the various teaching he has done. 'Confounding' refers to his earlier studies and his skill in debate. 'Propounding' refers to the works he has written, all short ritual texts.)

As for our Lama's powers of clairvoyance, [81] we begged him to give us a clear account, but he replied: 'How should I have powers of clairvoyance?' and would

---

[1] Concerning this term, see the Introduction, p. 27–8.

not tell us clearly. If we who were in his circle recall these matters in an orderly way and tell just a little, (then events such as this occurred:)

One day our precious lord looked unsettled and said: 'How sad! How sad!' A monk asked him why he looked unhappy, and he replied: 'What might it be? I had a visual impression of Squire *Sri-dar* and his brother surrounded by a lot of people. The Squire himself was saying "O Lama of Margom, mercy!" and he was in the posture of meditation upon his lama. He trembled violently down his sides and died. But it does not work out right.' We enquired afterwards, and matters were just as he knew them to be. (*Sri-dar* had died).

Another time when he was meditating, he said *Phaṭ*! violently several times.[1] A monk went to see what it was, and he said: 'Look up there quickly.' We went to look, and the monk Sombo had gone to get wood from the roof of the monastery and had fallen down. Our lama knew this.

Again one day he gave a dedicatory ceremony without a blessing. 'What is this?' we asked. 'I wonder if Her Ladyship at *dGa'-mi* has had an accident,' he said, 'it seems that some misfortune has come to the lady and her son.' (Later) we worked out the times and the day he gave that consecration, the lady had died.

Again if we did good or bad things however they were and then conspired together and prepared untrue statements, our lama would know and as soon as we began to speak, he would say: 'Don't tell lies. Speak the truth.' There was no place for lying and concealment, [82] and such things occurred innumerable times.

Again he would say: 'Today such and such a guest will come and there will be such and such presents,' and it would come about just as he said. Again when benefactors and monks were getting ready (to offer presents), thinking: 'We will give such and such' or 'We will not give such and such,' when they were adding things or taking things away, all this he saw clearly. He saw too the bodily postures of the monks, the way they meditated, whether they were making effort and trying hard or not. He clearly knew even how the monks slept, how each one as a result of dreams and night vagaries experienced a weakening of the *thought of enlightenment*, and how they experienced such a weakening as a result of obstructions in day-time. These and other things he knew quite clearly.

One day he said: 'Today two men are coming from Lower Lo to ask for a diagnosis.' Towards evening they arrived and asked for a diagnosis saying that the

---

[1] *Phaṭ* is the call that a lama uses in order to release the consciousness of someone just deceased. This monk Sombo had presumably fallen and killed himself.

young son was ill. They said: '*Sems-ma*[1] begs this time for a diagnosis by meditation and a diagnosis by butter-lamps and she has told us to bring a clear answer, so we beg you to tell us clearly whether he will die or not die!' Our lama replied: 'Whether I do the diagnosis or not is of no account. Her son is now scarcely a human being any longer. But look after him as well as you can.' Then the son died in their presence. Again some one was sent to ask for a blessing, and he said: '*Sems-ma* has told me to ask urgently what kind of birth her son will get, a high one or a low one.' He remained a moment in thought and then replied: 'Tell her that her son will not have a low birth this time.' [83] After he had left, the monks said: 'Where has her young son been reborn?' 'Why do you ask all these questions?' he replied, 'he has gained the body of a god.' Furthermore he knew what bodies creatures in the *intermediate state* would obtain, as well as people who had just died for whom dedicatory ceremonies were requested. These and other matters he knew directly, but except for some individual cases, he kept them secret. So in the case of our cup-bearer *Jewel Glorious and Good* he told us in the second week (of the after-death ceremonies) that this man had obtained a human body not worse than his previous one. In other cases although he knew everything in the past, future and the present, he acted as though he did not know, for he realized that (otherwise) there would be no concealment or privacy for his flock.

Furthermore, the spring of the Great Grotto of T'ha-kar and the large stream that flows down by *Char-chab* now, both these were produced by our lama, although there were no such large streams there before.

As for this large bronze pot used for passing water, once when our lama had passed water and was throwing it from the small window of his apartment at Margom, the pot seemed to slip from his hand and striking on the cliffs (which descended) in three great steps, it went down to the gorge of the Red Crag. Yet it was not broken, and this was just a sign that he could bring this about. That miraculous bronze pot is still existing now.

Furthermore the ways in which he contracted and overcame illness on just the two occasions that this happened, and the ways in which he repelled black magic on the two occasions that someone practised it against him, there are so many such like affairs, that I hesitate to write of them here.

Again the way in which he would suddenly come and go and do other such things on receiving the prophetic advice of *attendant goddesses*, this is so much talked about in this land as the cause and origin of these things, that how could I deal with all these matters?

[84] Once when a monk stole some woollen cloth and a ball of butter at T'ha-kar,

[1] *Sems-ma* is the same Lady *Sems-ma-lha-lha* mentioned above on p. 169.

our lama said: 'If the theft were revealed our shame would be very great. The cloth and the ball of butter are in such and such a place,' and things were just as he said.

Again one day at Margom the monk Urgyan had covered up some *chang* under some clothes, and the monk Shey-nyen in ignorance of this pulled up the clothes spilling the *chang* accidentally. The next day when the monk went to our lama's presence, he said: 'Yesterday a great disaster befell the monk Urgyan. In place of that (which he lost) take him this *chang*.'

Again on one occasion when instruction was being given for sharpening the intellect, the prior *Saviouress Religious Power*, the Reverend One of *lHab* and the monk *Accomplishment Glorious Protector* were discussing together whether concentrated meditation was the real thing and relaxation mere appearance, or whether relaxation was the real thing and concentrated meditation mere appearance, and whether all this was so or not. At noon as soon as they went to our lama's presence in the teaching enclosure, he said to them: 'There is no need for scruples in such matters. Whatever you are doing, whether moving around or sitting still, if you but remain firm in the *Great Symbol*, that is concentrated meditation. But although you meditate with the correct bodily posture, if various reflective thoughts occur to you, that indeed is relaxation.'

Again when the Lady *Saviouress* came to visit him on the first occasion, for her return journey she had decided to go through *Ban-tshang* and as she was setting out, our lama said: 'This time do not go through *Ban-tshang*. It is best to go to the North.' He sent his monk-attendant, and although it was displeasing to the lady and her servants [85] since they had left supplies in *Ting-khyu*, they travelled via the North and all went well. Otherwise the villagers of Shimen and *Ko-mangs* had decided to beat them up, for they had made a pact, saying that they had a grudge against the squire (her husband). However this did not come off. This matter too he appeared to know by clairvoyance.

Also when I was going to Central Tibet, other people advised me[1] saying: 'Last year there was very bad smallpox in the area of Central Tibet and as a result of this many people seem to have died, so now it would be better to wait.' But when I went to ask our Lama's opinion, he said: 'It is all right to go now. You wont get smallpox,' and he gave me a knotted kerchief which he threaded on my beads. Then he gave me a bead which was from the rosary of our Lord *Merit Intellect*, and said: 'Now there is no fear of smallpox.' As a result of this prophetic utterance I did not have smallpox on my travels, although my teacher had it very badly and I nursed him

---

[1] The writer who here refers to himself in the first person is the monk *Merit Intellect*, whose name also occurs in the colophon. See below pp. 181-2.

without shrinking. This was through the compassion of my Lama and just as he had prophesied. Thinking that there was nothing to obstruct his clairvoyance, my reverence for him was quite boundless. For it was not the kind (of illness) which never came, for when I afterwards returned to these parts it happened to me in *Zho-gam*.

Furthermore while I was frequenting the lotus-feet of these lordly lamas, both spiritual father and son.[1] I thought I would do a three-year session, so I asked my lama's permission. But he said: 'In general I should say that the Prior *Saviouress Religious Power*[2] is not strong, so don't take a vow.' Because of what he said, I stayed in retreat as before without taking a vow, and at the end of that winter it happened just as he had suggested (*viz*. the Prior died).

[86] Again one day in the course of taking tea in seated assembly with some of the monks, our Lama said: 'Today some tea will be brought. I wonder! Is this an old man's chatter?' As soon as the assembly had broken up there arrived from Central Tibet the master scholar Paljor-dar and Dorje of Mö bringing tea for general brewing.

Again '*Dza'i-'phan*, the King of Mon, besought him saying: 'In general, O Lama, may you remain strong in health — as firm as sun and moon — for the good of living beings! In particular I beg you to prophesy whether I shall gain the kingdom or not.'
Our lama remained a moment in thought and said: 'There is a good chance of your gaining the kingdom this year. Otherwise it will be hard to gain it.' Just as he said, that year he held the kingdom, but since he was uncircumspect, it was not permanent. These things happened just as our lama said.

Furthermore as for the way in which he received the prophetic advice of lamas and *attendant goddesses*, (it is related that) a few days after the Lord *Merit Intellect* had passed to another realm, his lama appeared to him one day at dawn dancing down from the heights of the heavens, and he said to him: 'Son, for the sake of the doctrine and living beings exert yourself indefatigably in teaching and prayer.' From that time on he beheld his lama's countenance again and again, and again and again he received prophetic advice.

---

[1] The 'spiritual father and son' are the Lama of Margom *Merit Intellect* and his favourite disciple, Lama *Religious Protector Glorious and Good*, one of whose disciples was the present writer, the monk *Merit Intellect*.
[2] One may note that the religious name *Saviouress* (*sGrol-ma*) may occur quite properly as a man's religious name.

Again when he was staying at the old T'ha-kar priory, he was sitting one day as though resting a little with his legs stretched out in the sun. No form was visible but a voice came from the sky saying: 'Draw up your legs!' On the edge of the roof [87] fire-wood was piled up and held down by a heavy stone. This wood was shaken by the wind and the stone fell down in the place from where he had drawn back his feet. This he told us himself. There were many prophetic occurrences of such a kind as this, but he only informed us of these few.

Then chiefly from rulers and officials and others, from the outer nomad lands of the north and from the southern region of *Zam-'phreng*, from every region from his faithful followers he received a great quantity of material presents, but except for food and clothing, fuel and minor items, in no way did he ever put any of it to improper use, such as passing things on to relatives and so on.

As for what was expended on good works in the matter of gift giving, one part out of five went on commissioning images, books and shrines. One part went on butter-lamps and tea-ceremonies. On the occasion of his first and his later visit to the Buddha's image (at Kyirong) he spent 24 drams of gold, and expenses went on more than forty tea-ceremonies at the three great monasteries of Central Tibet and at *Ngam-ring*. One part went on festivals and food-supplies during meditation, and this amount is uncalculable. One part went on gifts to ordinary people, and it was incalculable what went every year in measures (of grain) to the people of the outer and inner districts (of Dolpo), to Tarap, *Phod* and *Bi-cher*. But these four parts were grants on an equal basis.

One part (the fifth) was used for ceremonies, the most important of which were a thousand performances of *Hevajra*. Then there were performances of the *All-Knowing*, the *Imperturbable*, the *Universal Saviour*, altogether 183,000 performances.

[88] He instigated 200,000 sessions of special prayers, and furthermore there were litanies, good conduct prayers, confessions and all the rest, such as he instigated sometimes for three days, sometimes for four at the three upper and lower monasteries (*viz.* Margom, Yang-tsher and T'ha-kar). Then he gave a lot of small assistance, food supplies and so on, to those who could do nothing for themselves, to the incapacitated and to many people on pilgrimage. In short he acted in accordance with the ways of accepting and rejecting with regard to the process of cause and effect.

On one occasion the monk *Rare Refuge* said to him: 'Such actions and works resemble the ways of a perfected buddha.'

Our lama replied: 'If you measure them against my acts in my former births, there is no reason for enlarging upon my actions and works in this life.'

When he had altogether completed his acts in this life, at the age of 77 years he gave the appearance of being ill.[1]

> In the last autumn month of the Male Wood Rat Year
> Although the whole host of his disciples begged him to remain,
> He said: 'I go for others' good in the Female Wood Ox Year.'
> To him who thus prophesies coming events, we make supplication!

In the last autumn month of the Male Wood Rat Year his health seemed to be a little impaired, and although we inmates of the monastery begged him to remain, our lama replied: [89]
'I do not know whether your asking me to stay will act as a cause for producing or for not producing favourable circumstances. Very many thanks for your supplications, but in any case it will be difficult for an old man (like me) to live as long as the 2nd Month of next year.' Thus he would not consent to remain.

> Although the Powerbolt-Body *is neither born nor dies*,
> *Yet he shows the signs of illness so as to confute our clinging to ideas of permanence.*
> *We supplicate him who remains composed and motionless*
> *In the profound yoga of the dual* Process of Emanation and Realization.[2]

This means that although there cannot be such things as illness and death for the *Powerbolt-Body* in *absolute truth*, yet in order to produce ideas of impermanence in living beings who see things as permanent and in order to urge them on in their religious practice he showed the forms of illness in the delusive appearance of *relative truth*. He remained composed and motionless, traversing in one moment all the stages of activated and non-activated being. A few days later at dawn a large number of sentient beings and especially two old wolves came to make a full confession of what they had done in former times and they made fervent prayers such as: 'In all our births and life-series may we be born as members of your flock, O holy one.' This is what he told us. His monk attendant asked him: 'Were those genuine animals?' 'They are non-human creatures,' he replied.

> On the 14th day at dawn the Lady Mandāravā
> Together with the host of Urgyan's attendant goddesses,
> [90] Appeared in his sight and at once encircled his head.
> We make supplication to him whose disposition manifests itself as so pure!

At dawn on the 14th day of the 2nd month he said there was someone there who

---

[1] If we accept the fact that this Lama *Religious Protector Glorious and Good* died in a Wood Ox Year, this can only have been A.D. 1565, when he would have been 89 years old. See p. 76.
[2] Concerning these terms, see the Introduction p. 26.

looked like a nun, clad in red religious robes and holding a begging-bowl and a staff in her hands. The monk *Rare Refuge* asked him who it might be. 'It is the Goddess *Mandāravā*,' he said. 'She will come with the fourfold host of the *attendant goddesses* of the entourage of *Lotus-Born* of Urgyan. Encircled by eight *attendant goddesses* she has approached my head.' As he thus prepared to leave for other realms, we made urgent supplication to him, and he replied saying: 'If matters are so, I will remain until the 20th, and as that is the feast-day of the lamas, it will be easier for dealing with the ceremony. Our learned master (*viz. rGyal-mtshan chos-'phel*) need not stay with me today.' Thus he remained until the 20th. In the meantime we pupils of his together with our benefactors and the chief mourners and all the people, both lay and religious, supplicated him with one voice, saying: 'Give thought to the doctrine and to sentient beings, and you must consent to remain with us. As an offering in support of this request, you holy lama would not be well pleased with material gifts, so as a mere gesture towards an auspicious outcome we pupils will undertake a vow to stay in solitary retreat for three years, and we your benefactors will take a vow that all hunting shall be stopped on the mountains and in the valleys for a space of five years, and at all costs you must be pleased (to agree).' Our lama replied: 'As for your asking me to stay, you need someone who has power over birth and death. [91] I am not such a person. As for the vows you would make, generally speaking you would be doing youselves the greatest kindness, and in a special way I shall rejoice with you, for I would experience great happiness.' Thus he would not give his consent (to staying), and so we said: 'Then if you are not pleased (to agree), you must give a personal audience and detailed directives about how we should do our practice as well as notification of the (divine) realm to which we should direct our supplications.'

Our lama replied: 'One must die while one is still teaching or one must die while one is in solitary retreat. Now when our former lamas went to another realm, they received no one at all, some for a space of three years, some for a single year, and some for several months, and they manifested the signs of death while remaining in retreat. Now since I came into retreat, a few months have passed, and I was thinking that I would depart during this time, so it would not be suitable to see anyone. Do not be displeased about this. As for the way you should direct your practice, this is just as I have told you again and again. As a general consideration (we know that) all living beings must die. As a special consideration we do not know the time of our death. So let everyone renounce from his mind the activities of this life. Arouse a loving and compassionate disposition. Let religious practice on behalf of yourself and of others be the most important thing. As for the matter of the realm to which you should make supplication, as I am making a vow to remain working for the good of all creatures until all phenomenal existence with the three spheres of evil rebirth shall be emptied, I wonder how we can arrange this. Perhaps it will be all right wherever you make your supplications. The *Highest Heaven*, the *Womb of the Powerbolt-Queen*, [92] the *Elemental Sphere*, the *Realm of Bliss*, *Potala*, the *Western Land of Urgyan*, these are a list of terms, of which the meaning is one and the same. So make your supplications wherever the best association seems to be, the *Realm of Bliss*, *Potala* or the *Western Land of Urgyan*.'

> *When it was time to pass from sorrow, he prayed to his lama,*
> *And after remaining composed for thirty-five days*
> *In a cross-legged position, body composed with all the right gestures,*
> *He really became the* Threefold Buddha Body.
> *To him we make supplication!*

At twilight on the 20th day of the 2nd month, he made up his mind to depart for another realm, and those who were waiting upon him said: 'As it is the custom to wear religious garments and the Urgyan hat, please agree to this.' He replied: 'To wear religious garments is the custom of those who follow the way of monastic discipline. To wear the Urgyan hat and to eat elixir pills is the tantric custom. But an old man wants no artifices at all.'

Then he said: 'I supplicate the feet of *Merit Intellect*,' and he remained cross-legged with body composed and with all the right gestures according to the 'Seven Teachings of *Vairocana*', and having thus remained composed in the state of the *clear light* of the *Great Symbol* for the space of five weeks, he traversed at one go all the stages of the way and gained the rank of the *Great Powerbolt-Holder*, where the four buddha-bodies and the five wisdoms all coalesce.

> [93] *When the corpse was cremated the sky was clear*
> *And a shower of flowers descended with a sweet scented smell.*
> *The regions trembled and the sounds of music resounded.*
> *Such extraordinary wonders showed forth. To him we make supplication!*

Thereafter we honoured the corpse with cremation according to the ceremony of libations as given in the Tantra of the Glorious *Hevajra* together with the technical directives. At that time the sky was very clear and in different places showers of flowers descended and everyone saw them. A sweet scented smell pervaded everywhere. The regions of the earth trembled and loud sounds of music were heard. There were tent-shaped appearances of rainbow rays. These and other wonderful signs were manifested on a very large scale.

> *In order to guide the pure in heart he produced in very great numbers*
> *Relics of a special kind, such as a rounded skull,*

BIOGRAPHY OF LAMA RELIGIOUS PROTECTOR GLORIOUS AND GOOD 179

Effigies of the Lord of the World, *the* Laughing Powerbolt,
The syllable A and other such things. To him we make supplication!

When the cremation-urn was opened, the rounded skull was preserved as a relic in its normal form and there were many effigies, the Noble Lord *Glancing Eye* in his eleven-headed manifestation, the *Red Fury* of Urgyan, the tutelary divinity *Hevajra*, the Lord of Yogins *Laughing Powerbolt*, as well as many others. There were many verbal symbols, seed-syllables such as the letter A. As mental symbols, there were stupas and twisted bone-relics as described in the *Great Perfection* tradition. [94] These and other relics of a special kind were produced on a vast scale.

Furthermore as for his physical disposition he never parted from the 'Seven Teachings of *Vairocana*'. As for his speech, he avoided foolish talk consisting of such matters as the praising of oneself and the maligning of others, and he spoke only the great words of religion. As for his mental disposition, he remained in a state of great mental calm and with thoughts of love, compassion and enlightenment he worked on behalf of the doctrine and living beings. These activities of his were certainly a sign indicating the subtleness of his Body, Speech and Mind.

From the ocean-like quantity of biographical material of this holy guide of ours the oral accounts he gave us were in an ordinary style and sketchily told, and we have put them together without any artificial improvements. As there may be a host of faults in this work, we ask the worshipful ones to forgive us.

Afterwards in order to effect the fulfilment of the wishes of our religious communities, our lama had said: 'As I myself have made shrines and reliquaries, funeral ceremonies and so on, there will be nothing for you to do these things with.' As he had made frequent distributions of whatever material things he possessed, there was not much left over, but with the things that remained, together with the funeral offerings made by the teachers and students at the monasteries and our various benefactors, we performed offerings of worship, which were like this. In the first place the monks of the Five Communities[1] performed services for the space of five weeks. At *Grva* and *'Dul* they were performed for ten days, and at Margom for seven weeks, all in accordance with local customs. There was a distribution of his books and his clothes, [95] as well as general offerings and so on. Then there was an offering of religious gifts to the monks of *Nang-khong* and *Ban-tshang*, and offerings to various lamas, the Abbot of *Ja-tshang* and others. Thus we performed all the services that should be performed. Tea-ceremonies and a general distribution of

---

[1] The five communities are those of Margom (*dMar-sgom*), Yang-tsher (*gYas-mtsher*), T'ha-kar (*mTha'-dkar*), Rin-chen-gling (near *Bi-cher*) and *Ja-tshang* (also known as *Grva-tshang*).

gifts were performed at the various monasteries of Tarap, and fees for blessings were paid to various lamas. From *Re-la* to the *Ti-se* Mountains, as well as at the monasteries of *Ta-le*, at the Red Crag, *dGon-gsar* and *Songs*, at *Shug-dings* and other places, at *Mu-gum* and the monasteries of *Karma*, to the lamas and communities at these various places fees for blessings and the cost of tea-ceremonies were paid, as is the manner of performing such services. Distributions according to district were made to the people of the four districts of Dolpo.

While we were building the relic stupa named the 'Great Stupa whose Sight grants Release', and making 900 *maṇi*-stones, there was a distribution of the relics. On that occasion various local chiefs and religious teachers, the men of '*Phan-byi* and other benefactors of the doctrine experienced such devotion and purity of thought with regard to our holy lama, that they gave a great quantity of offerings of gold and copper and other things. So thinking that these things should not be wasted, and in order to fulfil the wishes of our holy lama, and in general to cause the spreading of the precious doctrine of the buddhas, to cause happiness for all living beings who exist throughout space, and in particular to complete the two accumulations (of merit and knowledge) of those disciples and various benefactors of the doctrine who have such special regard for this Great Guide *Religious Protector Glorious and Good*, [96] we thought that we should have made some very special images to serve as basis for our worship. We sent for some Newar (craftsmen) and so had made from the gold and copper an image of the Protector *Maitreya* one storey tall and profitable to gaze upon, also an image more than life size in the likeness of our holy lama himself, made of the most excellent materials, the six 'good things', various medicaments, gems and other things. It was a very wish-granting gem. We had scrolls painted one storey high, depicting the events of his life and serving to refreshen our faith.

Thereafter we offered butter to the value of thirteen drams of gold at the shrine of the Precious Buddha-Image of Kyirong and to the ruler of *Gung-thang* (*mNga'-ris chos-rgyal*) we offered a dram of butter, a dram of gold, a curtain of patterned cloth, a roll of muslin, and six squares of gold-coloured brocade silk.

After that we offered general tea-ceremonies and fees to the teaching staff for their special prayers at monasteries in Central Tibet, Sa-kya, *Ngam-ring*, the 'New Monastery' of *Ngor*, the Victorious *Thub-bstan* the Golden and *Thub-bstan Yangs-pa-can*.

In short from the time of his showing the way of uniting the buddha-realms (*viz.* from his death) until the feast-day (the 49th day) we had performed at the 'Isle of Enlightenment' at Yang-tsher 45,000 ceremonies. Our Dolpo benefactors commissioned an incredible number of things for the good intention of our holy

BIOGRAPHY OF LAMA RELIGIOUS PROTECTOR GLORIOUS AND GOOD 181

lama in accordance with their various means, twenty-three stupas of which just six were 'umbrella-shaped' ones, the *Sūtra* of the *Good Age* and also our lama's biography, 7,000 *maṇi*-stones with the six-syllable prayer, [97] also painted scrolls illustrating his life's story, bronze images, medicinal images, books and other things. These items just represent a list of what was done to fulfil our lama's intentions. The roots of merit derived from these things we dedicate (in the following verses) through the seven factors of enlightenment.

Saluting in devotion of body, speech and mind
Our lama, supreme guide, the very substance of the Three Precious Ones,
We confess all evils committed by force of the Three Evils
And we rejoice in all the merits accumulated throughout past, present and future.
We beg you to turn the Wheel of the Doctrine of the Three Vehicles
And to remain here for the benefit of the beings of the threefold world.
All the merits in the threefold world which are directed to no special intention,
May they be dedicated to the 13th Stage, that of the Powerbolt-Holder.

From the boundless biographical material of our glorious lama
We have taken just so much and set it down here.
The whole host of our errors and faults
We confess to the host of our lamas and attendant goddesses.
May the clouds of pure disposition gather and thicken
And the ambrosial rains of the merits that cleave there
Cause increase of the harvest of worthy converts
And may they delight in the riches of the treasury of the Threefold Buddha-Body!
May we too throughout our whole life-series
Be members of your flock, O holy guide!
May we complete our accumulation (of merit and knowledge) and perfect ourselves in buddhahood.
May we save all beings from the ocean of physical and metaphysical states!
By the grace of our own lama and the lamas of our tradition and of the Three Precious Ones,
By the power of the Defenders of Religion and the host of tutelary divinities,
Grant increase in all regions both of the doctrine and of knowers of the doctrine,
And the blessings of the light-giver, meritorious virtue!

From the boundless biographical material of this religious king of the threefold world, the guardian of men, this small work has been composed in face of the constant entreaty of the faithful disciples (of our Lama), the great textual authority *Merit Intellect*, the monk *Saviouress Religious Power*, the pure friend in religion

Buddha Powerbolt, the monk *Ocean of Intellect* and others. Through this work which has been composed during the white fortnight of the 7th month of the Male Wood Horse Year,[1] known as 'Victorious', may there be great benefit to the doctrine and to many living beings!

[1] This Wood Horse Year is likely to be A.D. 1594, and it will then refer to the main part of the biography that was put together from autobiographical material while Lama *Religious Protector Glorious and Good* was still alive. One of the 'compilers' who is named here, namely *Ocean of Intellect*, died before this Lama. See p. 169. The last part of the biography (from folio 81 of our MS, page 170 of the present translation) which deals in general with his powers of clairvoyance and in particular with his death and last rites, is a later addition of his disciple *Merit Intellect*, who is not to be confused with the great Lama of Margom *Merit Intellect*. See pp. 68–9.

Powerbolt-Terror

III

THE BIOGRAPHY

OF

THE SUPREME GUIDE GLORIOUS INTELLECT

entitled

The Door-opener to the Three Kinds of Faith

The Biography of the Supreme Guide

GLORIOUS INTELLECT

which is entitled

THE DOOR-OPENER TO THE THREE KINDS OF FAITH

We bow at the immaculate lotus-feet of our good master, who is the glory of all living beings in the threefold world, for he waves aloft the banner of the great secret teachings, and the fame of his presence equals that of the *Gentle Protector*.[1]

Excellent and precious, the glory of the ocean (of beings) of the Good Age,
He possesses the elixir of the accomplishments of inspired teaching and knowledge.
By means of his ocean-like intellect where springs forth the perfection of realization,
May the Buddhas' doctrine spread abroad in an ocean of great actions!
Like the Lord of a thousand rays in the great expanse of the heavens,
This glorious protector of all sentient beings triumphs in the Buddhist doctrine.
Among the Buddhist texts and inspired knowledge of the tantras which are like a
  vale of lotuses, there opens the smiling lotus of his pure intellect.
Taking the sweet nectar of the Buddhist sages, that bee-like host, he spreads forth a
  joyous feast of honey-like elixir.

We bow at the feet of the religious teacher *Glorious Intellect* who using the perfected bodily forms of Buddhist renunciation and knowledge, teaches religion to the three grades of sentient beings.

I will make known the flower-rosary of his wondrous acts, for it is wonderful how this precious teacher, giver of final perfection, bestows his blessings like a universal monarch, source of all desirable things.

---

[1] See p. 194 fn. 2.

He himself has said: 'I entered the door of religion and met with holy men. Having obtained the sacred teachings, I finished with all false views. I absorbed the meaning and gained some inner clarity. [2] Then I spread the teaching with a pure disposition. The manner of all this is the small matter of my knowledge and practice as a yogin.'

Thus speaking words of praise and promise, (I shall tell of) this sage so great, the teacher of the threefold world, Buddha throughout Past, Present and Future, guide of the three spheres of existence, whose name *Glorious Intellect* is as famous as the sun and moon. He is representative of all buddhas. He makes the doctrine of the *Great Vehicle* resound throughout all the ten points of the compass. Possessed of a mind so clear and of accomplishments so numerous, he thereby achieves on his own account the *Absolute Body* of buddhahood, while on account of others he displays various bodily forms, images, physical bodies and superior bodies, whatever form is necessary on whatever occasion for converting those who can be converted by means of bodily forms. Thus he acts continuously for the good of sentient beings until the whole circle of existence shall be void. As it is written in The *Sūtra of the Briny River*: 'Referring to images, rebirth and enlightenment, and also buddhas and would-be buddhas, they are said to assume various bodily forms, tigers, lions, hares, boats, bridges and so to act for the benefit of others.'

In the 'Treasury of *Dohā* Verses' it is said: 'In many forms, as hare or tiger, lion or elephant and so on, his compassionate mind intent on others' benefit, he makes the decision and comes into birth.'

'Furthermore he appears as a Buddha to convert buddhas, as a disciple to convert disciples, as Brahmā to convert the gods of the Pure Realm, as a king of the gods (*Indra*), as a heavenly musician (*Gandharva*), as a sprite (*yaksha*), as a divine lord (*īśvara*), as a great divine lord (*Maheśvara*), as a universal monarch, [3] as a flesh-eating demon, as a general, as a Brahman, as one who wields the powerbolt (*Vajrapāṇi*), as lama or teacher, as an ordinary religious friend, as father or mother, as brother or sister, as friend or as girl-friend, as aunt or uncle or nephew. Thus wherever there is converting to be done, he teaches religion with a mental disposition that accords with each potential convert.'

Also in the same work it is said: 'Who is the *Powerbolt-Being* you ask. It is he who takes the form of a teacher, and intent on benefitting sentient beings, keeps to this lowly form.'

In the *sūtra* of 'The Lord's Address to the Would-Be Buddha *Remover of Defilement*', he says: 'O noble son, the Great Being, the *would-be buddha*, the Lord *Glancing Eye* teaches the doctrine by displaying a form that accords with each sentient being of all the sentient beings existing to the ends of space. Thus for converting buddhas, he teaches as a Buddha. For some he teaches like one of the early disciples (*Śrāvaka*). For some he teaches as a Lone Buddha. For some he teaches as Brahmā. For some he teaches as the king of the gods. For some he teaches as a heavenly musician. For some he teaches as a sprite. For some he teaches as a divine lord. For some he teaches as a great divine lord. For some he teaches as a universal monarch. For some the teaches as a general. For some he teaches as a Brahman. For some he teaches as a wielder of the *powerbolt*. For some he teaches as lama or teacher. [4] For some he teaches as an ordinary religious friend. For some he teaches as brother or sister. For some he teaches as friend or as girl-friend. For some he teaches as aunt or as uncle. Thus he teaches religion in a way suitable for whomever he intends to convert.' Thus it is taught at great length in all the *sūtras* and *tantras* that all holy men and worthy lamas must be recognized as derived manifestations of the Buddha.

So (this lama of ours) took the form of a great friend in religion and converted whomever he had to convert, mean fellows the like of us. The wonderful tales of how he taught the doctrine in a way that accorded with the mental stature of each one, surpasses all thought and exceeds the very telling. His disciples however kept on begging him (to tell the story of his life) for it would encourage the faith of future converts, and now his replies and the submissions of us two (writers) have been correlated and set down in writing, as will be clear hereafter.

This holy lama of ours was nurtured by many other holy lamas, and among his innumerable rebirths, (we should mention) the preceding one which took place in the sacred land of Central Tibet. He was born as *gSal-ba dBang-phyug grags*, and he was the best pupil of the Lord *Victorious Banner of Fame*,[1] thus gaining great prowess through the insight and spiritual power of the head-lamas of Sa-kya, both the older and the younger.

CHAPTER I. (*The Events of his Birth.*)

As for the biography of his present life, first we must tell the manner of his birth. He came of the *Ga-se* family and the *Shu-rtsa* lineage, which ranks as a ministerial one for it goes back to the Uncle-Minister '*Bru-gsum* who lived in the time of King Song-tsan-gam-po. His birth-place was in Dolpo, at *rTsa* in Upper Nam.[2] His father was named *Peak of Merit* [5] and his mother *Gem of Beauty*, and they were both faithful and zealous, virtuous and wealthy. Of the three children that were born to them, this holy one was the youngest. When he was in his mother's womb,

---

[1] This is *rJe-btsun Grags-pa rGyal-mtshan*, who was Abbot of Sa-kya from 1172 to 1216 A.D.
[2] Tib. *Nam-stod*, viz. the upper part of *Nang-khong* above Namdo (*Nam-mdo*).

she saw in a dream a woman wearing a spotless white garment and adorned with precious jewelry. This woman was about the age of sixteen, and giving the mother a white flower with beautiful petals, she said: 'Look after him.' His mother's body was hallowed. She felt no pain during the process of giving birth and she was happy and joyful. At the time of the child's birth there were many wonderful accompanying signs, and even from the earliest age he avoided childish behaviour, and by force of awakening the karmic connections with his former lives, he acted as though making sacrificial offerings and reading religious texts, and if he saw a creature suffering unbearably, he would shed tears of compassion, manifesting himself as befitted the ways of a *would-be buddha*.

CHAPTER II. *Now as for his entering the door of the doctrine, we come to the second chapter about how he entered this door.*

To begin with he received — at the age of three years — in the presence of the learned lama *Gloriously Good* the vow of good conduct of a 'virtuous adherer'. At the age of thirteen in the presence of Abbot *Intellect Victorious* he received the vow of a novice. From the age of thirteen to that of twenty he stayed with Abbot *Intellect Victorious*, acting as his sacristan. He became proficient in the doctrines of the *Way and its Fruits* and the related supplementary texts, and he trained his mind towards the motionless condition of the *Great Vehicle*. He learned many *sūtras* and spells including the cycle of Ka-dam-pa[1] works, [6] and his lama treated him with great compassion. When he was twenty he went to *rGya-mdo*[2] for the religious festival of Upper Nam. The date was the 15th of the 4th Month. The evening of his return home, he appeared to be ill. *Phan-dar-'dzin* of *'A-pha*[3] was sent for, and having looked him over, he said: 'This is not very good. The learned *Gloriously Good* has greater spiritual power. Ask him to look.' He looked the patient over and said: 'This seems to be smallpox. You must take all the care you can.' My parents said to themselves: 'This disease has not originated in the village. Now it has come to him like this, he will probably die,' and so they were very sad.

[1] The Ka-dam-pa (*bKa'-gdams-pa*) Order (literally: 'order of the precepts') was founded by *Atīśa* and his disciple *'Brom-ston* in the latter half of the 11th century. Concerning their main literary works, see G. Tucci, *Tibetan Painted Scrolls*, pp. 98–9.
[2] The present site of *bDe-chen bla-brang*, where the gorge widens above Namdo.
[3] This man is a local seer. The term *'a-pha* is a doubtful word. The *bDe-chen bla-brang* Lama says it is a place-name, and it may be some *nepāli* name in Tibetan garb. I have therefore treated it as such. Local seers are elsewhere referred to in these texts as 'practitioners' *tib sgrub-pa* (p. 218) and respectfully as 'lord of religion' *chos-rje* (p. 213), a term of address commonly used for lamas. A woman seer is respectfully addressed as 'lady' *jo-mo* (p. 192). There seems to be no general term by which local seers are known. See also p. 238 fn 3.

(Our lama himself continues the story:)
In my own mind I prayed like this: 'Even if I die, I beg that this may not spread into the village, O Precious Ones. If I do not die, I will ask my lama and my parents, and at all costs I will go East' (*viz.* to Central Tibet).

In the event I did not die and the disease did not spread into the village. At that time the young squire *Good and Famous* was making a return visit to Central Tibet for some religious purpose, so I thought that I would go with him. I asked my parents about going, but they would not permit it. My father said: 'Go and ask the advice of your holy lama. If your lama tells you to go to Central Tibet, even if I prevent you, you will free yourself and go, and if he tells you not to go, even if I send you, you will not go. So go and ask him. Decide the matter like that.'

On the way to *Ja-tshang*[1] to ask his permission, I slept at *rDzong-kha-'jar* and in a dream I saw three beautiful women decked with jewelry, offering me a ladle full of elixir. On that occasion I received a clear sign that at all costs I should go to Central Tibet. [7]

My lama said: 'Although you are indispensable to me, if you go there for study, it will be of benefit both to the doctrine and to sentient beings, so it is certainly good that you should go.'

Again I explained to my parents in full how matters had gone. My mother shed tears of sadness and so on, and in order to comfort her my father read the stories of former buddhas. When I set out, she accompanied me for a short distance.

CHAPTER III. (*His Course of Study.*)

Without having any trouble on the journey, I reached the great monastic centre, the Victorious *Thub-bstan* which is the equal of (ancient) *Śrāvasti*.[2] I paid my respects to the Great Buddha-Abbot *Intellect-Born* and for fourteen years I applied myself to inspired teachings and the pursuit of knowledge at the feet of learned men.

As *Perfection of Wisdom* material I studied the *Abhisamayālaṅkāra*, and its basic commentary, also the *Uttaratantra*, the *Sūtrālaṅkara*, the *Madhyāntavibhaṅga* and the *Dharmadharmatāvibhaṅga*, representing the five treatises of Maitreya.[3] Also the 'Clarification of the Meaning of the Perfection of Wisdom' (*yum don rab gsal*)

---

[1] Concerning this monastery, see p. 201 fn.
[2] For references to this monastery, see p. 133. The Jetavana Monastery at Śrāvasti in northern India was established during the lifetime of Śākyamuni himself and became one of the chief Buddhist centres during the early period of the doctrine.
[3] Concerning this 'Perfection of Wisdom' literature, see Conze, *The Prajñāpāramitā Literature*, Mouton & Co., The Hague, 1960, pp. 93–106.

written by the great omniscient sage[1], the 'Great Commentary' (*rong krig bka' 'grel chen mo*) of *Rong-ston*[2], the four sets of great commentarial works[3] and other treatises.

As for texts on Logic, (I studied) the three main treatises which are as it were the body, and the four derived treatises which are like the limbs, making up the seven treatises (of *Dharmakīrti*), as well as the commentary written by the great omniscient sage, entitled 'Clarification of the Seven Treatises' (*sde bdun rab gsal*) and the 'Great Commentary All-Good'(*krig chen kun bzang*); [8] also the *Logic of Inference* (*rtags rig*) and the *Logic of Deduction* (*blo rig*) by the Great Kong-Po Pandit, the 'Treasury of Knowledge' and the author's (*viz.* the Sa-kya Pandit's) own commentary, the 'Clarification of the Treasury of Knowledge' and other works on logic.

As for the section on 'Monastic Discipline', (I studied) the *Vinayasūtra*, and the author's own commentary, the *Vinayasūtraṭīka*, the 'Four *Āgamas*', and the 'Essence of Monastic Discipline'.

As for the section on 'Philosophical Notions', (I studied) the *Abhidharmakośa* (*Treasury of Philosophical Notions*), the author's own commentary, also the 'Treatise of *Śāriputra*', the Seven Sections of *Abhidharma*, the Elemental Components and so on, the '*Abhidharma* Compendium' (*mngon-pa kun las btus-pa*) and other works.

As for the section on the 'Middle Way', (I studied) in the first place the *Prajñāmūla* of *Nāgārjuna*, also his 'Six *Mādhyamaka* Treatises' (*dBu-ma'i rigs tshogs drug*), the 'Collection of Praises' (*bstod-tshogs*), the 'Collection of Stories' (*gtam-tshogs*) and other works. Also Candrakīrti's *Mādhyamikāvatāra*, as well as the commentary on this work by the great omniscient sage, also his 'Four Condensations' (*bka' bsdu bzhi-pa*).[4] Also the 'Great Commentary on the Three Vows' (*sdom gsum krig chen*) and the 'Great Work on the exoteric meaning of the Three Vows', and *Śāntideva's Bodhicaryāvatāra*.

Having thoroughly studied and learned these theoretical works, I clarified for myself the teachings in this way. In the midst of numerous monks in the glorious monastery of *La-stod* in *gTsang*[5] District in the snowy land (of Tibet), a monastery

---

[1] The great omniscient sage is *Kun-mkhyen Shes-rab rGyal-mtshan*, who came from *Ban-tshang* in Dolpo. See the *Blue Annals*, p. 775 onwards, and also Ruegg, *Journal of the American Oriental Society*, vol. 83, no. 1, 'The Jo-nang-pas', p. 80 onwards. See also my Introduction, p. 11 fn.

[2] *Rong-sTon* (1367–1449), a famous Tibetan teacher and founder of Nālanda Monastery about 16 miles north of Lhasa. See *mKhyen-rtse's Guide*, p. 84 and the *Blue Annals*, p. 340.

[3] These four sets of great commentarial works refer to Logic (*tshad-ma*), Monastic Discipline ('*dul-ba*), Philosophical Notions (*mngon-chos*) and the philosophical teachings of the Middle Way (*dbu-ma*).

[4] Concerning this work, see Ruech, *op. cit.* p. 83 fn.

[5] The monastery referred to here is probably *Ngam-ring*, a Sa-kya establishment, founded in 1225. See *mKhyen-rtse's Guide*, p. 153.

Vajrāsana, tib. *rDo-rje-gdan*, the 'Powerbolt Throne' is another name of Bodhgayā, where Śākyamuni first gained enlightenment under the pipul tree. In mediaeval times there was a great monastery there. It was destroyed by the Muslims at the end of the 12th century.

THE BIOGRAPHY OF LAMA GLORIOUS INTELLECT 191

which is a second *Vajrāsana*, I took part in debates, and destroying the arguments and contentions of my antagonists, I was the joy of many learned men.

As for the section on 'Secret Spells', (I studied) the *Process of Emanation* according to the *Mahāyoga* and the *Process of Realization* according to the *Anuyoga* as well as other relevant works. Also the basic *Two-Part Tantra* (viz. *Hevajra-tantra*), the explanatory *tantra*, namely the *Powerbolt-Canopy* (*Vajrapañjara*), and the complementary *tantra*, the *Sampuṭa*.

[9] I studied all the *Father Tantras* and *Mother Tantras* together with their commentaries.

Thus he passed the time in the threefold manner of a clever man (viz. studying, learning and meditating), thoroughly studying the tantras and their various commentaries, the Dag lJon sKor gsum pa[1] and so on, and became even more famous than the other wise men of his time.

CHAPTER IV. *Now we come to the fourth chapter which tells how, having acquired this sacred learning, he removed all false notions by listening to holy religion at the feet of holy men.*

(The whole of this chapter, MS. page 9 line 6 to page 11 line 12 is omitted in this translation. Having listed in the previous chapter the works received from Blo-gros rnam-rgyal (*Intellect Victorious*), our lama now lists all the works he has received from seventeen other lamas, namely from:

bZang-po Dar-dar
Blo-gros 'Byung-gnas (*Intellect Born*),
'Bum-ram-pa Lama,
dKon-mchog lhun-grub (*Jewel Self-Created*),
Sangs-rgyas Seng-ge (*Buddha Lion*),
Shar-khang-pa Lama,
the Lama 'named Shā-kya', probably Shā-kya rNam-rgyal
sNa-tshogs rang-grol (*Variety Self-Released*),

[1] This name has been identified for me by sDe-gzhung Rin-po-che of Sa-kya, who is now in Seattle, as being the sPyi-ljon-brtag gsum. Dag (or brTag) refers to the Dag-ldan, a commentary on the Hevajra-Tantra (also known as brTag-gnyis, the 'Two Part' tantra). lJon refers to the work mNgon-rtogs ljon-shing. sPyi refers to the rGyud-sde spyi-rnam. The first two are by rJe-btsun Grags-pa rgyal-mtshan and the third by bSod-nams rtse-mo. They are included in the 'Complete Works of Sa-kya' (Sa-skya bka'-'bum).

'*Ja*'-*tshon phug-pa* Lama (*Rainbow Cave Lama*),
dKon-mchog rGyal-mtshan (*Jewel Victorious Banner*),
Blo-gros rNam-rgyal (*Intellect Victorious*),
bSod-nams blo-gros (*Merit Intellect*),
Shā-kya dPal-mgon, (*Shākya Glorious Protector*),
rDo-rje rGyal-mtshan (*Powerbolt Victorious Banner*),
bSod-nams Ye-shes (*Merit Knowledge*), Lama of the Mount of Realization,
the Great Translator, *Ratnabhadra*,[1]
the Great Lord of Margom *bSod-nams blo-gros* (*Merit Intellect*)

CHAPTER V. *This tells how I absorbed all this subject matter and gained a little insight, so it is called the fifth chapter about the absorbing of profound subject matter.*

When I was 36 years old I performed invocations of *Boundless Life* and the *Terror* (*Bhairava*) at *sTeng-chung*.[2] I was thinking of carrying out another set of invocations, when Bu-chung Zangpo Tson-druy became ill with smallpox. I went to ask '*Phan-dar-'dzin* of '*A-pha* and his brother to come. They came, but the youth had passed away. We asked the Priestess *Powerbolt Clear Light* to work out prognostics, and she said that my own life would be endangered.[3]

I went to *sTeng-chung* again, and from the 15th to the 21st I practised the 'life-fortifying' rite according to the tradition of *Ras-chung*, and on the 21st especially I offered some good butter-lamps and prayed to the Lamas and Buddhas.

[12] The butter lamps shone very clear and beautiful flowers appeared with them, and I had a vision of the protecting divinity *Boundless Life* as though seated clearly on my head. That night in my dreams I went with a slight feeling of fear along the upper *Sa-dkar* Valley and it was very dark except for one or two stars. In that mood I gained control of my dream, realizing that these were untrue appearances. Then as I moved this way and that up the cliffs, the sun's orb appeared as a mass of variegated brilliance in the east, and I seemed to have an experience of bliss and voidness. Then in that mood I went flying to the top of *Phug-gsum-mdo* and I saw the evil lake of *Reng*,[4] and I thought to myself: 'I must destroy this evil lake.' I transformed myself into a brilliant manifestation of *Powerbolt-Terror*. On the near side of the lake was a large boulder, and turning it into a ball of fire, I hurled it into

---

[1] This Sanskrit name refers to *Rin-chen bZang-po*, the famous Tibetan translator (A.D. 958–1055). See *Buddhist Himalaya*, p. 180 ff. *Glorious Intellect* met him in trance. See p. 206.
[2] This place is just above *Zel*.   [3] See p. 188 fn 3.
[4] Concerning Phoksumdo and this lake, see *Himalayan Pilgrimage*, pp. 58–63. The name *Reng* occurs in the name of the village of 'Ringmo' at the southern end of the lake.

THE BIOGRAPHY OF LAMA GLORIOUS INTELLECT 193

the evil lake. The evil lake boiled away and I saw dry ground where it had been before. Then I went up to the summit of the Dragon Crag,[1] and I thought: 'This is the palace of *Supreme Bliss*. I must pay my respects.' And I saw the palace of *Supreme Bliss*, scintillating with many colours. In that same mood I thought: 'I must pay my respects to the *Boar-Headed Goddess* at *bTsag-khang*.'[2] I went there and in a palace of gems there was a lady with beautiful jewelry, and I thought that she must be the *Boar-Headed One* and I went to pay my respects, making obeisance, and begged her to remove the danger to my life and to support me. Then I saw a white thread with 81 needles of the kind that come from India threaded upon it, and as I counted the needles on the thread, the 69th one had a broken eye. As I counted them back again, [13] the 69th again had a broken eye. With these thoughts in my head I went again to *sTeng-chung*. At the head of the valley there was a yellowish snake which blocked the valley. I transformed myself into the king of birds (*Garuḍa*) and swallowed it.

[*Biographer's note:*
The meaning of the needles was this. At the age of 67 he would have a bad illness, and then the Abbot of *Ja-tshang*, the sage named *Saviouress Religious Power*[3] and others, as well as many of his disciples would beg him to remain in the world, saying: 'Give us the good news that you will remain firmly here for the good of living beings.' He will give his word, and if no danger befalls him at the age of 69, he will remain until the age of 81, the number of the needles. Thus he explained things.]

Then I came to a place that seemed to be Margom, and I woke up. I realized that the snake was the one who was causing the danger, and I thought that the sign of the needles must refer to my number of years, and I was sure that I had overcome the Demon of the Lord of Death.

At that time Bu-chung Dorje, the scholar *Shākya-dpal* and his brother, and other people of Upper Nam arranged for some cultivatable land free of tax, and asked me to stay in the village. They looked after me very well indeed.

[1] A mountain near Shey.
[2] Literally 'the house of the red earth'. The Lama of *Zel* has a small meditation house at this place nowadays. It is up in the mountains behind *bDe-chen bla-brang*. The red colouring used for painting the exteriors of religious houses is still obtained from there.
[3] *Saviouress* represents Sanskrit *Tārā* (Tibetan *sGrol-ma*), who is the Great Mother Goddess of late Indian and so of Tibetan Buddhism. Her name, although feminine in form, is used as a religious name for men, as well as for women, very much as 'Maria' may be used in Italy as a second name for boys.
This is the same *Saviouress Religious Power* who was associated with the writing of Lama *Religious Protector*'s biography. See p. 181. Lama *Glorious Intellect* actually died at the age of 69. See p. 76. The square brackets are my insertion. The Tibetan text simply passes from first to third person and back to first again.

Then the Lama of Red Crag at Tarap said I must go there. When the invitation came, I had a prophetic intimation that Samdrup of Rashi would help me. As the invitation from Tarap was so urgent, I thought I should go there. While I was staying at Red Crag, a villager of Tak-kyu,[1] by name Tshe-wang Phan-dar became ill. I made an investigation of the auspices, [14] and realized that the harm came from (the local demon named) *Bya-'bag*. I trained my thoughts upon him and it was revealed that his place was a certain multicoloured rock-face. I transformed myself into *Powerbolt-Terror*, and uttering the cry PHEM, smashed the rock with the points of my horns. A large snake came out at the foot of the rock and circled itself around my arm. I hacked at it with my sword,[2] but it joined its body together again and disappeared into the rock. On many other occasions too I made use of a dream, training my thoughts upon him, but the matter did not come to a clear issue.

On another occasion a woman benefactor of mine went down to the *'Du-le* Valley and was ill there. Someone came to ask for an investigation of auspices (on her account), and having examined my dreams, I knew that it was the evil doing of the same demon. Again I transformed myself into *Powerbolt-Terror* and set off. There he was, his top half like a man and his lower half like a snake, in between two large cairns on the edge of a grey mountain-face. Looking very fearful, he blocked the way, not letting anyone pass. Flying up into the sky, I transformed his place into a mass of fire, and hurt him by burning him, throwing things at him and so on. I came upon him quite fearlessly, and this local divinity offered me a length of cotton cloth, saying: 'You have harmed me on many occasions. From now on I will serve you, but you must have compassion on me and give me a special sacrificial cake.' I replied: 'You are not to harm sentient beings, but you will not get a special sacrificial cake. You are to do no evil. You are to practise a generous disposition and practise this and other virtues, and I shall hold you under oath.' The good woman was cured of her illness.

Again on another occasion *Jo-bo Yul-lha* of Upper Nam[3] [15] came dressed in red and wearing a turban and accompanied by a large entourage. With the wafting of incense he invited me to seat myself on a high throne which he had set up in his stronghold. He offered me tea in a snow-white porcelain cup and milk in a skull-shaped cup of crystal.

[1] Concerning this place, see p. 165.
[2] The sword he was holding belongs to the accoutrements of *Powerbolt-Terror* (*Vajrabhairava*). This divinity is supposed to be the fierce manifestation of the *Glorious Gentle One* (*Mañjuśrī*), also known as the *Gentle Protector*, with whom Lama *Glorious Intellect* is equated in the opening verses of praise. See p. 185.
[3] Tib. *Nam-stod*, viz. the upper part of *Nang-khong* above Namdo (*Nam-mdo*). Concerning the local mountain-gods, see the Introduction, p. 15.

THE BIOGRAPHY OF LAMA GLORIOUS INTELLECT   195

Then a relative at *Ne-lde-sum-mdo*[1] was ill with a pain in the upper part of his body, and whatever ceremonies were performed, there was still no improvement. So it came about that I had to go there. Then in a dream that lasted just half the night, that local god came riding a white horse, dressed in red clothes and with his hair combed straight down. He was wearing conch-bracelets and he was accompanied by a large entourage. *Jo-bo Yul-lha* came again with his large following, and coming to my presence, he made salutations and sat down at one side. From the direction of *Wa-la-wa*[2] there came a group of demons riding black horses, black birds, black dogs and so on, and *lHa-btsan-pa*'s group came too in large numbers. *Lha-btsan-pa* had a wand in his hand, and after he had admonished them, he restored the 'soul' of the sick youth in the form of a sheep with a brown face.[3] After I had talked with them, the sick youth recovered. Then *Jo-bo Yul-lha* and all the others were filled with faith and devotion.

On another occasion I was invited by the lama of *Zhva-lding* (in Tarap). I went there, and while I was doing a drawing of Sa-kya Monastery under the portico at *Zhva-lding*, I had a prophetic intimation concerning Bu Lha-wang Dorje. After that the holy lama *Merit Knowledge* said that I should visit the abbot of the 'Isle of Blessings', but I asked to be excused and so he excused me. But having received a prophetic intimation that I should go to the 'Mount of Realization', I went there.[4] On one occasion when I was practising invocations of *Hevajra* and other divinities [16] I thought I saw the tutelary divinity reflected clearly in his own self-nature, a clear bluish colour, clear without and clear within, so that for one moment I saw all the vital channels of his body.

On another occasion a lot of women beautifully adorned and singing songs, made a procession around me in a clock-wise direction. Then they arranged in front of me vessels of jewels and suchlike filled with rice-gruel, fresh fruits, and many different kinds of food. The roof of the temple seemed to shine with gold and conch-shells, and all around outside there appeared to be ceremonial umbrellas, banners of victory, hangings of tassels of pearls and all kinds of ceremonial trappings. There were many such things, mere appearances without any real substance, and the place was full with these non-substantial things, like reflections which one cannot identify as such and such things, yet clear like a rainbow. Although I applied absolute non-attachment in their regard, meditating upon them as unreal appearances, yet they continued to appear as before and occupied most of my attention. I

[1] This is the name of the gorge where two rivers meet at the southern end of *Nang-khong* about two hours walk above *rTsa*. It is now quite uninhabited.
[2] *Wa-la-wa* is the name of the gorge near Yang-tsher. It is also the name of the local god of Yang-tsher.
[3] Concerning this kind of soul, see the Introduction, p. 28.
[4] Tib. *dNgos-grub-ri*, a place to the north of *dMu* and close to the present Tibetan frontier. 'Isle of Blessings' (*bKra-shis-gling*) was the name of the hermitage there.

wondered if these were just the signs of my having achieved some fervency in meditation, that is to say the manifestations of an unusual mental disposition.

Another night as I directed my dreams, I came to a dark and misty valley, where I transformed myself into an unusual form of *Lord of Yogins*.[1] I went up towards the summit of a high rock-face that was there, and as I went up ever higher and higher I changed into the *Glorious Gentle One*, then into *Powerbolt-in-Hand* and then into *Glancing Eye* in his one-headed four-armed form. When I reached the summit of the rock, the summit was so fine that I could find no place to sit, and jumping here and there in all four directions, I realized that one can find no reality, even as much as the point of a hair, in all physical and metaphysical manifestations, and I thought, this rock-face too must be an illusion. Thus illusive appearances of unimaginable kinds appeared to me.

[17] Furthermore by mastering my dreams I gained great powers at the 'Mount of Realization', sitting on the sun and moon like a carpet, going through the air and so on. I would have achieved very good application in virtues if I could have stayed there more than three years, but I could not stay more than that. Furthermore it was there that I practised the insight of the *Great Symbol*, and on many occasions I experienced the state of *clear light* of which the chief sign is absence of discriminating thought.

At that time the proprietor Palden of *dMu* attended upon my wants very well, and always from then onwards he continued to serve me. On that occasion Bu-chung Dorje said that I must go at all costs to a lonely place in Upper Nam, and as he invited me with such urgency and offered such service, I had to go without hesitation. Then when I reached *sKyid-kha*,[2] I had a small pain in my foot. Realizing that it was the local god of *rDzong-kha-'jar* who was vexing me, I directed a harmful spell at him, and that local god appeared carrying three arrows with vulture-feathers in their tops, and wearing torn liver-coloured clothes. He gave the arrows into my hand and said: 'I will be your subject. I will perform the works of your command. Of the sons of Bu-chung Dorje *Bu-chung bTsun-chung* will be the one who serves you best.' Then he vanished.

One day I said to my attendant Sherap Tenpa: 'There is a place up there called Hrap Monastery. We shall both go there for a rest.' So taking a joint of meat as sacrificial food, the two of us, master and pupil went to Hrap and stayed there a while. When we had finished the sacrificial offerings, I said: [18]
'How would it be if we founded a monastery here?'
'The place is rather narrow,' my attendant replied, 'and the village is very near.'

---

[1] This is a title of *'Bir-ba (Virūpa)*. See p. 131 fn.
[2] This is the village near Karang, which is normally simply written *Kyi*.

THE BIOGRAPHY OF LAMA GLORIOUS INTELLECT 197

'Many people have stayed here previously. It is said that half this present building is mine. My parents will look after it for me.'
'Let us then repair this hermitage.'
'We must perform the "refuge-seeking" prayer as well as we can, for it will be difficult to do as we are thinking.'

First of all I had to act as lama at *Zhva-lding* and the Red Crag for a few years, and I consumed many offerings both from the living and the dead. All things there in the monastery and the village flourished greatly. Then I had a sense of sadness, and following the advice of my Lama, I decided that I should stay at the 'Mount of Realization' without going anywhere and devote my life to meditation. But I could not stay there longer than three years. (Now we were at Hrap.)

My servant said: 'There is no place better for meditation or more solitary than this place.'

'That is just what I think,' I replied, 'for those two first years the combination of three things, the place, my lama's blessing and my fervent faith, have resulted in great benefit to my religious practice. I consider that skill in religious practice consists just in these things. I have succeeded a little in seeing myself "face to face".'
'What was this skill like?' he asked.
'During the second year I concentrated my "refuge-seeking" prayers upon *Aṣṭha*,[1] and one night it seemed as though the appearances of this world ceased, and the interior of the cave was filled with gods and goddesses. In particular the pores of my body and the hairs of my garments gleamed with gods and goddesses.
[19] 'Is *rGyal-po-phan* happy?' he asked.[2]
'It has been very good for us two to come here. Get the best out of the human body you have obtained. I can just remember my last three states of existence.'
'It does not happen that a man remembers his various states of existence,' he said.
'In my case it is so.'
It was then that I had prophetic premonitions that it would be very good to found a monastery in that place, and he asked me what I had to say about it.
'In my dreams there was a mountain behind this place and it rose up one ridge above another. On the mountain there was a circular lake with flowers growing round the edge, and a lot of people were there picking them. A middle-aged woman who was there, gathered the flowers together and said to me: "You be master of this place. It is certainly good that you have come here." So this place will be really well blessed in the matter of food and supplies.'

---
[1] These are the mystic syllables of the *All-Knowing* (*Kun-rig*), alias the supreme buddha *Vairocana*.
[2] The two speakers are presumably Lama *Merit Intellect* and his attendant Sherap Tenpa. *rGyal-po-phan* seems to be one of his favourite monks. See below, pp. 204–5. The present conversation seems rather inconsequential, but both my MSS agree in the text.

Then the two of us, master and pupil, returned to *sKyid-kha*. I said: 'Now we must certainly found a monastery at Hrap.' Thus this monastery was founded.

On another occasion I went to the 'Isle of Blessings' to visit the Lama of the 'Mount of Realization', and at the mere sight of his face I had feelings of respect and devotion properly due to a buddha. I stayed there for the space of one month, receiving many instructions, textual initiations and words of advice, and he gave me in the fullness of their perfection sacred teachings from both the *sūtras* and the *tantras*. On my return journey it was evening when I reached *lHas-nag*,[1] and *Jo-bo Yul-lha* brought all the local gods to meet me. A god named *Jo-bo sDugs* came riding a horse. He was splendid to look at and was wearing a turban round his head. When he reached me, he did not dismount from his horse, [20] so I reduced him to subjection, and from that time on, he always dismounts and makes an obeisance. All of them paid me honours and attended to me lavishly. *Jo-bo Yul-lha* and the others said to me: 'On the morrow, O Lama, you will have to perform services in good style,' and then they went away. 'What can it be?' I thought. The next day I went to *dGon-chung* and found myself in front of the corpse of the scholar *Shākya Glorious Protector*. He had been my former teacher, so I performed the services very well. It was this that those local divinities were referring to.

Then the son Padma of Bu Wang-chuk-dar was ill, and I was invited to *mDa'-chen*[2] to investigate. I went there, and when I had done all that was good, the boy recovered.

On the same occasion the good woman Drolma was ill and near to death, so I went to *Zha-ri*[3] to look into things. In my dream that night a woman wearing jewelled garments spoke to me saying: 'As the Lord of Margom is really the Teacher from Urgyan, go to pay your respects to him.'[4] Following upon that I awoke, and as it was both my own wish and the goddess's prophesy, I thought that I must go to see him, so I went to Hrap. That evening I controlled my dreams and went to look. Behind the monastery a ragged nomad came to meet me first of all. Then five beautiful women met me and made salutations. Then two monks burning incense led the way, and I entered a small room. The Lama was on a throne in the form of the *Horse-Necked God the Queller of Serpents*, brilliant to behold with a green coloured horse's head and neighing like a horse. Seeing him like this, I made obeisance and asked for his gracious favour.

[1] This is a grazing ground above *Ting-khyu*.
[2] *mDa'-chen* was just above *rTsa*. No one lives there now.
[3] *Zha-ri* was above Namdo. No one lives there now.
[4] The 'Lord of Margom' is Lama *Merit Intellect*, who is regarded as a physical manifestation of *Lotus-Born* (*Padmasambhava*), the Teacher from Urgyan. One of *Lotus-Born*'s fierce manifestations is the *Horse-Necked God* (*rTa-mgrin*) whom *Merit Intellect* sees in his dreams. On being advised to visit *Merit Intellect*, he first returns to his own hermitage at Hrap in order to test the advice.

The next day I went to visit him (viz. the Lama of Margom) and told him all about these things. He said: [21]
'I just transform myself into three forms, the Teacher from Urgyan, the *Horse-Necked God* and the *Red Fury*; those previous meetings came about from the auspicious circumstances produced by the good will of the local divinities, the *Five Sisters of Long Life*.' In a joyful mood I received the profound doctrine of the *Guru*, the *Red* and *Blue Perfecter of Thought* and other consecrations, textual initiations and instructions according to the rediscovered texts, and in the presence of this sage I lost all false notions, just as he disposed. He gave me in their entirety all the relevant texts and supplementary works, saying: 'You must go to *Grva-tshang*,[1] and there you can copy the books out and paint picture scrolls of the mystic circles. Since you have received in particular the command of the *Queller of Serpents*, you should start seven or eight courses of instruction according to this tradition.' He also pronounced good prophesies (for my future).

Then I went to *Zom-bshad*[2] in Upper Nam and practised invocations of the *Blue Perfecter of Thought*. From the fifth or sixth day onwards I experienced the various psychic states of *crossing the crest*.[3] One night mastering my dreams, I went to pay my respects to the Lord of Margom and made obeisance to him where he sat within a temple. 'Why have you come?' he asked. Having told him how the states of *crossing the crest* had arisen, I was transformed into the *Perfecter of Thought*. Pronouncing the sound HŪM, I danced upon the roof of the temple, and the mountains of Margom and the groves of trees swayed and rocked this way and that. Then the Lord of Margom too became transformed into the *Perfecter of Thought*, and the two of us, master and pupil, danced there, enunciating the sound HŪM. This is how I absorbed the *Perfecter of Thought* teachings.

[22] Again the Lord of Margom said: 'The absorbing of the *Red Fury* is like this,' and he appeared as the *Red Fury* with *Glorious Gentle One* at the top of his head, the *Horse-Necked One* at the throat. *Powerbolt-in-Hand* at the heart, the *Goddess of Knowledge* at the navel, and the Wrathful Yaksha *Me-wal* at the groin, representing Body, Speech, Mind, Qualities and Acts. It was a non-substantial body and visible in the same way as a rainbow.

That spring the *Songs-pa* Lama invited me to *Gro-tshang*, and because of his persistence I had to go. I set off. Near *La-chung* is the village of Tsharka, and although I had never met these Tsharka men before, the proprietor *Guru-bzang-po* and others of them came to meet me and did reverence to me and looked after me in fine style. I know now that they gave me this escort because they were urged to do it by the local divinities.

[1] *Grva-tshang* is an alternative name for *Ja-tshang*. See p. 201 fn.
[2] This is the name of a meditation-cave up the gorge opposite *bDe-chen bla-brang*.
[3] Concerning this term, see p. 139 fn.

(The biographer continues the story:)
Then on the way to *Songs* (we came to) Barbung where not a single drop of rain had fallen, so that all the crops had dried up and men were distraught with drought. By the grace of our Lama from that night onwards heavy rain began to fall, and everyone was filled with faith and devotion, and his renown spread abroad.

The day we arrived in *Songs* the lama and his followers met us with silk umbrellas, banners of victory, with pendants and with cymbals, and with so many different kinds of items of worship, and thus we came to *Songs*[1].

At the monastic house of *Songs* there was an abundance of things given in our honour and they made enormous offerings. Then we went on to *Gro-tshang*, and for the space of three months our Lama instructed those worthy disciples in the 'Profound Doctrine of the Sa-kya Lords, Father and Son, the perfect inspired teachings of the *Way and Release*, [23] as well as the *Sure Instructions of the Universal Saviour, the Great Compassionate One, Life Instructions* and *Transference Instructions*, the *Innate Yoga of the Great Symbol* and the *Inspired Teachings of the Rite of Self-Sacrifice*. From among the community there he bestowed upon about twenty, who were ready, the vows of monkhood, novicehood and so on, and performing these consecrations, he caused the Buddha's doctrine to extend in that monastic place.

On one occasion the proprietor *Phan-dar* of *dMu* was struck with a serious illness, but before anyone came to ask our Lama to make an investigation, *Khye-dom*, the local god of *dMu* appeared to him in a dream and begged him to come to *dMu*. Then our Lama mastered his dreams and going after him he surveyed this place and its various localities, seeing everything clearly. Then later he explained all the facts of the investigation as revealed in the dream to those who came asking for it. 'In particular on the edge of your village on a mound between two valleys there is a large boulder. At that place in accordance with your customs you must make offerings to your local god.' But although they made offerings in this way, it was of no use. So they came to invite our Lama again, and he went to *dMu* and bound *Khye-dom* under oath, and then the illness was cured. All the villagers came to believe in him.

On the way home we slept one night on the *bZu-lung* Saddle, and our Lama said to those around: 'Tomorrow a man will come from afar, so do not be in a hurry.' 'What is it' we asked. He replied: 'Last night a white man appeared in my dreams,

---

[1] *Songs* is in the Kāli Gandaki valley just below Jomosom (*rDzong-gsar-ba*). It is marked on the Survey of India maps as Syāng.
Gro-tshang I have not located, but I suspect it is below Tukucha near the place marked Lārjung on the S of I maps. There are several old Tibetan Buddhist temples in this area.

saying "Tomorrow morning someone will come, and I ask you to do the best you can for him. [24] You should take care of him and give him good service." Then he disappeared,' he said. The next morning as sun rose and we waited, the attendant Tshe-wang with about seven servants arrived from a journey to Jumla. He asked for an audience (with our Lama) which he received. Our Lama gave whatever good advice seemed necessary, and with a gesture of respect they made obeisance and put their heads at the Lama's feet. In particular the attendant Tshe-wang besought our Lama urgently and with many arguments that he should take charge of Shey. From that time onwards he performed too the most excellent services.

(*Our lama continues the story:*)
Then I went to my place of meditation at Hrap. But the lamas of *Nang-khong*, of *Ban-tshang*, masters and pupils, the great, the venerable and all the ordinary people begged me with great urgency to act as lama of *Ja-tshang*,[1] so I had to take charge of things there. At that time when I was teaching the whole assembly of monks, there was an epidemic in the village which began to spread to the monastery. Some of the monks were ill, and my attendant Sherap Tenpa in particular was worried. 'Will we be able to get through this course of instruction?' he thought, and was very anxious. I bestowed a blessing upon him, and then prayed one-pointedly to my lamas and to the Lord *Victorious Banner of Fame*.[2] The next morning, when I was making my devotions to him, the sun rose as a shining orb of variegated light and in the middle of a maze of sun-rays and rainbow colours was the glorious and wonderful form of the Lord *Victorious Banner of Fame*. Then I said: 'Sherap Tenpa, come! [25] Don't you want to change your opinion?' That day during the interval in the instruction I gave them the inspired teachings from the biography of the Lord *Victorious Banner of Fame*, and during these inspired teachings many of us, master and pupils together, shed tears of faith and devotion. On that occasion I gave them the special initiation of *Sha-ba-ri*,[3] and the epidemic ceased at once. Everyone was immeasurably happy.

Again when I was acting as steward at *Thub-bstan*, I was living in the west courtyard of the main building, and one night I dreamed that the outer door was opened forcibly and a black man with a patchy red face appeared. He had four overlapping fangs with yellowish points and an eye in his forehead and he looked quite fearful. I was very frightened, but although I prayed to my lama, it was no

[1] This monastery, now a ruin, is near Koma (*Ko-mangs*). Its name is spelt both as *Ja-tshang* and *Bya-tshang*, and since the pronunciation of these two words is the same in Tibetan, I have used the spelling *Ja-tshang* throughout my translation. It is also referred to as *Grva-tshang*, which simply means 'the monastery'. Since this is in effect an alternative name, I have kept this spelling wherever it occurs in the texts. See e.g., pp. 199 and 237.
[2] See p. 187 fn.
[3] This is another of the 84 Great Yogins. See p. 88 fn.

use. I meditated upon the ordinary form of *Bir-srung*, but this was no use. Still being very frightened I prayed one-pointedly to the Lord *Victorious Banner of Fame* with the thought: 'You are all-knowing.' The Lord's glorious form appeared in the sky before me. In his right hand he was holding a powerbolt and in his left hand he was ringing a bell. He cried out: 'Sum-bha' and scattered grain and the demon disappeared. That black man was a magical form of *Nyug-gdong rGyal-po*,[1] and the trouble which he was starting was clearly known by the Lord. From then on his manifestation faded away into universal space, but I had gained unbroken faith in the Lord *Victorious Banner of Fame*, and all this was a certain sign that I had clung to his lotus-feet in a former state of existence.

All this our lama told us. Then some of his disciples asked him: 'How did you cleave to his lotus-feet in a former birth?' [26] Our Lama said: '*rJe-btsun* had four disciples whose names ended in *Grags*, namely *Karma-shākya-grags*, *gSal-ba dbang-phyug-grags*, *dGa'-ston rdo-rje-grags*, *Dam-pa kun-dga'-grags* and I was *gSal-ba dbang-phyug-grags*, and I drank much of the elixir from the mouth of the Lord, who was the leader of our line.'

Another time when our Lama was at *Ja-tshang*, King '*Byid-ras* was ill and two valley-men came from Jumla to ask our Lama for a diagnosis. He said to them: 'You go to Bu-chung Dorje and I will send the results of the diagnosis,' and he sent them to *mDa'-chen*. Mastering his dreams, our Lama went to look at the king, and he was already dead. King *Dza-li-phan* had taken off his turban and was wearing an old *bir-kyi*.[2] Towards the south up the valley from where the king was, there was a lawn with pools of water here and there. The queen was there with the king's corpse. She was in great anguish of fear at being burned, and she was looking round-eyed at the king, hoping that he would say: 'Stay.' But the king did not say anything. Our lama said to the King: 'Do not let the Queen go to her death. She is suffering so much.' The King replied: 'She knows whether she will go to her death or not,' and remained there without speaking (to her). Our Lama had in mind to explain the doctrine of acts and retribution, but as he could not enunciate the speech of the valley-men, this explanation of the doctrine did not succeed. Then the Queen jumped to her death,[3] and although he felt limitless compassion in his heart, there was nothing he could do, he said. [27] When morning came, he sent his assistant Sherap Tenpa to *mDa'-chen* with the results of the diagnosis, for the two valley-men were waiting there. Our Lama sent a message by his assistant to Bu-chung Dorje

---

[1] The name of the local god, meaning perhaps 'King of Boastful Face' (by reading *myug* for *nyug*).
[2] This is a Tibetan phonetic spelling of Nepāli *birke* (*topi*), a small round black braided hat, seldom worn in Nepal nowadays, but frequently seen on the heads of Nepāli merchants in Darjeeling.
[3] She practises the self-immolation of a virtuous wife (*satī*) on the funeral-pyre of her husband. The kingdom of Jumla was formally Hindu. See the Introduction, pp. 9–10.

THE BIOGRAPHY OF LAMA GLORIOUS INTELLECT 203

saying: 'My dream was of such and such a kind. You decide whether it would be wise or not to tell the two valley-men.' Bu-chung Dorje replied: 'We must tell them about the dream quite clearly. They set out and came here on foot to ask for a diagnosis.' So he told them about it quite clearly. The two valley-men cracked their finger-joints (as a gesture of despair), and one of them returned looking quite grief-stricken. The other one went to Narakot,[1] and when he told about the affair of the diagnosis, the valley-men were amazed and from then on they used to say 'That Tibetan lama is a good fellow.' Later on one of these two valley-men returned to the lama's presence, bringing as presents a roll of cloth and some foreign molasses. 'It has happened as the Lama pronounced,' he said, and he begged to place his head at our Lama's feet. 'I beg that my relations and dependents may come within the protection of your responsibility,' he said.

On another occasion when he was performing special prayers for the old man *sKab-ma* at *Za-khud* on the *Ja-tshang* Saddle, a middle-aged woman appeared to him in a dream, saying: 'Tomorrow the *Canopy Guardian* will visit you, so make him happy with decorations, banners of victory, garments and such like articles of worship.' Then she vanished. At the moment of sunrise, [28] Squire *Blo-gros* of Shimen presented him with a black-edged painting (of the *Canopy Guardian*), and our Lord said: 'This accords with last evening's prophesy.' He had some prayer-flags made at once. Then just at noon the cleric *dPal-rdor* brought a painting of the *Canopy Guardian* and *Ge-sar* both together. 'I shall give this to the Lama,' he said. Our Lama made him some good presents. Then he had a temple built for the guardian divinities beside the monastic buildings at *Ja-tshang*, and over the Guardian's head he set up new decorations and prayer-flags, and he had banners of victory erected over the assembly-hall. Thus he made the divinities happy with ceremonies of propitiation and with articles of worship. It was on that occasion that he wrote the praises of solicitation for his two lamas,[2] 'The Pure Elemental Sphere' and 'The Two Accumulations from Former Times'.

Another time he went to meet the Lord of Margom at T'ha-kar one spring. He received from him the consecrations and instructions of *Nai-gu* and the *Eight-Word God*, and as he gave him the consecration of *Nai-gu Queller of Serpents*, the Lord said to him: 'The word of this tutelary divinity has descended upon you, so by these means do great things for living beings!' With this prophetic statement, he gave him

[1] Actual Tibetan spelling *Na-ra-bkod*. I have not identified this place and the *bDe-chen bla-brang* Lama said it was 'somewhere near Jumla'. He gave the same vague location for '*Gar-cha-bkod*, which probably stands for Jājarkot. See p. 238. Tibetan speakers are no better at reproducing Nepāli names in Tibetan than Nepāli speakers are at reproducing Tibetan names in Nepāli. Only for places of sufficient importance are there recognized pairs of names, e.g. Jumla and '*Dzum-lang*, Mustang and *sMon-thang*, Muktināth and *Chu-mig-brgya-rtsa*, etc.
[2] Namely for the Lama of Margom and the Lama of the 'Mount of Realization'.

the life-consecration of *Red Fury*, the consecration of the *Eight-Word God* once more, *Life-Body Red Fury*, the consecration of the Sage *sDong-grug*, all these and others our Lama received.

Later on when the Lord of Margom was about to pass to another sphere, he sent a messenger saying: 'Come for the ceremony of the Goddess *Cleanser of Defilements*.' The evening when I was preparing to go (our lama told us), I had a dream like this. I went to T'ha-kar to meet the Lama, [29] but a white man was blocking the top entrance of the room and would not let me pass. I flew inside through the roof-vent and saw the Lama who appeared to be ill. A vast orb of the sun rose above the mountains around T'ha-kar, and then it set. Then while I was thinking that another solar orb ought to be rising, the sun shone straight out from the top of the heavens, and from the roof of the house the white man, whom I had seen before, handed me a horn and told me to blow it. I blew it three times, and there were three loud notes.

Then (in the morning) I went to see the Lama and asked him about the visions that I had seen. He replied: 'The sun's rising and setting refers to me, for now I shall not remain here, I suppose. The sun's reappearance and the blowing of the horn represent an auspicious reference to your deeds.' Thereafter however much we performed the ceremonies of the *Cleanser of Defilements* and so on, he still did not remain with us and departed for the pure realms.

About five months afterwards I mastered my dreams one night, and I knew with certainty that the Lord (of Margom) was in the *Realm of Urgyan*,[1] so I went to pay my respects. There appeared a realm which I thought must be Urgyan, and in a divine palace of gems I met two beautiful women. 'Why have you come?' they said. 'I have come to see my Lama. Where is he?' I asked. 'We will lead you there,' they said. Then three white women decorated with all kinds of jewelry appeared. One of them said: 'He is in her womb,' and the woman concerned said: 'If you can see, he is here.' Then I saw in her womb a blue powerbolt shooting forth rays of different colours. I had faith that it was my Lama, [30] and I made respectful obeisance and asked for his gracious blessing. Such is his account of his visions.

Again in summer-time our Lama was going from *Ja-tshang* to Shey, and during a stay (en route) at *bTsag-khang*[2] the monk *rGyal-po-phan* and his assistant Sherap

---

[1] Lama Merit Intellect died in A.D. 1581. See p. 76. The Realm of Urgyan refers here to *Lotus-Born*'s paradise, known as the *Glorious Copper-coloured Mountain*. Urgyan is in fact a real place-name, for it is the Tibetan equivalent of *Uḍḍiyāna*, an ancient Buddhist land to the NW of Kashmir. It was probably the home-land of *Lotus-Born (Padmasambhava)*. But in Nying-ma traditions all real geographical and historical associations have been forgotten and it has simply become the name of his paradise.
[2] See p. 193 fn. 2.

Tenpa were waiting on him. He said to the monk *rGyal-po-phan*: 'Look at the foot of the wall and turn (the soil) back.' They both thought that this must be an important matter, and having quickly turned up the soil, they extracted a boulder that was there. Then there came out a large earthenware pot with good barley in it. They prepared it and the good woman *Tshe-ring* processed it (to make *chang*). Our Lama made preparations for giving the instructions of *Nai-gu*, and we prepared the sacrificial elixir. It had a very good taste and there was such a quantity of it that it seemed to be inexhaustible. Those who were there in attendance said: 'There has never been such good tasting *chang* before or such great quantities of it. There is still more of it,' they said. Our Lama said: 'The present amount will do. Last night the Sage-Magician *Khyung-po* Yogin came to me (in a dream), and said: 'That barley is intended for you to prepare. It is given to you. So give now the instructions of *Nai-gu* on a lavish scale. On this occasion you will see in outline the faces of the whole line of lamas of the "*Nai-gu* Tradition of the Seven Kinds of Gems" and other works. The boy *Blo-gros* will be of service to you.' I had the impression that he said all this, our Lama said.

At that time the scholar *Lord of Compassion*, who had taken up the '*Brug-pa*[1] doctrines, was telling about the many miraculous places at Shey and *gSer-phug*, [31] and that many great things had been told about these monasteries, which had been mentioned prophetically by sage-magicians. Bearing all this in mind, I mastered my dreams one night and went wandering around both places. I saw a vast palace of *Supreme Bliss*, far exceeding the one on the mountain of the previous occasion when I gained control over the evil lake of Reng. Furthermore there were many miraculous places, just as had been described by the scholar *Lord of Compassion*. Reflecting that he must be a good yogin, I experienced firm knowledge and pure insight, our Lama said. It was at that time that our Lama repaired our main monastery buildings, had paintings of the various paradises painted on the inner walls, and performed works of virtue on a large scale.

On another occasion when our Lama was gaining control over the 'Black Crag' of Saldang,[2] the local god of 'Black Crag' was a serpent-devil. So mastering his dreams, our Lama transformed himself into *Powerbolt-Terror* and uprooted the crag with his horns. The local god turned into a poisonous snake, and one had the impression that his head reached up to the limits of the physical world. Knowing that he was

---

[1] The '*Brug-pa* Order is a branch of the Ka-gyü Order. It was founded in the 12th century by *rJe-btsun Gling ras-pa* (*Blue Annals*, pp. 659–664) and is named after the monastery of '*Brug* which was founded by *Gling ras-pa*'s disciple, *Ye-shes rDorje* of Tsang (*op. cit.*, p. 669).

[2] The 'Black Crag of Saldang' is actually a short day's journey distant from Saldang village up beyond Namgung. Namgung itself is often referred to as 'Namgung of Saldang'. The interests of the Saldang villagers extend to Shey, which is the far side of a high pass and a day's journey from Namgung and a day and a half from Saldang.

not to be overpowered by violent means, our Lama went up to the top of the 'Black Crag', where he turned himself into the Supreme Lord *Glancing Eye*. A flow of nectar descended from the palm of his right hand and he meditated with thoughts of limitless love and compassion. The local god turned himself into a large (human) figure clad in dark brown, and from the roof of his citadel he made obeisance. Then he invited our Lama inside, leading the way respectfully, and set ready a great throne. Offering a ceremonial drink of *chang*, he showed our Lama great honour by the gift of treasures and so on, and he promised that he would cause no harm to living beings.

[32] Our Lama returned to *Bya-tshang*, and for the space of a year he did great good for the doctrine and for living beings by the discourses that he gave. Although he did not deal with all the monastery's affairs, he gave his tithes and other things to the general assembly of the monks. Then once more he went to Hrap.

On some (very much earlier) occasion when he was under instruction at the glorious monastery of *Evam Chos-ldan*,[1] he was preparing one evening for receiving the consecration of *Powerbolt-Terror* from the Lord *Buddha Lion*, and he thought to himself: 'Since this lama is the *Powerbolt-Holder*, the 11th occupant of the throne (of this monastery) as prophesied by *Kun-dga' bzang-po*, he is surely a manifestation of the Three Family Protectors.[2] Shall I investigate?' So mastering his dreams, he investigated, and he saw the lama as the Great Sa-kya Sage, and his hairs quivered with the faith of his devotion.[3] He (also) met the Great Translator *Rin-chen bzang-po* and asked for the special initiation of *Glancing Eye* and of other divinities as related above.

The night after performing the special ceremony of sixteen days' abstinence, there were signs in his dreams that all evil had been washed away. Blood from the nose and suchlike (impurities) seemed to flow down like a great flood from the sides of the *Potala* Mountain. The Great Translator was seated on the *Potala* and our Lama knew for certain that he was *Glancing Eye*. 'As which particular manifestation?' he wondered, so he controlled his dreams and investigated. He saw the Great Translator in the form of *Glancing Eye* with one head and four arms and the antelope skin covering his left breast and with a physical body quite clear in all its characteristics although it was really non-substantial.

On that same occasion on the night following the special ceremony of sixteen

---

[1] See p. 86 fn.
[2] These are the three great celestial *would-be buddhas*, the *Glorious One of Gentle Voice* ('*Jam-dpal-dbyangs*), *Glancing Eye* (*sPyan-ras-gzigs*) and *Powerbolt-in-Hand* (*Phyag-na rdo-rje*). For more about them see *Buddhist Himālaya*, pp. 65 and 116, where they are referred to under their Sanskrit names. *Kun-dga' bzang-po* was the founder of *Evam Chos-ldan*.
[3] The Great Sa-kya Sage is *Kun-dga' snying-po* (1092–1158). See G. Tucci, *Tibetan Painted Scrolls*, p. 100. Concerning the 'Great Translator', see above, p. 192 fn. 1.

days' abstinence, he had the impression that there was a greyish-coloured bridge on the right bank of a river just near a grassy plot, and that he walked over it. [33] As he went over the bridge, a swollen human corpse was carried along by the flow of the river. He pulled it out by its hair and it was his own mother. He had the impression that they both conversed together a little, and both mother and son seemed to be very happy.

On one occasion when he was staying at Hrap, he mastered his dreams and went to see the *Potala* Mountain. There was great expanse of yellowish-white flowers with clusters of trees, and all very pleasant. 'If only I could be born here in my next rebirth!' he thought. He paid his respects to *Glancing Eye* who was enthroned inside a heavenly palace of jewels. He made obeisance, offered worship and said prayers. *Glancing Eye* said: 'Not far distant from here in a westerly direction is the *Realm of Bliss*, so go there.' Following upon this prophetic statement, he saw the Great Buddha *Boundless Light* in his divine palace in the western *Realm of Bliss* with its parks and so on. He made obeisance, offered worship and made prayers, and the Buddha said: 'Go to the *Realm of the Heaped-up Lotuses*.' Following these prophetic words, he went to the *Realm of the Heaped-up Lotuses*, and there in a palace of jewels he saw the splendid and glorious form of the Guardian Buddha *Boundless Life*, and above his head was a revolving umbrella of gold. He bowed down, offered worship and said prayers, and he had the impression of receiving a consecration in verse-form, 'Life-consecration manifest in the body,' etc. Then he returned (in his dreams) to Hrap, and the sun rose in a mass of rays, and he awoke. Such things were always happening, he said.

[34] On most such occasions when I mastered my dreams, I had a great longing to visit the *Realm of Bliss*, and I used to have the impression of paying my respects to the buddhas, sometimes in their divine palaces and sometimes (as they sat) with their backs against the jewelled trees of paradise.
Moreover when I was mastering my dreams, I would think that I would go to visit the *Realm of Bliss*, and then in the next moment I would recognize my own mind, thinking: 'It is this that is the *Realm of Bliss*. What is the use of going (anywhere). I have grasped it here.' Thus by abiding in things as they ultimately are, this special and absolute certainty of knowledge arose in me. Sometimes the pure signs of this kind of comprehension would arise.

On other occasions when I was practising the fierce rite of self-sacrifice at *Jo-bo Yul-lha*'s place, and at other times on the many occasions of this rite, as I sounded my drum, a large number of *attendant goddesses* would appear in the sky, and I would have the impression of a general reverberating of drums and a rending of the crags and mountains.

Once when I was mastering my dreams at Hrap, the mountain-king appeared from the recesses of the Hrap gorge, riding an enormous horse one and a half storeys high. He was wearing red felt and a red broad-brimmed hat and he came with a large entourage. I transformed myself into *Powerbolt-Terror* and turning large stones into masses of fire, I hurled them (at him) and his entourage disappeared. The king himself fled up the gorge, so I turned the stones on that side of the mountain into masses of fire and hurled them (at him). He fled to my side of the mountain, so I turned the stones on this side into masses of fire and threw them. Finally he fled to the Do-ra Bridge and went to *Shi-se*. I have the impression that he has gone to other countries now.

[35] On another occasion in my dream (I saw) *Sri-dar*, a villager of Saldang and a benefactor of mine, sitting in a cave with his head bent low down. I mastered my dreams and thought to myself: 'If he dies seated like this in that cave, he is bound to be reborn as an animal.' So I called to him from the top of the cave, telling him to come up. 'I cannot come up,' he replied. With a feeling of great compassion I pulled him up by the hand into my own presence. Then I pointed with a finger in the direction of *rDzing-po-che* Monastery. 'Nor far away from there in a westerly direction lies the *Realm of Bliss*. Go there and pray to your lama,' he said. He seemed to go off in the direction of *rDzing-po-che*.[1]

In another dream at Hrap I thought I would see the four great continents from the summit of the heavens of the 33 gods, so I flew there and went up to the top of Indra's palace. From there I saw the four continents and the great outer ocean all blue and shimmering. I thought I would leave one body there, and in another body go to get jewels from the ocean. I went there, and from out of the ocean (came) one whom I supposed to be the Serpent-King, and he gave me a heap of stones like *lapis lazuli*. 'Take these,' he said. I sank back into my original body. I had all sorts of experiences like this, he said.

> At such wondrous doings as these
> Involuntarily we feel respect and devotion.
> The waters of grace shoot up in full force.
> To us thy devoted sons give a blessing!

Furthermore when I was at *sTeng-chung* performing invocations of the *All-Knowing One*, four great rivers seemed to flow down from the four sides of a high mountain. [36] 'Are these the waters of phenomenal existence?' I wondered, 'then I must rescue the living creatures that are in them.' Then I thought of the Great Compassionate *Glancing Eye*, and on the summit of the mountain I transformed

---

[1] *rDzing-po-che*, now a ruin, is high above Sham-tr'ak in *Nang-khong*.

myself into *Glancing Eye* in his one-headed and four-armed form. I recited the *maṇi* prayer, reciting it as I envisaged myself going round from the east in a clockwise direction. To the east and the west the sound of the *maṇi* recitation grew less, but to the south and north it grew loud.

Once when I mastered my dreams at Hrap, I flew to the summit of a high crag in a land which had many trees and meadows decked with all kinds of flowers. I remained sitting up there with my legs hanging down, thinking: 'In order to realize buddhahood, I must experience the *Absolute Body of Buddhahood*, and for this I must comprehend the true nature of mind. This is nothing else than abiding continuously in the unaffected uncreate.' So I composed myself and experienced quite clearly the excellent state of true nature in its infinite incomprehensibility. Then again I understood and I thought to myself: 'For the sake of others I should become a buddha with a physical shape, and first I must be the *Glorious Body* of the Highest Heaven, namely the *Powerbolt-Holder*. So I became just this, adorned with a precious crown and precious decorations and so on. Then in order to act the part of those *would-be buddhas* who stay in the pure stages of the buddha-way and work on behalf of the hosts of potential converts, both lay and religious, I must transform myself into an excellent *Physical Body*, I thought. Thus I had the impression of being the great *Śākyamuni*.[1]

If you think rightly about all this, our Lama clearly had gained control over appearances, and this is the sphere of activity of holy ones alone. In order to listen to the wonderful stories about our holy Lama, [37] in order to meet him and listen to his words, to remain in his presence and to absorb his teachings, for all this, one must have accumulated merit during three immeasurable world-ages, this you must surely believe.

On yet another occasion our Lama had to go to Tarap, for both the layfolk and the religious there, especially the people of *Zhva-lding* and the Red Crag, had asked him again and again. Just before going, when he was about to leave the *Ja-tshang* Monastery, in his dream a voice sounded from the sky saying: 'As it is said "The horse that leads is the best in the fair", so it will be good if you go to Tarap.' This was a sign of the disease that came to Upper Nam later on (and which we were able to attend to on our way).

Then when he was in *Man-thod*, where he intended to make a long stay, he dreamed that a large prayer-flag was set up over a boundary stone on the *Zhva-lding* Saddle. So he went there and founded the monastery of *bSam-grub-chos-sdings*. He stayed there several years and instructed his converts in the scriptures, in the

---

[1] Concerning the three bodies of buddhahood, see the Introduction, p. 21. Here we have another triad, *viz.* a nameless *Absolute Body*, the supreme buddha *Powerbolt-Holder* as *Glorious Body* and the historical buddha *Śākyamuni* as *Physical Body*.

Way and its Fruits, Life Instructions of the Great Symbol, the *Sure Instructions of the Great Compassionate Lord,* and other profound doctrines. Having given them many such consecrations, textual initiations and instructions, he brought to fruition the inner disposition of these converts. In particular (one day) when he was giving instructions in the *Innate Yoga of the Great Symbol,* a clump of hollyhocks sprang up quite spontaneously by the edge of the religious enclosure. Six of the flowers opened and they were very beautiful. As soon as they were opened, a lot of clumps sprang up spontaneously from the roots (of the first one).

(*Our Lama continues the story:*)

One night in a dream [38] the Lama of the 'Mount of Realization' came to the side of a stupa and drew with his hand a circular design on the ground. Inside this circle he stuck three sticks at random, and he said: 'If you are demonstrating the *Great Symbol,* you should demonstrate it by such means as these. This circle represents the universality of the Absolute, and as for the three sticks, in ignorance they represent the *Three Evils,* and in knowledge the *Three Buddha-Bodies.*'

At *bSam-grub-chos-sdings* I mastered my dreams and went to visit the *Golden Realm* of the North. In the midst of a vast plain which seemed to have the colour of gold there was a palace of gems in a blazing glory of light, and I seemed to see there a great figure adorned with a jewelled tiara and various other items of jewelry, and I thought it must be the *Lord the Victorious Banner of Fame.*

On another occasion at *bSam-grub-chos-sdings,* when I was offering sacrificial cakes one evening, I was sounding my bell for the praises of the *Defender* (which begin with the words) 'All ablaze', and had reached the praises of *Spuṭa,* when I seemed to see the *Defender*'s figure as a mingling of rainbow colours, and *Spuṭa,* the army-commander was with him, and the sky was filled with a great army-host, armed with different kinds of weapons, and they moved with dancing gestures.
This happened on many occasions, and from then onwards I had great faith in the *Canopy Guardian.* So I exerted myself especially in reciting the 'All ablaze' verses and the prayers of atonement a hundred times over and more.

Furthermore when I was practising invocations of the *Red Fury,* the sky seemed to be filled with masses of fire. Then when I mastered my dreams, the whole room below was filled with beetles which swarmed up towards me. I transformed myself into the Teacher from Urgyan and from the roof-vent I hurled down great stones which [39] turned into balls of fire. The room below seemed to be filled with flames. If that was not all an illusion, I wonder if it was a sign from the local god, he said.

There is no doubt that our Lama had overcome the Devil of Personality.

On another occasion when he was practising the *Great Symbol* at *bSam-grub-chos-sdings*, he thought that he should go to see the Lama of the 'Mount of Realization', so he prayed to the Lama, and the Lama said to him: 'Nowadays you are in good health, so you should provide some good instruction in order to assist your faithful disciples with their religious training.' He said to himself: 'I wonder how good they are at meditation,' and he went round their meditation-tents in turn. The good layman *Novice* was in his tent in a very tearful mood because he could not correlate his thoughts, and yet he sat there trying very hard with his body upright in the correct posture. Our Lama was pleased at this, and he thought: 'I must watch over him with great compassion.'

Again when he was 61, he was explaining the doctrine at *bSam-grub-chos-sdings* when he thought that he must go to see the Lama of the 'Mount of Realization', so he mastered his dreams and went. Two women wearing beautiful jewelry handed him a length of white cloth and said: 'If you want to go and see him, sit in this.' So they invited him into a dooly and he travelled in that. 'They are *Attendant Goddesses*', he said to himself. In the middle of an ashy-coloured place there was a jewelled palace with tiered roofs. The lama was seated inside.

(Our Lama himself tells the story:)
I went to see him, making obeisance and saying a prayer. 'Go away for a while,' he said, 'and train your thoughts on the Uncreate.' Then I thought I should go to see the Great Lama of *Ngor*, so I went.
[40] In a region which proclaimed itself as Urgyan there were a lot of beautiful women decked with jewelry. 'Where are you going?' they said. 'I am going to see my Lama,' I replied, 'where is he?' 'At the side of that assembly-hall with the tiered roof there is a tiered-roof temple. He is in there,' they said. I went there and I saw the Lama as a young man with all the beauty of youth. His hair was plaited around his head and he wore a garland of flowers and other adornments. I made obeisance and said a prayer, and he said to me: 'Just now we are absorbing the teachings of secret spells, so go away for a while.' Then I woke up, our Lama said.

(The biographer continues:)
Afterwards he went to Hrap, where he taught many profound doctrines to his worthy disciples, of whom the foremost were the qualified monks of Dolpo. He taught them the doctrines of the *Way and its Fruits*, the Six Doctrines of *Nai-gu* and other works. While he was staying at Hrap, Bu-chung Wang-chuk was laying the foundations of the *Zel* Fort, and one day he told us that the father of a certain Brahman was ill. This man came to ask for a diagnosis, and our Lama asked him:

'How long has your father been ill?' 'Three years,' he replied, 'whatever methods we have used, they have been of no use. O Lama, you must make a good diagnosis and let me have it.' 'My knowledge is not unlimited,' our Lama said, 'but I will do what I can tonight.' Bu-chung led off the Brahman.

(The next day) our Lama said: 'I have made a diagnosis and the vision was like this. Beside the Brahman's house there is a white boulder, a grass-plot and a stream. I looked to see where the Brahman's father was, and he was lying inside the house. By the head of his bed was a middle-aged woman who seemed to be a servant. I asked her what she was doing there. [41] She replied: "By force of a former vow I am waiting here until my expectations are fulfilled." It is such a one as this who is causing the harm. What kind of matter is this?'

The Brahman rang his hands and said: 'Lama, it is just as you say. That valley-woman says that we Brahmans all owe her worship.'

'Why is she owed worship?' our Lama asked.

'When she was dying, she gathered all classes of Brahmans together and they performed a ceremony, but they did not do it properly, for they said to themselves: "It will be a good thing if she dies." So she became spiteful and made an evil vow, saying: "If I die, I shall want the worship of all the Brahmans and a food-offering of whatever you eat, and I pray that I may be reborn as one who harms the lives of Brahmans!" Uttering this vow, she died, and as a result of that we Brahmans have to give her worship.'

Then he returned to his village, where he gathered all the Brahmans together, and when they had made offerings and worship to that woman, his father recovered from his illness. Thereafter every time this Brahman Kyi-su-ba met our Lama, he would say: 'Lama, I beg to go into the protection of your tutelary divinities together with my whole household,' and he was quite filled with faith in us, our Lama said.

About that time when it was the beginning of winter Bu-chung Wang-chuk Paljor Teng-shal was going down to the lower valleys (the south) and he stayed one day at *rTsa*. Our Lama said to Bu-chung Dorje: 'Maybe it is not right that you should send your brother to the south this year,' and Bu-chung Dorje looked rather unhappy. Our Lama gave his assistant Sherap Tenpa a round lump of butter and some natural-coloured homespun (to take) to Bu-chung Wang-chuk Paljor Teng-shal with the message: [42]

'Our Lama says take these things down south with you.' Bu-chung was very pleased and said to Sherap Tenpa: 'Now what gracious favour he shows me! I will stay down south for the winter, then in the spring when my illness is over, I will come up to visit him bringing a really good present. Until then I beg him to keep me in the protection of his tutelary divinities.' With that he set out down south. The assistant

Sherap Tenpa returned to our Lama and said: 'For the present Bu-chung is happy,' and he gave him an account of what had just happened at his meeting with Bu-chung. Our Lama said: 'By mastering my visions, (I see that) for three years past the life-force of Bu-chung Wang-chuk Paljor and of Bu-chung Tse-tan Dorje have passed into the hands of the local god. When they were building *Zel* Fort, they did not subdue the place properly. They set to work quickly and turned up the soil, and now the king down there is being spiteful.'

That winter Bu-chung died while he was down south, and Bu-chung Tse-tan Dorje died at *rDzong-lung* Monastery.[1] After that they asked the seer[2] Tsha-ram-pa to subdue the place at *Zel* Fort, and they kept on asking our Lama too to subdue the place. He went there one night, and having mastered his dreams, he could not see the local god very clearly. He transformed himself into *Powerbolt-Terror* and raised up the rock of *Zel* Fort with the tips of his horns. The mountain-king in glorious attire came out from the inner recesses of the fort together with a large entourage. In their fear they stayed there motionless. Again our Lama transformed himself into *Red Fury* and set *Zel* Fort on fire with balls of fire. The king disappeared into the lower part of *Zel* Fort, and after that he had no further wish to go there, our Lama said.

[43] While our Lama was still staying at Hrap, the uncle, named Lha-dar, of a certain monk *Tsheng-lhas-skyabs* (*alias* Lekpa), failed to obtain (another) body (after death). Lama *mKhar-pa* and his assistants had already started a fire-oblation, and the monk came himself in person to beg our Lama to take him under the protection of his tutelary divinities. Our Lama said: 'You keep the fire going from now on, and I will do whatever I can.'

Then at night he mastered his dreams, and went to Lekpa's house, where the lamas were performing the ceremony. 'Where can this fellow be?' he thought. He looked about and saw (the deceased) going round and round the sacrificial hearth. Our Lama was moved by feelings of boundless compassion, and so he went up to him with the intention of giving him some religious instruction. But he could not endure our Lama's overpowering presence. So he ran away and disappeared into the *Khyung-lung* Crag. Thinking that *Khyung-lung*[3] would get mastery over him, our Lama went up to the top of the Crag, and turning himself into *Powerbolt Terror*, performed a furious dance. The *Khyung-lung* Crag seemed to crumble and break apart. (The deceased) came out of the middle of the crag and made off towards *Zhva-lding*. 'Where has he gone?' our Lama thought. He looked around

[1] *rDzong-lung dGon-pa*, now a ruin, is above Shimen.
[2] See p. 188 fn. 3.
[3] This name refers both to the mountain, which is near *rTsa*, and to the local god who lives in it.

and saw that he had entered *Zhva-lding* Monastery, so our Lama went there to search him out. He was hiding in one of the lower rooms, but when he saw our Lama, he came out and went towards Upper Nam. 'Where has he gone now?' our Lama thought. He looked around and saw that he had gone into Lekpa's house. At the same time Lekpa, who was setting up a prayer-flag on a headless arrow plumed with vulture-feathers, came out onto the roof. Our Lama thought: 'What can this Lha-dar be doing?' and going onto the roof of Lekpa's house, he looked inside through an upper window.

[44] He was not there, but he saw the place where the sacrificial fire had been, all glowing red. At once he had a feeling of boundless compassion, and snapping his fingers, he prayed that the deceased might be reborn in the Pure Realms.

He told us:

'On one occasion when Kunga Tshe-phel of *rTsa* had died, I received a request for a special ceremony, so that night I mastered my dreams and went to the mart (at Tarap), where I made an investigation to see if he had obtained another body or not. (I saw that) he had not obtained a body and was inside an animal's horn lying by the side of the river. "Why are you staying here?" I asked. "I am waiting here to get alms from the valley-men," he said, "but they have not given me a single grain of rice or a single grain of barley." I said to him: "You are dead, so it is useless yearning for alms. However much you yearn for them, there will be no one to give them, so come along." So I took him along to *bSam-grub-chos-sdings*.'

When he was telling us the story of how the Teacher from Urgyan founded *Ri-bo-bum-pa*[1] and other tales, he told us that the special ceremony for that man (Kunga Tshe-phel) was a terrible case.

On another occasion when he was staying at Hrap, a benefactor (of ours, also named) Kunga died in Lo. Someone came to ask for a special ceremony with a message which read: 'Evil as I am, I beg you to make amends for me.' Our Lama understood clearly and felt very sad. He was pervaded with boundless compassion and at the beginning of that winter he started on one thousand rituals of the *Buddha Imperturbable* for the good intention of that particular benefactor. He had performed one full set of invocations of the *Buddha Imperturbable* and it was the night of the sixteenth day (since he began), when the darkened room (where he sat) was filled with murmurings and clamourings, and with roarings and neighings. While this was going on, [45] he concentrated his thoughts on our benefactor Kunga and continued with the invocations. 'Are these lamentations coming from our benefactor

---

[1] *Ri-bo bum-pa*, a small monastery just above Do in Tarap, is supposed to have been founded according to local tradition by *Lotus-Born* himself.

THE BIOGRAPHY OF LAMA GLORIOUS INTELLECT   215

Kunga?' he thought. A hand reached up at the window. Our Lama called out: 'Kunga, Kunga!' but there was no reply. Then he caught him by the hair, and pulled him up forcibly, and it was our benefactor Kunga who emerged. Thus Kunga received some small benefit on this occasion. As for sacraments, he had only received blessings (during his lifetime),[1] but all his generous gifts counted in his favour, our Lama said.

When he was 67 years old and still living at Hrap, he had a serious illness. In order to reinforce the auspicious intentions of all the special ceremonies that were held, he gave away all his paraphernalia to various lamas, and to the various monasteries of Dolpo he gave food-supplies and things useful as offerings. As for his gifts to the ordinary people, to the villagers of Tarap, *Ban-tshang*, *Nang-khong*, *Ku*, *Bi-cher* and so on, he gave away measures of grain and made general distributions on a large scale.

At that time he was practising meditation in strict seclusion.

When he mastered his dreams one night, the sun appeared immediately opposite Hrap and moved rapidly to the west. He transformed himself into the extraordinary form of the *Lord of Power*,[2] and pressed the sun flattish, so that it came out again as an oblong shape. This was to be understood as a sign that his life would be prolonged for three more years.[3]

Furthermore while he was staying at Hrap, he performed one thousand ceremonies of the *All-Knowing* and one thousand of the *Buddha Imperturbable*. He paid for the making of images, books and shrines, making religious craftsmen well content with the fees he paid. In short his works were what would be expected of just such an exalted one whose place is the ten stages of buddhahood. [46]

CHAPTER VI.   *An account of how he spread the Buddhist Doctrine.*

As for this pure minded spreading of the doctrine,
It is just the small matter of my knowing and doing as a yogin.

As for the meaning of this, our Lama said: 'Having first completed the study of all the *sūtras* and *tantras*, I learned their meaning by bowing at the lotus-feet of twenty worthy lamas and quenching my thirst with the elixir of their words, which I received with faith and devotion, absorbing their content by strict austerities and

---

[1] This is to say that he had received no consecrations with their fortifying power, but only simple blessings (*phyag-dbang*).
[2] This is '*Bir-ba* (*Virūpa*), also referred to as 'Lord of Yogins'. See pp. 101 and 196.
[3] Counting the first year and the last in accordance with normal Tibetan practice, this would make him 69 when he died. See pp. 76 and 193.

exertions in lonely places. Thus I brought to birth in my mind the special qualities of renunciation and understanding. As for the way I performed religious acts with my thoughts on the doctrine and on sentient beings, this is just as has been related above. Taking special account of the manner in which the inner disposition of others is brought to full developments, (one notes that) this is done by instruction and by performance. There was the Great Abbot *Jewel Religious Adornment*, a great sage and comprehender of the doctrine, handsomely adorned with good moral teachings and high-ranking by the excellence of his good qualities of inspired learning and understanding.

There was the Great Abbot *Magnificent Aim-Winner*, who was perfected in the five kinds of knowledge and had achieved stability in the processes of emanation and realization of the *Powerbolt Vehicle*. There was the Great Abbot *Saviouress Religious Power*, whose inner disposition was well schooled by study, learning and meditation, and who spread the teachings of tantric performance.

There was that secret yogin, the Great Abbot *Jewel Morality*, possessor of the Seven Noble Gems and upholder of the way of *Ku-su-lu*.[1] There were those two, the Great Abbot of *Zhva-lding*, *Excellence Glorious and Good*, and the Abbot of *Zhu-lag*, *Merit Life-Consecration*, who were the adornments of the triple doctrine, teaching faultlessly to others the teachings of their forebears.

There was the wise Abbot *Glorious Gem* and the scholar [47] *Merit Knowledge* together with his nephew.

There was the Sage, the Lama of *Songs*, together with his brother.

There was Master *Intellect Powerbolt* and Master *Jewel Victorious Banner* who possess the treasure of inspired teachings, knowledge and profound advice, and who have achieved a great measure of joy in the ten-stage path of study, learning and meditation.

There was the Master *All Joy Victorious Banner*, who was a repository of much learning, and very many others, who as friends of religion did all they should do for the doctrine, attaining to the very essence of the *Powerbolt Body*, for they were perfect in their control of the vital channels and the vital breath, self-characterized by their profound experience. Such were the Ascetic *Nam-mkha' Dar-po* and those later pupils who took to the way of active performance.

Then there were also many nuns, but fearing verbosity, we do not give the name of

[1] This is a curious term best defined by a quotation from the *Hermit Teachings*, 'Advice on Religious Retreat' (*ri-chos mtshams kyi zhal-gdams*): '*Ku-su-lu* is not the real form (of the word), for in the language of India it was Ku-sa-li. In Tibetan the term refers to the three notions of (1) food and drink (2) excretion and (3) getting supplies. Apart from these three a hermit should abandon all activities and practise contemplation. Nowadays this is referred to as Ku-su-lu. In India there were two (Great Yogins) named Kusali, the Elder and the Younger. In Tibet the name had been wrongly turned into Ku-su-lu, and it means the way of a yogin who lives like a hermit.' (folio 102b of the *bDe-chen bla-brang* MS copy.)

every one. I too, who am named *Puṇyamati*,¹ a saffron clad monk of this hidden border land of (Dolpo), also gained some little instruction. I have told here something of how our Lama spread the doctrine of the Victorious Buddha by referring to those (of his pupils named above).

On one occasion when he was at Hrap Monastery, giving instructions in the *Nai-gu* teachings of the *Great Symbol*, the 'rite of self-sacrifice' and such matters, to several of his disciples, of whom the foremost were the Great Abbot *Jewel Religious Adornment*, Master Tashi the Northerner and the Ascetic *Nam-mkha' Dar-po*, he thought to himself: 'Is this instruction excessive?' So he prayed to his lama, and controlling his dreams, set out (to find him). In the *Realm of Urgyan* he saw a lama with the form of an eight year old boy, who was explaining the methods of learning. Then he went on to see where the Lama of the 'Mount of Realization' might be, and he went and found him in the heavens.

(The next morning) when his assistant came to see him, our Lama said: 'Last night I saw two of my lamas, so I am very happy.'

His assistant asked him: 'What articles of worship are there in the realms where those lamas dwell?'

[48] Our Lama replied: 'How can words describe those jewelled palaces rich with adornments, where there is no apprehender and really nothing to be apprehended. The various kinds of worship transcend our thoughts altogether, for the lay-out of these realms is quite perfect.'

His assistant asked again: 'What did the lamas say in the matter of your doubts concerning the instructions that you have begun?'

'The gracious Margom Lama said: "The time has come for work on behalf of your converts." The Lama of the 'Mount of Realization' said: "It is good to pray to your lamas, for your work on behalf of others will then come about quite spontaneously". This is what our Lama told us.

On another occasion he was teaching the *Great Symbol* to the monk *rGyal-po-phan* and a few others. Having started the monk on a course of solitary meditation, he went away to take charge of a set of one thousand performances of the rite of the *All-Knowing* on behalf of the two Bu-chung Dorje Teng-shal brothers.² (Meanwhile) the monk got into difficulties. He himself was very upset and some of the others became excited. When our Lama had finished the performance of rites, he went (back to Hrap). Having given (the monk) a powerful blessing, he prayed to his lamas, and mastering his dreams, went to see the Lama of the 'Mount of Realiza-

¹ The writer *Merit Intellect* modestly quotes his own name in Sanskrit, which is a hidden language so far as most Tibetans are concerned. For other references to him, see pp. 68–9 and 182.
² See p. 213

tion'. The lama said: 'The way in which you gave the basic instruction was good, but you must explain things (to each pupil) in a manner that befits each case.'

So I was brought to realize (our Lama said) that I had explained things only in a general way. In accordance with my lama's advice, I explained things once again to the monk and his difficulties were resolved.

On another occasion the cleric *Blo-gros* was struck with some devilish complaint. However much he recited texts and spells and despite the supporting ceremonies that I performed, for some time he got neither better nor worse. 'Haven't we overcome this yet,' I thought. Then one night in my dreams (I saw) [49] a stream running here and there at the foot of a dark cliff and a white boulder on the hill-slope above. At the bottom of the valley there was a circular pool, and the cleric was in the middle of it tied up naked. I transformed myself into *Red Fury* and hurled balls of fire. The pool went up in steam and I could not see the cleric any more. Realizing that it must be an illusion created by the local god, I transformed myself into *Powerbolt Terror*. I must jab at the pool with my horns, I thought, so I pressed my horns into the pool, and it all dried up. The cleric came out looking very feeble, and I saw that a great many creatures had died. My thoughts were filled with boundless compassion, and I thought: 'What is this? Have I struck the blow perhaps?' But it was not I who struck the blow. Someone else was practising black magic against him. When one is dealing with illusions, the *Red Fury* and the *Terror* are the best, our Lama said. The cleric was cured of that disease which was caused by the local god.

On one occasion when our Lama was staying at *Zhva-lding*, (a villager named) Gu-ma was almost dying. Two local practitioners,[1] brother and sister, gave him their attention, but it was of no use. So they came to ask our Lama for a diagnosis. Having made it, he said: 'The place indicated is *mDa'-chen*. This needs my attention.' So he went there. It was evening and *Jo-bo Yul-lha* had brought together all the local gods from up and down (the valley). They came to meet our Lama and conducted him on his way. Then they discussed matters together, and brought a sheep, which they gave to him. It was the 'soul' of the sick man. He made them a mental offering of sacrificial *chang*, and the sick man recovered. Then the local gods made *chang*, tea and curdled milk, and said: 'We beg to enter the protection of your tutelary divinities, and we beg you to look after this sick man.'

Our Lama told us:

On one occasion when I was at the 'Mount of Realization', the master-scholar Namdrol was so ill that he was nearly dying, [50] and they said that I must go

[1] See p. 188 fn. 3.

there. 'Will it be of any use or not?' I thought. I made an investigation. At dawn I mastered my dreams, and went to see how Namdrol was. He was in his house on his bed, and a very ugly black woman was lying by the head of the bed. By her side there was a woman of *Khyung-lung*. The black woman wriggled with her feet and changed herself back into a serpent, twisting herself around my feet. It was a devilish piece of illusion, and I turned myself into *Red Fury* and hurled balls of fire. There was no certitude in her physical form. I asked the woman of *Khyung-lung* what all this might be.

'He was formerly the Lama of Shey,' she said, 'but he did not serve the monastery well. As a result of his acts in this former life he was harmed by the local god. I did something to counteract it.'

'What happened?' I asked her.

'He was struck in the stomach,' she said. 'You, O Lord, have seen things here for yourself, so please take charge of this affair. I am going.'

Then I woke up and thought the matter over. 'It may be some use,' I thought, so I went to the place. The master-scholar was still lying in bed, looking quite exhausted. 'How is it?' I asked him.

'I am unable to die,' he said and kept on crying.

'You seem to be under attack,' I said, 'what kind of building work did you do?'

'O gracious one, is this what your dreams indicated?' he said, 'I beg you to tell me.'

I told him how my dream had been, and he said: 'O gracious one, I am such a selfish person, that without giving thought I set about this work of construction.'

[51] Our Lama performed a rite for his intention, and this counteraction was effective, with the result that the Master's life was extended for three years. He gave some very good offerings in thanksgiving.

On another occasion when our Lama was at *bSam-grub-chos-sdings*, the chief man named *Saviouress*[1] came asking for a blessing, and said: 'A bad epidemic has broken out at *Phal* and *rTar* and many people are dead. It has not finished yet. The villagers have sent me to ask for your diagnosis about how matters will be, and whether it can be stopped or not.'

Our Lama replied: 'We are completely sincere with one another. I will make as good a diagnosis as I can.' Then he mastered his dreams and went to see the villages of *Phal* and *rTar*. At the end of the bridge in *Phal* there was a fearful-looking black dog tied up with an iron chain, and it prevented anyone from coming near. Realizing that this was a fiendish piece of illusion, he turned himself into *Powerbolt-in-Hand* and flew up into the sky. As he went along the *rTar* valley, he was met by *Jo-bo Yul-lha*, who was very unhappy, saying that he had been defiled.

[1] See p. 193 fn.3.

He invited our Lama up to the head of the valley to his castle, where he had set up a high throne. He invited our Lama to be seated upon it, and then offering him agreeable things (flowers, incense, etc.) and *chang* and many other things, he made obeisance, walked round him in a clockwise direction to show his respect, and said: 'I beg you, O Lama, to remove this defilement of mine.' 'I will do that,' said our Lama, and sprinkled him with holy water. He was delighted at this, and he and his whole entourage, wearing turbans of red silk and white cloth, fine garments and all kinds of adornments, sang and danced, and then offered to our Lama as a thanksgiving a skull-cup filled with elixir. Placing his head at our Lama's feet, he said: [52] 'I beg you to encompass me and my following with your compassion, O Lama.'

Our Lama said: 'In connection with your defilement great harm has befallen these villages. I am benefitting you, and you are the god of the village, so do not cause them harm, but produce a remedy for removing the epidemic.'

The local god brought forward an eleven year old boy, and said: 'Except for (returning) this boy, I will do what you say, O Lama. Those villagers defiled the place with dead bodies, and it was not very pleasant,' and he looked rather upset about it.

The Lama said: 'Give me this boy which you have brought here.'

He replied: 'I beg you to permit this, O Lama,' and he was unwilling to give up the boy. Then with many horsemen as escort, our Lama made his way back (to the village). The chief man *Saviouress* was on the roof of his house in the attitude of meditation. Below him there was (another) house with firewood all around the roof-edge, and a great gust of wind shook the wood and brought it all down. Our Lama thought: 'That boy who is in the hands of the local god was an occupant of that house,' and he had a feeling of boundless compassion for them. All over the village-fields and between the houses a lot of tents had been put up. There were a lot of ragged and wretched beggars there with a middle-aged monk in their company. Our Lama chased after him with a serpent-noose which he was holding (at the time) as a functional symbol, and with a loud roaring noise the monk fled. (Realizing that) the local god of *Phal* was the demon (behind all this), he transformed himself into *Powerbolt-in-Hand*, and brought the god to account. He was terrified and cried: 'O Great Wrathful One, I beg you to be patient. I will do what you say.' Then he came out to meet our Lama and escorted him in fine style, and the local gods of *Ting-khyu* as well came to escort him, showing their faith and devotion. Then *The-'or* too came to meet him, [53] and with clouds of incense and other good things invited him to his palace. A high throne was set up with curtains of white silk and pleasant things (flowers, incense, etc.) were set ready. They prepared offerings of many kinds of foods, and made many salutations and respectful circumambulations. Then (the mountain god) said: 'We beg that you would give us some religious teachings.'

So our Lama transformed himself into *Glancing Eye* in his one-headed, four-armed form. The place was filled with rays of light, and he taught them the doctrines of cause and effect as suitable for the occasion. The god had complete faith in him and made a vow not to take life or cause injury. Then with the sound of music this *The-'or* and other local gods came with an enormous following of military horsemen and escorted him as far as the *Tshos-la* Pass.[1] So he returned to his room, where he woke up. He told something of all this to the chief man *Saviouress* and said: 'Do not tell all the details.'

On another occasion the people of *Po-ldad* were afflicted by an epidemic and the monk *Firm Life* came to ask for a diagnosis. Our Lama mastered his dreams, and flying through the air, sat down on the mountain-side near *Jo-bo Yul-lha*. The sun rose straight up from the east, and our Lama made it into a seat and sat upon it. *Jo-bo Yul-lha* with a large following gathered around him and prepared the most wonderful things for worship, for the way in which our Lama used the sun as a seat and all the blaze of light impressed them very much. So all the local gods gathered together and the whole mountainside was filled with military horsemen. (*Jo-bo Yul-lha* addressed words) to them, saying: 'Ask for religious instruction. Offer him honour and service. Make salutations to him and respectful circumambulations,' and to the Lama he said: 'I beg that you would teach them about religion.' Then our Lama transformed himself into *Glancing Eye* and instructed them in religion, and they all rejoiced [54] and were glad, and they rose up and made salutations and respectful cicumambulations. Then they asked for the waters of purification, and so our Lama sprinkled purifying water from a crystal vase. After he had purified them all, they promised to help in furthering religious affairs, and that they would not take life and go hunting and so on, for they said: 'We will perform whatever command you give us.' Then they each made offerings and showed our Lama honour on a scale that quite surpasses one's thought. With things thus arranged, he went to see the village, where there was a stupa with a great raised platform, and he sat on the top of this. The sun shone over the village and everything was very bright, but towards the upper part of the valley there was a hazy mist. Becoming aware of this, our Lama transformed himself into the *Leaf-Clad Goddess*, recited a set of spells and sprinkled purifying water. The mist disappeared, and he addressed them, saying: 'You monks of this village, just perform this set of spells.' They did so, and the epidemic came to an end.

On another occasion the wife of Master Palzang was ill, and he came to our Lama to ask for a diagnosis. Our Lama mastered his dreams and set out. At the top

---

[1] The *Tshos-la* is the pass between *Ting-khyu* and Tarap.

of the *Tshos-la* Pass *Jo-bo Yul-lha* came to meet him with a large following and they were leading a sorrel horse, decorated with silks of five colours. They begged our Lama to ride on it, and made salutations and respectful circumambulations, they led the way. So our Lama came to the 'White Crag'. He was considering the situation, when *Jo-bo Yul-lha* approached him again, and said: 'I beg you to come to my palace.' They invited him with the accompaniment of music and incense, and from within the fort (they brought) a dooly made of a length of silk stretched out, and on this he went up to the fort. There was a throne on a set of thirteen tiered platforms, enclosed by curtains of white silk. A check-cloth [55] was arranged on the throne, and here the Lama seated himself. Then they offered him the esoteric worship of elixir in a crystal skull-cup and also other kinds of worship on a scale that quite surpasses thought, and the local god said to him: 'I beg you to give religious instruction to myself and my entourage, and to sprinkle purifying water in my palace.' Our Lama did as he asked, and they rejoiced and were glad and joined their hands in prayer. Then they invited him to take his place in a silken dooly, and they went down from *Jo-bo Yul-lha*'s peak to the Master's house. The door was firmly closed, but in the middle of it there was a peep-hole. They worked the door open and went inside. The woman of the house was lying down and by the head of the bed a monk was standing, but he ran away. Our Lama manifested the self-confidence of *Powerbolt-in-Hand* and went in pursuit, but only a short distance, for the monk disappeared in the middle of the village. Then they said: 'Good woman, get up!' and she got up feeling giddy. She said: 'I am going up onto the roof,' but she could not get up there. The result of the diagnosis was that she would not die, but there was the likelihood of the disease lasting a long time. Our lama said to them: 'Perform some good ceremony for the intention of that monk.'

On another occasion when he was staying at *Ja-tshang*, a cleric of Shimen, named Paljor Gyaltsan was very near dying, and someone came to invite our Lama there. He said: 'I will see tonight what kind of diagnosis I get.' Then mastering his dreams, he went to see the place. On the slope behind the house there was a gorge filled with water and nearby three men were chasing an *argali* (wild sheep). 'If only that *argali* might escape!' he thought. He tried to save it, but he could not do so, for they chased it across the rocky mountain-face. Our Lama transformed himself into the *Red Fury* and went across the mountain too. When they [56] saw him, they were frightened and went higher (up the mountain) and the *argali* fell (over the side). Our Lama felt great compassion and said a prayer. He thought that he should give its flesh to those (hunters), but although he looked around, they seemed to be nowhere. Then he went to see the cleric, and he was very near death. Our Lama said to him:

'*Compounded things are void of real existence.*
This thing called death is now upon you, so pray to a lama for whom you feel devotion.'

By a black rock-face near the village there was a clear stream, and a demoness who lived there had been affected by sour *chang* which had been thrown into it (by the cleric). She was very unhappy about this, and it was she who had caused the cleric harm. Our Lama gave her some religious instruction, but she said: 'I do not understand such things for I know nothing about them. I beg you, O Lama, to give me the blood of a living animal which you have first tasted.'
'I cannot get the blood of a living creature,' our Lama said.
'It will do if you just draw a little blood off any animal that comes to my door,' she replied.
So our Lama drew off a little blood (in this way), tasted it and then gave her ablution. Thus she was cured of her sickness and her sorrow. Then he recited to her a verse:
'*No evil must one do, but the very highest good.*'
She attained to great faith in him, and he induced her to do no harm to living creatures.
Then he awoke and said to the man who had come for the diagnosis: 'This time the omens were not good, but perform whatever good ceremonies you can.' When the man returned, the cleric was dead. He came again to see our Lama and met him on the way on the *Wa-gong* Pass.[1] 'I beg to come under the protection of your tutelary divinities,' he said.

On another occasion when our Lama was at *bSam-grub-chos-ldings*, he thought that he would go and see his lama, so mastering his dreams, [57] he set out. He went up over high alpine pastures thick with flowers, and there where the pasture ended and the bare mountain began there was a mare with her foal. He thought: 'It is remarkable that these horses should have come so high. Is a wolf on the way?'
He drove them downhill, but on the alpine slopes he was inattentive with his mind on other matters, and then the wolf came and carried off the foal. He tried to save it, but he could not, and so it was lost. Then the mare turned into a beautiful woman, and clinging to our Lama's feet, she wept in a state of great misery. 'It is no use being so unhappy,' our Lama said, 'I will pray (for your foal). You must not be distressed.' Then the woman changed back into a mare and disappeared over the crest of the mountain. Our Lama awoke. A messenger from Kāk[2] reached the monastery just about sunrise and asked for a diagnosis. He wanted to know how

[1] This lies between Shimen and *Ja-tshang*.
[2] Tib. *bKag*. This is Kāgbeni in the Kāli Gandaki valley. See *Himalayan Pilgrimage*, pp. 165-9.

matters would be with the (chief man's) son who was ill. Our Lama said that the night before he had such and such a dream. 'I wonder how things will be,' he added. 'O he will be dead now,' the man said and was very unhappy. 'I beg you to make a diagnosis tonight as well.'

So that night he mastered his dreams again and went to see the boy. On the south side of Kāk there is a track under the cliffs, and here there were a lot of horsemen. The boy was with them, riding a sorrel horse and wearing a round Mongol hat. As he rode, his horse stumbled a little. The white hat rolled away and was carried off by the current of the river. Our Lama went to catch the hat, but he could not. When he looked at the young man again, he was under his horse by the edge of the river. He pulled him away and put (his head) in the water. He came to and gained consciousness.

[58] Our Lama set him on his horse, but he could not stay there. So he led him along on foot and then set him forth on the whitish dusty track that goes towards Muktināth. Then our Lama went to see *Saviouress* the chief man (of Kāk). There were high stacks of wood and a lot of horses, but he could not see his lordship, although there were a lot of people mourning. At that point he awoke. 'The young man seems to be lost in this bad affair. His lordship himself will not have any troubles from outside for a few years, and he will be successful and rich and so on,' thinking thus, he said to the messenger: 'Both the first and the later dream are in agreement. The boy wont live, or else my dreams are false. There is no clear issue. I beg you to perform such and such a ceremony as well as you can. I too will do what I can.'

On another occasion when he was staying at Hrap, Bu-chung Tsun-chung was unwell. He came to the monastery, but whatever our Lama did in the way of benedictions and so on, it was all no use. Once again he made a diagnosis by means of dreams. Mastering his dreams, he flew to the summit of *Jo-mo rTogs-ldan-ma*,[1] where he had a vision of *Jo-bo Yul-lha*. The local god came with his entourage, and giving him a present of a roll of silk, invited him into his palace, where he offered him some dark-coloured tea. 'What's the use of tea of such a black colour?' our Lama said, and he threw the cup and its contents at him. The local god was terrified and went and got some clear-looking tea, saying: 'I beg you not to be displeased with me, but to give us some religious instruction.' So our Lama bestowed upon them the vows of the 'Three Refuges' and the 'Arousing of Thought', and they placed his feet on their heads and were filled with devotion. Then he went to *rDzong-'jar*, and the mountain god came wearing clothes of old brocade silk and a strange kind of hat,[2] [59] and carrying four arrows without heads on them. Reaching our Lama's

---

[1] This is the mountain above Hrap.   [2] The Tibetan term '*bar-zhva* remains unidentified.

presence, he made salutation and invited him inside. They went inside the castle, and our Lama said: 'Tell me, will Bu-chung Tsun-chung's life be cut short or not.' 'I don't know,' he replied, for he did not want to have to explain things clearly. Our Lama transformed himself into *Powerbolt-Terror*, and made a show of shaking the castle with his horns, so that the place trembled. Then he turned himself into *Red Fury*, and transforming a great boulder into a ball of fire, he hurled it, and it went straight downwards, falling into the centre of the ocean, and there was a sissing sound. Seeing that he could not quell this local god by fierce means, he turned himself into *Glancing Eye*, and brought the fellow within the scope of his compassion. The local god showed himself in his own form, smiling and taking our Lama's feet on his head. 'How will Bu-chung be?' our Lama said. 'I cannot very well say how he will be,' the fellow replied, and he offered our Lama a leg of meat. He accepted it and came away, and it turned into a left hand. Our Lama thought: 'Can Bu-chung live now, I wonder.' When he had completed the period of his solitary meditation, he gave Bu-chung the consecration of the *All-Knowing*. Bu-chung looked at him fixedly, and then burst into tears and seized the Lama's feet, crying: 'Except for you, Lama, I have no hope. You know what must be done.' For he was in great misery through his fear of dying. Our Lama said: 'Now Bu-chung, it is no use getting upset. Concentrate your thoughts within, and without feeling any attachment for anything, concentrate upon your lama, and pray to him. I will guide your consciousness and pronounce the prayers and all the rest as well as is possible, supporting you with the greatest compassion.' Then Bu-chung joined his hands in supplication, and his head sank down and down. The time for him to die had come, [60] and so whatever was done was of no use, and he died. The corpse was given as a ceremonial offering to the birds, and our Lama did all he could in the way of consecrations, prayers, rituals and so on.

In short this Lama of ours spent all his time on religious works, and by teaching and by meditation he caused the doctrine to spread and did good for living creatures. He had many visions too of the realms of pure buddhahood and other things that quite transcend our imagination. But fearing excess of words, we have told things rather sketchily.

CHAPTER VII.

Having finished his wonderful works in this present life, he began to think of converts in other realms, and so his body passed away into the elemental sphere. This is how it happened.

From the first autumn month of the Wood Female Sheep Year (A.D. 1535) onwards, here within the area of Hrap the splendour of the sun and moon was dimmed and in our soil the vitality of our grain and its ripening force were weakened, there was damage from frost and hail, and birds made all kinds of unpleasant calls, the wild animals who live around showed their unhappiness in many ways, and many empty sounds resounded from the sky. Then on the 28th day of the middle month of winter he showed signs of illness and up until the 18th day of the 1st Month of the Fire Male Monkey Year[1] (*alias* 'Year of Evil Countenance') his mind rested unmoved in the universal absolute, while in the eyes of us his imperfect pupils he gave the appearance of being ill.

In the meantime *rGyal-po-phan*, who is a fully qualified monk, the chief assistant Sherap Tenpa and other staff-members of our Lama's entourage, having in mind the intentions of his last rites, made a general distribution of his movable property. '*A-pha*[2] Paljor, the medical practitioner, who is quite expert in the knowledge of cures, and Master Pal-tshap gave him medical attendance of the best possible kind.

[61] From the 29th onwards until the 5th the whole assembly of monks of our monastery exerted themselves without any interruption in the ritual *Ocean of Accomplishments* and in a session of *The Divine Names*. I myself, who am the least of all, together with Master *Songs-pa*, three master-scholars and eleven of the brethren, started on the rite of atonement of *Glorious Black Powerbolt-Canopy Countenance*.

On the 5th the Master *Saviouress Religious Power* and his attendant Kunga, these two, both master and pupil, arrived.

From the 6th until the 8th some of us religious brethren performed the 'thousand-fold purificatory rites' of the *Destroyer*, the *Victorious Lady* and the *Fierce God with Up-turned Moustache*. We did these purifying rites for the person of our Lama, but he said: 'There is no means by which I can return (to the world) now, but since this will remove defilements on my path (towards buddhahood), perform purificatory rites, ablutions and the rest.'

From the evening of the 8th until the 11th we performed the rite of atonement of the *Guru Red Fury*. On the morning of the 11th his condition had deteriorated, and he said to the clerics, the teachers and their pupils: 'Tomorrow morning offer up sacrificial cakes.' They did as he said, and we religious brethren went to his side. He gave us rather sketchy instructions about what should be done with regard to his will, both in the matter of religious affairs, and in the affairs of normal life. All of us who were there in his presence felt very depressed and our eyes were filled with tears. Then he said: 'Let the Learned Master look after me. The fully-qualified

---

[1] Corresponding to A.D. 1596. See p. 76.   [2] See p. 188. fn.

monk Kunga and the rest of you, please begin now *Hevajra*'s ritual, while let the members of the community perform the ritual of *Buddha the Imperturbable*.'
On the latter of the two dates 11th[1] the teachers and pupils formally asked him to remain, but their request was not granted. The next morning there arrived from Margom [62] a message in verse asking him to remain in the world, a ceremonial scarf of auspicious import (this was the chief item) and a present of a set of seven articles, a copper *chang* jug and six other things. These were sent by that most excellent guide *Religious Protector Glorious and Good*.
We religious brethren also begged him to remain, but he said: 'Whatever is done now, my life will not be lengthened. However since such things have been sent from Margom, all I can say is look to it yourselves.'
We each made him a symbolic offering, asking him to stay with us: 'For the good of living creatures you must bestow upon us a favourable reply to the effect that your feet will remain firm (in this world).' 'From my early days onwards,' he replied, 'I have performed works of a religious kind as far as my strength allowed. Such has been my way of doing what good I could for the doctrine and for living creatures. Now however much we may all want things to be as you say, inevitably my time has come, and so I must depart. Is it not even said of our Teacher the Perfect Buddha with regard to (the last of) his twelve great acts:

"*Salutation to him who has passed from sorrow,*
Destroying his own physical body though it resembled an immortal powerbolt,
At that immaculate place, the City of Fine Grass (Kuśinagara),
And all for the sake of inspiring us lazy mortals".'

At dawn on the 14th while he was meditating upon the *clear light*, four women decked with jewelry appeared. He told us just so much, for he did not tell us everything clearly. Then he said: 'All of you should say the prayer of the *Realm of Bliss*.'
We recited once the prayer that begins with the words 'Not parting'. Then he said: 'You do not have to do it in full. Recite it as many times as you can from the words "The merit accumulated throughout past, present and future by myself and by others" onwards.'
Then he asked immediately: 'What date is it today? What lunar mansion are we in?' 'It is the 14th and the lunar mansion is that of the Fox,' we said.
[63] 'Then that doesn't do,' he said, and he looked doubtful.
Then on the 17th at dawn his mind was in a very happy state with all appearances

[1] The Tibetan calendar sometimes has two consecutive days of the same date, usually to compensate for inauspicious dates which have been omitted in a particular month.

resolving into themselves like bubbles into water, but something disturbing happened, and (again) he said: 'It doesn't do.'
At dawn on the 18th the signs worked out auspiciously, and he told us in what way to read off the promptings. Then he said: 'I have obtained clarity (of insight).'
Those who were standing around him asked: 'Which of the holy realms do you intend to go to? If disciples and followers who depend upon you as we do, wish to pray to you, where should they direct their prayers?'
Our precious Lama replied: 'If you wish to pray to me, then (know that) I have a desire to go to the *Realm of Bliss*, so say your prayers with that realm in mind.'
'Will you remain in meditation?' they asked.
'The best is to remain composed in the natural state of reality. As I intend to embark upon soul-transference, you will not need to give me a lot of promptings for the transference-process. Just the hand-gestures will be enough.'
From dawn until sunset he sat with his eyes set firm in the attitude of the *Powerbolt Holder*, remaining motionless in one long session of meditation. His physical appearance and his complexion were quite resplendent. In this condition his mind passed into the elemental sphere.

Now as for the after-events, preparations were made for the ceremonial burning of the corpse on the 18th day of the 1st Month, and when we were about to make this homage of fire in *Hevajra*'s mystic circle as accords with tantric practice, by merely touching the corpse with one tongue of flame, the fire consumed itself in self-ignition. It looked very beautiful with flames like lotus-petals, and there was a pleasant sound of burning like the humming of bees.

[64] The pleasant smell of incense was all-pervading, and all those who were assisting at the ceremony experienced religious insight and avertion to the world, unlike anything they had known before, and all kinds of wonderful notions. Moreover flowers rained down from the skies, and there were many extraordinary portents, rainbow colours in the form of a tent, and the sounds of music.
Moreover there were many extraordinary signs, flowers raining down from the skies, rainbow colours in the shape of a tent, and the sounds of religious music; it was a wonderful example for the guidance of men of pure heart.
Then on the 15th day of the 2nd Month they opened the funeral-urn. On the skull there were *Hevajra, Powerbolt-Terror, Gentle-Voice, Perfecter of Thought*, both *Blue* and *Red, Bir-srung* in his ordinary and extraordinary form, the Teacher *Nāgārjuna*, the Lord *Victorious Banner of Fame*, the Four-Armed Protector (according to the tradition of the concealed texts), the *Canopy Guardian* and *Glancing Eye*.
On the short ribs was the Lord *Śākyamuni*.

THE BIOGRAPHY OF LAMA GLORIOUS INTELLECT 229

On the thigh-bones were the nine goddesses of *Hevajra*'s troupe, namely *Gaurī* and the others.
On the jaw-bone were *Powerbolt-in-Hand* and *Caṇḍālī*.
Moreover there were other effigies which could not be identified. As symbols of the Buddha-Word there were a lot of embossed syllables, OṂ Ā HŪṂ, AṢṬHA and others.
As symbols of the Buddha-Mind there were little stupas to which pure-hearted converts and faithful disciples might say their prayers. These miraculous appearances had the effect of establishing the faith of disciples who were already under vows, and of nourishing the seeds of devotion of ordinary folk who had simply heard of the wonderful acts of our Lama, and so while some of them were just paying their respects to his physical remains, others were able to recognize the different divinities. The physical remains returned for the most part to normal forms, to curiously shaped bone-relics, but they were quite splendid ones. All this has been set down in outline without exaggeration or bias.

[65] *By just hearing the title of our Lama's biography*
May all future converts
Be cleansed from sin and all consequent effects
And quickly gain the state of omniscience!

We can give just a brief account of the events following upon our Lama's passage to the elemental sphere. From the 6th Month to the Autumnal (9th) Month ceremonies were performed continuously for the perfecting of his intentions, the ritual of *Hevajra*, the rituals of the *All-Knowing* and of the *Buddha Imperturbable*, as well as ceremonies by the qualified teachers of Dolpo and the monks of the monasteries. Stupas and reliquaries, written accounts of his life, paintings in gold, and a life-size image for his accustomed seat, all these and other such things were donated. Suitable offerings were made to the Lord of Religion at Margom and to other lamas and various renowned disciples who had been connected with our holy Lama. General distributions were made to the people of Dolpo. In the course of his lifetime our Lama had increased the meritorious value of the gifts which had been offered him by the faithful (by passing them on to those in need), but with the wealth that remained we did all we could with the object of perfecting our Lama's intentions.

This account is a mere drop of water
From the ocean of wondrous doings
Of our Good Lama Glorious Intellect,
But we pray that it may perfect his intentions,

That the flow of good intentions it produces,
May prosper the doctrine, bring happiness to living creatures,
And that all those who hold sway over them
May spend their lives performing the ten virtuous acts,
And that all may gain the stage of the Powerbolt-Holder!

The biography of this religious king of the threefold world, this second *Powerbolt-Holder* in this degenerate world-age, our own holy guide, the all-famous *Glorious Intellect*, [66] quite surpasses thought by its very wonder, and here we have set down its essence. Three of us who stayed for a long time in our holy Lama's presence, receiving, as though never contented, the flow of his words, so that the profound meaning arose in our hearts, namely his next representative, the Great Abbot *Jewel Religious Adornment* and the prior *Saviouress Religious Power* and I myself *Merit Intellect*, received these stories from our Lama just after he had made a symbolic offering of the universe. The small section after his passing is related by me wretched fellow who has the name of *Merit*, and by Master *Intellect Powerbolt*. The two of us composed all this at Hrap on auspicious days of the increasing moon in the Fire Male Monkey Year (A.D. 1596) known as 'Evil Countenance', having first offered worship at our Lama's precious reliquary.

IV

THE BIOGRAPHY

OF

LORD OF MERIT

entitled

Worthy Fulfiller of Hopes

The Biography of

LORD OF MERIT

entitled

WORTHY FULFILLER OF HOPES

Salutation to my precious lamas, to the gods and attendant goddesses!
O immaculate orb, knower of all knowledge, refined throughout past time,
Eternally sending forth countless progressions of hundreds of rays
Through the vast measureless depths of pure space,
Vast as the twin stocks of merit and knowledge which you have accumulated from past ages,
We bow to you, our protector, who gives birth eternally to the glorious brightness of knowledge,
Whose infinite activity destroys the darkness of the two obscurations,
Which bring men to evil rebirths produced by their past evil actions.

Possessing infallible knowledge of faultless religion,
You turn the wheel of the infinite doctrine, wheresoever you will,
In undifferentiating compassion for the innumerable hosts of converts.
We worship you in faith, O changeless Sage without peer!

We bow to the good teachers of his succession, who have realized perfect knowledge,
And having condensed as an essence the all-profound and immaculate scriptures,
Reveal them in virtuous activity as a wondrous substance of profound essentials,
Thus establishing their numerous converts in the profound and excellent way.

We praise all great sages who permeate the five elements with their dancing illusory forms.
Purifying the five impure components of personality, they are manifest eternally as a form of fivefold buddhahood.

Cognizing the group of the five evils, ignorance and the rest, they spread in all
   directions the light of wisdom in its fivefold form.
They purify the impure life-series of the five spheres of sentient beings
And bestow the glories of bliss by establishing them firmly in the excellent fivefold
   path of enlightenment,
Achieving the five special faculties which previously none had achieved.[1]
   Having offered these praises, we make our vow.
We make obeisance with great devotion of body, speech and mind
To him who is named *Jewel Self-Created*[2]
The omniscient manifestation at second remove of *Vairocana* and of *Ānanda*,
Ānanda that disciple of *Śākyamuni*, the Sage of the Good Age,
Who comprehended all things in himself, for he is indistinguishable from the
   Three Precious Ones, our infallible and excellent protectors.
We beseech your blessing for body, speech and mind!

   By dint of prayers throughout the series of my former lives and by force of exerting myself in the past to accumulate the twin stocks of merit and knowledge, I was born as the son of parents named Sonam, in this happy and blessed place, the glorious valley of *Ting-khyu* in the heart of the four districts of Dolpo, where holy religion has spread, [2] and in conditions ideally suited for practising the religious life. Although I shall tell a little of my story, an ordinary fettered mortal like myself really has nothing on which to base a biography. Especially during the fifth injurious period of this degenerate age it might be nothing but a cause of exaggerating and belittling and other false impressions. However the Religious King, our ruler, as well as the lamas who have taught me, my friends in religion, the whole assembly of monks, and my faithful benefactors, all organized a general celebration and made me presentations and urged me again and again. Thus not being able to resist any longer, I have written just this little.
   As for my lineage, there was in former times a king named Rupati, who came with his five hundred followers, all dressed in women's clothes, to the upper part

---

[1] Concerning most of these sets of five, see the Introduction, pp. 21–22. The 'five spheres of sentient beings' refer to the six realms of possible rebirth. Since they were originally five (without the titans), there is doctrinal justification for referring to them as a set of five when it happens to suit the context. The five (or six) 'special faculties' are the divine eye, the divine ear, knowledge of others' thoughts, knowledge of the previous existence of oneself and of others, magical powers, and (as the sixth item which is not required here) knowledge of the eradication of one's own imperfections. For more on this subject see Har Dayal, *The Bodhisattva Doctrine*, pp. 106–34.

[2] This Lama *Jewel Self-Created* (*dKon-mchog lhun-grub*) is presumably the great *Ngor-pa* lama who was once *Merit Intellect*'s teacher. See p. 86. *Vairocana*, of whom he is said to be an incarnation, lived in the 8th century and was a disciple of *Lotus-Born*. Another lama named *Jewel Self-Created* is mentioned below (p. 239), but it is unlikely that he would merit such special praise in these introductory verses.

of Nga-ri, where they made their home in Purang. While they were thinking of visiting Central Tibet, the king ascended the celestial cord.[1] Two of his followers, named *Ugly Face* and *Knowledgeable*, held on to the right and left of his garments, so that they all went up into the sky. They rested on the summit of *Kha'u-bya-'gyur* in Tsang, and one of the followers settled there and founded the *'Khon* lineage, from which the Sa-kya lineage comes. The other one settled on the summit of *Jo-mo Kha-rag* on the boundary of Tsang and Ü, and founded the *gNyos* lineage, which is that of my holy teacher.

The king continued his journey and descended on the summit of Mount *Yar-lha-sham-po*. He traversed *bTsan-thang-sgo-bzhi* and was met by some herdsmen. 'Where do you come from?' they asked. He pointed to the sky. The herdsmen said: 'As he has come from the sky, he must be a son of the gods. We will make him our king.' They came carrying him on a chair on their shoulders, so he was known as the *Shoulder Throne Strong One*.[2] He made the eldest of the herdsmen his minister, and this first of ministers was named *Byams-pa Thog-gi rGyal-mtshan*. His lineage continued and his descendant was Uncle-Minister under Song-tsan-gam-po. Under Ti-song-de-tsan a descendant of his was the Grandfather-Minister *Nyi-ma*, and thus the family-line continued, so that later members of the family were in the service of the monarch *'Od-srung*, settling in *Gu-ge* in the upper part of Nga-ri. In this line there were six brothers with the family name *'U*, and [3] and they preserved the later lineage with the name of *Me-zhang-stod-pa*, which continued the succession. They became very knowledgeable in traditional arts and medicine. In the time of *rGyal-ba bzang-po* they moved to Sa-kya. Then they settled in *Gung-thang*. In the time of *A-ma-dpal* they settled in Mustang. From there they spread to *Byi-phug*.

A member of the family was a minister of the Governor *A-mgon-bzang-po*. At that time the Governor and his brothers fell into dispute with the Grand Lama *Chos-dpal-bzang-po*, with the result that the Lama instituted harmful rites against the Governor's family and all his ministers. Especially on account of a fierce rite practised with a corpse, the families on our side suffered from shortened lives. The minister's wife herself, *Kun-dga' sgrol-ma* died at the age of 49. Of five sons the four elder ones all died, so they threaded some dog-hair through the ear of the youngest and named him *Khyi-ku* (Puppy).[3] At that time the Governor and the officials were at enmity amongst themselves, and everywhere there was robbery and murder, fear and loss. When he was eleven years old *Khyi-ku* was taken in charge by the learned lama *Merit Self-Created*, and as a result of studying his father's books on medicine, designing and painting, he became very skilful in medicine and

---
[1] viz. the king, considered as a divine being, returned to heaven, whence he had come.
[2] As quoted (and hence translated) in this text, the name represents a piece of Tibetan popular etymology. For the legend of this king (*gNya'-khri btsan-po*), see *Buddhist Himālaya*, p 127.
[3] By thus demeaning him, they hoped to make him proof against the malicious attacks of gods and demons.

in painting. He founded a temple at *Ru-thog* Black Rock, and thereafter he continued to serve his learned lama, founding many temples everywhere. When the lama was about to die, *Khyi-ku* asked him, saying: 'As a result of having so many enemies in Lo, I cannot settle here. So I beg you to give me a place in Dolpo, where salt wont run short in winter, and grain wont run short in summer.' He gave him the place called *sKom* in Dolpo, and he settled there. Thus we have descendants of his with the name *sKom-pa khyi-ku*.

As none of his children lived, he kept a piebald dog in his doorway and used to stoop under it when he went in and out. So in addition to the name derived from the dog-hair in his ear, he was now called *Piebald Puppy*. Afterwards he had a son, who was called *Piebald Life*. During the first part of his life this son stayed in *sKom*, where he had some religious texts copied. In the latter part of his life he came to *Ting-khyu*, finished the texts already started, as well as three major texts.[1] [4] He had five sons, of whom the two eldest died. The three youngest were named *rTsod-ma*, *rTsom-mchog* and *Kun-dga'-sgrol-ma*.[2]

rTsod-ma had a son named *Jewel Prosperity*, but he had no wealth. When he was hunting in *'Om-lung*, he saw a doe whose belly had been cut open by a jagged rock and was giving birth to a fawn. Both mother and offspring were crying pitifully, and overwhelmed with compassion, he wept many tears. He gave the fawn some of the mother's milk, and while she was dying he repeated continuously such prayers as he knew. When she was dead, he took her body together with the little fawn to the Lama *Good Deliverance*. Then he became a monk and sought religious teachings, renouncing desire and turning away from the world. He used to experience the *clear light* continuously, and when he died, his body remained in an upright posture of meditation for three weeks, for he was a great ascetic.

Kun-dga'-sgrol-ma, the youngest of the three, was an artist in painting, clay-modelling and carving, and the Mustang Governor was very fond of him. He died when he was 35.

rTsom-mchog had a son by his brother's wife. He was named *Deliverance Protector*, and there were descendants in his line.

Jewel Prosperity had four sons. Two of them, *Merit Prosperity* and *Saviouress Lord of Religion*, were born in their father's homeland. The other two, *All Joy Protector* and *Lord of Religion*, were born in *'Bri-gung*. *All Joy Protector* and *Saviouress Lord of Religion* were outstanding men of religion and did a great deal for the good of living beings, as everyone has heard.

[1] Namely *brgya-tog-gser*, which stands for *brgya-stong-pa*, the 'Perfection of Wisdom' sūtra in 100,000 verses, *tog-gzungs* which is the *Ratna-keṭu-dhāraṇī-mahāyāna-sūtra*, and *gser-'od dam-pa* which is the *Suvarṇa-prabhāsottama-rāja-sūtra*.
[2] They are all provided with girls' names with the same intention of demeaning them as in the case of the boy named 'puppy'.

Merit Prosperity had three sons. *Aim-Winner Gloriously Blazing* as eldest, *Victory-Banner of the Heavens* as second, and *Jewel* as the youngest. The second son was very skilful at medicine, painting and astronomy. He went to Central Tibet, where he learned, studied and practised all the *sūtra* and *tantra* texts, so that he was infallible in all branches of knowledge. Especially was he clever at the 'Profound Matter of Absolute Certainty' and he was the beloved successor of *Religious Protector Glorious and Good*. He experienced the *clear light* continuously and was fully competent in the practice of the *Great Symbol*. [5] He was generally recognized as being a reincarnation of the Yogin *mKhas-grub Khyung-po*.

Aim-Winner Gloriously Blazing had three sons, of whom the eldest was Tshe-wang Dorje, the second Sonam Phan-ne and the youngest *Jewel Prosperity*.

Sonam Phan-ne went to Central Tibet, where he completed the specialist course, and afterwards he became lama at *Zhva-lding*, *Grva-tshang*, Yang-tsher and other places. When he died, his body remained in an upright posture of meditation for fourteen days. In his will he wrote: 'As the second day of the month is the feast-day of the Lord *Victorious Banner of Fame*[1] burn my corpse on that day and make *tsha-tsha*'.[2] That summer rain had been very slight, but when his corpse was cremated very heavy rain fell for seven days. His spiritual power and grace were immense, and everyone had stories to tell about them. After the cremation his skull was like a small sacrificial vase and his bones had assumed all kinds of remarkable shapes as images, mystic symbols and so on, so that everyone was filled with devotion.

The eldest son Tshe-wang Dorje in his turn had seven sons, of whom the eldest was Sonam Phun-tshog. He had three sons, of whom the middle was one myself.

My father belonged naturally to the family of *would-be buddhas*. He was zealous in his service of the *Precious Ones*. He had great faith in men of religion. He was affectionate to his parents, brethren, friends, kindred and retainers. He was long-suffering, modest and reliable. He would grant success to others and kept failure for himself. It is not just I myself, who claim that he was such a man of natural virtue, for everyone here is aware of it.

My mother's lineage on her father's side was that of the *gNam-ru*. Her name was Sonam-dzom. She belonged naturally to the family of the *Attendant Goddesses of Action*. Her complexion was of a bluish golden hue, and she had a mark between her eye-brows, reddish gold in colour and the size of a mustard-seed. Above her left breast there were three marks suggesting a trident, and on the inside of her left thigh there were marks in a criss-cross pattern. She had great faith. She was affectionate to our retainers. She was clever in all worldly activities, and she never

---
[1] Concerning this lama, see p. 188 fn.   [2] Concerning *tsha-tsha*, see p. 99 fn.

bore a grudge. She was skilful in taking care of our possessions, and she was completely honourable. She attended to my father's parents and his brothers, [6] and she was kind and generous to the poor and needy, as everyone here knows. When I entered the womb of such a mother, there were wonderful dreams and portents, but there is no purpose in writing them down in detail.

When ten months had passed I was born in the Male Iron Rat year (A.D. 1660) under the 4th sMe-ba, the green one, and under the sPar-kha kham.[1] It was a Thursday and also the season of the 8th lunar mansion (puṣya). I was taken to my great-uncle Sonam Phan-ne for the purification and naming ceremonies. He said: 'This boy has been born under an auspicious star. Such was the birth-star of Śākyamuni himself. Let him be given the name rGyal-po Don-grub.[2] If he practises religion, he will be outstanding.' Such was his prophesy. My father and mother gave a birthday-feast, and my uncles on both sides and our other relations all gave 'long-life goats' and 'long-life sheep'. I was continuing to grow and get very big, when someone asked prophesy of a soothsayer who came from Jājarkot.[3] He was possessed by his local god, and he brought a cloth, saying: 'This child who dwells in Ting-khyu is my teacher reborn. Give good thought to this!' As a result of this pronouncement, I became very difficult to care for. My father and mother had to take it in turns to spend the night without sleep, nursing me in their arms. Whenever I was possessed by this spirit from Jājarkot, they had to scatter offerings of flour pellets and parched grain all mixed together. As I was passing from my third to fourth year I had a severe attack of dysentery, so that I was very difficult to look after. I had a Khampa nurse named A-pi-dung-ril, and because she gave me her breast when it was dry, I contracted a very serious disease of pollution. I could not sleep at night, for if I settled down to sleep just a little, the house seemed to collapse, or I was carried off by water, or burned by fire, or I fell down a precipice, and other such terrible fears and anguish. Finally it seemed that the whole house [7] was filled with butter-lamps. Then at the end I would fall into a deep sleep and remain like one dead until half the day had passed. So evening would come and I would remember those terrors all over again.

Towards the end of the 8th Month of the Water Hare year that man of Jājarkot went back to his home, and my father gave him a young goat, some rice, milk and

---

[1] For these signs of divination, see Waddell, Lamaism, pp. 456–64. See also p. 77 above.

[2] Don-grub 'Aim-Winner' corresponds to Sanskrit Siddhārtha, which was the personal name of the historical buddha Śākyamuni. The first part of the name rGyal-po 'King' is used throughout the first part of the biography as the personal name of Lama Lord of Merit.

[3] Written in Tibetan as 'Gar-cha-bkod. See p. 203 fn. Concerning Jājarkot, see Himalayan Pilgrimage, pp. 17–20. The word which I have translated as 'soothsayer' is Tibetan blon-po, which normally means officer or minister of state. The bDe-chen bla-brang Lama had no explanation for this unusual meaning of the word. It is unlikely to be a MS error for bon-po, since this term is not normally used of soothsayers who are not Tibetans. See also p. 188 fn. 3.

butter, and a few other things. When he reached Shimen, he killed a goat that he had taken with him, and sent back its meat together with the end of a roll of cloth and a head-scarf as presents. When the family was eating this meat, Yang-jom gave me his share, and as a result of eating it I developed a fierce fever and became more dead than alive. A tall fat monk used to appear. He had a long beard and wore a big hat like that of a wandering mendicant. 'Come, come!' he would say, as he offered me what seemed to be a bracelet, a piece of amber or turquoise, and then he would drag me by the arm. I remember how I used to call out in my terror, and sometimes my parents would call me a wretched little orphan and would slap me, or sometimes they would call upon the names of the *Three Precious Ones* and seek their protection.

From then on that monk used to appear as a vision or mental image, and the impression was so strong, that I would not go outside even as far as the threshing-floor. Until the men came home from work, I would stay in the lap of *A-pi-dung-ril*, and even when they gathered in the room I would still stay in her lap. Although my father, my uncle and others called me, I would not go to them, but stayed where I was. 'He is a self-willed young fellow,' they would say. I really was not so. I was just frightened.

In the autumn no nourishment seemed to come from my food, and I was shaken with fear and anguish. Then during the second and third months of the following year, which was that of the Wood Dragon, there was a pollution of the water-spirit, resulting in an outbreak of a very bad disease, which no one had had before, and some people died. [8] Both my brother and sister were near death, and my parents called the monk *Nyi-ma* to make ceremonies of offerings and sacrifice to the water-spirits. My mother said: 'Both the good uncle who helped us in the affairs of this world and the good lama who helped us in the affairs of the next world are dead. Our small daughter who was like a child of the gods is dead. This seemingly ill-augured boy is not likely to survive. Do not take offense at us, learned monk, but please stay and recite some texts as a supplication for this boy.' Then she gave him some cloth as a present, and he recited canonical texts for the space of one month, with the result that I grew strong and well.

Then my uncle Gyamtso, who had just finished some paintings for the abbot of *Grva-tshang*, arrived home. He said to the monk: 'Just shake the dust from the pages of these volumes for me,'[1] and as an advance fee he gave him a dram of gold and a square of mottled silk. I became happy, thinking: 'Now there is no need to be afraid.'

The next year the Khams Lama *Jewel Self-Created* was invited by the villagers, and while they were receiving a community blessing, there developed within me extraordinary faith and devotion towards the lama. When he was giving the 'life-

[1] That is to say: 'Sit here and read them through for me' as a meritorious religious act.

consecration' I had visual impressions of him enveloped in dazzling brilliance. I became very happy, thinking: 'Now I shall live a long time.'

The next morning my parents offered the lama a silver coin, one bushel and five measures of barley, and a length of cloth, saying: 'This is our one surviving child. At night he is overwhelmed with terror and cannot sleep at all. We beg you to give him an amulet and your blessing and to let him take the vows of a "virtuous adherer".' We presented a name-card with our presents and all bowed down with signs of great devotion. I myself bowed down a lot of times and then sat in the row with the others. The lama looked at us all each in turn, but at me in particular he looked with a fixed steady gaze, so that I felt very frightened.

[9] As the others were leaving, he gave a glance to Uncle Monk, and said to him: 'Keep the small boy here a moment,' so my uncle and I stayed. I repeated after him the vow of a 'virtuous adherer' together with a profession of faith in the Buddha, the Doctrine and the Community, and the lama showed signs of great pleasure. Then he said: 'This boy is being tormented by the evil spirit of some potentate or monk. I can protect him against such harm. Do you intend to send him to *Thub-bstan*?'[1] My father and uncle promised that I should be sent there. 'In that case,' said the lama, 'bring the boy here this evening at twilight.'

So that evening my father, my uncle and myself all went into the lama's room. First he performed the ceremony for dispelling demons. Then it seemed to me as though he were not there. There was a mass of fire with smoke bellowing from it, and in the middle a black man with fire shooting from his mouth, nose and eyes. I was terrified and buried my face in my father's breast. My father said: 'The lama is blessing you. Do not be afraid,' and he turned me round to face the lama. But the lama seemed more fearful than before. He had four or five hands with what might have been a wand in one right hand. For a moment I was overpowered with an impression of a mass of blackness which appeared to my vision, and from out of this there came an extraordinary blueness. I seemed to be shivering with cold, and at that moment the lama appeared over the cushion on which my head rested, and touched all my body in the act of blessing me, with his wand and magic dagger. Then he gave me the combined consecration of the two divinities *Boundless Light* and *Horse-Neck*, and confirmed the evil-spirits in their vow (to leave me in peace). My body felt gently happy and my mind surged with bliss. The lama looked me in the eyes and said: 'This small boy is now realeased from evil spirits and demons. Let him be named *Meritorious Promoter of Religion*. Let him be taught religious texts, and learn to recite them continuously. That will protect him from all plagues.'

The next morning the young squire *Jewel King* was receiving a special initiation of the *Anchoress*, [10] so I asked to receive it with him.

[1] Concerning this monastery, see p. 133 fn.

That evening my Uncle Gyamtso was teaching to our whole household the invocations of the *Victorious One*, of the *All-Knowing Lama* and of the *Anchoress*. I soon knew them all, and my uncle was delighted, saying: 'The lama says that he will make a good man of religion, and his knowledge is developing already.' That evening I lay against Uncle Monk's lap and practised recitation, so that in the morning I was very good at it. My father, uncles and all the members of the family were amazed. From then on I had no more terrors and I grew up strong and big.

Then in the 6th month of the Wood Dragon year I ate some cooked rice mixed with cold ewe's milk, with the result that my stomach was upset. A quack-doctor[1] was called from *Kyi*, and as a result of spell-impregnated water that he gave me and some meat-leavings that *A-pi-dung-ril* gave me, all the knowledge that I had previously gained was lost. I went with my Uncle Monk to see the Monk *rGyal-mtshan dkar-mo*, and he gave me spell-impregnated water for a period of seven days, which had the effect of clarifying my mind a little.

Then at the end of the 10th month of the Horse year when I was six, we invited the great abbot of *Grva-tshang*, *Intellect Glorious and Good*, to perform a ceremony which would counteract the effects of tittle-tattle. We also requested the special initiation of the *Glorious Gentle One Arapacana*.

That winter my father taught me to spell, and the subtle influences of religion awoke in me a little. I felt great faith and devotion towards the lamas, boundless compassion for sentient beings, and great zeal for the religious life. As I was young and my parents were wealthy, I passed three years feeding and caring for our calves and sheep.

Then in the Male Iron Dog year when I was ten years old, our whole family went to visit the Lama of Hrap, whose name was *Gloriously Good*. We asked for instruction in the law of cause and effect, for the initiations of the *All-Knowing* and of the *Queen of Success*, and also for the *maṇi* initiation. From then until I went to Lo, I exerted myself in *maṇi* recitations.

When I was eleven, I went to the Nomad Country with my Uncle *Chos* to look after our animals. [11] All that time I was joyfully enthusiastic about my religious practice, so that I continued practising the texts while I was following the animals. Thus I learned how to read.

The next year I went again to the Nomad Country with my Uncle *sGrub-pa*, who taught me the *Confession of a Would-be Buddha* and other texts, but I did not learn much because we had so much work.

When I was 13 years old my parents entertained the Artist *sKyab-pa* with meat and *chang*, and begged him: 'Please give this boy a good final training in reading.'

---

[1] The Tibetan word is '*gar-ba*, perhaps for *mgar-ba* meaning 'smith'. It could well be that the smith at *Kyi* happened to be renowned for medical skills.

Thus I learned the printed style and the manuscript style of writing, both how to write the letters, and how to read them singly and grouped together in words. I was even allowed to act as teacher to other children.

That spring I went with my uncles and some young friends to look after the animals in the Nomad Country. When I was leaving, my teacher said to me: 'I believe that you will know your religion well, so now do not forget the refuge-prayers, which I have been teaching you intermittently. I am giving you these two books, so you must be determined in your reading practice.' So saying he gave me a philosophical text with many contracted spellings and an incomplete copy of 'Calling upon the *Excellent Goddess of the White Parasol.*' So my uncles and our whole group went to *dGon-chung* in the Nomad Country, and while looking after the animals, I made effort in my reading practice as my teacher had told me, so my uncles were very pleased. Thus I learned the ritual of the *Goddess of the White Parasol* as well as the *Essence of Wisdom.*

When I was 14, there was an outbreak of body-sores and smallpox, and my elder brother was very ill indeed, so I acted as his nurse. The disease spread everywhere, and although my elder brother recovered, both my youngest and eldest uncle died, and we were all very sad. Finally I myself had a light attack, and I thought: 'Now I am glad that I shall not die, but at all events I must be a good man of religion.' I intended that autumn to settle to my religious practice, [12] but we had a great deal of snow and rain then, and because of our many domestic animals Uncle Gyaltsan and myself and two servants went to *Phal-rtar*. During the first part of the winter I collected our interest on loans in *Phal-rtar* and debts due in hay, and gave some to the animals. During the second half of the winter I had to just dig up gorse roots and give it to them, and with all this I was extremely tired. But I bestirred thoughts of loving-kindness and exerted myself in their care all day long. Then at night I would practise my reading with a lamp, and thus I got to know the 'Praises of the Five Great Sa-kya Lamas' and the religious writings of the Lama of Margom. I was then so zealous for religion, that I was practising reading in my dreams, in my waking condition, as well as when I was fully awake. My uncle said to me: 'You are reciting texts in your sleep. When you make mistakes, I call out to you, but you do not listen at all.' I was very surprised.

Then that summer on the 23rd day of the 5th month my father died, and we were all very sad. For the first week we called in a group of monks (and all was well), but we did not have enough grain for continuing ceremonies until the end of the 7th week, so Uncle Gyaltsan took seven yaks and went to Kāk, and Uncle Nam-rin took six yaks and went to Tarap, so we had a lot of grain. In the autumn we made a great distribution to the poor and performed the after-death ceremonies properly with name-cards, presents and offerings in all the monasteries.

From then until I was 16 I had to do the milking, but I continued my exercises in the texts uninterruptedly. All my uncles were very pleased, especially Uncle Monk Tshe-ring Gyaltsan who gave me a small field of the size requiring 3½ measures of barley seed, and Uncle Gyamtso who gave me one of a size requiring 4 measures.

[13] By working them carefully I increased them to a combined size requiring 10 measures. Moreover I became so skilled in all the everyday activities, looking after the animals and producing our food-crops, that all my uncles and other relatives were filled with joy and respect.

At that time the Monk *dGe-'dun bzang-po* was appointed abbot of *Grva-lung*, and Uncle Monk provided the feast at the enthronement ceremony. My uncles, myself and others went to arrange an appointment for the giving of consecrations and so on, and the Lama said: 'If you will send that boy to Central Tibet, I will provide the consecrations and whatever else is needed.' With this in mind, I begged my uncles to let me go for religious training, and they replied: 'It will be possible for you to go, but first you must study the texts of the *All-Knowing One*.'

On the 27th of the next month I went with my uncles to the Lama and received the consecration of the *All-Knowing One*. We received explanations and full instructions in the meaning of the consecration, and I was filled with great devotion. When the consecration was finished, my uncles bowed down and said: 'We beg you now to teach this boy the rituals and techniques of the *All-Knowing One* in full.' The Lama replied: 'I was intending to spend this winter in solitary retreat, but now I will do as you say. But you must also do as I say, and send this boy to Central Tibet.' Thus I studied the *All-Knowing One* with him, and learned the rituals and techniques.

Then when the Lama was invited to preside over the after-death rite and ceremonies of the deceased *Pad-rgyal*, he told me to accompany him, and since we performed the ceremonies for five days, I became very well practised in the *All-Knowing One*.

During that time there came the feast-day of the Supreme Guide *Religious Protector Glorious and Good*, which is on the 20th (of the 2nd month), and on that occasion I asked for the consecration and textual initiation of the *Universal Saviour* and for the textual initiation of the *Ma-ṇi bka'-'bum*.

In the spring of my 17th year in the 3rd month we had no salt to give the cattle, so we went to get some salt-deposit. At *rGad-pa gSer-phreng* we met some men carrying salt-deposit, [14] so we returned home quickly. We gave a little to our own cattle and oxen and to those of others, making no discrimination, so everyone was satisfied.

The next year a lot of *Ting-khyu* people went to *gSer-kha*, and my uncles said that I ought to go too, so I took with me ten yaks, three horses and four dzo, and went. A calf of one of the female dzo was very weak and could not go at all. The sun was right up in the sky, and I felt so sorry for the creature. I took it on my back and carried it the rest of the way to *gSer-kha*. Half-way there Koncho Gyaltsan of Shimen had a very serious attack of serpent-sickness.[1] He could not eat meat, so I gave him two bowls of milk every day from two of my female dzo who had some fine calves. We went on to sell our dzo, but the sick man became even worse and everything around his bed was covered with pus and blood, so that no one could go near. I felt an irresistible sense of compassion, so I gave him food and drink and attended to him in all ways without considering the difficulty and the horror.

At that time there was an embargo on salt and wool, and we said to one another: 'Perhaps we might get a little.' The chief man Gyamtso cast lots, and the lots fell out well, so we young men went to Tsharka to get salt. When we had finished our trading, we each went to collect some small sums which we had not yet received. I went to get the price of a woollen rug from someone, but the house-holder had disappeared. There was a pregnant woman there, about to bear her child that evening or the next morning. She had no food and possessions, for someone else had taken them away, and except for my rug she had nothing to wear and she had nothing to eat. She said: 'You have left your rug with me. Now have mercy! If I do not die, I will repay the price in full.' I felt irresistible compassion for her and said: 'Listen, you poor woman. Wear my rug, and do not give the price to anyone but to me. In these degenerate times it is difficult to trust people.' She clung to my feet, saying: 'How great is your kindness!', and burst into tears. [15] Then on our way back the man who was sick was advised by his companions: 'It is no good for you to load up salt, for we shall not help you to load it. There is a saying: "Of one hundred heads one's own is the most precious. Which ever of your ten fingers you cut off, it hurts the same." That is so, isn't it?'

But he paid no heed to them, and so loaded his yaks according to their size. However when we had gone five days' journey, his hands had become torn with the ropes and were a mass of open sores dripping with blood and pus. I had a feeling of irresistable compassion and with a piece of rag which I found on an old camp site I made bandages for his hands from one half, and wrapping the other round my own hands, I helped him load and unload his loads. My uncles and cousins said to me: 'Don't put an end to our family by helping this fellow with his leprous sores!'
'Is this true what they say?' I wondered.
When we reached *Tshva-lto* a young man named Gyaltsan Dorje said to me:

---

[1] For a similar case, see p. 108. This disease is supposedly caused by the serpent-divinities (*klu*) who watch over the springs and streams. One may have displeased them by inadvertently polluting the water.

'Squire rGyal-po, if you come with me to *Khung*, you will meet your Lama Uncle. It will be all right if I give you a present for him.' Although I wanted to go, my uncles and cousins as well as my elder brother and others prevented me. So travelling over the *Ma-khan* Pass, we reached our own village and were met by my mother, my uncles and other relations. Moreover that man who was sick made more than twice the profit on the salt which has no value in the north, than on the merchandise which he had brought from his own village. Our trading companions told everyone: 'Squire *rGyal-po* seems to be well practised in the *thought of enlightenment*.'[1]

At that time my uncle Nam-rin and myself went to Lo to get grain, and on the way my uncle was very ill. Returning to our village I sought the assistance of Kunga Palzang, and taking a horse with us, we put my uncle on it and sent him home. Then the two of us went on to Lo and fetched the grain. On the way back one of the yaks reared as I was loading it. The load was thrown back into my grasp, straining my kidneys very badly, and because I was not careful afterwards I was ill for a very long time. Then when I was nineteen, [16] we invited Lama *Jo-bo* who was on his way back from visiting Lama *U-rgyan dPal-bzang*. He had visited him in order to get the hidden teachings found by *bDud-'dul rDo-rje*. As a general initiation for the village he performed the *Union of the Precious Ones*, and as a special initiation for us that of the *Queen of Success*. When he was explaining the meaning of the initiation, I had an extraordinary feeling of devotion. Then when we were consecrating a set of canonical books, I thought: 'I must make a solemn entreaty in the presence of so special an object,' and so I prayed thus:

'May I keep near the lotus-feet of this lama, and so obtain in their entirety the profound doctrinal cycles of the Oral Tradition!

'Having obtained them, may I absorb them, and may there come about great benefit for others, so that both myself and others shall together come to the released state of fruition!

'Having gained fulfilment, may I act as a religious guide for all the beings of the realms of the universe, until the whole of phenomenal existence shall be void!'[2]

The lama did not say anything, but he just smiled. The Monk *dPal-bzang* was there, and he said: 'Son, may your entreaty be fulfilled!'

Later when the tax-gatherers came from Lo they brought an order for my uncles to go to Tsarang quickly to paint a temple there. Setting out in haste, my uncles and I travelled to *dPon* together with the tax-gatherers. There I offered several presents of which the most important was a mare with an unborn foal, to the precious and honourable '*Jam-dbyangs mGon-po Don-grub*, reincarnation of the great Sa-kya scholar, and he bestowed upon me in their entirety the vows of a 'virtuous adherer.'

[1] See the Introduction, p. 30–31. [2] This is a typical vow of a *would-be buddha*. See p. 30.

Such in brief were the ways of my worldly doings of which the story is now finished.

Being a man of property, whoever you are, you burn in a pit of fire.
Leaving home for a homeless state, whoever you are, you are cool.
Having abandoned the place of this fire-pit, wherever it is,
We delight in adopting the ways of poverty, whatever they are.

Now I shall give a brief account of the ways of my religious doings, telling first how I practised my mind in study and learning.

[17] From *'Jam-dbyangs mGon-po Don-grub* I learned the 'Invocations to the Abbots of *Thub-bstan*' together with the *Lama Rite* of the Sa-kya Order and also the first chapter of the *Ornament of Comprehension*. In the autumn I returned to my own village with my uncles, and there I practised reading the rest of the *Ornament of Comprehension* as well as *Treasury of Knowledge of Logic*. The same autumn the accomplished *Khro-bo bKra-shis* came to collect offerings of copper for the great image of *Maitreya* in Lo, and afterwards I returned with him to Lo. I went to see my honourable and precious lama, and he said: 'You must practise reading.' Then giving me the *Three Grades of Religious Vows* and the *Items of Confession* together with their commentaries, he said: 'Now exert yourself. I will make provision for your food.'

Thus I practised reading at the side of the lama's room. From dawn until midday and again from midday until midnight I worked at my books, and thus I learned the 'Four Difficulties' quite well. Every evening the lama would come three times to listen to me read. Then one evening he called me to him and said: 'Have you learned these books?' 'I have learned them,' I said, 'but I am not well practised in them.' 'You must be competent in logical philosophy,' he replied. 'If you are not competent in this, it will be hard to hold your own in the midst of the general assembly of monks. You must be so well practised, that you do not forget where you are, even if you were chased by seven full grown dogs. Now sit on the east side of the balcony or walk round the veranda, practising meanwhile. From time to time look at this,' he said giving me the *Treasury of Philosophical Notions*.

I practised reading this, but I only learned two chapters, the one on the five components of personality and the one on the eighteen bases of sense experience, although I also worked a little on the chapters concerning phenomenal existence and the subtle and vast elements. My lama asked me if I had learned it, and I replied that I had not grasped it. Then he said: 'As you are tired, practise for a while the texts you learned before and just recite a little from the *Treasury*.'

At that time one of my benefactors, named *Tshe-ring dPal-bzang* arrived from my village together with his servant. [18] He brought a message from my uncle: 'As they will probably send you to Central Tibet this year and Uncle Monk is ill, come home once whatever happens, and see your mother.' He sent a lump of butter, which I offered to my Lama and explained matters to him. 'Do as they say' he said, and I came away with supplies which he gave me for the journey. I asked him for a blessing, and he gave me generous provisions and candy heaped on a silver plate. Then he gave me excellent advice and instructions, and so sent me off very well indeed.

I left with two companions, and when we reached the village of *Phal-ba* by *Shar-tse*, we were met by my cousin Tshe-ring Palmo. After she had asked how I was, she told me that Uncle Monk was dead, and she stood there crying. At that time I was so tired, that I could not apply my mind to grief. Then I went to her home, where they made great celebrations for my reception, and brought curds and butter for my two friends as well. They told me in detail how Uncle Monk had died, and I cried a great deal and felt very unhappy. From there I made my way to my own village, where I met my mother and all my other relatives. I intended to return quite quickly, but they insisted that I stayed for the making of *chang*. I went to see Monk Kunga, and stayed a few days with him, practising recitation. Then I returned to Lo and met my Lama and other important people. At that time the youth Pal-zang-po said: 'Squire, you seem very unwell. Ask leave from the Lama and we will both go down to the warm medicinal streams. I will provide seasoning and cereals, so it will be all right.' So we went, and I benefitted greatly. After that I practised recitation very hard for seven days, and then asked if I could undergo an examination in the 'Four Difficulties'. 'If you can do it,' my Lama said, 'do this examination at Sa-kya. It wont do here.' 'I will do it there,' I replied. But in fact later on when I was at Sa-kya [19] the time was not quite propitious, so I could not take the examination, and the Lama and his colleagues were rather displeased about it.

Then when I was 21, I set out for Central Tibet with three friends and a large group of monks from *Tshe-lnga-pa* Monastery. In order to consecrate the merits accruing from the founding of his temple and of the great image of *Maitreya* and other things to the supreme end of universal enlightenment, my Lama sent a gift of nine good things to the Glorious Sa-kya Lama, of which the most important was an image of the *Horse-Necked* and the *Boar-Headed* divinity made from 300 silver coins. To the four of us he gave general presents, and to me in particular he gave an under-jacket, a gold coin, five sheep for carrying things, seasonings and cereals for the journey and whatever else I wanted. Then we went to see the Mustang Ruler and the Queen. They gave us generous presents, of which the most important was 20 notch-weights of indigo. 'Take whatever else you want,' they said. 'My Precious

Lama has given us things, so we need nothing,' I said, 'but I would ask for a sheep to carry this indigo.' So they gave us a letter authorizing us to receive a sheep from their chief bailiff who was in the north. Thus they sent us off very well.

Following the *Chu-mig dKar-mo*, we crossed the *Be-kyu* Pass, and so visited my cousin Tshe-ring, who gave us tea, butter and cheese and so on, whatever we wanted for the journey. After 20 days we reached Sa-kya and met the Grand Lama. We offered him the presents sent by our Precious Lama. He gave us free maintenance for seven days, and we visited all the shrines and temples.

Then gradually we made our way to Shigatse, and there I went to look for my uncle's former lodging-keeper, who was named Dar-gyä of the West Gate. He himself had died, but his sons and daughters were there, and I made them a present of four square yards of cloth. 'You men of Dolpo are faithful in your contacts,' they said, and they looked after me very well. 'Have you all the tea for general offerings which you will need?' they asked. 'I have not much tea,' I replied, 'and I have to give general tea offerings in the university,[1] [20] so please help me to buy some good tea.' 'We will do that,' they said, and they bought me a brick of excellent tea, for which I paid 12 tankas,[2] and it really was outstanding.

Then in three days we reached *Thub-bstan rNam-rGyal*. On the 10th day of the month we met Lama *bZang-po rGyal-mtshan*. On the 13th I took my vows as a monk. On the 14th I made a general offering of tea, and on the 19th a special one for the Nga-ri College. On the 20th I distributed gifts and on the 21st I offered tea in the Dolpo College. Everyone was delighted with the excellent tea.

As my Lama and his colleagues had so ordered, I asked the professors and others about the necessity of going to Sa-kya to undergo an examination in the 'Four Difficulties'. According to their argument, they urged me thus: 'Unless you want distinction and fame, it is all the same whether you take the examination or not. But if you make effort in your studies, that is what will please your Lama and his colleagues.' So because of what they said, I did not take the examination.

Then I said to them: 'Well if you are really not displeased, I beg you, since today is propitious, to start my instruction in the *Chrestomathy*.' Some said: 'Ask (such and such) a doctor' but he told us to ask someone else. Thus they made excuses one to the other. A master-scholar named *Intellect* said: 'Since today is propitious, Doctor, please instruct us in the argument concerning the three buddha-bodies. Tomorrow I will take him to Doctor *Tshe-brtan*.' Thanks to the doctor's instruction I knew by that evening the exposition of the three buddha-bodies. The next day the master-scholar *Intellect*, having prepared an offering of good tea, introduced

---
[1] Tib. *grva-sa*. Concerning the various academic titles and my conventional translations of them, see the Introduction, p. 73.
[2] A small silver coin worth about an old (pure) silver sixpence.

me to Doctor *Tshe-brtan*, and said: 'This nephew of mine comes of good family and is the nephew of worthy lamas. Everyone sets great hopes on him, so I beg you to help with his instruction.' The doctor said: [21] 'There's no difference in our accomplishments, and it would be all right if you taught him. But since you ask me to teach him, why should I not do so? I will do as you say.'

To begin with he instructed me in the first section about elements from the seven-part work 'What things are and what they are not', and in one day and a half I knew this. From then on I spent a day and a half on each part of this work. In each part of this seven-part work there are seven sub-sections, and at the end of nine days I knew all forty-nine sub-sections. Meanwhile I was always present at the main ceremonies, reciting clearly the invocations of the *Victorious Lady* and of the *Destroyer*. Some of the others would look at me and laugh: 'This fellow recites our invocations and just muddles them up.' But others said: 'He recites our spells clearly, and is really an accomplished fellow.' So they were uncertain about me.

Then as the winter term progressed I was able to give the required answers to others concerning the thirty odd general and special expositions and the forty-nine sub-sections of 'What things are and what they are not.' During the second winter term, which coincided with the Great Prayer Festival, I learned how to debate.

During the first and second spring terms I learned how to make spontaneous reply in debating and extemporaneous exposition.

My teacher said: 'Now I shall teach you the sixteen kinds of characteristics and indications,' and so I went with my friends in religion into a reading-retreat. But there were so many rooms in the Dolpo College, that we were occupied just with repairing holes in the roofs, so that study was neglected. However we continued learning each syllogism in turn, and I became skilful at logical deductions and their antitheses. On occasions I worked on logical expositions based both on direct observation and on inference. Then my teacher said: 'During the winter terms you must learn to recite the basic text, so take the *Four Bases*.' But I did not grasp it very well, but learned mainly from the *Chrestomathy*. I entered into debate with any student of logic whom I met. Some of them gave me replies. Some did not reply, but went off angrily.

I was now twenty-three [22] and in the first winter term I began to learn by heart the short part of the *Chrestomathy*. In the second term I began the middle part, but there were so many tea-offering ceremonies that I could not work at it for more than one day. However by means of oral practice I learned it all right. Then during the first and second spring terms I learned to recite the large *Chrestomathy*, and even underwent a test.

Later the *lHo-ri* master-scholar set out on his way home, and we friends in religion went to visit the Monastery of *Ngor*. We visited the abbot *Glorious Spontaneous Achievement* just as he was giving the special blessing of the *Red Fury Sure and Short* according to the tradition of the *Nyang* Translator, and so we received this too. The master-scholar was very pleased and said: 'It is very good that such a combination of circumstances should come about without any arrangement.'

Then we visited the shrines at Tashilhunpo, and travelling via Shigatse, we reached *Thub-bstan*.

The master-scholar was carrying out a commission for me to the scholar Sonam Palzang in Lo, so I saw him off in good style. Also he carried letters to my relatives enquiring after their health, and especially to the Lama my maternal uncle I sent a letter with a present and enquiries about his health. 'Holy protector, closely related to me in affection, think of me with compassion. I pray that we may indeed meet in this life, and if we should not, that we may meet in our next one.' This was the way I wrote.

Then the master-scholar eventually reached Dolpo, where he gave my present and letter to my Lama Uncle. After he had asked about the progress in my studies, he read the letter and wept, for we would not meet again in this life. He knew this, he said, and he displayed great sadness, they told me.

I was then twenty-four and in the second spring term Doctor *bKra-shis* of *sGrol-mtshams* returned home and my two friends went off to a reading-retreat, [23] so that I was left alone. At that time the abbot and the prior took counsel together and summoned the teachers from the Nga-ri College. They explained that the rooms of the Nga-ri College that had fallen into disrepair, must be restored, and that they should extend an invitation to the Prelate *Nectar Spontaneously Produced*. At this Professor Palzang of Lo and Professor Sonam Raptan of *Se-rib* fell into unmitigated strife, especially the Professor of Lo, who said: 'Unless we repair our own college first, we will not repair the Nga-ri College.' He just talked in this disorderly way, and the Professor of *Se-rib* struck him with a key with the result that his head was cut. Thus Lo and *Se-rib* struggled against one another, and one man of *Se-rib* was wounded. 'Not only is work on the College not done, but things come to such a pass as this,' I thought and I was terribly sad. The next morning I asked the two Professors of *Ru-'brog* to come, and took counsel with them. They said: 'Religion is being destroyed, and those two, Lo and *Se-rib*, are responsible. There is nothing we can do, but in any case we will discuss the matter at the end of the general tea-offering.'

I did not go to the tea-offering, but I took a pot of tea and went to see the Professor of Lo. Having asked him how he was, I argued that this was a matter of the abbot's command, I explained what we gained and lost in the matter, and urged that a man of religion must practice forebearance.

'What you say is all very well,' he replied, 'but the action of the Professor of *Se-rib* might have made me a corpse. Until this matter has been decided in court, there is nothing to be done.'

I begged him to consider that we had for once obtained a precious human body with all the advantages for practising religion, and that to destroy religion and to accumulate evil actions would not do at all.

Then I went to see the Professor of *Se-rib* [24] and talked to him of these eventualities in just the same way, but he said: 'The Professor of Lo has been guilty of all sorts of misdemeanors, and there is no reason for me to be afraid, because I cut open his head. This case must be heard at Lhasa.' Thus they would not listen at all.

Then as third member of the group I took counsel with the two professors of *Ru-'brog*. The two of them had already conferred together, and decided that there was nothing to be done except to have the two professors of Lo and *Se-rib* removed. 'However it may be, you take some tea, young squire,' they said, 'and go to the Abbot and urge him politely that Doctor *Swastika Long-Life* of Lo and the Master-Scholar *Victory* of *Se-rib* should be appointed professors.' This was done and the two teachers of Lo and *Se-rib* were removed. Their case was decided by eighteen representatives.

Then I addressed all the assembled professors and said: 'Before we invite the Prelate, we must repair the college. Let each group contribute three bushels of barley, and thereafter let everyone as groups and as individuals do whatever they can according to their faith. I myself will give as much *chang* as can be made from seven bushels of barley.'

Everyone was very pleased and said: 'Let us do like that.' But although the college premises were soon repaired, the Professor of Lo began to quarrel with me for no reason. He caused various disputes and attempts were even made on my life. I thought to myself: 'I have simply been serving the doctrine, so it seems unjust that they should bear me malice. However this must be the effect of my actions in the past.' Thus I did my best to protect myself. Relying on the prior's advice and my own expedients, I practised very great forebearance, and the prior was very pleased.

Then I went to the New Monastery, which lies to the east of ours, and carried out a reading-retreat for three months under *Byams-chen bKra-shis lhun-grub*. At the midday periods [25] I received from him the profound consecration of the *Sky-Farer Nāropa* together with instructions, and as my main studies I learned the four modes, necessity and the other three, of the *Perfection* Literature, the precepts, the methods of practice, the *Three Precious Ones*, the raising of the *thought of enlightenment*, the *Perfection of Wisdom*, the state of *nirvāṇa* and the eight principal subjects.[1]

At that time I was twenty-five. During the first winter term I learned by heart the schema of the short essential teachings, and during the second term the schema of the medium-length essential teachings. Then during the first and second spring terms I did oral practice with other scholars on both the former prescriptions and the present prescriptions of monastic discipline and on the 3rd section of the *Treasury*.

Then I gave tea to everyone who was staying in the Dolpo College, and appointed duties to each individual. I sent the chief master-scholars *Intellect* and *Deliverance* to Dolpo to raise a new intake of students. I myself entered upon a reading-retreat under *Byams-chen bKra-shis lhun-grub*. I grasped the 2nd and the 3rd principal subjects very well. Then in the first summer term I returned to visit my lama. He said: 'An official letter has come from the government, and since it is a matter of a general tea-offering, they tell me to send a reliable messenger. It seems that you should go, Squire.' So I went there and handed over to the lamas and the provosts this tea-offering from the government together with subsidiary presents. There were six packs, each containing six bricks of good tea, and quite considerable presents, of which the chief was a gilded saddle.

At that time there was very heavy rain and the roofs of the Dolpo College fell in. I prepared *chang* from ten bushels of barley and flour from another thirteen bushels, and when I was beginning to do the repairs, presentations were made to us from the Lower Lamas' House and both Lo and *Se-rip* helped us with the rebuilding, so that work was finished very quickly. I bought meat with the extra flour, and made a display of the extra *chang*, and there was such a fine spread for the workmen, that they were all delighted.

Then in the second summer term the nephew *Aim-Winner* of *'Or-rlon* of *sGrol-mtshams* arrived with goods from the north loaded on four donkeys. [26] 'Squire *rGyal-po*,' he said, 'my mother and the family send you a message saying, come and stay for a while, since you have had so tiring a time this year.' So I took some books and went. My study prospered, and I felt happy. Then returning to my monastery, I stayed there a while. Then again they invited me to *'Or-rlon*, so I went there. I learned by heart *The Four Performances for Quiet Study* and *The Precise Teachings* in their extended form. I recited the latter works and worked on the first chapter of the commentary of *Rong-sTon Chos-rje*.[2]

[1] These eight principal subjects are those of the *Ornament of Comprehension* (tib. *mngon-rtogs-rgyan*, skr. *abhisamayālaṃkāra*). See E. Obermiller, *Analysis of the Abhisamayālaṃkāra*, Luzac, London, 1933, and especially the English translation by Edward Conze in the *Serie Orientale Roma* VI, Rome 1954.

[2] Concerning *Rong-sTon*, see p. 190 fn. 2.

THE BIOGRAPHY OF LAMA LORD OF MERIT

I came back for the first winter term. Two of the chief graduates had arrived, bringing twelve new novices, and as I was rather disturbed by the party of welcome and by their return hospitality and so on, my study did not go too well. At that time I was twenty-six.

Then there came an invitation to recite two good texts as religious readings for the *Lug-ra-ba* family in *Phyin-'bras*. So one of the chief master-scholars went with me, and in the course of fifteen days we recited the *Padma thang-yig*, the *Ma-ṇi bka'-'bum* and other works. Having thus seen (in our reading) the wonderful works of Lhasa and *bSam-yas*, I wanted to go there very much.

I returned for the spring term and learned to recite from works on monastic discipline and from the *Treasury*. At that time there was an attack of smallpox, and one of the chief master-scholars died while engaged in the invocations of the *All-Knowing One*. I did my best in the way of last rites and funeral ceremonies.

I had asked the Abbot for the 108 divine evocations and for the set known as 'The Ocean'. I arrived when he was giving the evocations of the 21 forms of the *Saviouress*, but someone made trouble so in the end I failed to get five of them. Then I asked Lama *Victory Glorious and Good* for the Six *Nai-gu* Doctrines complete, for the Way Consecration and the Cause Consecration of *Hevajra* and for the complete consecration and teachings of the *Sky-Farer*.

I then intended to go on pilgrimage, but Lama *Victory Glorious and Good* was giving the profound matter of the *One Mother*, and the Abbot was giving the *Drag-rDzong-ma* teachings, [27] and so thinking that I should ask for them too, I stayed. Then the Lama told Dr. *bKra-shis lhun-grub* and me to go and give the Prelate *Nectar Spontaneously Produced* advance advice that he should visit us that autumn. So the two of us went there, and he promised to come in the autumn. Then on our return, we asked for the *Sky-Farer* teachings.

When these were finished, we asked the Lama to check the auspices, and then set out in a group of six friends on pilgrimage.

We reached *bDe-legs-gling* in *sNye-mo*,[1] where we met the chief lady of Sa-kya. We stayed there in quiet study for half a month, and learned by heart the thirty pages of the great work on the Tantric Vow by *Chos rNam-rgyal*. Then we went out to the *sNye-mo* estate, and underwent tests in the Three Vows and disputed together.

Then gradually we came to *mTshur-bu*[2] in *sTod-lung*, where we met the Red Hat Karmapa *Ye-shes sNying-po* and I asked for special prayers for my father and uncle. I also asked both the *rGyal-tshab* Incarnation and the Black Hat Lama *Ye-shes rDo-rje* for special prayers, but I received no actual blessing with their hands although I saw them face to face.

---

[1] *sNye-mo*, a tributary valley of the Tsangpo, just *NE* of Shigatse. See end map. I am grateful to Mr. Hugh Richardson for checking the place-names on this pilgrimage.   [2] See *mKhyen-rtse's Guide*, p. 74.

Then we met *dPa'-bo Rin-po-che* at *gNas-nang*.[1] We asked him for special prayers and visited the shrines.

Then we went on quickly to Lhasa, where we stayed about five days, made over a hundred circumambulations, visited the shrines carefully, and said our prayers properly. We made circumambulations of *dMar-po-ri*, *lCags-po-ri*, visited the shrines and said prayers properly.

Then we came to *Yer-pa*[2] and visited all the shrines except for the Moon Cave.

Then gradually we came to *gYa'-ma-lung*[3] near *Brag-dmar*, visited the shrines there and said prayers.

Then gradually we came to *bSam-yas*,[4] where we made circumambulations, visited shrines carefully, and said prayers.

Then we went to the royal place of *Lha-stod*[5] and visited the palaces of the religious kings. Then we reached the Nga-ri College and visited the shrines there. Then we came to an estate belonging to the *sDe-srid bZang-ri-pa*, where we took part in ceremonies and the making of religious offerings. [28] When the monks who were staying there left, they gave us all the tsamba which they had in excess, so we obtained a lot of supplies for the journey.

Next we went to the *Phag-mo* Hermitage,[6] and said some prayers. We asked where the *Phag-mo* Lama had gone, and they said that he had gone to look after his goats, so we did not meet him.

Then we went to *gDan-sa-mthil*,[7] where we visited the shrines founded by the lordly Lama *Phag-mo gru-pa* and especially the one containing his own relics, called 'Effective on Sight'. We said a lot of prayers.

Then we went to *Zangs-ri khang-dmar*,[8] where we visited the image of the *One Mother* and other shrines, and said prayers there. We intended to go to *rTsa-ri*,[9] but were so tired that we did not reach there, so we made obeisances from a distance and said a lot of prayers.

Then travelling via *bZo-thang* we came to *rTse-thang*,[10] where we visited the many Ka-dam-pa and Sa-kya shrines there and said our prayers.

Then we reached *Khra-'brug*,[11] where we met the text-discoverer of Ü, whom I asked to say special prayers for my father and my uncle. Just then they were performing on behalf of the government a special rite directed against malign influences, and 108 monks were there from Nalanda for the supporting ritual. The Lama told me to engage in debate with them, and so I did so. They debated in a

---

[1] See *mKhyen-rte's Guide* p. 74.
[2] *op. cit.*, p. 43 and pp. 103–4.
[3] *op. cit.*, pp. 44 and 113.
[4] *op. cit.*, pp. 44–6 and 113–4.
[5] This is probably the area around *Yar-lung* eastwards to *Lha-rgya-ri. op. cit.* map A, 29°N, 92°E.
[6] *op. cit.*, p. 47.
[7] *op. cit.*, pp. 47 and 120–1.
[8] *op. cit.*, pp. 47–8.
[9] Wylie, *Geography of Tibet*, pp. 94–6.
[10] *mKhyen-rtse's Guide*, pp. 48–9.
[11] *op. cit.*, pp. 50 and 124–5.

THE BIOGRAPHY OF LAMA LORD OF MERIT 255

very ill-tempered manner, but at each show of ill-temper, I waved my beads three times round my head, at which the text-discoverer was delighted. I engaged in much other disputation besides this. When I left, I made a prayer that I might meet with the text-discoverer again.

Then we came to lower *Yar-lung So-kha*, and leaving our things there, we went to visit *Ri-bo khyung-lding*,[1] where there are Marpa's relics and so on, various shrines of all three kinds and very wonderful religious things. We were filled with extraordinary faith and devotion and said many prayers.

Then we visited *Ombu bla-mkhar*,[2] where we made prostrations, circumambulations and many prayers. Then we visited *bKra-shis chos-lde*[3] and the cave of *Ras-chung*, [29] visiting the shrines and saying prayers. Next we visited the College of *Ras-chung*'s Cave. We made prostrations before the five or six stupas of *lHa-lcam-ma*, which mark historical sites, and we made circumambulations and said prayers.

Then we came to the Crystal Rock of *Yar-lung*,[4] visiting all the upper and lower hermitages. There is a sacred cemetery there, which is quite the equal of the *Śītāvana* (in India), and so we slept there. The next morning we visited the shrine with the mystic circle of *Hevajra* where the Lord *Victorious Banner of Fame* had meditated, as well as the Crystal Rock with its two peaks.

Then we made another visit to *bSam-yas*. At *sGra-bsgyur-gling*[5] the Lama Incarnation of *rDo-rje'i brag* was performing a rite directed against malign influences on behalf of the government. He said: 'Monks from *Thub-bstan* are very welcome here,' and seemed very pleased indeed. He pointed out things himself, saying: 'These are the places where the King stayed, the Great Teacher stayed, the scholars and translators stayed. Make circumambulations, and as you go, recite the Song of Happiness.' With his own right and left hands he set up a stand for the drum and a stand for the conch. Then holding in both hands the cymbals, the drum-stick and the bell, he played all these instruments together. The others joined in in like manner, and we felt great faith and devotion and said many prayers.

Then we went to *Zur-mkhar*[6] and made prostrations from a distance in the direction of the palace.

Next we visited *Brag-dmar*, where there were ten monks, of whom the chief were the prior in the service of the household of the Karmapa lama *Chos-dbyings rDo-rje* and the nephew of *Ye-shes rDo-rje*, also performing on behalf of the government a rite directed against evil influences, so we made their acquaintance.

---

[1] Possibly the same as *Ri-bo chos-gling*, as mentioned by G. Tucci, *Lhasa and Beyond*, pp. 136–7. *Yar-lung So-kha* remains unidentified, but it is clearly in this same area, namely the lower *Yar-lung* Valley.
[2] This is *Yum-bu bla-mkhar* of *mKhyen-rtse's Guide*, pp. 50 and 125.
[3] See Tucci, *Lhasa*, pp. 138–9.
[4] *Yar-lung Shel-brag. mKhyen-rtse's Guide*, p. 51.   [5] *op. cit.*, p. 65.   [6] *op. cit.*, p. 46.

We visited all the shrines of the former Karmapa lamas, as well as other especially sacred things, the images of the Great Teacher and so on where we said prayers.

Then we came to *sGrags* and *Yongs-rdzong*,[1] where we visited all the old and new places, [30] especially the foot-prints of the Buddha *Maitreya* and the places of meditation of the Great Teacher.

Having visited the shrines of *rDo-rje brag*, we came to *Ra-ba-smad*.[2] *Lha-gnang*, a monk of Dolpo, acted as our guide and we visited everything properly. Then having visited the places of meditation and the shrines of *Chu-bo-ri*,[3] we made our way round to the right and came to *lCags-zam*, where we saw the image of *Thang-ston rGyal-po*.[4]

Then we came to *Chos-'khor yang-rtse*,[5] where we visited shrines and said prayers. The next morning we reached *bZhang-ri skyid-tshal*,[6] where we visited shrines.

Then we reached *bDe-legs-gling* in *sNye-mo*, where we studied quietly for half a month, learning by heart the rest of the great work on the Tantric Vow. Then we reached *Thub-bstan*, where we paid our respects to our Lama.

About that time I went to *'Or-rlon* for quiet study and learned to recite the *Precise Teachings* in their extended form and the commentary. Following upon that we invited the Prelate *Nectar Spontaneously Produced* and recited the commentary in both the upper and lower colleges and had tests.

In the second winter term I was intending to take my degree, but my colleagues presented me with meat and *chang* and some mottled silk and asked me to go to Dolpo in order to encourage a new intake of monks.

I set out for Nga-ri with two Karmapa novices, and so reached Mustang. The Honourable Lama was not there, but we paid our respects to the king and queen, and then went on to Dolpo. One of the novices was suffering from serpent-sickness and on the way he became seriously ill, so that when we reached Black Springs (*lu-ma nag-mo*), he could not go at all. I asked our other companion to help me to carry him, but he said: 'Whatever the Squire says, I will do, except carry him as he is now,' and so he would not carry him. But I had a feeling of irresistible compassion, and carrying him on my back, I reached Lo-Way Springs (*Glo-lam chu-mig*). Being very tired, I left them both there and went on ahead to my village to get a yak. [31] I met my relatives and my younger brother let me have a yak, which I sent to fetch the sick man. Thus he reached the village, where he regained his health a little.

---

[1] *Yar-lung Shel-brag. mKhyen-rtse's Guide*, p. 46. [2] See Wylie, *Geography of Tibet*, p. 89.
[3] See *mKhyen-rtse's Guide*, p. 71. [4] *op. cit.*, p. 90.
[5] On the north bank of the Tsangpo opposite *lCags-zam*. It is mentioned by Waddell, *Lhasa and its Mysteries*, p. 431 fn.
[6] Unidentified.

Then I went to visit Lama *dGe-'dun bzang-po* at T'ha-kar and he said: 'Don't go back to Central Tibet this time. Stay here. Our lordly lama (*Ngag-dbang rnam-rgyal* of Namgung) can make even the birds meditate. It would be good to learn and practice religion with him.' In reply I explained the necessity of my returning just this once.

Then I went to Hrap and Namgung, paid my respects to the two lamas and gave them the messages I had brought.

Then I went to Yang-tsher, where I met Lama *Tshe-ring dPal-bzang*. I gave him messages, and the Lama himself and the whole community treated me very well.

Then I went to Karma, where I stayed about a month, learning off the invocatory descriptions of divinities. I found three for the new intake, but they arranged a time for coming later, while I came on ahead. On the way I cut my foot on a piece of slate, and although it became very bad, I kept on reciting the series of divine descriptions and other texts I knew by heart. I reached Yang-tsher, where I met the Lama, and he gave me a monk to accompany me as far as Shimen. Then I went to my own village, where I stayed a few days. From there I went to Tarap, but I did not get a single recruit. On the way back I visited the lamas of Hrap and Namgung, and then went on to Yang-tsher, where some men and women from Karma had arrived. Together with Palden, the nephew of Lama *Tshe-ring dPal-bzang*, I went on to *Ting-khyu*. I sent the novices to beg for alms and so collected food-supplies. Then together with the nephew of Lama *bSod-nams rGyal-mtshan*, making a group of eight companions in all, we set out on our journey. People said that we should beware of the *'Bong-pa* people of *Bi-ri*, so we came to an arrangement with Lord of Religion *Lung-rig*, who was going to Tashilhunpo, [32] and going by way of *rNam-rgyal-lha-rtse*, we came to *Sra-dum*, where we stayed a few days, making prostrations and circumambulations and saying many prayers. Then our anxiety being over, we travelled gradually to *Thub-bstan*, where we paid our respects to the old abbot and the new one, to the worthy lama, to the prior and all the others, making general tea-offerings and religious offerings in return for blessings.

Then during the first winter term I practised well at debating, and so at the age of twenty-seven I passed my degree. About that time a friend of mine was robbed of something that had been entrusted to him, so quickly taking with me the things that had been entrusted to me I set out for Ü with the nephew of Lama *Tshe-ring dPal-bzang* as my companion. I handed over everything properly to the Karmapa Red Hat Lama, to the *rGyal-tshab* Incarnation and to the *dPa'-bo* Incarnation, as well as asking for their blessings. Then I arrived in Lhasa at the time of the Great Prayer Festival, where I benefitted greatly from the general distributions and the affairs of the great public ceremonies, and also visited shrines and said prayers carefully. Next I visited *Yer-pa* and from there went on to *bSam-yas*. Then I went to *sMin-grol-gling*, but because of a serious outbreak of smallpox, I did not have an audience for seven days. Then the *rNam-sprul* Lama and the *Thugs-sprul* Lama arrived seeking religious instruction, and so I was received in audience together with them.

I obtained the consecration, inspired teaching and instructions in the *Heart-Drop of the Knowledge-Holders*, the textual initiation of *Powerbolt-Being*, the instructions in the essence of the *Profound Matter of A-ti*, the consecration, textual initiation and instructions in *Padma dBang-rgyal's Essence of the Blessed Ones of the Eight-Word God*, the consecration and textual initiation in the *The Life-Effecting Concentration of Pure Essence*, etc.

Then leaving the lama's nephew at *dPal-ldan* College, my two other companions went round on pilgrimage, while for seven days I sat copying out the *Heart-Drop of the Knowledge-Holders*, and then asked for the consecration and instructions of *Powerbolt-Being*, the teachings concerning the *transfer of consciousness*, the consecration in *Self-Release on the Thought of the Tranquil and Fierce Divinities*, and *Lama-Yoga of the Heart-Drop Meditation*.

[33] Then I returned to *Thub-bstan*, where I received from Lama *bZang-po rGyal-mtshan The Way and its Fruits* in its full form, also *Bir-srungs* and the special initiation of the *Eight Canopy Gods*, and other texts besides, all of which are clearly listed in a certificate.

Then at the age of twenty-eight, not being able to resist my lama's insistence, I became chief disciplinarian. About that time too I received from Lama *rDo-rje rNam-rgyal* the works entitled *Up-turned Moustache*, *Spirit Quelling* and the *White Gentle Voice*. Then as the door of the Dolpo assembly-hall was not firm, I made a flight of steps and put the door to the east.

Then during the first summer term my study went very well, and in the second summer term I passed on the duties of chief disciplinarian to someone else. Thus in the presence of Lama *bZang-po rGyal-mtshan*, Lama *rNam-rgyal bZang-po* and a full complement of monks I was consecrated a fully ordained monk. Then I asked Lama *bZang-po rGyal-mtshan* for *Hevajra*'s 'Way Consecration', for instructions in the ordinary and special *Lama-Yoga*, for *Drag-rdzong-ma*'s consecration, the special initiation of the *Four-Faced* Divinity and the consecration of the *All-Knowing One*.

Then at the age of twenty-nine I returned to my own village and saw all my relatives again. Then two men of T'ha-kar were sent to me with the message: 'The Master must come to T'ha-kar, and if he is going to practise meditation, we beg him to meditate at T'ha-kar. I consented to this, and went to Namgung, where I asked the Lama to give me the 'Six Teachings of the Oral Tradition' in accordance with my former entreaty. He replied: 'As I must carry out my vow of seclusion for another half month, it will not do while this is in progress. But it will certainly be in order from then on, so in the meantime learn this.' He gave me the *Lama-Yoga* and *Dohā* verses, which I learned. Then when he came out from his seclusion he started instruction in the Six Teachings, and as the preliminary part I obtained the *dPe-chos-spungs* and *Dvags-po lha-rje's Thar-rgyan*. As the process of maturation I obtained the consecration of the Sixty-Two [34] and of the Fifteen Divinities, of the Five Divinities, of the Innate, of the *Boar-Headed Goddess* and of the *Innate Goddess*. As the main part of this instruction I received the sixty sections of the old and the new 'Oral Tradition', and as a complimentary work *The Golden Rosary of the Ka-gyü Order* according to *Brag-dkar* and to Margom (*dMar-sgom*). Everything is listed in full in a certificate. Thereafter I received:

'The Golden Distillation of the Secret Way,'
'The Religious Cycle of the bodiless Sky-Farers'
'The Single Flavour of the Secret Practice'
instructions in both the old and the new 'Four Letters of the Great Symbol',
the consecrations of the *Red Fury* and the *Protector*,
the verbal initiation in the *Perfecter of Thought* according to the tradition of the *Eight-Word God*,
the four complete consecrations of the *Queen of Success*, together with the special initiation and all the rest, namely consecrations, verbal initiations and instructions.

I also received:
consecrations, verbal initiations and instructions in the *Universal Saviour*,
consecrations, verbal initiations and instructions in the *One Mother Wrathful and Black*,
the life-consecration of the *White Saviouress*,
consecration and verbal initiation in the *Unity of the Blessed Ones*,
Religious History of the Ka-gyü Order,
'The Primary Topic, Clarifier of the Essence of the Doctrine of the Great Vehicle' by '*Bri-gung-pa*,
and other works which are all listed clearly in a certificate.

Then at the age of twenty-nine, thinking that I must absorb all I had learned, I went into seclusion at T'ha-kar for a period of three years. First I performed invocations for quelling spirits for one month. Then I invoked the *Universal Saviour* for two months, the *All-Knowing* for four months, and then *Hevajra* for nine and a half months. I performed the number of invocations as indicated in each text.

During this period my vital fluid waxed and waned and I had psychic experiences and spiritual visions, but there is no need to write of all this. Then as an act of supererogation I sat invoking *Hevajra* for several months.

When I came out from all this, a ceremony of oblations was performed, and as a result of drinking a lot of *chang* without eating tsamba [35] I had a serious illness affecting all the humours, accompanied by various psychic experiences, which there is not space to write about here.

About that time I received from Lama '*Brug-pa rDo-rje* the combined consecration of *Boundless Life* and *Horse-Neck*, the consecration and verbal initiation of the *Fierce Dart*, the *Consecration in substance of the Four Consecrations*, the *Six Teachings of Mixture Transfer*, the *Wish-granting Gem of the Oral Tradition* as transmitted by *Dvags-po lha-rje*, the *Wheel of the Network of Channels and Vital Breath*, and the *Religious History of the Ka-gyü Order*.

At that time while I was in seclusion my mother died, and I arranged for her funeral ceremonies using all I possessed. After that I remained invoking the *All-Knowing* for three months for my mother's intention. I knew that my mother's consciousness and my own mind were inseparable, and so I made great efforts in religious practice and in special prayers.

Then when those full three years were over, we made a great 'coming out' feast. As soon as this was finished, we read a great number of texts for my mother's intention, thirty volumes of *sūtras*, the three major texts (*brgya-tog-gser*),[1] the *Ratnakūṭa* and so on.

Then they said that I must take on the abbacy at Yang-tsher, and kept on sending messengers. Although they insisted, I replied: 'I have no thought of being a superior being in this life. I just want to practise meditation towards the end of my life. So I beg you all not to take offence at me.' But they would not listen. I referred the matter to my uncles and my holy lordly lama. My lama told me to test the auspices, and as they would not listen to my protests, I did so. The test decided in favour of acceptance, and as no one would listen to what I said, I had to become abbot of Yang-tsher, despite my lack of learning and knowledge, despite my lack of contemplative experience, despite my lack of proficiency in philosophy, meditation, religious practice and religious accomplishments, and all those other qualities associated with renunciation and understanding.

Thus at the age of thirty-three, although I was not ready for it, I had to attend a little to the affairs of others. Lama '*Brug-pa rDo-rje* (of T'ha-kar) performed the purificatory rite and the consecration, and thus on the 12th day of the 6th month, as I came escorted by monks from Margom, [36] the monks of T'ha-kar formed an orderly accompanying procession. Then the people of Shimen met me and

[1] See p. 236 fn.

escorted me in orderly manner. When I reached *Tshe-zhabs* Lama *Karma Chos-grub* met me, performed auspicious actions and showed his great pleasure. Then we continued and the people of Nyisal and the monks of Margom formed an escort in proper order. On the 14th I was consecrated and enthroned in the presence of the whole assembly of monks.

With these matters the brief account of the way in which I practised my mind with learning, reflecting and meditating, is finished.

We rejoice at this Bestower of the Title of Clear Knowledge,
Who brings together the vital profundities of all pure doctrine,
And spreading for people of many kinds, a feast of whatever pleases
Establishes them in the perfect way of release and salvation!

Now if we recount just a little how I acted on behalf of others, then it was the way of uniting both teaching and meditating. When I became abbot of Yang-tsher, some six monks who had been enclosed for three years were released from their meditation, and many benefactors came to the festival. A lot of them presented name-cards for blessings and presents for such services, and I contented them all by giving them the 'life-consecration' and the consecration of the *All-Knowing*. I gave them explanations of the consecrations, explained the intentions, and described the experiences, all in detail. They were all delighted, and the Lama (*Karma Chos-grub*) heard of it and said: 'We set such great hopes on him, and it has all worked out that way,' and he was very pleased.

Thereafter I stayed for four months in meditation on the *Red Fury*. Then I had a very severe illness, and as a result of the medical diagnosis and so on and the ceremonies I performed, there was some small improvement. I meditated for two and a half months on the *Protector*, and during these sessions I had many visions and visitations and so on, [37] but they are not described here.

The crops were poor that autumn, and since the monastery-tithes were not very much, my uncles and other family-members made me a loan of thirty-seven bushels of barley. Then I remained invoking the *Life-Effecting Concentrations of Pure Essence* for one month and seven days, and I experienced feelings of compassion and grace, and saw many portents and unusual signs. From that time my severe illness passed away like a light autumn cloud, and that is the reason why nowadays I am still absolutely devoted to the *Knowledge-Holder, the Master of Hidden Texts of Ling*.[1] Thereafter I felt very happy and performed in due order the

[1] This is *'Gyur-med rdo-rje*, a text-discoverer (*gTer-ston*) of *sMin-grol-gling* (according to the *bDe-chen bla-brang* Lama).

external practice, the internal practice and the combined practice of *The Heart-Drop of the Knowledge-Holders*, and of these too the indications and signs were most wonderful. Then I sat invoking the *Innate Supreme Bliss* for two months and seven days, and the *Boar-Headed Goddess* for three months, and my religious practice greatly improved.

Then when I was thirty-six I instructed the general assembly of monks in the 'Four Letters' and gave them the initiation of the *Boar-Headed Goddess*. On that occasion the nectar boiled (miraculously in its bowl) and overflowed and one of the butter-lamps burned for four days without diminishing. The monk *rGyal-mtshan dPal-bzang* noticed it, and he told everyone: 'Four days have passed, yet it does not get less. How very wonderful!' As a result (of his talking about it) that butter-lamp was very quickly consumed. These things were manifested as auspicious signs that I should have a long life and watch over this monastery for a long time.

Then when I was thirty-seven I performed the atoning ceremony of the *Universal Saviour*, and instructed the general assembly of monks and four nuns who had come from Lo, in the teachings of the *Innate Yoga of the Great Symbol*. Also I gave consecrations and instructions according to the *One Mother Wrathful and Black* and some special initiations in the *Triad of the Mighty Sage and his Two Disciples*, in the *Saviouress* [38] and in other rituals.

Then I went into retreat for the winter and my religious practice succeeded well. The next autumn five nuns came from Sikkim, and they said: 'Lama, you must come to Sikkim, and now we have come to make prior arrangements.' I instructed them together with those of our monastery who had been in retreat for three years, in *Life Instructions* and in the *Single Flavour of Secret Practice*. In the winter I performed an atoning ceremony for the *Red Fury*, and one for the *Protector*, and on that occasion we performed for four days the ceremony of consecration of the *Red Fury* and the *Defender* in the whole assembly of monks, and since I remained in firm concentration, my religious practice succeeded well.

Then for the space of six months I instructed the whole assembly in the teachings of the *Six Teachings of the Oral Tradition*, and as complimentary teachings I gave *The Golden Rosary of the Ka-gyü Order* and the biographies of the Margom series. At that time three marigolds remained fresh for two months and seven days, and everyone was amazed. This was a clear indication that it had been auspicious to teach this Oral Tradition so much.

Then I went to visit the Lama at Namgung and asked him for the rest of his teachings. I asked in particular for the *Six Adornments and Five Excellences* together with the precepts, and I also asked for the personal precepts written by Karma Lobsang. That year I made effort in the essentials of the practice of vital breath and the mystic circles, and meanwhile I asked Lama *dGe-slong* for the three tantras of the *Great Compassionate Lord* and for the verbal initiation into the *Innate Yoga of the Great Symbol*. All these works are listed in detail in a certificate.

The next year the Lama said that I must come for the consecration of a prayer-wall, so I went to Namgung (again), met the Lama and performed the consecration ceremony. He gave me the *Six Adornments and Five Excellences* of *rGod-tshang ras-chen* and *Byams-pa Phun-tshogs*, and furthermore he said: 'Now I shall not live for long, [39] so please look after Namgung and Yang-tsher, and be assiduous in the care of reliquary-shrines and in benefitting sentient beings.' Saying this, he gave me a horse in its prime together with the harness. Furthermore he gave me useful things for every purpose as well as a hat and a begging-bowl. But although I promised to act in accordance with the irresistible urging of the Lama, later circumstances made it impossible, so that I could not act accordingly.

That summer both the Eastern and the Western Kings[1] came, making many presents and acting as patrons. The Eastern King in particular put up many flag-masts for the monasteries and made considerable offerings for my house and quarters, as well as giving a copper coin to each monk and two such coins to those who were in solitary meditation. We made large distributions with these and other gifts.

That autumn my Uncle Gyamtso was approaching death, and since he asked me to visit him, I went to *Ting-khyu*. But although I performed many ceremonies, the 'life-consecration', prayers of atonement and so on, I could not save his life. I performed the funeral ceremonies properly, and on that occasion also gave a general consecration with name-cards, benedictions and blessings, so that everyone was satisfied. Then I returned to my monastery. At that time I went to see the Lama at Namgung and made him a selected offering of presents I had myself received, asking for a blessing for my uncle's intention. Although I intended to stay a few days, a messenger came from Lo, saying that the Boy *Phun-tshog* had committed a ritual offence and had become ill, and asking me for special prayers and for the protection of my tutelary divinities, so I quickly returned to my monastery, and having performed special prayers, purificatory ceremonies and propitiatory rites for the serpents, I brought some benefit to the youth.

Then I gave instruction in the *Six Teachings of Mixture Transfer* to the general assembly of monks, some others from *Mu-gum* and some from *Gro-phug*.

[40] I spent some time instructing them in the consecrations, inspired teachings and instructions of the *One Mother Wrathful and Black*. Then the holy Lama[2] showed signs of physical weakness and his spirit departed for the celestial spheres accompanied by extraordinary signs and portents, and I performed properly all religious offerings and funeral rites.

[1] Namely the 'King of Jumla' and the 'King of Mustang'. See the Introduction, pp. 8–10.
[2] This is presumably Lama '*Brug-pa rDo-rje* of T'ha-kar.

At that time a great number of nuns came from Lo with two teachers in charge of them, and I gave instruction both to them and the general assembly of monks in the *Universal Saviour*, the *Great Symbol*, the *Heart-Drop*, etc.

The following year we invited Lama *Karma Chos-grub* and asked him to bestow upon us the consecrations, inspired teachings and instructions of both the White and the Black *One Mother*, the inspired teachings of *The Source of all Necessities*, the instructions in the *Immaculate Transference*, and *Transference according to the Margom way* as transmitted by *sGrol-ma Chos-dbang*. All these and other teachings we asked of him. In return I offered him the *Universal Saviour*, the *Perfecter of Thought*, the *Innate Supreme Bliss*, the consecration of the *Boar-Headed Goddess*, and other consecrations. Our minds were united and he was very happy about it all.

At that time the men of T'ha-kar said I must go there at all costs, so I went, and gave instruction to those who were staying in the monastery and to a great number of the faithful who had come from all directions, giving them the full teachings of the *Universal Saviour*, the *Great Symbol*, the *Heart-Drop*, etc. As complimentary works I gave them the transmitted biographies of the Father and Son of Margom,[1] the *Ma-ṇi bka'-'bum*, the *Podma thang-yig*, and inspired teachings of whatever kind anyone wanted as part of his religious practice. Moreover I made them happy by giving them whatever they wanted, consecrations with name-cards, benedictions, blessings, etc. I consecrated Lama *Chos-'phel* as head of T'ha-kar, and then made my way back, contenting everyone in Shimen, *Ko-mangs* and Nyisal with benedictions, blessings and so on. Having reached my own monastery, I settled down to invoke the *One Mother Wrathful and Black*, and my religious experience was greatly advanced. [41] On that occasion I pleased many of the faithful who gathered there, both men and women, by giving them consecrations, inspired teachings and so on.

Later on Lama *Karma Chos-sgrub* said: 'Make a full measure of invocations to the *Wrathful and Black One*, and when you emerge from this bout of invocations, perform in full the ceremony of tranquil libations. As sacrificial offerings use all the internal parts complete of a wild deer, and the auspicious circumstances will be just right.' So afterwards I made a full measure of invocations to the *Wrathful and Black One*, and when I had come out of this retreat and was performing a two-day ceremony of libations, a nun named *Ling-brgyan* set up as sacrificial offerings the whole corpse of a wild deer which had turned up, and the circumstances worked out auspiciously, as the lama had foretold.

At that time I was giving instruction to the whole assembly of monks, and rain being very scarce, the people of *Kyi* came asking me to come and make rain. So the monk Gyaltsan and I went on a circuit through the mountains. We came first to

---

[1] These are the biographies of *Merit Intellect* and *Religious Protector Glorious and Good*.

Cha-ling and although the 'excitation' was only moderate, there was a great deal of rain. Then the people of Ka-rang said we must go there, so we went to Ka-rang and contented them all with general consecrations, name-cards, benedictions and so on. Then they said we must go to Kyi, so we went there and contented them with general consecrations, name-cards, benedictions and so on. Then the people of Nyisal said we must go there, so we went to Nyi-phug. There was a good fall of rain and a new well of water sprang forth. The 'excitation' succeeded very well, and thereafter the people of Nyisal had water in plenty. Then making a gradual circuit of such wild places as the Eightfold Stream of Mount Shi-se, we returned to our monastery.

Some people came from Mu-gum, asking for instruction, so I contented them with the consecrations and inspired teachings of the Universal Saviour, the One Mother and so on.

Then I went to Byas and exerting myself in the matter of sacrificial offerings and special prayers, I made good the harm suffered by local divinities, [42] and there were many signs of resulting benefits. Then returning to my monastery, I went into strict solitude and my religious practice succeeded well.

Then I went to see the Lama bsTan-'dzin Ras-pa at Shey, and I asked him for the consecrations of the Great Symbol and the Fire of Internal Heat, the consecration of the two-headed Boar-Headed Goddess, the consecration of Bla-ma sgrub-pa, the inspired teachings from the works of Dvags-po Lha-rje and so on. Then returning to my own monastery, I contented the many worthy faithful who had gathered there with consecrations, textual initiations, religious instruction and so on. Then as I had resolved to go into strict seclusion, I went to the lower monastery and passed a winter retreat there. My religious practice succeeded well and I felt very happy, but once again the general assembly of monks, people from the inner and outer districts, representatives of the governors and so on, all of them refused to listen to my excuses, so I returned to the upper monastery, and contented these ready-listeners with consecrations, textual initiations and whatever they wanted.

At that time my brother became severely ill, and whatever I did in the way of consecrations, ceremonies, medical diagnosis and so on, he did not survive. With the monks providing a procession, I performed the funeral ceremonies very well, and everywhere I made donations in the name of the deceased with name-cards and gifts as fees for benedictions.

Then a month later my younger brother had a severe illness, and whatever I did in the way of medical diagnosis and ceremonies, he did not survive. So if one thinks on the worldly side of things, the misery of it is unbearable. But thinking on the religious side of things, I reflected that the life and happiness of all sentient beings in the threefold world is impermanent and inconstant, and such is the true nature of phenomenal existence. Thus I recovered myself, and exerting myself in religious works, benedictions and prayers and so on, I performed the donations on behalf of the deceased very well. From that time onwards I was completely taken up by weariness for the world, and I made great effort in solitary meditation, remaining in seclusion both summer and winter. Especially this meditation, the essence of which is Voidness and Compassion, [43] is a way of meditation which should be uninterrupted through all times and all occasions, but sometimes I would do whatever was best for the good of sentient beings in the way of summer instruction and winter instruction, consecrations, textual initiations, instruction, advice and so on.

Then on one occasion when I was getting ready to go to Lo following upon the receipt of a command from the Ruler of Lo, my own people and some villagers said: 'It does not seem that rain will come this year, and taking into account the business of rain making, it will not do for you to go to Lo.' But I replied: 'In any case I must go this year, and since it is certain that there will be a lot of rain this year, there is no need for you to be so miserable about it.' Then in the course of the journey to Lo, I exerted myself in spells for rain and in profound meditation, and that year the rains came in the right season. Having reached Lo, I went to see everyone in the proper order, and first I went to see the old king who said to me: 'You must give the consecrations and inspired teachings of the *Eight-Word God* in the *Knowledge-Holder* version to the nuns of *dGe-lung*.' So I gave two series of consecrations at *dGe-lung*. Then a representative of the Ruler came, saying that I must go to Tsarang quickly, so I went to Tsarang and met the King and Queen together, and on the 21st I offered two tea-ceremonies at the monastery and made general distributions of presents. Then I went on to Mustang and visited the Incarnate Lama and his mother. Next I went to *Gar-ma*, where I made offerings and visited the shrines. Then the local governor said I must visit Red Crag, and I sealed the Lady *Sems-ma* and her son in solitary meditation and gave blessings and so on. I received a large number of various things. Then they said that I must go to *dGa'-mi*, so I went there and gave to the nuns and to various religious who had come from round about, [44] first the consecration of the *Innate Supreme Bliss*, and instructions in the *Great Symbol*, then the consecrations, textual initiations and instructions in the *Universal Saviour*, then the consecrations, textual initiations and instructions in the *One Mother Wrathful and Black*, and so made them contented with whatever they wanted. On that occasion I contented the villagers of *dGa'-mi* with general consecrations, name-cards and blessings, etc., and I received a lot of all kinds of things. Then a messenger came from the villagers of *Tshugs*, giving many reasons why I should go there, but I replied saying: 'This time I cannot come. I beg you not to take offence,' and I did not go.

THE BIOGRAPHY OF LAMA LORD OF MERIT 267

Then when I was about to return, I went to see the Ruler and his son and other gentry, offering each one a sprinkling of sanctifying water. They asked me to consecrate the images and books, etc. of all the local governors, so I performed a proper consecration, and they made me wonderful presents and gave me their patronage. When I was returning to Dolpo they accompanied me on the way, one group taking over from another. Some nuns assisted me on the way to Tsharka, and the people of Tsharka conducted us, and asked for benedictions, and formed an escort and so on, doing it all very well. Then continuing my journey, I made all the people of Shimen and *Ting-khyu* happy with consecrations, name-cards, benedictions, blessings and so on. Then the people of *Ko-mangs* said I must go there, so I went there and contented them with general consecrations, name-cards, benedictions and blessings.

Then I reached my monastery, and having seen all the monks, I went into retreat for the winter, and this religious practice succeeded very well. The following year I summoned *dBon-chung rDo-rje* and his son from Lo and relatives of mine from *Ting-khyu*, and we repaired the entrance-chöten at Do-ra properly. I also had some picture scrolls, mystic circles and ritual cards painted, performing the consecration ceremonies on a large scale with festivals and general distribution of gifts. Then Lama *bsTan-'dzin Ras-pa* summoned me, so I went to Shey, and as soon as I met him, [45] he recited a religious song. I asked him questions and received answers in an orderly manner, and then the Lama said to me: 'Just tell me about the three divisions of the scriptures, the *Vinaya*, the *Sūtras* and the *Abhidharma*,[1] about the four doctrines of the *Vaibhāsikas, Sautrāntikas, Cittamātras* and *Mādhyamikas*,[2] and about the four kinds of tantras, *kriyā, caryā, yoga* and *anuttarayoga*.[3]' I explained their meaning in due order. He was delighted and our minds were united as one.

The following morning I made a circular tour of the holy places, making offerings at the four quarters, and I delighted in the weather and in the landscape. Then I returned and the Lama asked me what impressions I had. I explained my impressions in an orderly way, and he was very pleased.

Then on my way back, they said I must visit Namgung, so I went there and visited the shrines, and everyone showed me respect and escorted me properly on my way. Then continuing on my way, I made everyone happy in Saldang and *Ti-ling* and other places with name-cards, benedictions, prayers and so on, and then I reached my own monastery. That winter I remained in strict seclusion, and my religious practice benefitted and great insight arose within me.

Then when I was 54 years old, I went to the upper monastery and sealed myself

---
[1] The three sections of the Indian Buddhist canon, viz. Monastic Discipline, Doctrinal Treatises and Philosophical Notions.
[2] The four main philosophical schools of later Indian Buddhism.
[3] *Viz.* Rites, Religious Practice, Yoga and Supreme Yoga.

off from the world for three years. I passed two months in atoning invocations of the *Red Fury*, then three months in invocations of the *Stirrer of the Pit of Existence*, and three months in invocations of the *Sky-Faring Goddess*, then two months in atoning invocations of *Hevajra*, then three months in invocations of the *Canopy Guardian*. Continuing thus, my religious practice benefitted greatly. In between these series of invocations and at the urgent entreaty of the faithful, I gave instructions in the *Universal Saviour*, the consecrations of the *Red Fury* and the *Canopy Guardian*, the consecration of the *Stirrer of the Pit of Existence*, instructions in the *Golden Distillation of the Secret Way*, [46] the 'life-series' consecration and the 'way' consecration of *Hevajra*, the consecration, textual initiation and instructions of the *Sky-Faring Goddess*, the consecrations of the *Canopy Guardian*, so satisfying the intentions of the faithful. Then as a festival for the ending of my three years' retreat, I arranged ceremonies lasting for five days at both the higher and the lower monasteries, and as religious gifts I made large offerings of cotton and woollen cloth, etc., which was worth a hundred silver pieces. Furthermore I gave parties and presents at all the monasteries in *Nang-khong* and *Ban-tshang*.

Then although I had the intention of practising meditation in the solitude of the mountains, the lamas who were my friends in religion, the whole assembly of my own monks and all sorts of people from the inner and outer districts of Dolpo urged me so strongly that I had to stay, working great good for sentient beings by giving consecrations, textual initiations and instructions and the rest to these faithful disciples of mine.

The next year Lama *bsTan-'dzin Ras-pa* said I must come for the consecration ceremony of a silver shrine, so I went to Shey. I met the Lama and we had many discourses on religion. We consecrated the silver shrine properly and there were wonderful presentations of offerings and a most joyful festival. Then on the way back I received all sorts of presents from the faithful village folk in return for benedictions and the consecrating of name-cards.

Then I reached my own place and went into retreat for the winter. From that time on I made many faithful people happy with consecrations, textual initiations, instructions, with advice and practical teachings, and it would not do to try and write about each case in turn.

The next year the Chief Lady came from Lo and asked me for the consecrations and textual initiations of the *Sky-Faring Goddess*, as well as those of *Bir-srungs* and the *Profound Way*. I asked them to excuse me from giving *Bir-srungs* and the *Profound Way*, as it would not be suitable on this occasion.

[47] 'As for the inspired teachings of the *Sky-Faring Goddess*,' I said, 'since your command does not permit refusal, it would be only suitable to give them.' So I gave one set of consecrations to the nobility and their entourage, and another set to the

servants, making two sets together with the textual initiations, and they were well content. They made religious offerings and donations and acted as the most wonderful patrons.

Although I intended to retire to a mountain retreat that year, the King and the Incarnate Lama of Lo both urged me so strongly, that I agreed to remain available for three years. The following year the Incarnate of Lo came and in accordance with his order that I should give the consecration of the *Great Symbol* to the officials and their entourage, I gave them instructions in the *Innate Yoga* of the *Great Symbol*, and they gave me many donations and offerings. At that time the monks of T'ha-kar said that I should assume charge of both Margom and T'ha-kar, and because of the urgency of their request, I promised to do this, so I looked after both monasteries, making everyone contented with consecrations, textual initiations, instructions, advice and practical teachings. On my journeys between the two places, the villagers of *Ting-khyu* and Shimen and other places would ask me to come, and I would go there for a few days, making them all happy with general consecrations, name-cards and benedictions and blessings and the initiation of the *maṇi* formula.

Then when I was 64 years old, Lama *bsTan-'dzin Ras-pa*'s spirit departed to the celestial spheres. Since he gave instructions in his last testament that I should come and perform the funeral ceremonies, I went to *Gro-phug*, where I honoured the corpse by ceremonial burning. There were the most wonderful signs and portents, for the heart, the tongue, the eyes and the heart and so on were all preserved. I performed the proper ceremonial offerings, and in the following winter I had relic shrines made, [48] which we consecrated properly with a joyful festival.

In the first part of the following summer I gave instruction in the *Heart-Drop*, and in the latter part of the summer I gave the full version of the special initiation with the rite known as *rGya-tsa rgya-mtsho*. Afterwards while I was in retreat, a messenger came from the North, saying that the Karmapa Lama had arrived in *Gro-shod*. So I quickly went to *Gro-shod*, where I met the Karmapa Lama and his spiritual heirs, and together with fees for benedictions and presents I offered more than one hundred tanka[1]. Good prayers were said for the special intention of all beings throughout space and in particular for those nearest to me. I asked for the *Great Symbol* teaching, known as *The Four Letters*, written by the (former) Karmapa Lama *Don-yod rdo-rje*. Furthermore we received benedictions and blessings, and presents and so on, and with such good things they made us all very happy.

Then on the return journey I fulfilled the wishes of many faithful people with benedictions, retreats, blessings, the initiation of the *maṇi* formula and so on. On that occasion Shākya of *Phan-phyi* had said that I must at all costs visit his settle-

[1] A small silver coin worth about an old silver sixpence.

ment on the way back, and I had promised to do this. Then *Kun-bzang* of *sGom-mo*, Tashi Dondrup of *Sra-brtan*, Nga-dan of *gNam-ru*, Gar-wa of *sGom-mo* and the cousins of Uruba all said that I must go to their places, so I went and contented them all with benedictions, retreats and blessings and so on. Then I reached the settlement of Shākya of *Phan-phyi*, where beginning with the chief himself and his family, I gave benedictions, retreats, blessings, the initiation of the *maṇi* formula, etc., to many faithful people, so satisfying the wishes of everyone. Then as I came on my way, Tashi Gonpo of '*A-ba* said I must go to see him, so I went there and made many faithful people happy with benedictions, retreats and so on. In these places I received all sorts of things.

[49] Then I came quickly back to Dolpo, where the devoted villagers met me, and the householder Kon-chok said: 'At all costs you must stay in my house this night.' So I stayed there, and the next morning I made everyone happy with general consecrations, special consecrations, blessings and so on. Then continuing on my way, I was met and properly escorted by the villagers of Nyisal and by my own monks, and having reached my place, I remained happily in that state which knows no separation from religious aspiration.

Thus having settled in my monastery, I have been teaching up to the present time, giving consecrations, inspired teachings, instructions, advice and practical guidance, using the following works:

The Six Teachings of the Oral Tradition,
The Single Flavour of Secret Practice,
The Golden Distillation of the Secret Way,
The Universal Saviour,
The One Mother White and Black,
The Master Red Fury,
The Four-Armed Knowledge Protector,
The Blue Perfecter of Thought,
The Heart-Drop of the Knowledge-Holders,
The Stirrer of the Pit of Existence,
Hevajra,
The Wheel of Supreme Bliss,
The Boar-Headed Goddess,
The Canopy Guardian,
The Sky-Faring Goddess,
The All-Knowing,
The Destroyer,
Boundless Life, both the *New* and the *Old,* etc.

So I passed my time in teaching, especially during the summer and winter sessions, when I continued uninterruptedly. Some times I would start reading two or three commentaries and explain them. But how would it be possible to write about each of these matters in turn?

On the occasions of these consecrations and religious instructions, I composed many songs for various faithful pupils who asked me for them, and these are written up separately. In short by means of the teaching and practice of religion, I did whatever I could for the doctrine and for sentient beings. Nor did I waste the offerings of the faithful, for I spent them on the service of the Buddhas and the Religious Community, and in gifts to the poor and needy, and in the making of images, books and shrines. As for images [50] I had made two entrance-stupas at Do-ra, two paintings in gold of the *Buddha of Boundless Life* in 108 manifestations, a painting of the *Wrathful Black One*, a painting of *Maitreya*, a silver image of *Śākyamuni* to the size of a small man, a gilded image of *Glancing Eye* to the measure of a small man, as well as other smaller images and paintings and ritual cards and so on. There were so many of them, that it will not do to write about each of them.

As for books, I completed the missing sections from our set of canonical *sūtras*, I had copied the biographies of the 84 Great Yogins, the commentaries on the three *tantras* of the *Great Compassionate Lord*. I had about 15,000 *maṇi* formulas written.

As for shrines, I had repair work done on numerous stupas. Then I gave presents to the keepers of the great conch at Sa-kya, and at *Thub-bstan*. I made many tea-offerings and gave fees for benedictions.

Then I made four great distributions in the outer and inner districts of Dolpo, giving away horses, shields, turquoises, gold, and silver and flour among other things. Then I had numerous ceremonies performed for the fierce defenders of the doctrine, as well as the ceremonies of the *Heart-Drop*, the *Buddha of Boundless Life*, the *All-Knowing, Lama Worship*, the *Universal Saviour* and so on. It would be impossible to write about them all.

EPILOGUE

As for the rest, he spent his time in acts of pure goodness, doing whatever was of benefit to the doctrine and to living beings, at all times and in all ways and attending to the service of the Buddhas. Then when he was 72 years old — in the Female Iron Pig Year (A.D. 1731) — while he was at T'ha-kar, he gave the appearance of being rather unwell, and however much all his disciples besought him to remain, his health did not improve and he certainly intended to go to other realms. Those who were standing around begged him saying: 'Holy Lama, if you really will not stay with us, please let your thoughts rest a while, directing them to the benefit of the doctrine and of sentient beings.'

He replied: 'We have travelled a long journey together and you my pupils are weary. So I did not intend to rest my thoughts in meditation. But as you urge me so strongly, it would be unseemly if my robes of office were not arranged in a meditating posture.'

Again those around him asked: 'Which of the pure realms will you go to, O Lord? Since we who remain behind will make supplications to you there, we beg you to treat us with compassion.'

He replied: 'First I shall go to the *Glorious Copper-Coloured Mountain*. Then I shall ask leave of *Lotus-Born* and go to the feet of *Maitreya* in the *Joyful Realm*. So it will do, wherever you make your supplications.'

At what time the king of the birds and other creatures were heard calling. A rainbow appeared in the form of a tent. Flowers showered down and there was the sound of music. There was a sweet smell of incense and various other wonderful signs. The Lord said: 'The whole sky is filled with the tutelary divinities, the valiant gods and the attendant goddesses. I shall go away with them. At all times and in all ways you must cleave to your religious aspirations.' Saying this, his spirit was absorbed into the celestial sphere and his robes of office remained in the upright posture of meditation. When the corpse was to be honoured by ceremonial burning, the fire kindled of its own accord, and the tongues of flame had the shape of ritual powerbolts and lotuses and the letter A and of such signs and syllables. There were pleasant sounds and sweet odours and fine rainbow colours, as well as showers of beautiful flowers and similar manifestations made manifest to worthy persons. Then after seven days the funeral urn was opened with acts of worship and purification, and all sorts of relic images were found, his heart, tongue and eyes, images of *Supreme Bliss, Hevajra*, the *Protectors of the Three Families, Lotus-Born, Boundless Life, Śākyamuni, Horse-Neck*, the *Wrathful Black One*, the *Crow-Headed Protector, Jambhala*, the *World-Protector*, and the *Precious Finder of Texts*. Also a lot of mystic letters were found, VAJRA GURU, and letter A and so on. Many relics were found on the skull and the thigh-bones, while the other parts remained in their natural state. They too had assumed many remarkable shapes. Furthermore at each period of seven days many wonderful signs were manifest, the sky was clear, there was a rainbow, a smell of incense, the sound of music, showers of flowers and so on.

> Since he was perfected in the monastic rules of religious discipline,
> Sweet smells of incense are wafted everywhere.
> Since he was perfected in the *would-be buddha*'s vow of raising the thoughts towards enlightenment,

The sounds of birds and other creatures are heard.
Since he was perfected in the spell-bond of the *Knowledge-Holders*,
Music is heard and flowers shower down.
Since he is perfected in his assumption of the *Physical Body* of the *Process of Emanation*,
Rainbows and lights shine in all directions.
Since he is perfected in the assumption of the *Absolute Body* of the *Process of Realization*,
The sky is clear and free of clouds and the wind is gentle.
Since he is perfected in the assumption of the *Glorious Body* of the *Two-in-One*,
There is a continual manifestation of good and wonderful signs.

How should any creature possessed of an intellect fail to have faith in face of such wonderful signs and accomplishments?
Here I have taken just one drop from the whole ocean of wonderful doings of that Teacher, and may such merit as accrues bring to us limitless beings absolution for our sins, accumulations of merit and the final realization of enlightenment!
The biography of *Lord of Merit*, entitled 'Worthy Fulfiller of Hopes' is finished.

Double powerbolt in the form of a cross

TIBETAN INDICES

These Tibetan indices are arranged according to the order of the Tibetan alphabet, and for this and the system of transliteration used, see *Buddhist Himālaya*, p. 300. Since the order of the Tibetan alphabet is based upon radical (not initial) letters, I have normally used capital letters for radical letters in the first syllable of names, e.g. *gZhis-ka-rtse* (anglicized version: Shigatse). This is both helpful to the general reader who is thus assisted towards recognition of some connection between the correct spellings and the various 'phonetic' spelling in use, and also to the Tibetan reader who is enabled to tell by glancing at the radical letters (in capitals) as they appear in the indices, just what part of the alphabet he is looking at. See also p. 72 fn.

The items in the Tibetan indices are numbered throughout and access is available to them in many cases by cross-reference from the general index, where the Tibetan item numbers are quoted in square brackets. The three-figure references in round brackets (e.g. III.9.[10]) which occur very occasionally throughout the indices, relate to the actual Tibetan MSS which will be published in a separate volume.

DIVINITIES

1. *Kun-dga'-skyabs* 'Refuge of All Joy', 15, 151
2. *Kun-tu bzang-po* 'All Good' (*Samantabhadra*), 21, 81
3. *Kun-rig* 'All Knowing' (*Sarvajña* = *Vairocana*), 87, 118, 119, 131, 132, 135, 137, 144, 151, 175, 215, 217, 225, 229, 241, 243, 253, 258–61 pass, 170, 171
4. *Kye-rdo-rje* (*Hevajra*), 24, 85, 88, 96, 131, 132, 136, 140, 153, 175, 178, 179, 195, 227–29 pass, 255, 258–60 pass, 265, 268, 270, 272
5. *dKar-mo nyi-zla* 'White Goddess of Sun & Moon' (III.9¹)
6. *dKon-mchog-gsum* 'Three Precious Ones' (*Triratna*), 163, 169, 181, 234, 239, 252
7. *bKa'-brgyad* 'Eight-Word God', 85, 99, 105, 131, 144, 203, 204, 259, 266
8. *Khro-bo yaksha me-wal* 'Wrathful Yaksha Me-wal', 199
9. *Khros-nag* 'Wrathful Black One', 103, 272 [cp. 67]
10. (*Phyag-rdor*) *Khyung-khra* 'Hawk King of Birds', 132
11. *mKha'-'gro-ma* 'Attendant Goddess' (*ḍākinī*), 84, 85, 86, 103,

104, 114, 122, 128, 136, 148, 172, 174, 176, 177, 207, 211, 237
12. *mKha'-spyod-ma* 'Sky-Farer' (*khecarī*), 103, 251, 253, 268, 270
13. *'Khor-ba dong-sprugs* 'Stirrer of the Pit of Existence', 99, 100, 103, 106, 119, 268, 270

14. *Gu-ru drag-dmar* see *Drag-dmar*
15. *Gu-ru zhi-ba* 'Tranquil Master', 100, 103, 105
16. *Gur-mgon* 'Canopy Guardian', 203, 210, 228, 268, 270
17. *Gur-mgon lcam-dral* 'Canopy Guardian Brother & Sister', 88
18. *Gur-lha brgyad* 'Eight Canopy Gods', 258
19. *Grub-rgyal-ma* 'Queen of Success', 103, 106, 131, 137, 241, 245, 259
20. *mGon-dkar* 'White Protector', 96
21. *mGon-po* 'Protector', 104, 228, 259, 261, 262
22. *mGon-po phyag-bzhi-pa* 'Four-Armed Protector', 228, 270
23. *mGon-po bya-rog gdong-can* 'Crow-Headed Protector', 272
24. *mGon-ser* 'Yellow Protector', 154
25. *'Gro-ba kun-sgrol* 'Universal Saviour', 106, 118, 184, 149, 151, 154, 161, 175, 243, 259, 262, 264, 265, 266, 270, 271
26. *'Gro-ba-drug-sgrol* 'Saviour of the Six Spheres of Existence', 119
27. *'Gro-ba 'dul-ba* 'Converter of Sentient Beings', 119
28. *'Gro-ba bzang-po* 'Fair Farer', (a *ḍākinī*), 115
29. *rGya-glang 'khor-ba* (local god of *Mu-gum*), 114

30. *sGrol-ma* 'Saviouress' (*Tārā*), 24, 96, 116, 253, 262
31. *sGrol-dkar* 'White Saviouress', 88, 104, 259

32. *bCu-gcig-zhal* 'Eleven-Headed Glancing Eye', 132

33. *Chos-skyong* 'Defenders of Religion', (*dharmapāla*), 84, 117, 151, 181
34. *'Chi-bdag 'joms-pa* 'Destroyer of Death' (*Yamāntaka*), 87, 106, 119

35. *Jambhala*, 272
36. *Jo-bo sdugs* (a local god), 198
37. *Jo-bo yul-lha* (local god of Upper Nam), 15, 194–95, 198, 207, 218, 219, 222, 224
38. *'Jam-dpal* 'Glorious Gentle Lord' (*Mañjuśrī*), 129, 196, 199 (see next items)
39. *'Jam-dbyangs* 'Gentle Voice' (*Mañjughosha*), 132, 228, 241
40. *'Jam-dbyangs dkar-po* 'White Gentle Voice', 258
41. *'Jam-dbyangs nag-po* 'Black Gentle Voice', 116

42. *'Jigs-byed* see *rDo-rje 'jigs-byed*

43. *rTa-mgrin* 'Horse-Neck' (*Hayagrīva*), 240, 247, 260, 272
44. *rTa-mgrin nā-ga klu-'dul* 'Horse-Necked Subduer of Serpents', 106, 107, 198, 199
45. *rTa-mgrin yang-khros* 'Horse-Necked God Doubly Wrathful', 100, 106

46. *Thugs-sgrub* 'Perfecter of Thought'

(Blue & Red), 103, 131, 137, 151, 199, 228, 259, 264
47. *Thugs-rje chen-po* 'Great Compassionate One', 84, 116, 148, 152, 161, 168, 169
48. *Dur-khrod bdag-po* 'Lord of the Cemetery', 154
49. *bDag-med-ma* (*Nairātmyā*), 88, 140
50. *Drag-po ki-la* 'Fierce Dart', 260
51. *Drag-dmar* 'Red Fury', 97, 98, 99, 103, 104, 105, 106, 112, 131, 140, 154, 179, 199, 204, 210, 222, 225, 226, 259, 261, 268, 270
52. *Drag-dmar dmar-chung* 'Red Fury Sure & Short', 104, 106, 218–19, 250
53. *Drag-rdzong-ma*, 258
54. *gDugs-dkar* 'Goddess of the White Parasol', (*Sītātapatrā*), 242
55. *bDe-mchog* 'Supreme Bliss', (*Saṃvara*), 24, 88, 96, 131, 193, 205
56. *rDo-rje-'chang* 'Powerbolt-Holder' (*Vajradhara*), 21, 93, 95, 109, 121, 122, 123, 151, 178, 181, 228, 230, 262, 264, 266, 270, 272
57. *rDo-rje 'jigs-byed* 'Powerbolt-Terror' (*Vajrabhairava*), 88, 133, 192, 192, 194, 205, 206, 208, 213, 218, 225, 228
58. *rDo-rje phag-mo* 'Boar-Headed Goddess' (*Vajravārāhī*), 103, 105, 193, 247, 259, 262, 264, 265, 270
59. *rDo-rje sems-dpa'* 'Powerbolt-Being' (*Vajrasattva*), 81, 82, 147, 154, 157, 186, 258
60. *Na-rag dong-sprugs* 'Stirrer of the Pit of Hell', 119
61. *rNam-rgyal-ma* 'Victorious Lady' (*Vijayā*), 226, 249
62. *rNam-'joms* 'Destroyer', 87, 116, 154, 226, 249, 270
63. *rNal-' byor-ma* (*Yoginī*), 88, 106
64. *sNa-tshogs-yum* 'Mother of Variety', 96, 116
65. *sNang-ba mtha'-yas* 'Boundless Light', 116 (='*Od-dpag-med*)
66. *dPal rdo-rje nag-po gur-zhal* 'Glorious Black Powerbolt Canopy Countenance', 226
67. *dPung-khros-nag* 'Protector Wrathful & Black', 264 [cp. 9]
68. *sPyan-ras-gzigs* 'Glancing Eye' (*Avalokiteśvara*), 21, 33, 105, 106, 112, 119, 132, 179, 186, 206–9 pass, 221, 225, 228, 271
69. *Phyag-rdor* 'Powerbolt-in-Hand' (*Vajrapāṇi*), 88, 103, 132, 186, 196, 199, 206, 209, 219–20, 222, 229
70. *Byams-pa mgon-po* 'Protector Maitreya', 180, 246, 247, 256, 271, 272
71. *'Bir-srungs*, 106, 202, 258, 268
72. *Ma-gcig* 'One Mother', 53, 94–6 pass, 103, 112, 132, 136, 137, 157, 253, 254
73. *Ma-gcig dkar-nag* 'One Mother White & Black', 106, 262, 264, 270
74. *Ma-gcig khros-nag* 'One Mother Wrathful & Black', 263, 264, 266, 271
75. *Ma-gcig zhi-drag* 'One Mother

TIBETAN INDICES — DIVINITIES

Gentle & Violent', 114, 136, 151, 153, 158, 259

76. *Mi-'khrugs* '(Buddha) Imperturbable' (*Akshobhya*), 88, 119, 144, 175, 214, 215, 227, 229

77. *rMe-brtsegs* 'God of the Up-Turned Moustache', 132, 226, 258

78. *gTsug-tor rnam-rgyal-ma* 'Victorious Lady of the Chignon' (*Ushṇīshavijayā*), 88, 104, 204

79. *Tshe-sku drag-dmar* 'Life Body Red Fury', 104, 106

80. *Tshe-dpag-med* 'Boundless Life' (*Amitāyus*) 24, 96, 133, 135, 137, 167, 192, 207, 260, 270–72 *pass*

81. *Tshe-ring-ma* 'Long Life Goddess', 103

82. *Tshe-ring mched-lnga* 'Five Sisters of Long Life', 123, 199

83. *mDze-ta-ri* (*Jetari*), 87, 103, 132, 167

84. *Wa-la-wa* (a local god), 15, also a place-name

85. *Zhal-bzhi-pa* 'Four-Faced God', 88, 104, 258

86. *Za-byed mkha'-'gro* 'Consuming Ḍākinī', 106

87. *'Od-dpag-med* 'Boundless Light', (*Amitābha*), 21, 33, 240

88. *Yang-khros* 'Doubly Wrathful' [see 45]

89. *Yul-'khor-skyong* 'World-Protector', 272

90. *Ye-shes-kyi mkha'-'gro-ma* 'Goddess of Knowledge', 199

91. *Ri-khrod-ma* 'Anchoress' (*Śavarī*), 88, 96, 240

92. *Ri-khrod-ma lo-ma-can* 'Leafy Anchoress' (*Parṇaśavarī*), (see next item)

93. *Lo-ma gyon-ma* 'Leaf-Clad Goddess', 96, 116, 221

94. *gShed-dmar* 'Red Killer', 88

95. *Sam-pu-ṭa* (*Samputa*) (I.9^1)

96. *gSang-'dus* 'Secret Unity' (*Guhyasamāja*), 131, 132

97. *Seng-ge gdongs-ma* 'Lion-Headed Goddess', 116, 132

98. *lHa-btsan-pa* (a local god), 195

99. *lHan-cig skyes-ma* 'Innate Goddess', 259

100. *U-rtsa* (title of *Phyag-rdor*) (I.10^{17}, II.9^9)

TEXTS AND RITUALS

101. *Kye-rdo-rje'i rgyud* (*Hevajra-tantra*), 191 (as ed. & transl. by D. L. Snellgrove, Oxford 1959)
102. *dKa'-bzhi* 'Four Difficulties', 246, 247
103. *bKa'-brgyad bde-gshegs snying-po* 'Essence of the Blessed Ones of the Eight-Word God', 258
104. *bKa'-brgyad gsang-ba yongs-rdzogs* 'Quite Secret Eight-Word God', 99
105. *bKa'-brgyud chos-'byung* 'Religious History of the Ka-gyü Order', 259, 260
106. *bKa'-brgyud gser-'phreng* 'Golden Rosary of the Ka-gyü Order', 136, 143, 259, 262
107. *bKa'-gdams glegs-bam* 'Volume of Precepts', 132
108. *bKa'-bsdu bzhi-pa* 'Four Condensations', 190

109. *dGongs-pa zang-thal* 'Unobstructed Intentions', 158, 166
110. *dGos-pa kun-'byung* 'Source of All Necessities', 264
111. *mGon-dkar yid-bzhin nor-bu* 'Wish-granting Gem of the White Protector', 96
112. *rGya-gar mkha'-'gro'i gdams-pa bco-lnga* 'Fifteen Admonitions of the Indian Attendant Goddesses', 135
113. *rGyan-drug mchog-lnga* 'Six Adornments & Five Excellences', 262, 263
114. *rGyud-sde-lnga'i dbang-mo-che* 'Great Consecration of the Five Tantric Series', 103
115. *rGyud-bla-ma* (*Uttaratantra*), 189
116. *sGrub-thabs brgya-rtsa* 'Hundred-odd Invocations', (III.9⁹)
117. *sGrol-dkar yid-bzhin nor-bu* 'Wish-granting Circle of the White Saviouress', 104
118. *brGya-tog-gser* 236 fn, 260

119. *Nges-don zab-mo'i don* 'Profound Matter of Absolute Certainty', 237
120. *mNgon-rtogs-rgyan* (*Abhisamayālaṃkāra*) 'Ornament of Comprehension', 128, 246, 252 fn
121. *mNgon-pa kun-las btus-pa* '*Abhidharma* Compendium', 190
122. *mNgon-pa-mdzod* (*Abhidharmakośa*) 'Treasury of Philosophical Notions', 190, 246, 252 (See *l'Abhidharmakośa* de Vasubandhu traduit et annoté par L. de la Vallée Poussin, Paris 1923–31)
123. *sNgags-sdom chen-mo* 'Great Work on the Tantric Vow', 253
124. *sNgags-lam-rim* 'Order of the Way of Secret Spells', 100
125. *lNga-ldan* 'The Fiver', 149, 157

126. *gCod* 'Rite of Self-Sacrifice', 25, 161, 166, 200, 217
127. (*Tshe-dpag-med*) *lCam-rgyud-ma* 'Lady Tradition (of Boundless Life)', 132

128. *Chos-nyid rnam-'byed* (*Dharmadharmatāvibhaṅga*), 189
129. *'Chi-med* 'The Deathless', 96

130. *sNyan-brgyud chos-drug* 'Six Teachings of the Oral Tradition', 258–9, 262, 270
131. *sNyan-brgyud yid-bzhin nor-bu* 'Wish-granting Gem of the Oral Tradition', 260
132. *sNying-po don-gyi rgyud* 'Tantra of Essential Import', 118
133. *sNying-po don gsum gyi khrid* 'Instruction in the Three Essential Subject-Matters', 96

134. *Ṭig-chen kun-bzang* 'Great Commentary — All-Good', 190
135. *gTam-tshogs* 'Collection of Stories', 190
136. *gTor-chen* 'Great Offering of Sacrificial Cakes', 116
137. *rTags-rig* 'Inference', 190
138. *bsTod-tshogs* 'Collection of Praises', 190

139. *Thabs-lam* 'Way of Method', 112
140. *Thar-rgyan*, 259 (= 'The Jewel Ornament of Liberation' by sGam-po-pa as translated by H. V. Guenther, Rider & Co, London 1959)
141. *Thugs-rje chen-po'i dmar-khrid* 'Sure Instructions of the Great Compassionate One', 88, 200, 210
142. *Thugs-thig gi bla-ma rnal-'byor* 'Lama-Yoga of the Heart-Drop', 258
143. *Thub-dbang gtso-'khor gsum* 'Triad of the Mighty Sage & his Two Disciples', 262
144. *Theg-chen bstan-pa'i snying-po gsal-byed/sngon-byung-gi gling-gzhi* 'Clarifier of the Essence of the Doctrine of the Great Vehicle, Primary Topic, 259

145. *Dag-ljon-skor*, 191 *fn*
146. *bDud-bzhi rang-grol* 'Self-Release of the Four Evil Ones', 95, 153
147. *bDe-mchog lhan-skyes* 'Innate Supreme Bliss', 262, 264, 266
148. *bDe-gshegs kun-'dus* 'Unity of the Blessed Ones', 259
149. *mDo-sde-rgyan* (*Sūtrālaṃkāra*), 189
150. *mDor-bstan* 'Precise Teachings', 252, 256
151. *'Dul-ba mdo-rtsa* (*Vinayasūtra*), 190
152. *'Dul-ba'i snying-po* 'Essence of Monastic Discipline', 190
153. *rDor-sems snying-thig* 'Heart-Drop of the Powerbolt-Being', 144, 146, 157, 168

154. *sDe-brgyad gnad-kyi shog-ril* 'Vital Scroll of the Eight Spirits', 98
155. *sDe-bdun rab-gsal* 'Clarification of the Seven Treatises', 190
156. *sDom-gsum* 'Three Grades of Religious Vows', 246
157. *sDom-gsum ṭig-chen* 'Great Commentary on the Three Vows', 190
158. *sDom-gsum spyi-don chen-mo* 'Great Work on the exoteric meaning of the Three Vows', (III.8[12])
159. *bsDus-ra* 'The Chrestomathy', 248, 249

160. *Padma thang-yig*, 132, 253, 264 (= 'Le Dict de Padma' as translated by G. C. Toussaint, Paris 1933)
161. *dPe-chos-spungs-pa* 259 (=*dPe-chos rin-chen spungs-pa* as published by Guru Deva, Tibetan Monastery, Sarnāth, India 1965)
162. *dPe-mtshams-pa'i sgrub-pa bzhi* 'Four Performances for Quiet Study', 252
163. *sPu-gri'i zur-kha* 'Razor's Edge' (III.9[10])
164. *sPyan-ras-gzigs yang-'dus* 'Glancing Eye — Further Unity', 160
165. *sPros-med* 'The Non-Activated', 106

166. *Pha-chos bu-chos* 'Inspired Teachings of Father & Son', (I.9[11])
167. *'Pho-ba ka-dag-ma* 'Immaculate Transference', 264
168. *'Pho-khrid* 'Transference Instructions', 200
169. *'Pho-ba* (*sMar-sgom-lugs*) 'Transference — the Margom Way', 264
170. *'Phyug-med* 'The Unerring', 96

171. *Ba-tshva-can chu-klung-gi mdo* '*Sūtra* of the Briny River', 82, 186
172. *Bar-do 'phrang-sgrol* 'Release on the Path through the Intermediate State', 147, 153, 161, 165
173. *Byang-chub ltung-bśags* 'Confession of a Would-be Buddha', 241
174. *Byang-chub-sems-dpa'i spyod-pa la 'jug-pa* (*Bodhicāryāvatāra*), 190 (text published by the Asiatic Society, Calcutta, 1960; translated as *Introduction à la pratique des futurs bouddhas* by de la Vallée Poussin, Paris 1907)
175. *Bla-ma'i mchod-pa* 'Lama Rite', 117, 246
176. *Blo-sbyong don-bdun-ma* 'Purifying the Mind — seven part work' (III.9[9])
177. *Blo-rig* 'Deduction', 190
178. *dBang-bzhi don-dbang* 'Consecration in substance of the Four Consecrations', 260
179. *dBu-ma la 'jug-pa* (*Mādhyamikāvatāra*), 190
180. *dBu-ma'i rigs tshogs drug* 'Six Mādhyamaka Treatises', 190
181. *dBus-mtha' rnam-'byed* (*Madyāntavibhaṅga*), 189
182. *'Byung-po 'dul-byed* 'Spirit Quelling' (III.10[6]), 258

TIBETAN INDICES — TEXTS 281

183. *Ma-ṇi bka'-'bum*, 111, 132, 148, 243, 253, 264

184. *rTsa-dbu-ma'i khrid yum-bka'-la brten-pa* 'Instructions in the Central Channel according to the Mother-Word', 88
185. *rTsa-ba shes-rab (Prajñāmūla)*, 190
186. *rTsa-rlung drva-mig 'khor-lo* 'Wheel of the Network of Channels & Vital Breath', 260

187. *Tshad-ma rig-gter* 'Treasury of Knowledge of Logic', 90, 246
188. *Tshe-khrid* 'Life Instructions', 200, 210, 262
189. *Tshe-sgrub yang-snying kun-'dus* 'Life-Effecting Concentration of Pure Essence', 258, 261

190. *Zhal-gdams-kyi yig-chung* 'Small Book of Precepts', 137
191. *Zhal-shes-kyi yig-chung* 'Small Book of Oral Teachings', 137
192. *Zhi-khro dgongs-pa rang-grol* 'Self-Release on the Thought of the Tranquil & Fierce Divinities', 258
193. *Zhi-khro sgyu-'phrul* 'Illusion of the Tranquil & Fierce Divinities', 132

194. *Yi-ge bzhi-pa* 'The Four Letters', 259, 262, 269
195. *Yum-don rab-gsal* 'Clarification of the Meaning of the Perfection of Wisdom', 189
196. *Yul-bzhi* 'The Four Bases', 249

197. *Ri-chos skor-gsum* 'Hermit Teachings — three parts', 144, 146, 157, 169, 216 *fn*
198. *Rig-gter gsal-byed* 'Clarification of the Treasury of Knowledge', 190
199. *Rig-'dzin thugs-thig* 'Heart-Drop of the Knowledge-Holders', 258, 262, 264, 269, 270
200. *Rlung-gi tshe-sgrub* 'Life-Perfecter of Vital Breath', 106

201. *Lam-grol* 'Way & Release', 200
202. *Lam-'bras* 'The Way & its Fruits', 131 *fn*, 132, 143, 167, 168, 188, 210, 211, 258
203. *Lam-bsdus thun-gnyis* 'The Concentrated Way in Two Phases', 106
204. *Lam-zab* 'The Profound Way', 106
205. *Lung-sde bzhi* 'Four *Āgamas*', 190
206. *Lus-med mkha'-'gro chos-skor* 'The Religious Cycle of the bodiless Skyfarers', 259

207. *Shā-ri-bus mdzad-pa'i bstan-bcos* 'Treatise of Śāriputra', 190

208. *Shes-rab snying-po* 'Essence of Wisdom', 243

209. *So-sor thar-pa* 'Items of Confession', 246
210. *gSang-spyod ro-snyoms* 'Single Flavour of the Secret Essence', 112, 259, 262
211. *gSang-lam gser-gyi yang-zhun* 'Golden Distillation of the Secret Way', 259, 268, 270
212. *bSre-'pho chos-drug* 'Six Teachings of the Mixture Transfer', 260, 263

213. *lHan-cig skyes-sbyor* 'Innate Yoga', 136, 153, 157, 168, 169, 200, 210, 262, 263, 269

214. *A-ti zab-don* 'Profound Matter of *A-ti*', 258

PERSONAL NAMES

215. *Karma chos-grub*, 261, 264
216. *Karma blo-bzang* 'Karma Lobsang' 262
217. *Kun-dga' rgya-mtsho* 'Ocean of All Joy', 104
218. *Kun-dga' 'phan-dar*, 123
219. *dKon-mchog-skyobs* 'Jewel Protector', 90
220. *dKon-mchog rgyal-po* 'Jewel King', 240
221. *dKon-mchog rgyal-mtshan* 'Jewel Victorious Banner', 192, 216
222. *dKon-mchog chos-rgyan* 'Jewel Religious Adornment', 216, 217, 230
223. *dKon-mchog dpal-bzang* 'Jewel Glorious & Good', 172
224. *dKon-mchog lhun-grub* 'Jewel Self-Created', 239
225. *dKon-mchog lhun-grub* 'Jewel Self-Created' (=*Ngor-chen*) 83, 86, 87, 104, 191, 211, 234
226. *bKra-shis-mgon*, 8, 84, 85
227. *sKye-sa gdan-sa*, 85

228. *Khyung-po rnal-'byor*, 205
229. *Khro-bo bkra-shis*, 246
230. *mKhas-grub khyung-po*, 237

231. (*Chos-rje*) *Gvra-lung-pa*, 110
232. (*rJe-btsun*) *Grags-pa rgyal-mtshan* 'the Lord the Victorious Banner of Fame', 187, 201, 202, 210, 237, 255
233. *Grol-mchog* 'Supreme Release', 96
234. *Glang-ri thang-pa* (III.10⁹)
235. *Gling* (*gTer-bdag Gling-pa*) 'Master of the Hidden Texts of Ling', 261
236. *dGe-'dun bzang-po*, 243, 257

TIBETAN INDICES — PERSONAL NAMES

237. *dGe-legs rgyal-mtshan*, 83
238. *dGe-legs bshes gnyen* 'Excellent Virtue Religious Friend', 87
239. *rGod-phrug*, 103, 137
240. *rGod-tshang Ras-chen*, 263
241. *rGya-so-pa*, 86
242. *rGyan-thang-pa*, 96
243. *rGyal-po don-grub* (= *bSod-nams dbang-phyug*), 238
244. (*dGe-slong*) *rGyal-mtshan dkar-mo*, 241
245. *rGyal-mtshan chos-'phel*, 177
246. *rGyal-mtshan dpal-bzang*, 262
247. *rGyal-mtshan-'bum*, 102
248. *rGyal-mtshan rin-chen*, 10
249. *sGam-po-ba* (*Dvags-po lha-rje*) 95, 259, 260, 265
250. *sGrol-ma chos-dbang* 'Saviouress Religious Power', 173, 174, 181, 193, 216, 226, 230

251. *Ngag-dbang rnam-rgyal*, 11, 257
252. *Ngor-chen* see *dKon-mchog-lhun-grub*
253. *dNgos-grub ri-ba* [see 426]
254. *mNga'-bho-pa*, 87

255. *Chos-skyabs dpal-bzang* 'Religious Protector Glorious & Good', 3, 11–13, 16, 49, 51, 54, 68–70, 74, 76–7, 123, 129–230, 237, 243
256. *Chos-rgyal bsod-nams* 'Religious King Merit', 83, 128
257. *Chos-rnam-rgyal*, 253
258. *Chos-dbang*, 99
259. *Chos-dbyings rdo-rje*, 255

260. *'Jag* (I.9¹⁸)

261. *'Jam-dbyangs mgon-po don-grub*, 245
262. (*rJe*) *'Ja'-tshon phug-pa*, 192
263. *gNyan*, 104
264. *gNya'-khri btsan-po* 'Shoulder-Throne Strong One', 235

265. *Ti-lo-pa*. 95
266. *gTer-chen-po sprul-sku* 'Great Text-Revealer Incarnate', 133
267. *rTogs-ldan rin-po-che*, 10
268. *bsTan-'dzin ras-pa*, 11, 265, 267, 278, 269

269. *Thang-ston rgyal-po*, 256
270. *Thugs-rje dbang-phyug* 'Lord of Compassion', 205
271. *Thugs-rje seng-ge* 'Lion of Compassion', 133
272. *Thub-pa bzang-po* 'Good Sage', 86, 87, 88
273. *mThu-stobs dbyang-phyug* 'Lord of Power' (= *'Bir-ba*), 215

274. *Dvags-po lha-rje* see *sGam-po-ba*
275. *Don-grub rdo-rje* 'Aim-Winner Powerbolt', 167
276. *Don-grub dpal-'bar* 'Aim-Winner Gloriously Blazing', 237
277. *bDud-'dul rdo-rje*, 245
278. *bDud-rtsi lhun-grub* 'Nectar Spontaneously Produced', 250, 253, 256
279. *rDo-rje rgyal-mtshan* 'Powerbolt Victorious Banner', 192
280. *rDo-rje sgrol-ma* 'Powerbolt Saviouress', 132

281. *Nā-ro* (*Nāropa*), 27, 95, 137

282. Nai-gu, 27, 96, 97, 103, 132, 134, 143, 168, 203, 205, 211, 217, 253
283. Nam-mkha' dar-po, 216, 217
284. rNam-grol bzang-po, 'Good Deliverance', 6, 10, 11, 51, 84, 94, 99, 104
285. rNam-rgyal dpal-bzang 'Victory Glorious and Good', 253
286. rNam-rgyal bzang-po, 258
287. sNa-tshogs rang-grol 'Variety Self-Released', 191

288. Pad-ma-gling, 104
289. Pad-ma dbang-rgyal, 98, 258
290. Pad-ma 'byung-gnas, 'Lotus-Born', 21, 33, 81, 83, 98, 99, 109, 111, 128, 134, 166, 177, 198, 199, 210, 214, 272
291. dPa'-bo rin-po-che, 254
292. dPal-skyid 'Glorious Gladness', 130
293. dPal-ldan blo-gros 'Glorious Intellect', 2, 11, 12, 28, 49, 50, 69, 71, 74, 76–7, 185–230
294. dPal-ldan bzang-po 'Gloriously Good', 188, 241
295. dPal-ldan lhun-grub 'Glorious Spontaneous Achievement', 250
296. dPal-' byor grags-pa 'Magnificence Renown', 130

297. Phag-mo grub-pa, 254

298. Ba-la tsa-dra (Balacandra), 103
299. Ba-lung-pa, 95, 100
300. Byams-chen bkra-shis lhun-grub, 251–52
301. Byams-pa thog-gi rgyal-mtshan, 235

302. Byams-pa rab-brtan 'Loving Firmness', 133
303. Bla-ma dge-slong, 262
304. Blo-gros rgya-mtsho 'Ocean of Intellect', 144, 155, 169, 182
305. Blo-gros rgyal-mtshan 'Intellect Victorious Banner', 96
306. Blo-gros rnam-rgyal 'Intellect Victorious', 96, 132, 188, 191, 192
307. Blo-gros dpal-mgon 'Intellect Glorious Protector', 104
308. Blo-gros dpal-bzang 'Intellect Glorious & Good', 241
309. Blo-gros dbang-phyug 'Lord of Intellect' (biographer of bSod-nams dbang-phyug), 59
310. Blo-gros dbang-phyug 'Intellect Might', 84, 94, 97, 99, 104
311. Blo-gros 'byung-gnas 'Intellect Born', 133, 189, 191
312. 'Ba'-ra (also spelt Ba-ra-ba), 102, 137
313. 'Bir-ba (Virūpa), 131, 196 fn
314. 'Bum-ram-pa, 191
315. 'Bri-gung-pa, 259
316. 'Bru-gsum, 187
317. 'Brug-pa rdo-rje, 260

318. Mar-pa, 103, 155, (see also p. 27 fn 2)
319. Mai-tri mkha'-spyod see mKha'-spyod-ma
320. Mi-la ras-pa, 16, 95, 111

321. rTsal, 103

322. Tshe-rgyal 'Life Conqueror', 90
323. Tshe-ring dpal-bzang, 246, 257

TIBETAN INDICES — PERSONAL NAMES 285

324. bZang-po rgyal-mtshan, 248, 258
325. bZang-po dar-dar, 132, 191
326. Yang-dgon-pa, 102
327. Ye-shes snying-po, 253
328. Ye-shes rdo-rje, 253, 255
329. Yon-tan dpal-mgon 'Accomplishment Glorious Protector', 173
330. gYung drung tshe-ring 'Swastika Long-Life', 251

331. Rva-lo-tsa-ba (rDo-rje grubs-pa) (III.9²¹)
331a Ras-chung-pa, 103, 255
332. Rin-chen-dpal 'Gem Splendour', 85
333. Rin-chen bzang-po, 192, 206
334. Rig-'dzin gter-bdag gling-pa see Gling
335. Rong-ston chos-rje, 252

336. Lung-ston gtsug-tor rgyal-po, 129
337. Legs-pa bkra-shis 'Excellent Blessing', 85
338. Legs-pa dpal-bzang 'Excellence Glorious and Good', 216
339. Lo-chen sprul-sku 'Great Translator Incarnate', 133
340. Lo-nag-dril see p. 88 fn

341. Sha-ba ri-pa (Śabaripa), 201
342. Shā-kya dpal-mgon 'Shākya Glorious Protector', 192, 198
343. Shā-kya rnam-sgrol, 169
344. Shangs-pa, 132
345. Shar-khang-pa, 87, 191
346. Sher mKhan-po, 10, 26, 85, 88, 89, 92
347. Sa-chen (= Sa-skya paṇḍita), 104, 190

348. Sangs-rgyas rdo-rje 'Buddha Powerbolt', 181
349. Sangs-rgyas seng-ge 'Buddha Lion', 87, 133, 191, 206
350. Sangs-rgyas lhun-grub 'Buddha Spontaneous Achievement', 122, 147
351. Sems-ma, 169, 172, 266
352. Srong-btsan sgam-po, 129, 185, 235
353. bSam-'grub rdo-rje 'Thought-perfecting Powerbolt', 169
354. bSod-nams rgyal-mtshan, 257
355. bSod-nams chos-'phel 'Meritorious Promoter of Religion', 240 (= bSod-nam dbang-phyug)
356. bSod-nams blo-gros 'Merit Intellect' (Lama of Margom), 3, 4, 10, 11, 12, 13, 16, 23, 24, 26, 31, 50, 68–71, 74, 76–7, 81–123, 128, 173, 174, 178, 192, 203 fn, 204 fn, 264
357. bSod-nams blo-gros 'Merit Intellect' (biographer), 68, 69, 181, 182 fn, 217, 230
358. bSod-nams dbang-phyug 'Lord of Merit', 4, 69–70, 77, 233–73
359. bSod-nams tshe-dbang 'Merit Life Consecration', 216
360. bSod-nams ye-shes 'Merit Knowledge', 192, 195, 216
361. bSod-nams seng-ge 'Lion of Merit', 153, 155
362. bSod-nams lhun-grub 'Merit Self-Created', 88, 235

363. Lha-'bum, 84
364. Lhun-grub dpal-bzang 'Spontaneous Achievement Glorious and Good', 132, 133, 138

365. *A-mgon bzang-po*, 235
366. *A-ma-dpal*, 235
367. *As-skyab*, 107
368. *U-rgyan dpal-bzang*, 245

PLACE NAMES

(Abbreviations; AV = Anglicized version; SI = Survey of India spelling).

369. *Ka-rang*, 2, 3, 5, 15, 158, 265
370. *Karma (-rong)*, 4, 97, 180, 257
371. *Ku* (Kuwāgaon SI), 3, 15, 157-8, 215
372. *Ku-ṭi* (Kuti AV), 84, 89, 90
373. *Ko-mangs* (Koma SI), 3, 145, 264, 267
374. *Ko-yol*, 135
375. *Kyi*, 2, 135, 148, 158, 264-5
376. *Klu-brag* (Lubra SI), 14, 84 *fn*
377. *bKag* (Kāgbeni SI, Kāk AV), 7, 8, 14, 36, 223-4, 242
378. *bKra-shis chos-sde*, 255
379. *bKra-shis-gling* ('Isle of Blessings'), 195, 198
380. *bKra-shis-lhun-po* (Tashilhunpo AV), 250, 257
381. *sKom*, 236
382. *sKyid-kha*, 196, 198
383. *sKyid-rong* (Kyirong AV), 4, 99, 105, 107, 151-2, 175, 180

384. *Kha-rag*, 88
385. *Khang-dkar*, 88, 89, 90, 91, 98, 107, 108, 120, 153
386. *Kha'u-ba-'gyur*, 235
387. *Khung*, 151, 161, 167-8, 245
388. *Khyas*, 116
389. *Khyung-lung*, 14, 84
390. *Khra-'brug*, 254
391. *Khrim-nyer* (Trhim-nyer AV, Darengaon SI), 43, 56
392. *mKha'-ra-lung*, 115
393. *Gang-tsher*, 167
394. *Gad-dkar* (Gä-kar AV), 44, 54
395. *Gad-ring* ('Long Bluff'), 84, 107
396. *Gar-ma*, 266
397. *Gu-ge*, 8, 235
398. *Gung-thang*, 8, 85, 180, 235
399. *Gung-bu*, 158
400. *Grva-'dul*, 168, 179
401. *Grva-tshang* see *Ja-tshang*
402. *Grva-lung*, 10, 94, 100, 108, 110, 243
403. *Gro-phug*, 263, 269
404. *Gro-tshang*, 199, 200
405. *Gro-shod*, 4, 269
406. *Grod-lung*, 51
407. *Glo* also spelt *Klo* and *Blo* (Lo AV, Mustāngbhot or Lho Mantang SI), ix, 7, 8, 9, 10, 14, 16, 26, 36, 85, 88, 90, 153-5, 161, 164, 166-7, 214, 245, 247, 250, 266-9
408. *Glo-lam chu-mig* 256
409. *dGa'-mi*, 154, 166, 171, 266
410. *dGung-khung*, 136

TIBETAN INDICES — PLACE NAMES

411. dGun-sa (Günsa AV), 40–42, 55, 64–5
412. dGe-lung, 153–4, 166, 266
413. dGon-chung, 94, 153, 155, 165, 242
414. dGon-gsar, 169, 180
415. 'Gar-cha-bkod (Jājarkot), 238
416. rGad-pa gser-phreng, 243
417. rGya-mdo, 188
418. rGyal-thang, 96
419. sGom-mo, 270
420. sGra-bsgyur-gling, 255
421. sGrags, 256
422. sGrol-mtshams, 250, 252

423. Ngam-ring, 175, 180, 190
424. Ngor see Evam Chos-ldan
425. dNgul-mkhar, 84
426. dNgos-grub-ri ('Mount of Realisation'), 195, 196, 198, 211, 217–8
427. mNga'-ris (Ngari AV), 8, 87, 92, 235, 256

428. lCags-po-ri, 254
429. lCags-zam, 256
430. lCam-pa, 116, 117

431. Cha-ling, 95, 256
432. Char-chab, 156, 172
433. Chu-bo-ri, 256
434. Chu-mig dkar-mo, 248
435. Chu-mig-brgya-rtsa (Muktināth SI), 224
436. Chos-'khor yang-rtse, 256
437. Chos-grva chen-po ('the great monastery'), by Bi-cher 135

438. Ja-tshang, Bya-tshang or Grva-tshang, 69, 145, 179, 189, 199, 201, 209, 222, 237

439. Jo-mo kha-rag, 235
440. Jo-mo rTogs-ldan-ma, 224

441. Nyi-phug, 265
442. Nyi-gsal (Nyisal AV), 3, 6, 11, 14, 15, 261, 264, 265, 270
443. sNye-mo, 253, 256

444. Ta-le'i-sgrub-sde, 180
445. Ting-khyu, 3, 10, 14, 16, 94, 152, 153, 165, 173, 234, 236, 257, 263, 267, 269
446. Ti-ling (Tiling AV), 15, 164, 267
447. Ti-se, 180
448. rTa-rab (Tarap AV), 2, 3, 4, 6, 15, 42–5, 54, 56, 57, 63–5, 164–5, 168, 175, 180, 194, 209, 215, 242, 257
449. rTag-kyus or rTag-rgyus (Takkyu AV), 165, 194
450. sTeng-chung, 192–3, 208
451. sTod-lung, 253

452. Thub-bstan rnam-gyal, 133, 180, 189, 201, 240, 248–51, 256, 257, 258, 271
453. Thub-bstan Yangs-pa-can, 180
454. mTha'-dkar (T'ha-kar AV), 3, 11, 14, 15, 68, 69, 119, 137, 139, 141, 143–5, 147, 149, 151–3, 155–7, 161, 165, 172, 175, 203–4, 257–60, 264, 269

455. gDan-sa-mthil, 254
456. bDe-chen bla-brang ('The residence of great happiness'), viii, 11, 47, 50, 54, 56–9, 61–2, 65–6, 69, 188 fn
457. bDe-legs-gling, 253, 256

458. *mDa'-chen*, 198, 202, 218
459. *mDo* (Do AV), 44, 56, 165
460. *'Du-le-rong*, 194
461. *rDo-rje-brag*, 256
462. *rDo-ra gsum-mdo* (Do-ra-sum-do AV), 2, 3, 6, 10, 119, 135, 267

463. *Na-ra-bkod* (Narakot AV), 203
464. *Nang-khong* (Nangung SI), viii, 2–6, 11, 15, 46–7, 94, 129, 152, 179, 187, 215, 268
465. *Nam-mdo* (Namdo AV), 2, 4, 14, 15, 48, 56, 63, 187
466. *Ne-lde gsum-mdo*, 195
467. *Ne-lung*, 100
468. *gNam-gung* (Namgung AV), 3, 11, 48, 53, 66, 140, 257, 258, 262–3, 267
469. *gNam-ru*, 270
470. *gNas-nang*, 254
471. *rNam-kha*, 94
472. *rNam-rgyal lha-rtse*, 257

473. *Po-ldad*, 3, 10, 95, 152, 153
474. *dPal-sdings*, 158
475. *dPon*, 245
476. *dPon-spang-lung*, 137
477. *sPang-phu*, 158
478. *sPu-hrangs* (Purang AV), 8, 11, 14, 84 *fn*, 235

479. *Phag-mo*, 254
480. *Phan-phyi* or *'Phan-byi*, 157, 166–67, 170, 180, 269–70
481. *Phal-ba*, 247
482. *Phal-rtar*, 3, 137, 145, 152–3, 165, 219, 242
483. *Phug-gsum-mdo* (Phoksumdo AV), 2, 5, 49, 192

484. *Phod* (Phopāgaon SI), 3, 4, 15, 157–8, 175
485. *Phyi-mo*, 156
486. *Phyin-'bras*, 253
487. *Ba-lung*, 95, 100
488. *Ban-tshang*, 2, 3, 4, 6, 11, 15, 47, 58, 94, 137, 143, 152, 155–6, 161, 173, 179, 215, 268
489. *Bar-rong* (Barbung SI), 3, 7, 15, 36, 37, 43, 55–6
490. *Bar-lag*, 36, 37
491. *Bin-du-la*, 152
492. *Bi-cher* (Phijor SI), 2, 3, 5, 6, 10, 14, 15, 45, 54, 132, 157–8, 175, 215
493. *Bi-ri*, 257
494. *Be-kyu-la*, 248
495. *Bya-tshang*, 206
496. *Byang-sgo*, 133
497. *Byang-chub-gling* ('Isle of Enlightenment') at Margom, 167, 180; at *Ze-phug*, 136, 155
498. *Byas*, 265
499. *Byi-phug*, 89, 91–2, 235
500. *Brag-gyam* (Tr'a-gyam AV), 52, 65, 69
501. *Brag-dmar* ('Red Crag') in Lo, 154, 180, 266
502. *Brag-dmar* ('Red Crag') in Tarap, 194, 197, 209
503. *Brag-dmar* in Central Tibet, 254, 255
504. *Brag-dmar* near *dMar-sgom*, 172
505. *Blo-bo* see *Glo*
506. *dBu-legs*, 152
507. *'Bo-tran*, 95
508. *'Bras-mo-bshongs* (Sikkim), 262
509. *'Bri-gung*, 236

TIBETAN INDICES — PLACE NAMES 289

510. *'Brug-brag* ('Dragon Crag'), 193
511. *'Brog* ('the Nomad Country'), 241–2
512. *sBal-pa-thang*, 116
513. *sBrang-dir*, 93

514. *Ma-khen-la*, 245
515. *Man-thod*, 209
516. *Mar-yul*, 8, 85
517. *Mu-gum* (Mugu AV), 4, 10, 11, 31, 97–99, 108–9, 113–5, 117–8, 134, 180, 263, 265
518. *Mon*, 9, 90, 109 *fn*, 115, 153, 166 *fn*, 170
519. *dMar-sgom* (Margom AV), 11, 15–16, 68, 108, 119, 134, 135, 139, 143–6 *pass*, 148, 153, 155, 157, 165, 167, 168, 172, 173, 175, 179, 193, 229, 259, 261, 269
520. *dMar-po-ri*, 254
521. *dMu*, 195–6, 200
522. *dMos* (Mo AV), 3, 15
523. *rMad-lha-khang*, 91
524. *sMon-thang* (Mustāng SI), 3–4, 7–9, 35, 37, 54, 84, 129, 154, 166, 235, 247, 256, 263, 266
525. *sMan-rdzing dgon-pa*, 168
526. *sMin-grol-gling*, 259

527. *gTsang-rang* (Tsarang AV), 154, 166–7, 245, 266
528. *bTsag-khang*, 193, 205
529. *bTsan-thang gong-ma*
530. *bTsan-thang-sgro-bzhi*, 235
531. *rTsa* (Tsa AV), 2, 6, 11, 47, 187, 212
532. *rTsa-ri*, 254
533. *rTse-thang*, 254

534. *Tshva-lto*, 244

535. *Tshar-kha* (Tsharka AV), 3–4, 7, 15, 36, 43, 46, 49, 64, 65, 199, 244
536. *Tshugs*, 266
537. *Tshe-lnga-pa*, 247
538. *Tshe-zhabs*, 261
539. *Tshos-la'i-la*, 221–2
540. *mTshams*, 145
541. *mTshur-bu*, 253
542. *mTsho-bar*, 152

543. *rDzing-phu*, 137
544. *rDzing-po-che*, 208
545. *rDzong-kha* (Jongkha Dzong SI), 4, 152
546. *rDzong-kha-'jar* or *rDzong-'jar*, 189, 196, 224
547. *rDzong-lung*, 168, 213
548. *rDzong-shod*, 95
549. *rDzong-gsar-ba* (Jomosom SI), 35, 36, 65, 67
550. *'Dzum-lang* (Jumla SI), ix, 4, 9, 117, 153, 170, 202, 263 *fn*

551. *Wa-gong*, 223
552. *Wa-la-wa*, 147, 195

553. *Zha-ri*, 198
554. *Zhva-lding*, 195, 197, 209, 213, 218, 237
555. *Zhu-lag*, 216
556. *Zho-gam* or *Zho-sgam*, 10, 15–16, 134–5, 144, 174
557. *Zho-tsal*, 145, 147, 161
558. *gZhis-ka-rtse* (Shigatse AV), 248, 250
559. *bZhang-ri-skyid-tshal*, 256

560. *Za-khud*, 203

561. *Zangs-ri mkhar-dmar*, 254
562. *Zam-'phreng*, 175
563. *Zur-mkhar*, 255
564. *Ze-phug*, 136, 155
565. *Zel*, 14, 15, 48, 50, 59, 211, 213
566. *Zom-bshad*, 199
567. *bZu-lung*, 200
568. *bZo-thang*, 254

569. *'A-pha*, 188, 192, 226
570. *'A-ba*, 270
571. *'Om-bu bla-mkhar*, 255
572. *'Om-lung*, 236
573. *'Or-rlon*, 252, 256

574. *Yar-lung*, 255
575. *Yar-lung so-kha*, 255
576. *Yar-lha sham-po*, 235
577. *Yul-smad* (Lower Valley of *Nang-khong*), 158
578. *Yongs-rdzong*, 256
579. *Yer-pa*, 254, 257
580. *gYa'-ma-lung*, 254
581. *gYas-mtsher* (Yang-tsher AV), 2, 3, 6, 11, 14–15, 50–51, 59–61, 68–9, 168, 175, 180, 195, 237, 257, 260–1, 263
582. *gYung-drung*, 45

583. *Rva-lding*, 144
584. *Ra-ba-smad*, 256
585. *Rva-sho*
586. *Rab-rgyal-rtse* ('Victory Peak'), 90
587. *Ri-bo khyung-lung*, 255
588. *Ri-bo bum-pa*, 214
589. *Rin-chen-gling* ('Isle of Gems'), 158, 179
590. *Rin-spungs*, 85
591. *Ru-thog*, 236

592. *Ru-'brog*, 250, 251
593. *Re-la*, 180
594. *Reng*, 192, 205

595. *La-chung*, 199
596. *La-stod*, 190
597. *Lab-phyi*, 16, 108, 135
598. *Lu-ma nag-mo*, 256

599. *Shar-tse*, 247
600. *Shi-min* (Shimen AV), 3, 58, 145, 239, 257, 260, 264, 267, 269
601. *Shi-se*, 208
602. *Shug-dings*, 180
603. *Shes* (Shey AV), 1–3, 6, 11, 60, 140–1, 158, 201, 204, 265, 267–8

604. *Sa-dkar*, 192
605. *Sa-dga'*, 93
606. *Sa-ldang* (Saldang AV), 2, 3, 15, 47, 48, 50, 61, 63, 94, 140, 164, 168, 205, 267
607. *Sa-skya* (Sa-kya AV), 180, 187, 235, 247, 248, 271
608. *Sang-dag* (Sangdak AV), 7, 35–7, 40, 45–6, 56, 64, 65, 67
609. *Se-rib*, 166, 250–1
610. *Seng-ge-lung*, 129
611. *Songs*, 180, 200
612. *Sra-brtan*, 270
613. *Sra-dum*, 257
614. *gSal-ba dBang-phyug grags*, 187
615. *gSum-mdum*, 96
616. *gSer-kha*, 243–4
617. *gSer-rdo-can*, 116
618. *gSer-phug*, 122, 158, 205
619. *bSam-gling* (Samling AV), 2, 10, 14, 45, 53, 54, 66
620. *bSam-grub-gling*, 91

621. *bSam-grub-chos-sdings*, 209, 211, 214, 219, 223
622. *bSam-yas*, 253–5, 257
623. *Hrab* (Hrap AV), 2, 5, 11, 47, 59, 69, 196, 198, 201, 207–9, 211, 213–5, 217, 224, 226, 241, 257
624. *lHa-stod*, 254
625. *lHa-sa* (Lhasa AV), 251, 253, 254, 257
626. *lHas-nag*, 198
627. *lHo-ri*, 3, 65, 147–8, 250
628. *lHab*, 173
629. *Evam Chos-ldan* or *Ngor*, 86, 91, 112, 180, 206, 211, 250

GENERAL INDEX

Numbers in square brackets refer to the relevant items in the Tibetan Indices, where the required page-references will be found. In other cases the General Index provides direct access to page-references

Abhidharmakośa [122]
Abhisamayālaṃkara [120]
accumulations (of merit and knowledge), 28, 122, 127, 162, 180, 181, 233, 234
Accomplishment Glorious Protector [329]
Aim-Winner Gloriously Blazing [276]
Aim-Winner Powerbolt [275]
All Good (Buddha) [2]
All Joy Victorious Banner (Kun-dga' rgyal-mtshan), 216
All-Knowing [3]
All-Knowing Lama (Kun-mkhyen bla-ma), 241
A-ma-dpal, 235
amulets, 13, 29, 113, 116, 170, 240
Anchoress [91]
animals, care of, 5, 6, 48–9, 241–3 *pass*, 248
animations and excitations, 95, 132, 265
Annapūrna, 36
attendant goddess(es) (*ḍākinī*) [11], 84, 103, 122, 134 *fn*, 172, 174, 176–7, 188, 189, 198, 207, 211, 237
aupicious presents, 29, 109–111, 136, 227
austerities, 25, 94, 95, 98, 136
Avataṃsakasūtra (*Phal-po-che*), 82

Balacandra, 103
Barbung [489]
Bar-do see *Intermediate State*
begging, 94, 97, 99, 169, 257
Bheri, 7, 8
'*Bir-srungs*, 106, 202, 258, 268
Black GentleVoice [41]
black magic, 107, 172, 218, 235
Black Springs (*Lu-ma nag-mo*), 256
Blue Annals (of *gZhon-nu-dpal*, translated by Roerich, 2 vols, Calcutta 1949 & 1953), 11 *fn*, 103 *fn*, 190 *fn*, 205 *fn*
Blue Perfecter [46]
Boar-Headed Goddess [58]
Bodhicaryāvatāra [174], 190
Bon, 10, 29, 32 *fn*, 45, 84–5
Boundless Life [80]
Boundless Light [65, 87]
brahmans, 186, 187, 211–212
breath-control, 27, 101–3, 108, 109
Bu-chung family, 168, 192, 195, 196, 198, 202–3, 211–12, 212–13, 217, 224–5
Buddha Lion [349]
Buddha Spontaneous Achievement [350]
Buddha Powerbolt [348]
buddha-bodies, 21, 33, 81–3, 121, 127, 128, 186, 209, 210, 248

GENERAL INDEX

buddhahood, concept of, 12–13, 25, 29–31, 33, 121–2, 179, 186–8, 228–9, 233–4, 248
building, 148–9, 168, 205, 213, 219, 249, 250, 251, 252, 258; *see also* houses *and* monasteries

Canopy Gods [18]
Canopy Guardian [16]
cause and effect *see* karma
Central Tibet (*dBus-gtsang*), 4, 66, 83, 86, 91, 92, 108, 114, 129, 133, 168, 173, 175, 180, 189, 243, 247, 253–6 (pilgrimage of the holy places)
Chrestomathy [159]
clairvoyance, 12, 111, 116–7, 170–75; *see also* prognosis, dreams, *and* portents
Clarification of the Meaning of the Perfection of Wisdom [195]
Clarification of the Seven Treatises [155]
Clarification of the Treasury of Knowledge [198]
Clarifier of the Essence of the Doctrine of the Great Vehicle [144]
Cleanser of Defilements (*sGrib-sel*) a ḍākinī, 204
clear light, 100–1, 102, 134, 142, 178, 196, 227, 236, 237
coalescence, 150; *see* two-in-one
compassion, 18–19, 26, 89, 92, 93, 96, 115, 138, 165, 170, 175, 179, 188, 206, 211, 213, 222, 236, 241, 244
The Concentrated Way in Two Phases [203]
Confession of a Would-be Buddha [173]
consecrations, 23–4; personal, 54, 85, 97, 99, 100, 131, 202–3, 243; general, 112, 147–8, 151–68 *pass*, 261–71

pass; as an abbot, 243, 160–61; 'violent release consecration', 98, *see* violent method
Consecration in the substance of the Four Consecrations [178]
Consuming Ḍākinī [86]
Conze, Edward, 27 *fn*, 189 *fn*, 254 *fn*
cord, celestial, 235
Converter of Sentient Beings [27]
cremation *see* funeral rites
crops, 5, 6–7, 66, 91–2, 107, 243, 261; *see also* harvesting
crossing the crest (*thod-rgal*), 139, 140, 199
Crow-Headed Protector [23]

dates, 75–7, 85, 113, 123, 130, 176, 182, 188, 226, 230, 238
death, of high ranking lamas, 116–7, 145, 177–8, 204, 228, 263, 269, 272; of others, 167, 169–70, 171, 208, 213, 214–5, 223, 225, 242, 247, 260, 263, 265–6
Deathless ('*Chi-med*) [129]
debating (*rtsod-pa*), 22 *fn*, 191, 249, 254–5, 257
defenders of religion [33]
defilement, 15, 110, 219–20, 223, 238, 239, 263
Destroyer [62]
Destroyer of Death [34]
detachment, 96, 113, 130, 159, 162
Dharmadharmatāvibhaṅga [128], 189
Dharmakīrti, 190
Dhaulagiri, 4, 7, 35, 36
disease: epidemics, 13, 31, 115–8, 201, 219–221, 239, 242, 253; individual illness undefined, 99, 110, 145, 176, 218, 261, 265–6; small-pox, 115–8, 173–4, 188–9, 192; 'serpent-sickness',

108, 244; disease of tongue, 155–6; from food & drink, 239, 241, 260; too much meditation, 98
divination *see* dreams
'Divine Cave', 111
Divine Realms, 33, 116–7, 146, 177–8, 207, 208, 210, 217, 228, 272
Dolpo, specific references in the biographies, 92–3, 108, 118, 129, 157, 180, 187, 211, 234, 236, 248, 250, 256, 268, 270, 271
Dolpo College (at *Thub-bstan*), 4, 248, 249, 252, 258
Dohā verses, 82, 186, 259
lDong (family name), 14, 83
Doubly Wrathful [45]
Do-ra Bridge [462]
Do-ra-sum-do [462]
Dragon Crag (*'Brug-brag*), 193
dreams: divination and prognosis, 95, 100, 109, 112, 113, 130, 139–41, 146–7, 155, 192–214 *pass*, 218–25; prophetic, 95, 100, 122, 113–4, 146–7, 204; as sign of religious advancement, 109, 130, 142–3

Eight Canopy Gods [18]
Eight-Word God [7]
Eleven-Headed Glancing Eye [32]
Essence of the Blessed Ones of the Eight-Word God [103]
Essence of Monastic Discipline [152]
Essence of Wisdom [208]
Evans-Wentz W. Y., 21 *fn*, 24 *fn*, 25 *fn*, 27 *fn*
Evil as fivefold *see* fivefold equations
Evil Ones (*Māra*), 127
Excellence Glorious and Good [338]
Excellent Blessing [337]

Excellent Virtue Religious Friend [238]
excitations *see* animations
elixir *see* sacrificial *chang*
exorcism, 98, 240
expounding, confounding, propounding, 22 *fn*, 81, 127, 170

'face to face', 23, 100, 134, 164, 197
Fair Farer [28]
family-relationships, 14, 15, 43, 58, 86, 87, 89, 91, 92, 93, 144, 189, 207, 237–45 *pass*, 250, 253, 260, 265; *cp* religious relationships
Fierce Dart [50]
fierce rites, 131 *see also* black magic
Fifteen Admonitions of the Indian Attendant Goddessess [112]
fire of internal heat (*gtum-mo'i me*), 265
'flock', 83 *fn*
Five Buddhas, 21
Fivefold equations of Buddhahood, Evil, Wisdom etc., 21–3. 233–4
the Fiver [125]
food, 5, 38, 45, 49, 50, 59, 63, 99, 107, 152, 195, 196, 245, 247, 248, 252, 254
Four Āgamas (*Lung-sde bzhi*) [205], 190
Four-Armed (Knowledge) Protector [22]
Four Bases [196]
Four Condensations [108]
Four Difficulties [102]
Four-Faced God [85]
Four kinds of action, 121 (see *Buddhist Himālaya*, 257–62)
Four Letters (of the Great Symbol) [194]
Four Performances for Quiet Study [162]
funeral and after-death rites, 62, 99, 117, 144, 145–6, 169–70, 171, 208, 225, 242, 243, 260; cremation, 178–9, 228–9, 237, 269, 272

GENERAL INDEX 295

Gä-kar (in Tarap), 44, 54
Ga-se (family name), 187
Gem Splendour [332]
Gentle Protector, 185, 194 fn2 [= 38/39]
GentleVoice [39]
Glancing Eye [68]
Glancing Eye — Further Unity [164]
Glorious Black Powerbolt Canopy Countenance [66]
Glorious Copper-Coloured Mountain see Divine Realms
Glorious Gem (dPal-ldan rin-chen), 216
Glorious Gentle Lord [38]
Glorious Gladness [292]
Glorious Intellect [293]
Glorious Spontaneous Achievement [295]
Gloriously Good [294]
Goddess of Knowledge [90]
Goddess of the White Parasol [54]
goddesses, ḍākinī see attendant goddesses
Golden Distillation of the Secret Way [211]
Golden Rosary of the Ka-gyü Order [106]
Good Deliverance [284]
Good Sage [272]
Gorkha, 8–9
Great Bliss (Realm of) see Divine Realms
Great Commentary All-Good [134]
Great Commentary on the Three Vows [157]
Great Compassionate One [47]
Great Consecration of the Five Tantric Series [114]
Great Offering of Sacrificial Cakes (gter-chen), 116
Great Perfection (rDzogs-chen), 21 fn, 54, 102, 106, 138, 149
Great Prayer Festival, 249, 257

Great Symbol (Phyag-rgya chen-po), 27, 100, 101, 103, 109, 134, 173, 210, 211
Great Text-Revealer Incarnate [266]
Great Translator Incarnate [339]
GreatVehicle, 32, 93
Great Work on the Exoteric Meaning of the ThreeVows [158]
Great Work on the TantricVow [123]
guardian-divinities see defenders of religion and protectors
Guru Red Fury [51]

Har Dayal, 30 fn, 234 fn
harvesting, 36, 44–5, 151
Hawk King of Birds [10]
Heart-Drop of the Knowledge-Holders [199]
Heart-Drop of the Powerbolt-Being [153]
heavens see Divine Realms
Hermit Teachings [197]
Hevajra [3]
Hevajra-tantra [101]
hidden texts (gter-ma), 99, 104, 245, 261
Horse-Neck [43, 44, 45]
houses, 37, 38–9, 44–5, 57, 148–9; see also building
Hrap [623]
human-body, advantages & disadvantages, 18–19, 150, 159, 162
Hundred-odd Invocations [116]
hunting, 16, 119, 135–6, 155, 156, 158, 166, 168, 177, 221, 222, 236

illness see disease
illusion, 20, 142–3, 151, 192, 195–6, 219; see also dreams
Illusion of the Tranquil & Fierce Divinities [193]
Immaculate Transference [167]

images, 99, 145-6, 180-81, 246
impermanence, 17, 66-7, 83, 148, 176, 265
Imperturbable (Buddha) [76]
Innate Goddess, [99]
Innate Supreme Bliss, [147]
Innate Yoga [213]
Insight/Concentration/Results, 151
Instructions in the Central Channel according to the Mother-Word [184]
Instructions in the Three Essential Subject-Matters [133]
Intellect Born [311]
Intellect Glorious & Good [308]
Intellect Glorious Protector [307]
Intellect Might [310]
Intellect Victorious [306]
Intellect Victorious Banner [305]
intermediate state (bar-do), 27, 102, 172
Isle of Blessings, 195, 198
Isle of Enlightenment (Margom) [497], 167, 180
Isle of Enlightenment (Ze-phug), 136, 155
Isle of Gems [589], 158, 179
Items of Confession [209]

Jājarkot, 203 fn, 238
Jambhala, 272
Jetarī [83]
Jewel Glorious & Good [223]
Jewel King [220]
Jewel Prosperity (dKon-mchog phandar), 236
Jewel Protector [219]
Jewel Religious Adornment [222]
Jewel Self-Created (renowned lama of Ngor) [225]
Jewel Self-Created [224]

Jewel Victorious Banner [221]
Jo-bo-sdugs, 198
Jomosom [549], 35-6, 65, 67
Jongkha Dzong, 4, 152
Jumla ('Dzum-lang), ix, 4, 9, 117, 153, 170, 202, 263

Ka-dam-pa, 130, 188
Kāgbeni or Kāk [377]
Kāli Gandakī, 4, 7, 8, 35, 40, 65
Kathmandu, 8, 35, 55, 67
karma (cause & effect), 13, 28-9, 89, 91, 93, 96, 129, 130, 150, 159, 188, 233, 251
Karmapa Lama, 269
'mKhyen-rtse's Guide', 72 fn, 86 fn, 133 fn, 190 fn, 252-6 fn
Khyung-po (family name 14, 84; (yogin) [228, 230], 205, 237
Khang-dkar-ba, 88, 89, 90, 91, 107, 108, 153
Knowledge-Treasury of Logic [187]
Kunga, 152, 154, 214-5
Ku-su-lu, 216
Kuti (Ku-ṭi), 84, 89, 90
Kyirong [383]
Kyi-tse La, 40, 64

Lady Tradition [127]
Lama-Rite [175]
Lama Yoga of the Heart-Drop [258]
Laughing Powerbolt (dGyes-pa'i rdor-rje), 179
Leaf-Clad Goddess [93]
Leafy Anchoress [92]
Lhasa, 251, 253, 254, 257
life-consecration, 28 fn, 49, 60, 98, 239-40, 261, 263
Life-Effecting Concentration of Pure Essence [189]

life-force, 12, 27–8, 195, 218
Life Instructions (of the Great Symbol) [188]
Life-Perfecter of Vital Breath [200]
life-series, 18–19. 27–8, 170, 234
Lion of Compassion [271]
Lion-Headed Goddess [97]
Lion of Merit [361]
Lion Vale (*Seng-ge lung*), 129
Lo (Mustangbhot) [407]; governor/ruler/king of, 8, 89–90, 91, 92, 152, 154, 157, 166, 169, 247–8, 256, 263, 266–7, 269
local gods, 15, 28–9, 109, 114, 141–2, 147, 166, 170, 194–202 *pass*, 205–6, 207–8, 210, 213, 218, 219–222, 224–5, 238, 265
Long Bluff (*gad-ring*), 84, 107
Long Life, Sisters of [82]
Long Life Goddess [81]
Lord of the Cemetery [48]
Lord of Compassion [270]
Lord of Merit [358]
Lord of Power (*mThu-thob dbang-phyug*), 215
Lord of the World ('*Jig-rten dbang-phyug*) [=68], 179
Lord of Yogins (*rNal-'byor dbang-phyug*), 196
Lotus-Born [290]
Loving Firmness [302]
Lo-Way Springs (*Glo-lam chu-mig*), 256
Lubra [376]

Mādhyamikāvatāra [179], 190
Mādhyāntavibhaṅga [181], 189
Magnificence Renown [296]
Mahāyāna see vehicles

Maitreya (*Byams-pa*), 180, 246, 247, 256, 271, 271
maṇḍala *see* mystic circle
Mandāravā, 176–7
manuscripts, 43, 45, 49–51 *pass*, 54, 57, 61, 65, 67, 68–71, 181, 271
Māra *see* Evil Ones
Margom [519]
Marpa [318]
Means & Wisdom, 30, 32, 33, 149
meditation, 22–25, 87–88, 94, 95, 98, 109, 137–40, 141, 211, 217–8, 259–60, 261, 266, 267–8
Merit Intellect (Abbot of Margom) [356]
Merit Intellect (biographer) [357]
Merit Knowledge [360]
Merit Life-Consecration [359]
Merit Self-Created [362]
Meritorious Promoter of Religion [355]
Mon [518]
Monasteries, Dolpo foundations, 10–11, 137, 148, 168, 197–8
Mother of Variety [64]
Mount of Realization [426]
Muktināth [435], 224
Mugu [517]
Mung (family name), 129
Mustang [524]
Mustangbhot (Lo) [407]
mystic circle, 20, *22–4*, 26, 85, 97
Nāgārjuna, 190
Nai-gu or Ne-gu [282], 97, 100, 112, 120, 132, 217, 253
Nairātmyā (*bdag-med-ma*), 88, 140
Namdo [465]
name-day, 238
gNam-ru, 237, 270
Namgung [468]
Narakot, 203

Nā-ro Sky-Farer, 103, 251, 253
Nāropa (Nā-ro) [281], 95, 112, 120, 137
Nectar Spontaneously Produced [278]
Newars, 180
Ngari [427]
Nomad Country [511]
nomads ('brog-pa), 4–5, 37–40 pass, 41, 43, 46, 48–9, 54, 65, 57, 58, 60, 61, 64, 151, 152, 156, 157, 165, 167
Non-Activated [165]
novices (dge-tshul), 56, 135, 188, 253, 257
Nyi-ma Tshe-ring, 47–50, 52–4, 61–2
Nyisal [442]

Ocean of All Joy [217]
Ocean of Intellect [304]
'Od-srung, 255
offerings, 16, 49, 53, 60, 97, 106, 109, 111, 137, 144–5, 151, 152, 167, 175, 179–80, 195, 197, 200, 220–21, 229, 264, 265, 268, 271
Olo, a Mustang Chief, 161–4, 167
One Mother [72]
One Mother Gentle & Violent [75]
One Mother White & Black [73]
One Mother Wrathful & Black [74]
Order of the Way of Secret Spells [124]
ordinations, 83, 87, 133, 258
Ornament of Comprehension [120]

Padma of Urgyan (= Lotus-Born) [290]
painting, 50, 54, 57, 58, 67, 146, 156, 161, 180, 199, 203, 236, 237, 239, 245, 267, 271
partner, 27, 33, 85, 102, 103
Pasang Khambache, vii, 34, 66–8
Perfecter of Thought [46]

Perfection of Wisdom literature, 27 fn, 32 fn, 189–90, 251–2
Phan-byi [480]
Phijor [492]
Phoksumdo [483]
Phyug-'khor (family name), 14, 85
polution see defilement
portents, 85, 93–4, 95, 100, 110, 114, 130, 140, 141, 144, 146–7, 187–8, 189, 192, 193, 226, 227–8, 262, 272
Potala see Divine Realms
Potopa, author of dPe-chos-sprungs-pa, (III.9^9)
powerbolt (skr vajra, tib rdo-rje), 33, 98, 202, 216
Powerbolt-Being [59]
Powerbolt-in-Hand [69]
Powerbolt-Holder [56]
Powerbolt-Saviouress [280]
Powerbolt-Terror [57]
Powerbolt Vehicle, 33, 146, 216
Powerbolt Victorious Banner [279]
Prajñāmūla [185], 190
prayer, 13, 46, 110, 111, 116, 123, 175, 181, 189, 197, 242, 253–7 pass
prayer-flags, 50, 59, 203, 263
prayer-wall, 263
Precious Ones, Three (Buddha, Doctrine & Community), 90, 107, 108, 129, 151, 156, 163, 166, 169, 181, 189, 234, 237, 239, 240, 252, 266
Precise Teachings [150]
Process of Emanation & Realization, 26, 97, 138, 273
Profound Matter of Absolute Certainty [119]
Profound Matter of A-ti [214]
Profound Way [204]

GENERAL INDEX 299

prognosis, 10, 115, 151–2, 155, 156, 166, 172, 253, 260; *see also* dreams
Protectors (*mGon-po*) of the Doctrine [21, 22, 23, 24, 67]
Purang [478]
Purifying the Mind [176]
Queen of Success [19]
Quite Secret Eight-Word God [104]
quittances (*mdos*), 144

rain, 13, 29, 200, 264–5, 266
Rainbow Cave (Lama), 192
Rare Refuge (*dKon-skyabs*), 175, 177
Ratnakūṭa (*dKon-brtsegs*), 260
Realms: of Bliss, Glorious Copper-Coloured Mountains, of Heaped-up Lotuses, Joyful, Lotus-Flower Realm of Light, Potala, Sheer Joy *see* Divine Realms
rebirth, connections with former lives, 18–19, 27–8, 94, 95, 130, 139, 172, 213–5, 219
Red Crag (of Lo) [501]
Red Crag (of Margom) [504]
Red Crag (of Tarap) [502]
Red Crag (of Central Tibet) [503]
Red Fury [51, 52, 79]
Red Killer [94]
Refuge of All Joy [1]
reincarnation, 81–2
Release on the Path through the Intermediate State [172]
relics, 13–14, 29, 99, 178–9, 180, 229, 237, 254, 239, 272
Religious Cycle of the bodiless Skyfarers [206]
Religious History of the Ka-gyü Order [105]
Religious King Merit [256]

Religious Protector Glorious & Good [255]
religious relationships of master & pupil, 16, 26, 91–98 *pass*, 136–9 *pass*, 144, 174, 189, 199
Residence of Great Happiness (*bDe-chen bla-brang*) viii, 11, 47, 50, 54, 56–9, 61–2, 66, 69, 188 *fn*
Richardson, Hugh E. 72 *fn*, 253 *fn*
Rite of Self-Sacrifice *see* self-sacrifice

sacrificial cakes, 5, 49, 53, 59, 60, 106, 116, 194, 226; =elixir, 95, 98, 189, 220, 222
sacrificial *chang*, 57, 59, 205, 206; =elixir, 95, 98, 189, 220, 222
Sa-kya [607]
Saldang [606]
Śākyamuni, 140, 143, 189 *fn*, 209, 228, 234, 238, 272
Samling [619]
Saṃvara [55]
Sangdak, 7, 35–7, 40, 45–6, 56, 64, 65, 67
Saviour of the Six Spheres of Existence [26]
Saviouress (*Tārā*) [30, 31]
Saviouress Religious Power [250]
Secret Unity [96]
Self-Release of the Four Evil Ones [146]
Self-Release of the Thought of the Tranquil & Fierce Divinities [193]
self-sacrifice (*gCod*) rite of [126] 25, 109, 161, 166, 200, 207, 217
seminal fluid as controlled in the process of meditation, 27, 31, 33, 101–3, 138, 260
Seven Kinds of Gems (*rin-chen sna-bdun*), 143
seven noble gems (of virtue), 128, 162
Shākya Glorious Protector [342]

Sham-tr'ak, 47–50 pass
Sherpa Tenpa, 210, 202, 204, 212, 226
Shey [603]
Shigatse [558]
Shimen [600]
Shu-rtse (family name), 187
Sikkim, 4, 262
Single Flavour of the Secret Practice [210]
Sisters of Long Life [82]
Six Adornments & Five Excellencies [113]
Six Doctrines (of Nāropa & Nai-gu), 27, 97, 100–103, 109, 112, 120, 132, 137, 145, 151, 153, 168, 211, 217, 253
Six Mādhyamaka Treatises [180]
Six Teachings of the Mixture Transfer [212]
Six Teachings of the Oral Tradition [130]
Sky-Farer, Sky-Faring Goddess [12]
Sky-King (nam-mkha' rgyal-po), 131
Small Book of Oral Teachings [191]
Small Book of Precepts [190]
Song-tsan-sam-po (Srong-btsan-sgam-po) 129, 187, 235
soothsaying, 188, 192, 213, 218, 226, 238
soul, 27–8, see life-force
soul-series see life-series
Source of All Necessities [110]
Spirit-Quelling [182]
Spontaneous Achievement Glorious & Good [364]
Stirrer of the Pit of Existence [13]
Stirrer of the Pit of Hell [60]
stocks of merit and knowledge, see accumulations
stūpas (mchod-rten), 99, 133, 146, 161, 180–81, 229, 263, 267, 268, 271
succession, religious, 11, 14–15, 26–7, 50, 95, 146–7

suffering, 20, 88–93 pass, 131, 150, 162, 265
Sun Cave (nyi-ma phug) a temple, 137
Supreme Bliss [55]
Supreme Release (Grol-mchog), a lama, 96
Sure Instructions of the Great Compassionate One [141]
students, intake of, 252, 253, 256, 257
Sūtra of the Briny River [171]
Sūtrālaṃkāra [149], 189
Swastika Long-Life [330]

Tak-kyu [449]
Tantra of Essential Import [132]
Tarap [448]
Tashilhunpo (bKra-shis-lhun-po), 250, 257
taxes, 8, 9, 168, 193, 245
tea & tea ceremonies, 5, 50, 117, 135, 137, 155, 157, 158, 166, 175, 194, 224, 248, 250, 251, 252, 257, 271
Terror [57]
T'ha-kar [454]
Thought of Enlightenment, 30, 31, 93, 163, 171, 245
Three Bodies of Buddhahood see buddha-bodies
Three Evils, 22, 181, 210
Three Grades of Religious Vows [156]
Thought-Perfecting Powerbolt [353]
'Three Storeys' (thog-gsum), 85, 111, 172
Tibrikot
Tichu-rong, 5, 43, 49, 63
Tilopa, 95
Tingri, 40, 65
Ti-song-de-tsan (Khri-srong-de-btsan), 235

Trä, 2
trading, 5, 165, 243–5
Tr'a-gyam [500], 52–3, 65, 69
Tranquil Master [15]
transfer of consciousness (*'pho-ba*), 27, 101–2, 228, 258
Transference Instructions [168]
Transference according to the Margom Way [169]
Translator's Cave (*Lo-tsha phu-gu*), 111
Treasury of Knowledge (of logic) [187]
Treasury of Philosophical Notions [122]
Treatise of Sāriputra [207]
Triad of the Mighty Sage and his two disciples [143]
truth, absolute & relative, 22, 176
Tsarang [527]
tsha-tsha, 99, 237
Tsharka [535]
Tucci, Giuseppe, 99 *fn*, 131 *fn*, 188 *fn*, 206 *fn*
Tukucha, 35, 55
tutelary divinities, 23–5, 98, 100, 181, 195
two-in-one, 26, 149, 273
Tyson, John, 1, 3, 4 *fns* (*see also his* 'Three Months in West Nepal', *The Alpine Journal* LXVII no. 304 May 1962 & John Cole 'West Nepal Expedition 1964' *ibid* LXX no. 311 Nov 1965)

Ü (*dBus*), Madman of, 102; Text-Discoverer of, 254
Uncle *Chos*, 241
Unéle *sGrub-pa* 241
Uncle Gyaltsan, 242
Uncle Gyamtso (*also* called Uncle Monk), 240, 241, 243
Uncle Nam-rin, 242

the Unerring [170]
Union of the Precious Ones, 49, 56, 60
Unity of the Blessed Ones [148]
Universal Saviour [25]
Unobstructed Intentions [109]
Up-turned Moustache [77]
Urgyan, 204, 211 *see also* Divine Realms; Lama of = Lotus Born [290]
Uttaratantra [115], 189

Vairocana, 178–9, 234
Variety Self-Released [287]
vessel & elixir, 20, 26, 163
vehicles, 32–3
Victorious Banner of Fame [232]
Victorious Lady [61]
Victorious Lady of the Chignon [78]
Victorious One (*Chos-rnam-rgyal*), 241
Victory Glorious & Good [285]
Victory Peak (*rNam-rgyal-rtse*) [586]
Vinayasūtra [151], 190
Vinayasūtraṭīka, 190
violent method, 101–3, 109
'virtuous adherer' (*dGe-bsnyen*), 85, 131, 154, 188, 240, 245
Virūpa [313]
Vital Scroll of the Eight Spirits [154]
Volume of Precepts [107]
vows, 83, 89, 94, 99, 105–6, 117, 131, 143, 156, 166, 177, 200, 212

Way & its Fruits [202]
Way of Method [139], 112
Way & Release [201]
weather, 4, 6–7, 36–40, 43–4, 46, 58–9, 62–3, 141, 242, 267
What things are & what they are not (*rdzas-ldog*) a subject of metaphysics 249

Wheel of the Network of the Channels & Vital Breath [186]
White Gentle Voice [40]
White Goddess of Sun & Moon [5]
White Protector [20]
Wish-granting Circle of the White Savioress [117]
Wish-granting Gem of the Oral Tradition [131]
Wish-granting Gem of the White Protector [111], 96
world, nature of, 19–20, 208

World-Protector (Yul-'khor-skyong) [89], 272
would-be buddha, 26, 30–33, 83 fn, 89, 96, 121, 186, 188, 237, 272
Womb of the Powerbolt-Queen (rDo-rje btsun-mo'i bha-ga) a divine realm, 178
Wrathful Black One [9]

Yang-tsher (gYas-mtsher) [581]
Yellow Protector [24]
Yoginī [63]; *also see* partner

ILLUSTRATIONS

from the author's own photographs

Plates 39–46 are of temple-banners (*thang-ka*)
painted by the Lama of the 'Residence of Great Happiness'

1. Ascending the valley leading from the upper Bar-rong (Barbung) valley to the pass towards Tarap. The author on his way into Dolpo in October 1960.

2. Taken from just below the main pass separating Bar-rong (Barbung) from Tarap. View eastwards towards the upper Bar-rong valley and the great massif, north-east of Dhaulagiri separating Dolpo from the Kālī Gandakī. Pasang Khambache in the foreground.

3. Bridge across the Bar-rong (Barbung) River at Trhim-nyer.

4. *The village of Tsharka.*

5. *Breaking camp in the upper Bar-rong (Barbung) valley.*

6. *Final ascent of the pass towards Tarap.*

7. Descending the other side of the main pass from Bar-rong (Barbung) to Tarap. View north-westward towards the great watershed (the head of the horseshoe—see p. 4) which separates inner Dolpo from Tarap.

8. Sonam Panden and the author on the pass between Tarap and Nang-khong (December 1960).

9. The Nang-khong Valley. View southwards from above Saldang (June 1961).

10. The 'Residence of Great Happiness' at Namdo in Nang-khong (June 1961).

11. Water-supply for men and animals from the frozen river at the 'Residence of Great Happiness' (January 1961).

12. Our host, the Lama of the 'Residence of Great Happiness' with Pasang Khambache.

13. *Our second Sherpa assistant Pasang at Nyisal.*

14. Yang-tsher Monastery. View south-west towards the range that separates Nang-khong from Bi-cher.

15. Nyisal Village on its 'alp' overhanging the gorge (below Ban-tshang).

16. Reciting the liturgy at Yang-tsher (January 1961). The Abbot is on the extreme right, and next to him is Pasang Khambhache.

17. Images and torma (sacrificial cakes) on the altar at Yang-tsher.

18a. The ransom-offering in the form of an effigy of a yak, moulded of tsamba and butter.

18b. Placing the ransom-offering on the temple-roof at Yang-tsher.

19a

19b

20. Two religious brethren of Tarap.

19a. Women (wearing home-spun blankets) and men dancing in the courtyard of Yang-tsher Monastery.

19b. Masked dancers.

21. *A Dolpo woman weaving woollen home-spun.*

22. Norbu and the second Pasang by the 'tomb' of our horse Tshering in the lower Nang-khong Valley.

23. *Nomad refugees from the north (Byang-thang) encamped outside the 'Residence of Great Happiness' (January 1961).*

24. View of Harp Monastery high up the gorge oppsite Tsa (June 1961).

25. *The mummified corpse of the Precious Lama of Shang in Tr'a-gyam Monastery at Namgung. (See p. 65.)*

26. Image of Chos-skyabs dpal-bzang ('Religious Protector Glorious and Good'), made soon after his death; (see p. 180.)

27. *Women of Nyisal, replaiting hair after a monthly wash.*

28. *The young niece of the Lama of the 'Residence of Great Happiness'.*

29. The scribe, Tshe-ring Ta-shi. (See p. 70.)

30. Washing a length of newly woven home-spun.

31. Nomad women with children and a nun (centre).

32. Nyi-ma Tshe-ring, chief man of Dolpo until his death in 1963.

33. *Images at Yang-tsher Monastery. Central seated figure is Shākyamuni with 'Powerbolt-in-Hand' on his left and 'Lotus-in-Hand' on his right.*

34. *Temple-banner of the Buddha 'Boundless Light'.*

35. 'Lotus-born'.

36. 'Red Fury' with 'Lotus-born' above him and the 'Lion-headed Goddess' below.

37. Eleven-headed 'Glancing Eye'.

38. The 'One Mother'.

39. Lama 'Merit Intellect'.

40. Lama 'Religious Protector Glorious and Good'.

41. Detail of Plate 40:
a. Concentrating upon the Five Buddha, 'Lotus-born' in his paradise, and the Defender Rāhu.
b. Cremation of Lama 'Religious Protector' at Yang-tsher (p.178).

42. Lama 'Glorious Intellect'.

43. Detail of Plate 42:
a. Receiving instruction from the Lama of the 'Mount of Realization', and manifest as 'Powerbolt-Terror' as he quells the local god Bya-'bang (p. 194).
b. Meditating upon Hevajra (p. 195).
c. Receiving the Nai-gu teachings from Lama 'Bum-ram-pa (p. 191).
d. Meditating upon the Buddha 'Boundless Life' and quelling the local god of the Reng Lake (p. 192).

44. Lama 'Land of Merit'.

45. Detail of Plate 44:
   a. Being received as Abbot of Yang-tsher, and giving instruction to the monks inside the monastery (p. 261).
   b. Returning home to Dolpo, where he is greeted by his mother, and inviting the Prelate 'Nectar Spontaneously Produced' (p. 256).

46. *Mystic Circle of the Fierce Divinities.*

MAPS

NOTE ON PLACE-NAMES

In order to ensure the maximum consistency Tibetan place-names are all given in their correct Tibetan spellings simply transliterated into the Roman alphabet (see pp. 72–3). The only exceptions are LO (for which possible Tibetan literary spellings seem to be KLO, GLO and BLO, the initial consonant being in every case silent) and possibly DOLPO (for which the spelling RDOL-PO occurs).

Listed below are place-names for which I have used conventional phonetic spellings or translations in the main text of this book, together with their correct Tibetan spellings. They are listed here so that they may be readily identified on the maps.

Barbung	BAR-RONG	Red Crag	BRAG-DMAR
Do-ra-sum-do	RDO-RA-GSUM-MDO	Saldang	SA-LDANG
Hrap	HRAB	Shey	SHES
Kāk	BKAG	Shigatse	GZHIS-KA-RTSE
Kyirong	SKYID-RONG	Tak-kyu	RTAG-KYUS
Margom	DMAR-SGOM	Tarap	RTA-RAB
'Mount of Realization'	DNGOS-GRUB-RI	Tashilhunpo	BKRA-SHIS-LHUN-PO
Namgung	NAM-GUNG	T'ha-kar	MTHA'-DKAR
'Nomad Country'	'BROG	Tsang	GTSANG
Nyisal	NYI-GSAL	Tsarang	GTSANG-RANG
Nga-ri	MNGA'-RIS	Tsharka	TSHAR-KHA
Purang	SPU-HRANGS	Ü	DBUS

Nepalese and other non-Tibetan place-names are given in brackets.

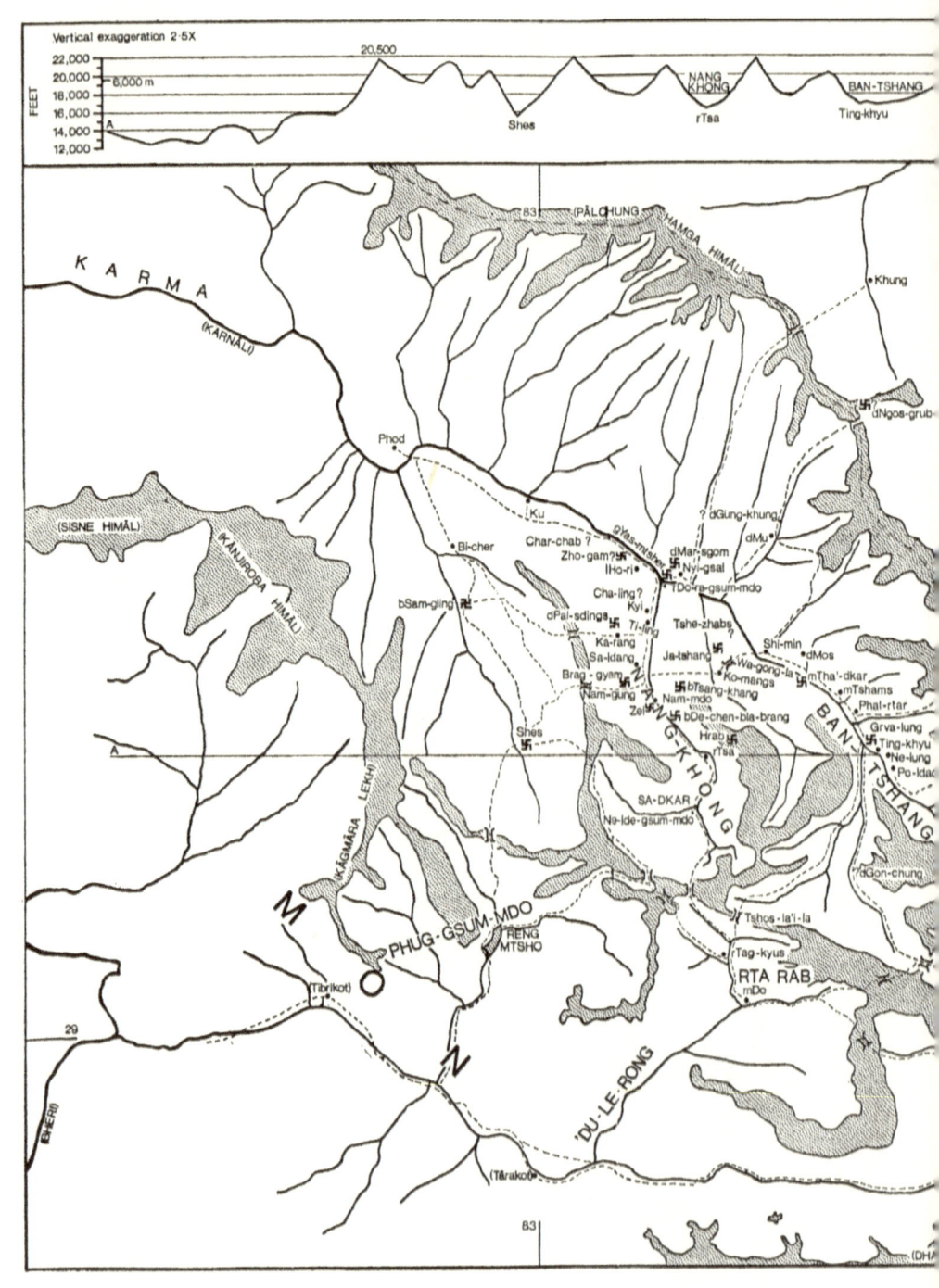

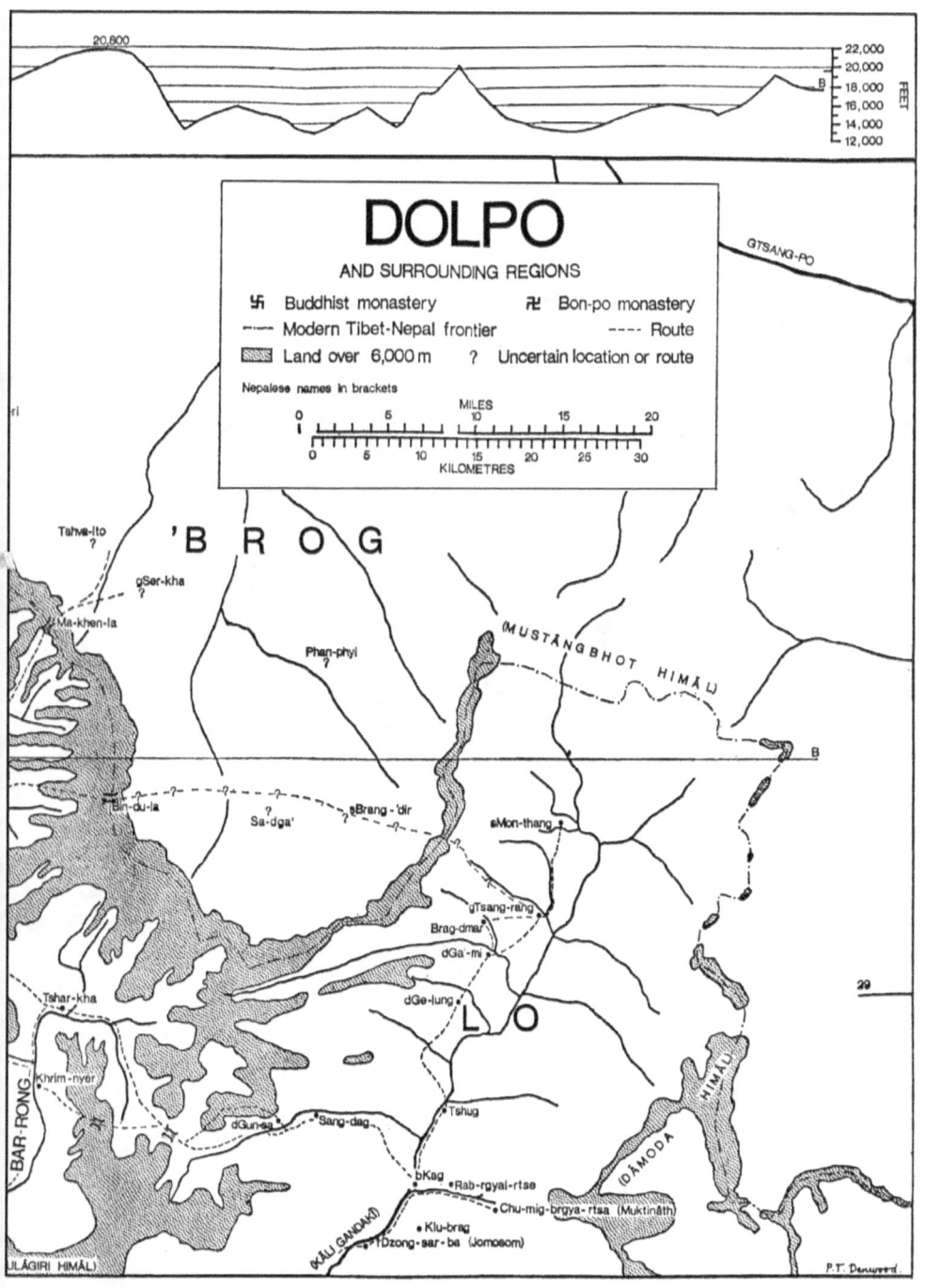

MAP 1

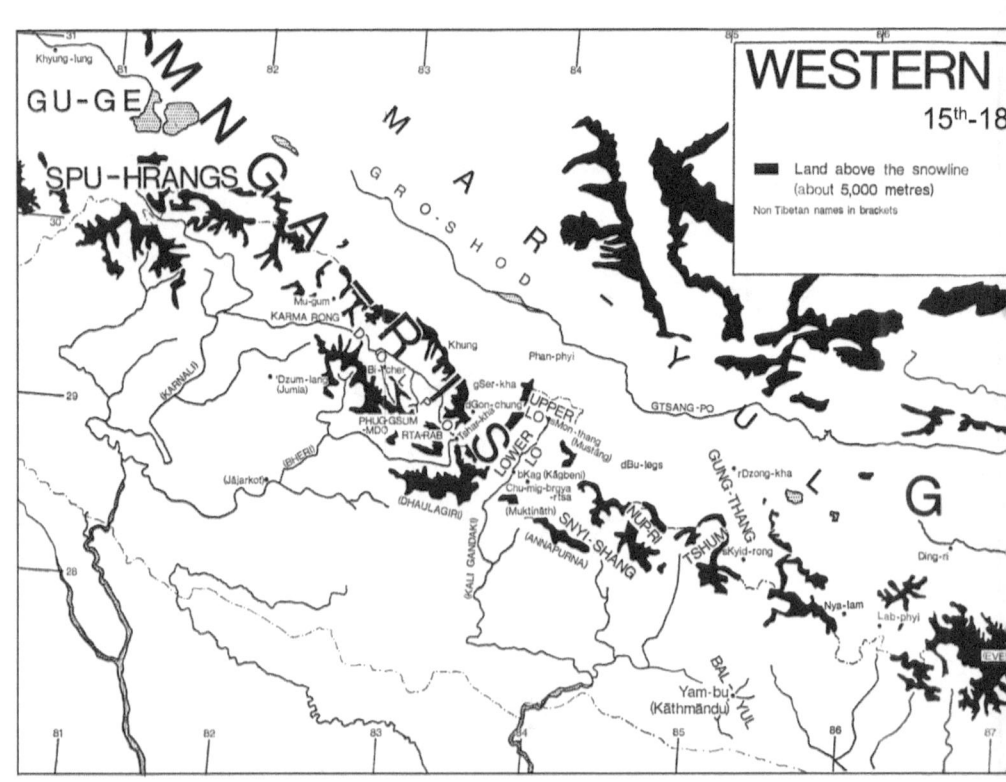

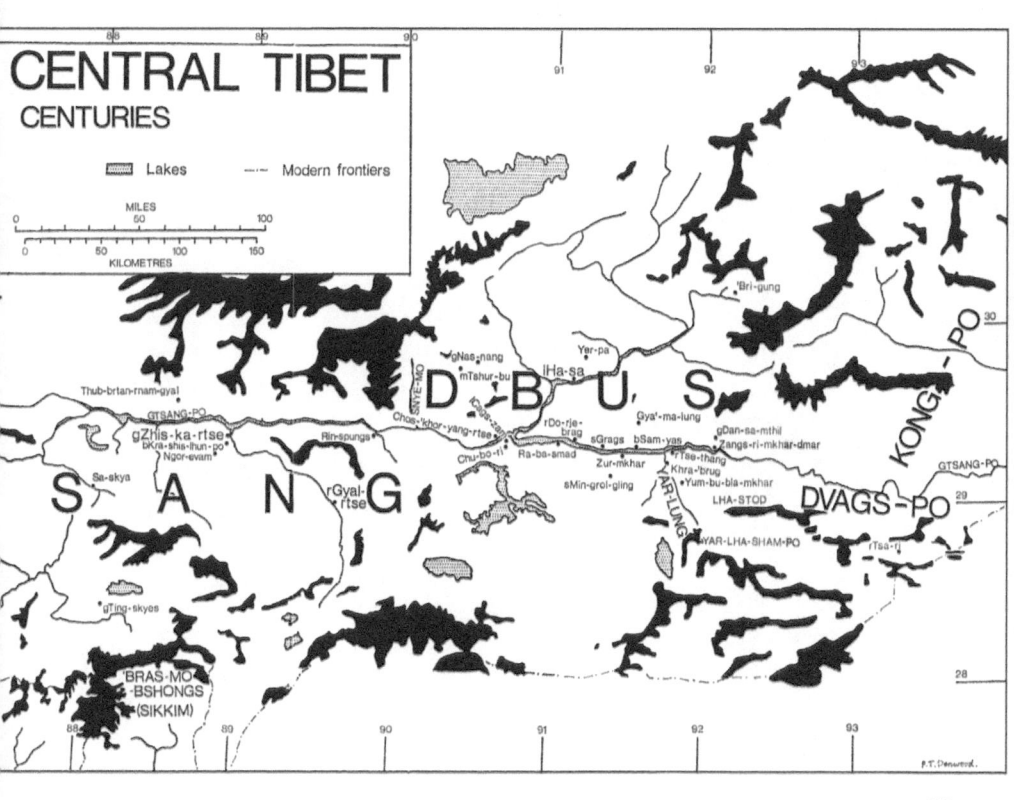

MAP II

ABOUT THE AUTHOR

David Snellgrove is renowned for his ability to convey the spirit as well as the textual interpretation of Sanskrit and Tibetan texts relating to the history of Buddhism. Following his retirement from teaching commitments in 1982, and a career-long interest in Tibetan peoples and cultures, Dr. Snellgrove transferred his scholarly focus to South-East Asia, primarily Indonesia and Cambodia, where he resided for over ten years.

David Snellgrove is a Doctor of Literature in the University of Cambridge, Professor Emeritus of the University of London and a Fellow of the British Academy. Dr Snellgrove currently resides in Italy.

David Snellgrove has been a prolific author throughout his long career. In addition to the present volume, Orchid Press is proud to have published the following partial list of his works :

> Asian Commitment: Travels and Studies in the Indian Sub-Continent and South-East Asia (1st ed., 2000)
> Khmer Civilisation and Angkor (1st ed., 2001/03)
> (with Hugh E. Richardson) The Cultural History of Tibet (3rd ed., 2003)
> Indo-Tibetan Buddhism (2nd ed., 2004)
> Angkor Before and After: A Cultural History of the Khmers (1st ed., 2004)
> Religion as History – Religion as Myth (1st ed., 2005)
> The Nine Ways of Bon: Excerpts from the *gZi-brjid* (2nd ed., 2010)
> The Hevajra Tantra (2nd ed., 2010)
> Himalayan Pilgrimage (3rd ed., 2011)
> Buddhist Himalaya: Travels and Studies in Quest of the Origins and Nature of Tibetan Religion (2nd ed., – forthcoming)

www.ingramcontent.com/pod-product-compliance
Lightning Source LLC
Chambersburg PA
CBHW021339300426
44114CB00012B/1009